From Exception to Promotion

International Environmental Law

Series Editor

Makane Moïse Mbengue

VOLUME 16

The titles published in this series are listed at *brill.com/iel*

From Exception to Promotion

Re-Thinking the Relationship between International Trade and Environmental Law

By

Elena Cima

BRILL
NIJHOFF

LEIDEN | BOSTON

This book received funding from Swiss National Science Foundation (SNSF).

Library of Congress Cataloging-in-Publication Data

Names: Cima, Elena, author.
Title: From exception to promotion : re-thinking the relationship between international trade and environmental law / by Elena Cima.
Description: Leiden ; Boston : Brill Nijhoff, [2022] | Series: International environmental law, 1873-6599 ; volume 16 | Based on author's thesis (doctoral - Graduate Institute of International and Development Studies (Geneva, Switzerland), 2020). | Includes bibliographical references and index.
Identifiers: LCCN 2021038804 (print) | LCCN 2021038805 (ebook) | ISBN 9789004467552 (hardback) | ISBN 9789004467569 (ebook)
Subjects: LCSH: Foreign trade regulation–Environmental aspects.
Classification: LCC K3943 .C56 2022 (print) | LCC K3943 (ebook) | DDC 343.08/7–dc23
LC record available at https://lccn.loc.gov/2021038804
LC ebook record available at https://lccn.loc.gov/2021038805

Typeface for the Latin, Greek, and Cyrillic scripts: "Brill". See and download: brill.com/brill-typeface.

ISSN 1873-6599
ISBN 978-90-04-46755-2 (hardback)
ISBN 978-90-04-46756-9 (e-book)

This book is printed on acid-free paper and produced in a sustainable manner.

To my parents

Contents

Acknowledgments XI
List of Figures and Tables XII
Table of Cases XIII
Table of Treaties and Legislations XVIII
Table of Documents XXV
Abbreviations XXXVI

1 **Introduction** 1
1 Vantage Points 4
2 The Untold Story of the Trade/Environment Nexus 5
2.1 *Transcending the 'Trade and …' Debate* 6
2.2 *The Importance of Historical Inquiry* 9
3 The Hidden Thread 13
3.1 *Trade Is a Means to an End* 13
3.2 *The International Trade Regime Is Historically Contingent* 15
3.2.1 The Emergence of Free Trade thought—The 1850s 16
3.2.2 Post-War Economic Reconstruction and the GATT 17
3.2.3 The 1980s and the WTO Project 19
3.2.4 A New Rationale? 20
3.3 *Individuals and Communities Contribute to Changes in Collective Ideas* 21
3.3.1 Right Conditions, Right Environment 22
3.3.2 The Trade Policy Elite: The Creation of an Environment Un-Conducive to Learning and Change 24
3.3.3 Making Learning Possible 26
4 What Lies Ahead 28
4.1 *Choices* 28
4.2 *A Cartography* 29
4.3 *Structure of the Book* 30

2 **First Came Economic Cooperation: The Genesis of the Nexus** 34
1 The Moral Value of Trade and the Need for International Trade Cooperation 35

1.1 *The Senator from Tennessee and the International Dimension of Trade Policy* 36
1.2 *'When Goods Don't Cross Borders, Soldiers Will'* 39
1.3 *The Call for an International Trade Conference* 42
1.4 *Anglo-American Trade Collaboration: The Atlantic Conference* 45
1.5 *Anderson's Circus* 48
1.6 *Meade's Multilateral Approach to Trade Agreements* 50
1.7 *Havana* 53
2 International Cooperation to Protect Our Spaceship Earth 55
2.1 *The Utilitarian Approach to Environmental Protection* 56
2.2 *"We Have Met the Enemy and He Is Us"* 58
2.3 *Spaceship Earth* 59
2.4 *The 'Internationalist' from Oak Lake* 63
2.5 *On the Road to Stockholm* 64
3 The Environment as a Late-Comer 70
3.1 *Mr. Clean—The Senator from Maine* 71
3.2 *The Commerce Clause and the Limits to Federal Environmental Law-Making* 75
3.3 *The Economic Purpose of Early European Environmental Efforts* 79
3.4 *The Environment Overlooked at Havana* 81
3.5 UNEP *and the Organizational Challenge* 83
3.6 *The Environment as an 'Add-On': The Origin of the Nexus* 85

3 **The *Exception-Based* Model** 87
1 The Environment Cornered in Exception Clauses 88
1.1 *The Environment Seen through Free Trade Glasses* 89
1.2 *Who's Afraid of Environmental Measures?—Part I. Environmental Measures as Non-Tariff Barriers* 93
1.3 *Who's Afraid of Environmental Measures?—Part II. The Harmonization Agenda* 96
1.4 *The Exception to the Rule* 98
1.5 *The Real Story of 'Environmental' Exceptions or 'On How They Became Environmental'* 101
1.6 *The Indeterminacy of Trade Law and The Neoliberal Turn* 104
2 Rivalry 108
2.1 *Dialogue of the Deaf* 110
2.2 *Everyone for Themselves* 115

2.3 *Between Two Fires* 118
2.4 *Development First* 121
2.5 *To Each His Own Fear* 124
2.6 *Like Riding Bicycles* 127
3 How Exceptions Work: The Environment Upstaged 129
3.1 *A Clause to Prevent All Abuses* 130
3.2 *A 'Narrowly Defined' Exception* 135
3.3 *Who Bears the Risk of Non-Persuasion?* 141
3.4 *Judges with Limited Mandate and Expertise* 143
3.5 *Trade Liberalization First* 146

4 The Evolution of the Nexus: The Quest for Balance 148
1 The Need for Balance 150
1.1 *Lady Jackson* 151
1.2 *Same Game, New Rules* 153
1.3 *Which Takes Precedence, Environment or Development?* 154
1.4 *Trade Too Can Harm the Environment* 157
1.5 *Assessing Environmental Impacts* 159
1.6 *Maquiladoras, Hazardous Waste, and the Pollution Haven Package* 163
1.7 *This Is Not Solely an International Story* 166
2 Finding Balance 167
2.1 *Free Traders and Environmentalists: Together at Last* 169
2.2 *The Committee on Trade and Environment: WTO's 'Softer' Version of Institutional Integration* 171
2.3 *Seven 'Faceless Foreign Judges'* 175
2.4 *Finding Balance through Interpretation* 180
2.5 *FTAs and the Introduction of 'Updated' Exceptions* 185
2.6 *An Exception and Nothing More* 190
3 Beyond Exceptions 194
3.1 *The (Not So) Thin Line between Exceptions and Exemptions* 195
3.2 *The Right to Protect the Environment* 201
3.3 *FTA s' Environmental Framework* 204
3.3.1 Environmental Principles 204
3.3.2 Environmental Obligations 206
3.3.3 Dispute Settlement 207
3.4 *The Road Ahead* 210

5 **Can Trade Work for the Environment?: The *Promotion-Based* Model** 212
1 Tables Have Turned 213
1.1 *The Instrumental Role of Trade* 216
1.2 *A Global Green New Deal* 220
1.3 *Trading Places: A Brief History of Means and Ends* 222
2 Negotiating Trade Rules with the Environment in Mind 225
2.1 *Plenty of Fish in the Sea?* 226
2.2 *The Untapped Green Potential of the Subsides Agreement* 232
2.3 *Three Ways to Protect the Environment* 235
2.4 *Trade Sanctions and Forests Protection* 240
2.5 *A New Kind of Environmental Bargain* 244
2.6 *The EU's Sustainable Commercial Policy* 247
2.7 *From Exception to Promotion* 249
3 The Power of Ideas 253
3.1 *From Weak to Strong Integration* 254
3.2 *Watching the Seeds Grow* 257
3.3 *The Development Factor* 261
3.4 *It's Not All about the Environment* 264
3.5 *Two Birds with One Stone* 268
3.6 *Missed Opportunities* 272

6 **Conclusions** 278
1 Ideational Change 280
2 Historical Contingency 284
2.1 *The GATT and Embedded Liberalism* 284
2.2 *The WTO and the Resurgence of Neoliberalism* 285
2.3 *The 2030 Agenda and the Instrumental Role of Trade* 286
3 A New Trade Story 287
3.1 *The Trade Regime: Can't Live without It* 288
3.2 *Asking the Right Question* 289
3.3 *An Organizing Principle for the Trade Regime* 291

Bibliography 295
Index 330

Acknowledgments

During the preparation of this book, I have been fortunate enough to benefit from the help, guidance, and support of many friends and colleagues. My gratitude goes, first and foremost, to Joost Pauwelyn, my PhD supervisor, whose patience, motivation, and knowledge have accompanied me throughout this journey. Second, my thanks go to Jorge Viñuales, for his constant support and inspiration, James Salzman, for having contributed to the completion of this book with insightful and valuable suggestions, and Attila Tanzi, for his precious comments. I am grateful to the entire faculty of the Graduate Institute, and in particular to Andrea Bianchi, for the interest he has always shown in my research and in my academic growth. Special thanks to Makane Mbengue, whose work and character have been an important inspiration for me. I am fortunate to have such a mentor, colleague, and friend. My gratitude goes to Dan Esty, for his support during the first crucial stages of this project and for always being an important source of inspiration. My thanks also to the following people from which I learnt a great deal: Laurence Boisson de Chazournes, Elizabeth Boomer, Jean d'Aspremont, Ginevra Le Moli, Dario Piselli, Giulia Raimondo, Chiara Redaelli, Jason Rudall, Thomas Schultz, and Fuad Zarbiyev.

Figures and Tables

Figure

1 Environmental 'Framework' within trade agreements 205

Table

1 Environmental obligations in FTAs 207

Table of Cases

General Agreement on Tariffs and Trade

Report of the GATT Panel, *Canada—Administration of the Foreign Investment Review Act*, B.I.S.D. 30S/140 (Feb. 7, 1984).

Report of the GATT Panel, *Canada—Measures Affecting Exports of Unprocessed Herring and Salmon,* L/6268-35S/98 (Mar. 22, 1988).

Report of the GATT Panel, *Thailand—Restrictions on Importation of and Internal Taxes on Cigarettes,* DS10/R-37S/91 (Nov. 7, 1990).

Report of the GATT Panel, *United States—Imports of Sugar from Nicaragua,* L/5607-31S/67 (Mar. 13, 1984).

Report of the GATT Panel, *United States—Measures Affecting Alcoholic and Malt Beverages,* B.I.S.D. 39S/206 (June 19, 1992).

Report of the GATT Panel, *United States—Prohibition of Imports of Tuna and Tuna Products from Canada,* L/5198-29S/91 (Feb. 22, 1982).

Report of the GATT Panel, *United States—Restrictions on Imports of Tuna,* DS21/R-39S/155 (Sept. 3, 1991).

Report of the GATT Panel, *United States—Restrictions on Imports of Tuna,* DS29/R (June 16, 1994).

Report of the GATT Panel, *United States—Section 337 of the Tariff Act of 1930,* B.I.S.D. 36S/345, 385 (Nov. 7, 1989).

Report of the GATT Panel, *United States—Taxes on Petroleum and Certain Imported Substances,* L/6175, 34S/136 (June 17, 1987).

Report of the GATT Panel, *United States—Trade Measures Affecting Nicaragua,* L/6053 (Oct. 13, 1986).

World Trade Organization

Appellate Body Report, *Australia—Measures Affecting Importation of Salmon,* WT/DS18/AB/R (Oct. 20, 1998).

Appellate Body Report, *Brazil—Measures affecting Imports of Retreaded Tyres,* WT/DS332/AB/R (Dec. 3, 2007).

Appellate Body Report, *Canada—Certain Measures Concerning Periodicals,* WT/DS31/AB/R (June 30, 1997).

Appellate Body Report, *Canada—Measures Affecting the Renewables Energy Sector,* WT/DS412/AB/R (May 6, 2013).

Appellate Body Report, *Canada—Measures Relating to the Feed-In Tariff Program*, WT/DS426/AB/R (May 6, 2013).

Appellate Body Report, *China—Measures Affecting Trading Rights and Distribution Services for Certain Publications and Audiovisual Entertainment Products*, WT/DS363/AB/R (Dec. 21, 2009).

Appellate Body Report, *China—Measures Related to the Exportation of Rare Earths, Tungsten, and Molybdenum*, WT/DS431/AB/R (Aug. 7, 2014).

Appellate Body Report, *China—Measures Related to the Exportation of Various Raw Materials*, WT/DS394/AB/R (Jan. 30, 2012).

Appellate Body Report, *European Communities—Customs Classification of Certain Computer Equipment*, WT/DS62/AB/R (June 5, 1998).

Appellate Body Report, *European Communities—Measures Affecting the Prohibition of Asbestos and Products Containing Asbestos*, WT/DS135/AB/R (Mar. 12, 2001).

Appellate Body Report, *European Communities—Measures Concerning Meat and Meat Products (Hormones)*, WT/DS26 & 48/AB/R (Jan. 16, 1998).

Appellate Body Report, *European Communities—Regime for the Importation, Sale and Distribution of Bananas*, WT/DS27/AB/R (Sept. 9, 1997).

Appellate Body Report, *European Communities—Trade Description of Sardines*, WT/DS231/AB/R (Sept. 26, 2002).

Appellate Body Report, *India—Certain Measures Relating to Solar Cells and Solar Modules*, WT/DS456/AB/R (Sept. 16, 2016).

Appellate Body Report, *Japan—Measures Affecting Agricultural Products*, WT/DS76/AB/R (Feb. 22, 1999).

Appellate Body Report, *Japan—Taxes on Alcoholic Beverages*, WT/DS8/AB/R (Oct. 4, 1996).

Appellate Body Report, *Korea—Measures Affecting Imports of Fresh, Chilled and Frozen Beef*, WT/DS161/AB/R (Dec. 11, 2000).

Appellate Body Report, *Philippines—Taxes on Distilled Spirits*, WT/DS403/AB/R (Dec. 21, 2011).

Appellate Body Report, *Thailand—Customs and Fiscal Measures on Cigarettes from the Philippines*, WT/DS371/AB/R (June 17, 2011)

Appellate Body Report, *United States—Import Prohibition of Certain Shrimp and Shrimp Products*, WT/DS58/AB/R (Oct. 12, 1998).

Appellate Body Report, *United States—Import Prohibition of Certain Shrimp and Shrimp Products. Recourse to Article 21.5 of the DSU by Malaysia*, WT/DS58/AB/RW (Oct. 22, 2001).

Appellate Body Report, *United States—Imposition of Countervailing Duties on Certain Hot-Rolled Lead and Bismuth Carbon Steel Products Originating in the United Kingdom*, WT/DS138/AB/R (May 10, 2000).

Appellate Body Report, *United States—Measure Affecting Imports of Woven Wool Shirts and Blouses from India*, WT/DS33/AB/R (April 25, 1997).
Appellate Body Report, *United States—Measures Affecting the Cross-Border Supply of Gambling and Betting Services*, WT/DS285/AB/R (Apr. 7, 2005).
Appellate Body Report, *United States—Measures Concerning the Importation, Marketing and Sale of Tuna and Tuna Products*, WT/DS381/AB/R (May 16, 2012).
Appellate Body Report, *United States—Standards for Reformulated and Conventional Gasoline*, WT/DS2/AB/R (Apr. 29, 1996).
Appellate Body Report, *United States—Tax Treatment for 'Foreign Sales Corporations'—Recourse to Article 21.5 of the DSU by the European Communities*, WT/DS108/AB/RW (Jan. 14, 2002).
Panel Report, *European Communities—Measures Affecting the Approval and Marketing of Biotech Products*, WT/DS291/R (Sept. 29, 2006).
Panel Report, *Japan—Taxes on Alcoholic Beverages*, WT/DS8/R (July 11, 1996).
Panel Report, *United States—Import Prohibition of Certain Shrimp and Shrimp Products*, WT/DS58/R (May 15, 1998).
Panel Report, *United States—Import Prohibition of Certain Shrimp and Shrimp Products—Recourse to Article 21.5 of the DSU by Malaysia*, WT/DS58/RW (June 15, 2001).
Panel Report, *United States—Standards for Reformulated and Conventional Gasoline*, WT/DS2/R (May 20, 1996).

Arbitral Tribunals

Adel A Hamadi Al Tamimi v. Sultanate of Oman, ICSID Case No. ARB/11/33 (Nov. 3, 2015).
Arbitration between the United States and the United Kingdom related to the Rights of Jurisdiction of United States in the Bering's Sea and the Preservation of Fur Seals, Aug. 15, 1893, XXVIII R.I.A.A. 1.002.
Chemtura Corporation (formerly Crompton Corporation) v. Government of Canada, ICJG 464 (PCA 2010) (Aug. 2, 2010).
Lake Lanoux Case (France v. Spain), Nov.16, 1957, 12 R.I.A.A. 281; 24 I.L.R. 101.
Mesa Power Group, LLC v. Government of Canada, UNCITRAL, PCA Case No. 2012-17.
NAFTA Arbitral Panel Established Pursuant to Chapter Twenty: In the Matter of Cross-Border Trucking Services (Secretariat File no. USA-MEX-98–2008–01).

Parkerings-Compagniet AS v. Republic of Lithuania, ICSID Case No. ARB/05/8 (Sept. 11, 2007).
Trail Smelter Case (US v. Canada), Mar. 11, 1941, 3 R.I.A.A. 1938.

Other International Cases

Maritime Delimitation and Territorial Questions Between Qatar and Bahrain (Qatar v. Bahr.) 2001 I.C.J. 40 (Mar. 2001).
North Sea Continental Shelf (Ger. v. Den.), 1969 I.C.J. 3 (Feb. 1969).

European Court of Justice

Case C-7/68, Commission v. Italy, 1968, E.C.R. 423.
Case C-13/68, Salgoil v. Italian Ministry of Foreign Trade, 1968, E.C.R. 453.
Case C-95/81, Commission v. Italy, 1982, E.C.R. 2,187.
Case C-113/80, Commission v. Ireland, 1981, E.C.R. 1,625.
Case C-120/78, Rewe-Zentral AG v. Bundesmonopolverwaltung fiir Branntwei, 1979, E.C.R. 649.
Case C-169/00, Commission of the European Communities v. Republic of Finland, 2002 E.C.R I-02433.
Case C-229/83, Leclerq, 1985, E.C.R. 1.
Case C-302/86, Commission v. Denmark, 1988 E.C.R. 4607.

United State Cases

US Supreme Court

Carter v. Carter Coal Co., 298 U.S. 238 (1936).
Champion v. Ames, 188 U.S. 321 (1903).
Chemical Waste Management, Inc. v. Hunt, 504 U.S. 334 (1992).
C&A Carbone Inc. v. Town of Clarkstown, 511 U.S. 383 (1994).
Dean Milk v. Madison, 340 U.S. 349 (1951).
Fort Gratiot Landfill v. Michigan Dep' of Natural Resources, 504 U.S. 353 (1992).
Gibbons v. Ogden, 22 U.S. 1 (1824).
Heart of Atlanta Motel, Inc. v. United States, 379 U.S. 241 (1964).
Hipolite Egg Co. v. United States, 220 U.S. 45 (1911).
Hodel v. Virginia Surface Mining Ass', 452 U.S. 264 (1981).
Hoke v. United States, 227 U.S. 308 (1913).

Houston E. & W. T. Ry. Co. v. United States, 234 U.S. 342 (1914).
Katzenbach v. McClung, 379 U.S. 294 (1964).
NLRB v. Jones & Laughlin Steel Corp, 301 U.S. 1 (1937).
Oregon Waste Sys. v. Environmental Dep't, 511 U.S. 93 (1994).
Perez v. United States, 402 U.S. 146 (1971).
Philadelphia v. New Jersey, 437 U.S. 617 (1978).
Pike v. Bruce Church, Inc., 397 U.S. 137 (1970).
Railroad Retirement Board v. Alton Railroad Co., 295 U.S. 330 (1935).
Schechter Poultry Corp. v. United States, 295 U.S. 495 (1935).
Solid Waste Agency of Northern Cook County v. Army Corps. of Eng'rs, 531 U.S. 159 (2001).
Swift & Co. v. United States, 196 U.S. 375 (1905).
United States v. Darby, 312 U.S. 100 (1941).
Wickard v. Filburn, 317 U.S. 111 (1942).

Federal Courts

Public Citizen v. Office of the U.S Trade Representative, 804 F. Supp. 385 (D.D.C. 1992).

Table of Treaties and Legislations

International Treaties and Conventions

Basel Convention on the Control of Transboundary Movements of Hazardous Wastes and their Disposal, Mar. 22, 1989, 1673 U.N.T.S. 57, 28 I.L.M. 657.
Cartagena Protocol on Biosafety to the Convention on Biological Diversity, Jan. 20, 2000, 2226 U.N.T.S. 208.
Convention for the Protection of Birds Useful to Agriculture, Mar. 19, 1902, 191 C.T.S. 91.
Convention for the Protection of Migratory Birds, Aug.16, 1916, 39 Stat. 1702-1704.
Convention for the Protection of the Ozone Layer, Mar. 22, 1985, 1513 U.N.T.S. 123.
Convention on Biological Diversity, June 5, 1992, 1760 U.N.T.S. 79; 31 I.L.M. 818.
Convention on Environmental Impact Assessment in a Transboundary Context, Feb. 25, 1991, 1989 U.N.T.S. 309.
Convention on International Trade in Endangered Species of Wild Fauna and Flora, Mar. 3, 1973, 993 U.N.T.S. 243.
Convention on the Prevention of Marine Pollution by Dumping Wastes and other Matter, Nov. 13, 1972, 1046 U.N.T.S. 120.
Havana Charter for an International Trade Organization, 1948, U.N. Doc. E/CONF.2/78.
International Convention for the Abolition of Import and Export Prohibitions and Restrictions, Nov. 8, 1927, 46 Stat. 2461, U.N.T.S. 811.
International Convention for the Conservation of Atlantic Tunas, May 14, 1966, 673 U.N.T.S. 73.
International Convention for the Prevention of Pollution of the Sea by Oil, May 12, 1954, 327 U.N.T.S. 3.
International Convention on the Harmonized Commodity Description and Coding System, June 14, 1983, 1503 U.N.T.S. 3.
International Plant Protection Convention, Dec. 6, 1951, 150 U.N.T.S. 67.
International Tropic Timber Agreement, Jan. 27, 2006, 2797 U.N.T.S. 75.
Kyoto Protocol to the United Nations Framework Convention on Climate Change, Dec. 11, 1997, 2302 U.N.T.S. 162.
League of Nations, Covenant of the League of Nations, Apr. 28, 1919.
London Convention relative to the Preservation of Fauna and Flora in their Natural State, Nov. 8, 1933, 172 L.N.T.S. 241.
Minamata Convention on Mercury, Oct. 10, 2013.
Montreal Protocol on Substances that Deplete the Ozone Layer, Sept. 16, 1987, 1522 U.N.T.S. 3.

Nagoya Protocol on Access to Genetic Resources and the Fair and Equitable Sharing of Benefits Arising from their Utilization to the Convention on Biological Diversity, Oct. 29, 2010, UNEP/CBD/COP/DEC/X/1.

North Pacific Fur Seals Convention, July 7, 1911, 37 Stat. 1542-1543.

Paris Agreement to the United Nations Framework Convention on Climate Change, Dec. 12, 2015, T.I.A.S. No. 16-1104.

Rotterdam Convention on the Prior Informed Consent Procedure for Certain Hazardous Chemicals and Pesticides in International Trade, Sept. 10, 1998, 2244 U.N.T.S. 337.

Stockholm Convention on Persistent Organic Pollutants, May 22, 2001, 2256 U.N.T.S. 119.

Tokyo International Convention for the High Seas Fisheries of the North Pacific Ocean, May 9, 1952, 205 U.N.T.S. 65.

Treaty for the Preservation and Protection of Fur Seals, June 7, 1911, 37 Stat. 1542.

United Nations Convention on the Law of the Sea, Dec. 10, 1982, 1833 U.N.T.S. 397.

United Nations Framework Convention on Climate Change, May 9, 1992, 1771 U.N.T.S. 107, 31 I.L.M. 849.

Vienna Convention on the Law of Treaties, May 23, 1969, 1155 U.N.T.S. 331.

Washington Convention on Nature Protection and Wildlife Preservation in the Western Hemisphere, Oct. 12, 1940, 161 U.N.T.S. 193.

Washington International Convention for the North-West Atlantic Fisheries, Feb. 8, 1949, 157 U.N.T.S. 157.

Washington International Convention for the Regulation of Whaling, Dec. 2, 1946, 161 U.N.T.S. 72.

GATT and World Trade Organization Agreements

Agreement on Government Procurement, Apr. 14, 1994, Marrakesh Agreement Establishing the World Trade Organization, 1869 U.N.T.S. 508.

Agreement on Sanitary and Phytosanitary Measures, Apr. 15, 1994, Marrakesh Agreement Establishing the World Trade Organization, Annex 1A, 1867 U.N.T.S. 3.

Agreement on Subsidies and Countervailing Measures, Apr. 15, 1994, Marrakesh Agreement Establishing the World Trade Organization, Annex 1A, 1869 U.N.T.S. 14.

Agreement on Technical Barriers to Trade, Apr. 15, 1994, Marrakesh Agreement Establishing the World Trade Organization, Annex 1A, 1868 U.N.T.S. 120.

Agreement on Trade-related Aspects of Intellectual Property Rights, Apr. 15, 1994, Marrakesh Agreement Establishing the World Trade Organization, Annex 1C, 1869 U.N.T.S. 299, 33 I.L.M. 1197.

Decision on Trade and Environment, Apr. 14, 1994, Marrakesh Agreement Establishing the World Trade Organization, Annex 1C, 33 I.L.M. 1267.

General Agreement on Tariffs and Trade, Oct. 30, 1947, 61 Stat. A-11, 55 U.N.T.S. 194.

General Agreement on Trade in Services, Apr. 15, 1994, Marrakesh Agreement Establishing the World Trade Organization, Annex 1B, 1869 U.N.T.S. 183.

Understanding on Rules and Procedures Governing the Settlement of Disputes, Apr. 15, 1994, Marrakesh Agreement Establishing the World Trade Organization, Annex 2, 1869 U.N.T.S. 401.

World Trade Organization, Ministerial Declaration of 14 November 2001, WT/MIN(01)/DEC/1, 41 I.L.M. 746 (2002).

World Trade Organization, Hong Kong Ministerial Declaration, Dec. 22, 2005, Annex D: Rules I. Anti-Dumping and Subsidies and Countervailing Measures including Fisheries Subsidies, WT/MIN(05)/DEC.

World Trade Organization, Fisheries Subsidies. Ministerial Declaration of 13 December 2017, WT/MIN(17)/64, WT/L/1031 (Dec. 18, 2017).

Bilateral and Regional Trade Agreements

Agreement on Environmental Cooperation, Canada-Chile, Feb. 1997.

Agreement on the European Economic Area, EU-EFTA States, Jan. 3, 1994.

Asia-Pacific Trade Agreement, July 31, 1975.

Australia-Chile Free Trade Agreement, July 30, 2008.

Australia-China Free Trade Agreement, June 17, 2015.

Australia-Papua New Guinea Free Trade Agreement, Nov. 6, 1976.

Canada-Colombia Free Trade Agreement, Nov. 21, 2008.

Canada-EU Free Trade Agreement, Oct. 30, 2016.

Canada-Panama Free Trade Agreement, May 14, 2010.

Canada-Peru Free Trade Agreement, May 29, 2008.

Canada-Republic of Korea Free Trade Agreement, Sept. 22, 2014.

Canada-Ukraine Free Trade Agreement, July 11, 2016.

Chile-Malaysia Free Trade Agreement, Nov. 13, 2010.

China-Singapore, Free Trade Agreement, Oct. 23, 2008.

China-New Zealand Free Trade Agreement, Apr. 7, 2008.

Costa Rica-Colombia Free Trade Agreement, May 22, 2013.

Costa Rica-Singapore Free Trade Agreement, Apr. 6, 2010.

Dominican Republic-Central America-United States Free Trade Agreement, Aug. 5, 2004.

EFTA-Bosnia Herzegovina Free Trade Agreement, June 24, 2013.

EFTA-Canada Free Trade Agreement, Jan. 26, 2008.
EFTA-Georgia Free Trade Agreement, June 27, 2016.
EFTA-Philippines Free Trade Agreement, Apr. 28, 2016.
EU-Caribbean Forum Free Trade Agreement, Oct 15, 2008.
EU-Colombia-Peru Free Trade Agreement, June 26, 2012.
EU-Chile Free Trade Agreement, Nov. 18, 2002.
EU-Georgia Free Trade Agreement, June 27, 2014.
EU-Iceland Free Trade Agreement, Dec. 19, 1972.
EU-Japan Free Trade Agreement, July 17. 2018.
EU-Moldova Free Trade Agreement, June 27, 2014.
EU-Norway Free Trade Agreement, May 14, 1973.
EU-Republic of Korea Free Trade Agreement, Oct. 6, 2010.
EU-SADC Free Trade Agreement, June 10, 2016.
EU-South Africa Free Trade Agreement, Oct. 11, 1999.
EU-Switzerland-Liechtenstein Free Trade Agreement, July 22, 1972.
EU-Ukraine Free Trade Agreement, June 27, 2014.
Global System of Trade Preferences among Developing Countries, Apr. 13, 1988.
India-Japan Free Trade Agreement, Feb. 16, 2011.
Japan-Australia Free Trade Agreement, July 8, 2014.
Japan-Peru Free Trade Agreement, May 31, 2011.
Latin American Integration Association, Aug. 12, 1980.
Mexico-Panama Free Trade Agreement, Apr. 3, 2014.
North American Agreement on Environmental Cooperation, US-Can.-Mex. 32 I.L.M. 1482 (1993).
North American Free Trade Agreement, US-Can.-Mex, Dec. 17, 1992, 32 I.L.M. 289 (1993).
Peru-Mexico Free Trade Agreement, Apr. 6, 2011.
Republic of Korea-New Zealand Free Trade Agreement, Mar. 23, 2015.
Republic of Korea-Vietnam Free Trade Agreement, May 5, 2015.
South Pacific Regional Trade and Economic Cooperation Agreement, Jan 1, 1981.
Switzerland-China Free Trade Agreement, July 6, 2013.
Treaty of Commerce, Italy-Switzerland, 1904.
Treaty of Commerce and Navigation, Sweden-Germany, 1911, Martens, N.R.G., 3rd Ser. VIII, 435.
Turkey-Chile Free Trade Agreement, July 14, 2009.
Turkey-Singapore Free Trade Agreement, Nov. 14, 2015.
United States-Australia Free Trade Agreement, May 18, 2004.
United States-Canada Free Trade Agreement, 27 I.L.M. 281 (1988).
United States-Chile Free Trade Agreement, June 6, 2003.

United States-Israel Free Trade Agreement, Apr. 22, 1985.
United States-Jordan Free Trade Agreement, Oct. 24, 2000.
United States-Mexico-Canada Free Trade Agreement, Nov. 30, 2018.
United States-Morocco Free Trade Agreement, June 15, 2004.
United States-Oman Free Trade Agreement, Jan. 19, 2016.
United States-Peru Free Trade Agreement, Apr. 12, 2006.
United States-Republic of Korea Free Trade Agreement, June 30, 2007.
United States-Singapore Free Trade Agreement, May 6, 2003.

EC and EU Treaties

Consolidated Version of the Treaty on the Functioning of the European Union, May 9, 2008, 2008 O.J. (C 115) 47.
Single European Act Amending the Treaties Establishing the European Communities, July 1, 1987, 1987 O.J. L 169/1.
Treaty Establishing the European Coal and Steel Community, Apr. 18, 1951, 261 U.N.T.S. 140.
Treaty Establishing the European Economic Community, Mar. 25, 1957, 298 U.N.T.S. 11.
Treaty of Amsterdam Amending the Treaty on European Union, the Treaties Establishing the European Communities and Certain Related Acts, Oct. 2, 1997, 1997 O.J. (C 349) 1.
Treaty of Lisbon Amending the Treaty on European Union and the Treaty Establishing the European Community, Dec. 13, 2007, 2007 O.J. (C 306) 1.
Treaty of Nice amending the Treaty on the European Union, the Treaties Establishing the European Communities and Certain Related Acts, 2001 O.J. C 80/1.

EC and EU Secondary Legislation

Regulations

Regulation 722/97 on Environmental Measures in Developing Countries, 1997 O.J. L181/1.
Regulation 443/2009 on Emissions of Passenger Cars, 2009 O.J. L140/1.

Directives

Directive 70/157, 1970 O.J. (L 42).
Directive 73/350, 1973 O.J. (L 321).

Directive 77/212, 1977 O.J. (L 66).
Directive 79/409, 1979 O.J. (L 103/1).
Directive 84/372, 1984 O.J. (L 196).
Directive 84/424, 1984 O.J. (L 238).
Directive 87/354, 1987 O.J. (L 192).
Directive 89/491, 1989 O.J. (L 238).
Directive 92/97, 1992 O.J. (L 371).
Directive 96/20, 1996 O.J. (L 92).
Directive 1999/101, 1999 O.J. (L 334).
Directive 2007/34, 2007 O.J. (L 155).

National Legislation

Canada

Fisheries Act, R.S.C., 1985.

Chile

Law No. 20962, Sept. 30, 2016, Diario Oficial [D.O.]

France

Décret no. 96-1133 relatif à l'interdiction de l'amiante, pris en application du code de travail et du code de la consommation (Jan. 1, 1997).

Peru

Forest and Wild Fauna Law, No. 29763, July 22, 2011.

United States

Clean Air Act, 42 U.S.C. § 7401 et seq. (1970).
Clean Water Act, 33 U.S.C. § 1251 et seq. (1972).
Coastal Zone Management Act, 16 U.S.C. § 1451 et seq. (1972).
Endangered Species Act, 16 U.S.C. § 1531 et seq. (1973).
Federal Insecticide, Fungicide, and Rodenticide Act, 7 U.S.C. § 136 et seq. (1972).
Federal Land Policy and Management Act, 43 U.S.C. § 1701 et seq. (1976).
Forest Rangeland Renewable Resources Planning Act, 16 U.S.C. § 1600 et seq. (1974).
Lacey Act, 16 U.S.C. §§ 3371-3378 (1900)
Marine Mammal Protection Act, 16 U.S.C. §§ 1361-1423h (1972).
National Environmental Policy Act of 1969 § 102, 42 U.S.C. § 4332 (2006).
Noise Control Act, 42 U.S.C. § 4901 et seq. (1972).

Outer Continental Shelf Lands Act, 43 U.S.C. § 1331 et seq. (1978).
Resource Conservation and Recovery Act, 42 U.S.C. § 6901 et seq. (1976).
Safe Drinking Water Act, 42 U.S.C. § 300 et seq. (1974).
Superfund Amendments and Reauthorization Act, 42 U.S.C. § 9601 et seq. (1986).
Surface Mining Control and Reclamation Act, 30 U.S.C. § 1201 et seq. (1977).
Tariff Act of 1930, 19. U.S.C. 4 (1930).
Toxic Substances Control Act, 15 U.S.C. §§ 2601-2629 (1976).
Trade Act of 2002, H.R. 3009, 116 Stat. 933, 19 U.S.C. §§ 3803–3805 (2002).
United States Constitution, effective Mar. 4, 1789.

Table of Documents

United Nations

General Assembly Resolutions

Institutional and Financial Arrangements for International Environmental Cooperation, 2997 (XXVII) (Dec. 15, 1972).

Problems of the Human Environment, 2398 (XXIII) (Dec. 3, 1968).

Programme for the Further Implementation of Agenda 21, A/RES/S-19/2 (Sept. 19, 1997).

The Future We Want, A/RES/66/288 (Sept. 11, 2012).

Transforming Our World: The 2030 Agenda for Sustainable Development, A/RES/70/1 (Sept. 25, 2015).

United Nation Conference on the Human Environment, 2581 (XXIV) (Dec. 15, 1969).

World Charter for Nature, A/RES/37/7 (Oct. 28, 1982).

Economic and Social Council

Drafting Committee of the Preparatory Committee of the United Nations Conference on Trade and Employment—Draft Report of the Technical Sub-Committee, E/PC/T/C.6/55 (Feb. 5, 1947).

Drafting Committee of the Preparatory Committee of the United Nations Conference on Trade and Employment—Report of the Technical Sub-Committee, E/PC/T/C.6/55/Rev.1 (Feb. 11, 1947).

Economic and Social Council Resolution, *Question on Convening an International Conference on the Problems of Human Environment,* 1346 (XLV) (July 30, 1968).

Preparatory Committee of the International Conference on Trade and Employment—Committee II—Technical Sub-Committee—Report of Rapporteurs on Item I of Provisional Agenda, E/PC/T/C.II/W.20 (June 11, 1946).

Preparatory Committee of the International Conference on Trade and Employment—Committee II—Note of the Delegations of the Netherlands and of the Belgian-Luxembourg Economic Union, E/PC/T/C.II/32 (Oct. 30, 1946).

Preparatory Committee of the International Conference on Trade and Employment—Committee II, E/PC/T/C.II/50 (Nov. 13, 1946).

Preparatory Committee of the International Conference on Trade and Employment—Verbatim Report of the Fifth Meeting of the Sub-Committee

of Committee II on Quantitative Restrictions and Exchange Control, E/PC/T/C.II/QR/PV/5 (Nov. 18, 1946).
Second Session of the Preparatory Committee of the United Nations Conference on Trade and Employment, E/PC/T/A/PV/30 (July 16, 1947).
Second Session of the Preparatory Committee of the United Nations Conference on Trade and Employment—Draft Charter, E/PC/T/142 (Aug. 1, 1947)
Second Session of the Preparatory Committee of the United Nations Conference on Trade and Employment—Report of the Legal Drafting Committee on Articles 16—23 and 37, E/PC/T/154 (Aug. 6, 1947).
Second Session of the Preparatory Committee of the United Nations Conference on Trade and Employment, Amendment proposed by the Australian Delegation, E/PC/T/W/264 (Aug. 6, 1947)
Third Committee: Commercial Policy, E/CONF.2/C.3/SR.35 (Feb. 14, 1948).

United Nations Conference on the Human Environment

An Action Plan for the Human Environment, A/CONF.48/5 (Feb. 9, 1972)
Annotations to the Provisional Agenda, A/CONF.48/2 (Apr. 27, 1972).
Declaration on the Human Environment, U.N. Doc. A/CONF.48/14/Rev.1.
Development and Environment, Report by the Secretary General, A/CONF.48/10 (Dec. 22, 1971).
Draft Declaration on the Human Environment, A/CONF. 48/4 (1972)
Educational, Informational, Social and Cultural Aspects of Environmental Issues, Report by the Secretary General, A/CONF.48/9 (Dec. 21, 1971).
Environmental Aspects of Natural Resources Management, Report by the Secretary General, A/CONF.48/7 (Jan. 26, 1972).
Founex Report on Development and Environment (1971).
Identification and Control of Pollutants of Broad International Significance, A/CONF.48/8 (Jan. 7, 1972).
International Organizational Implications of Action Proposals, Report by the Secretary General, A/CONF.48/11 (Jan. 10, 1972).
Planning and Management of Human Settlements for Environmental Quality, Report by the Secretary General, A/CONF.48/6 (Dec. 23, 1971).
Provisional Rules of Procedure, A/CONF.48/3 (Dec. 28, 1971)
Report of the United Nations Conference on the Human Environment, Stockholm, 5-16 June 1972, A/CONF.48/Rev.1.
The UN System and the Human Environment, A/CONF.48/12 (Dec. 17, 1971).

Other Conferences

United Nations Conference on Environment and Development, Rio de Janeiro, Brazil, June 3-14, 1992, *Rio Declaration on Environment and Development,* U.N. Doc. A/CONF.151/26/Rev.1 (Vol. I), Annex I (Aug. 12, 1992).

United Nations Conference on Environment and Development, Rio de Janeiro, Brazil, June 3-14, 1992, *Agenda 21: Programme of Action for Sustainable Development,* U.N. Doc. A/CONF.151/26 (1992).

United Nations and United Nations International Conference on Financing for Development, Monterrey, Mexico, March 18–22, 2002, *Financing for development: Monterrey Consensus of the International Conference on Financing for Development: the final text of agreements and commitments adopted at the International Conference on Financing for Development.*

United Nations, Follow-up International Conference on Financing for Development to Review the Implementation of the Monterrey Consensus, Doha, Qatar, Nov. 29—Dec. 2, 2008, *Doha Declaration on Financing for Development: outcome document of the Follow-up International Conference on Financing for Development to Review the Implementation of the Monterrey Consensus,* A/CONF.212/L.1/Rev.1.

World Summit on Sustainable Development, Johannesburg, South Africa, August 26-September 4, 2002, *Plan of Implementation of the World Summit on Sustainable* Development, U.N. Doc. A/CONF.199/20, Annex (Sept. 4, 2002).

GATT and World Trade Organization

GATT Documents

Analytical Index: Notes on the drafting, interpretation and application of the Articles of the General Agreement (3rd edition, 1970).

Decision on Dispute Settlement Procedures, GATT B.I.S.D. (31st Supp.) (1984).

GATT Activities in 1960-61 (Geneva, 1962).

GATT Activities in 1972 (Geneva, 1973).

GATT Activities in 1973 (Geneva, 1974).

GATT Activities in 1980 (Geneva, 1981).

GATT Activities in 1986 (Geneva, 1987).

GATT Activities in 1990 (Geneva, 1991).

GATT Council Meeting, 6 February. C/M/247 (1991).

GATT, The Uruguay Round and the Environment, 85 GATT Focus (Oct. 1991).

Industrial Pollution Control and International Trade, Note by the GATT Secretariat, L/3538, June 9, 1971.

Note on the First and Second Sessions of the Preparatory Committee of the United Nations Conference on Environment and Development, L/6892, Aug. 25, 1991.

Note on the Third Session of the Preparatory Committee of the United Nations Conference on Environment and Development, L/6892/Add.1, Nov. 25, 1991.

Outline of Points for Structured Debate on Environmental Measures and Trade, Spec(91)21, Apr. 29, 1991.

Report by Ambassador H. Ukawa (Japan). Chairman of the Group on Environmental Measures and International Trade to the 49th Session of the Contracting Parties, GATT B.I.S.D. (40th Supp.) (L/7402) (1994).

The Activities of GATT 1959/60 (Geneva, 1960).

Trade and Environment, L/6859, May 29, 1991.

Trade and Environment. Factual Note by the Secretariat, L/6896, Sept. 18, 1991.

Trade and Environment. Statement by the Delegation of the European Union, Spec(91)20, Apr. 30, 1991.

Understanding Regarding Notification, Consultation, Dispute Settlement and Surveillance, GATT B.I.S.D. 200 (26th Supp.) (1980)

GATT Standing Group on Environmental Measures and International Trade

The GATT and the Trade Provisions of MEAs. Submission from the EC, TRE/W/5 (1992)

Report of the Meeting Held on 19 November 1992. Note by the Secretariat, TRE/8 (1992).

Report of the Meeting Held on 4–5 February 1993. Note by the Secretariat, TRE/9 (1993).

Report of the Meeting Held on 5–7 July 1993. Note by the Secretariat, TRE/12 (1993).

Report of the Meeting Held on 5–6 October 1993. Note by the Secretariat, TRE/13 (1993).

Trade Negotiations Committee

Communication from Austria, Finland, Iceland, Norway, Sweden and Switzerland, MTN.TNC/W/47 (Dec. 3, 1990).

World Trade Organization

Observer Status for International Intergovernmental Organizations in the WTO, July 25, 1996, Rules of Procedures for sessions of the Ministerial Conference and Meetings of the General Council, Annex 3, WT/L/161.

2006 World Trade Report.

WTO Committee on Government Procurement

Decision on the Outcomes of the Negotiations under Article XXIV:7 of the Agreement on Government Procurement, GPA/113, Apr. 2, 2012.

WTO Committee on Trade and Environment

Communication from the CBD Secretariat to the Committee on Trade and Environment. Response of the Executive Secretary of the Convention on Biological Diversity (CBD) to the Chair of the CTE, WT/CTE/W/149 (June 28, 2000).

Communication from UNEP to the Committee on Trade and Environment. UNEP Fisheries Subsidies Workshop. Chairman's Summary, WT/CTE/W/187 (Mar. 15, 2001).

Draft Rules of Procedures for the Meetings of the CTE. Note by the Secretariat, WT/CTE/W/13 (1995).

Environmental and Trade Benefits of Removing Subsidies in the Fisheries Sector. Submission by the United States to the Committee on Trade and Environment, WT/CTE/W/51 (May 19, 1997).

Environmental Benefits of Removing Trade Restrictions and Distortions. Note by the Secretariat, WT/CTE/W/67 (Nov. 7, 1997).

Environmental Benefits of Removing Restrictions and Distortions: The Fisheries Sector-Item 6 of the Work Programme. Note by the Secretariat to the Committee on Trade and Environment, WT/CTE/W/167 (Oct. 16, 2000).

Environmental Benefits of Removing Restrictions and Distortions: The Fisheries Sector-Item 6 of the Work Programme. Note by the Secretariat to the Committee on Trade and Environment, WT/CTE/W/167/Add.1 (June 19, 2001).

Existing Forms of Cooperation and Information Exchange Between UNEP/MEAS and the WTO, TN/TE/S/2/Rev.2 (Jan. 16, 2007).

Japan's Basic Position on the Fishery Subsidy Issue, Item 6. Submission by Japan to the Committee on Trade and Environment, WT/CTE/W/173 (Oct. 23, 2000).

Non-Paper by the European Communities on Item 1 (Feb. 19, 1996).

Non-Paper. Submission by Switzerland on Item 1 (May 20, 1996).

Non-Paper. Submission by Korea on Item 1 (June 12, 1996).

Non-Paper. Submission by The Arab Republic of Egypt on Item 1 (June 18, 1996).

Non-Paper. Submission by India on Items 1 and 5 (July 23, 1996).

On the Environmental Impact of Fisheries Subsidies. Submission by Iceland to the Committee on Trade and Environment, WT/CTE/W/111 (Mar. 11, 1999).

Recent Roundtable on Promoting Development and Sustainability in Fisheries Subsidies Disciplines. Statement by UNEP at the Regular Session of the Committee on Trade and Environment of 6 July 2005, WT/CTE/GEN/20 (July 13, 2005).

Report (1996) of the Committee on Trade and Environment, WT/CTE/1 (Nov. 8, 1996).

Report (1997) of the Committee on Trade and Environment, WT/CTE/2 (Nov. 26, 1997).
Report of the Meeting Held on 6 February 1995. Note by the Secretariat, WT/CTE/M/1 (Mar. 6, 1995).
Report of the Meeting Held on 12 September 1995. Note by the Secretariat, WT/CTE/M/4 (Oct. 10. 1995).
Report of the Meeting Held on 21-22 May 1997. Note by the Secretariat, WT/CTE/M/14 (June 26, 1997).
Report of the Meeting Held on 22-24 September 1997. Note by the Secretariat, WT/CTE/M/15 (Nov. 20, 1997).
Report of the Meeting Held on 30 June 1999. Note by the Secretariat, WT/CTE/M/21 (July 26, 1999).
Report of the Meeting Held on 12 October 1999, WT/CTE/M/22 (Oct. 29, 1999).
Report of the Meeting Held on 5–6 July 2000. Note by the Secretariat, WT/CTE/M/24 (Sept. 19, 2000).
Report of the Meeting Held on 28 October 2003. Note by the Secretariat, WT/CTE/M/35 (Nov. 19, 2003).
Report of the Meeting Held on 20 April 2004. Note by the Secretariat, WT/CTE/M/36 (May 19, 2004).
Report of the Meeting Held on 6 July 2005. Note by the Secretariat, WT/CTE/M/40 (Sept. 2, 2005).
Report of the Meeting Held on 18 December 2006. Note by the Secretariat, WT/CTE/M/43 (Feb. 12, 2007).
Report of the Meeting Held on 30 November 2007. Note by the Secretariat, WT/CTE/M/45 (Jan. 9, 2008).
Report of the Meeting Held on 3 November 2008. Note by the Secretariat, WT/CTE/M/46 (Jan. 12, 2009).
Report of the Meeting Held on 10 July 2009. Note by the Secretariat, WT/CTE/M/47 (Aug. 31, 2009).
Report of the Meeting Held on 20 November 2009. Note by the Secretariat, WT/CTE/M/48 (Jan. 12, 2010).
Report of the Meeting Held on 17 February 2010. Note by the Secretariat, WT/CTE/M/49 (Apr. 7, 2010).
Report of the Meeting Held on 9 November 2010. Note by the Secretariat, WT/CTE/M/51 (May 31, 2011).
Report of the Meeting Held on 6 July 2011. Note by the Secretariat, WT/CTE/M/52 (Sept. 6, 2011).
Report of the Meeting Held on 14 November 2011. Note by the Secretariat, WT/CTE/M/53 (Jan. 27, 2012).

Report of the Meeting Held on 5 June 2013. Note by the Secretariat, WT/CTE/M/55 (Aug. 16, 2013).

Report of the Meeting Held on 16 October 2013. Note by the Secretariat, WT/CTE/C/56 (Jan. 31, 2014).

Report of the Meeting Held on 30 June 2014. Note by the Secretariat, WT/CTE/M/57 (Sept. 30, 2014).

Report of the Meeting Held on 23 October 2014. Note by the Secretariat, WT/CTE/M/58 (Mar. 23, 2015).

Report of the Meeting Held on 30 June 2016. Note by the Secretariat, WT/CTE/M/61 (Oct. 14, 2016).

Report of the Meeting Held on 14 and 15 November 2016. Note by the Secretariat, WT/CTE/M/62 (Mar. 20, 2017).

Report of the Meeting Held on 20 June 2017. Note by the Secretariat, WT/CTE/M/63 (Sept. 27, 2017).

Report of the Meeting Held on 30 November 2017. Note by the Secretariat, WT/CTE/M/66 (Mar. 22, 2019).

The Relationship between the Provisions of the MTS and Trade Measures for Environmental Purposes, including those Pursuant to MEAs. Submission by New Zealand, WT/CTE/W/20 (1996).

The Relationship between Trade Measures Pursuant to MEAs and the WTO Agreement. Proposal by Japan, WT/CTE/W/31 (1996).

Trade Liberalization and the Environment: A positive Agenda for Trade Reform. Submission by Australia to the Committee on Trade and Environment, WT/CTE/W/105 (Feb. 2, 1999).

WTO Committee on Trade and Environment Special Sessions

Statement by the Chairperson of the Special Session of the Committee on Trade and Environment to the Trade Negotiations Committee, TN/TE/1 (Apr. 12, 2002).

WTO Council for Trade-Related Aspects of Intellectual Property Rights

Minutes of Meeting Held in the Centre William Rappard on 1 March 2011, IP/C/M/65 (May 10, 2011).

WTO General Council

Communication from Iceland to the General Council, Preparations for the 1999 Ministerial Conference: Fisheries Subsidies, WT/GC/W/229 (July 6, 1999).

Communication from Australia, Iceland, New Zealand, Norway, Peru, Philippines and United States to the General Council, Preparations for the 1999 Ministerial Conference: Fisheries Subsidies, WT/GC/W/303 (Aug. 6, 1999)

WTO Negotiating Group on Rules

A Cap-Based Approach to Addressing Certain Fisheries Subsidies. Submission of Australia and the United States, TN/RL/GEN/197 (Mar. 25, 2019).

ACP Group Text Proposal, Fisheries Subsidies Discipline. Submission from Guyana on behalf of the ACP Group, TN/RL/GEN/192 (July 14, 2017).

Advancing Toward a Multilateral Outcome on Fisheries Subsidies in the WTO, TN/RL/GEN/181 (Oct. 18, 2016).

Comments from the People's Republic of China on the United States Proposal on Fisheries Subsidies to the Negotiating Group on Rules, TN/RL/W/88 (May 1, 2003).

Contribution to the Discussion on the Framework for Disciplines on Fisheries Subsidies. Paper from Brazil to the Negotiating Group on Rules, TN/RL/W/176 (Mar. 31, 2005).

Contribution to the Discussion on the Framework for Disciplines on Fisheries Subsidies. Paper from Brazil to the Negotiating Group on Rules, TN/RL/GEN/56 (July 4, 2005).

Discipline and Prohibition on Subsidies to IUU-Fishing. Communication by Norway, TN/RL/GEN/191 (June 26, 2017).

Draft Consolidated Chair Text of the AD and SCM Agreements, TN/RL/W/213 (Nov. 30, 2007).

Fisheries Subsidies Working Document. Communication from the Chair. Revision, TN/RL/W/274/REV.6 (Nov. 14, 2018).

Fisheries Subsidies. Compilation Matrix of Textual Proposals Received to Date. Introduction by the Chair, TN/RL/W/273 (July 28, 2017).

Fisheries Subsidies. Submitted by Antigua and Barbuda, Belize, Fuji Islands, Guyana, the Maldives, Papua New Guinea, Solomon Islands, St. Kitts and Nevis to the Negotiating Group on Rules, TN/RL/W/136 (July 14, 2003).

LDC Group Fisheries Subsidies Text Proposal. Submission of Cambodia on behalf of the LDC Group, TN/RL/GEN/193 (July 17, 2017).

Fisheries Subsidies: Limitations of Existing Subsidy Disciplines. Submission from New Zealand to the Negotiating Group on Rules, TN/RL/W/12 (July 4, 2002).

Proposal for Disciplines on Fisheries Subsidies. Communication from Argentina, Colombia, Costa Rica, Panama, Peru, and Uruguay, TN/RL/GEN/187/Rev.2 (July 24, 2017).

Proposed MC11 Fisheries Subsidies Disciplines: Implementing SDG *Target 14.6.* Communication from Iceland, New Zealand, and Pakistan, TN/RL/GEN/186 (Apr. 26, 2017).

Proposed Disciplines on Prohibitions and Special and Differential Treatment for Fisheries Subsidies. Proposal from Indonesia. Revision, TN/RL/GEN/189/Rev.1 (July 12, 2017).

Report by the Chairman to the Trade Negotiations Committee, TN/RL/9 (June 25, 2004).

The Doha Mandate to Address Fisheries Subsidies Issues. Submission from Australia, Chile, Ecuador, Iceland, New Zealand, Peru, Philippines and the United States to the Negotiating Group on Rules, TN/RL/W/3 (Apr. 24, 2002).

WTO Fisheries Subsidies Disciplines. Architecture on Fisheries Subsidies Disciplines. Paper from Fiji, Papua New Guinea and the Solomon Islands to the Negotiating Group on Rules, TN/RL/GEN/57 (July 7, 2005).

WTO Fisheries Subsidies Disciplines. Architecture on Fisheries Subsidies Disciplines. Paper from Fiji, Jamaica, Papua New Guinea, and the Solomon Islands to the Negotiating Group on Rules, TN/RL/GEN/57/Rev.1 (Aug. 4, 2005).

WTO Fisheries Subsidies Disciplines. Architecture on Fisheries Subsidies Disciplines. Paper from Antigua and Barbuda, Barbados, Dominican Republic, Fiji, Grenada, Guyana, Jamaica, Papua New Guinea, St, Kitts and Nevis, St. Lucia, Solomon Islands, and Trinidad and Tobago to the Negotiating Group on Rules, TN/RL/GEN/57/Rev.2 (Sept. 13, 2005).

EC and EU Documents

Commission Communication on a Sustainable Europe for a Better World: A European Union Strategy for Sustainable Development, May 15, 2001, COM(2001)264 Final.

Commission Communication on Building the Single Market for Green Products, Apr. 9, 2013, COM(2013)196 Final.

Commission Communication on Global Europe: Competing in the World, Oct. 4, 2006, COM(2006)567.

Council Resolution of May 28, 1969, 12 O.J. C 76/1 (1969).

Council Review of the EU Sustainable Development Strategy, June 9, 2006, 10117/06.

Declaration of the Council of the European Communities and of the representatives of the Governments of the member States meeting in the

Council of 22 November 1973 on the programme of action for the European Communities on the environment, O.J. C112/1 (1973).
European Court of Justice, Opinion 2/15, May 16, 2017.
European Parliament Resolution on Climate Diplomacy, July 3, 2018.
European Parliament Resolution on the 2018 UN Climate Change Conference in Katowice, Poland (COP24), Oct. 25, 2018.
Opinion of Advocate General Sharpston, Dec. 21, 2016.

United States Documents

Environmental Quality: The President's Message to the Congress Recommending a 37-Point Administrative and Legislative Program, 6 *Weekly Comp. Pres. Docs.* 160 (1970).
Exec. Order No. 13,141, 64 Fed. Reg. 63,169 (Nov. 16, 1999).
H. R. Con. Res. 246, 102d Cong., (1st Sess. 1991).
Pub. L. 102-582, 106 Stat. 4900, Sec. 203 (1992).
Remarks of President Nixon on Signing Public Law 91-604, Dec. 31, 1970, 7 *Weekly Comp. Pres. Docs.* 11-12 (1971).
Truman, Harry S., *Proclamation 2761: Carrying Out General Agreement on Tariffs and Trade Concluded at Geneva*, Oct. 30, 1947.
US Dept. of State, *Proposals for Expansion of World Trade and Employment*, State Department Publication No. 2411, Dec. 1945.
US Dept. of State, *Suggested Charter for an International Trade Organization of the United Nations*, State Department Publication No. 2598, Sept. 1946.
US Dept. of State, *A Constitution for World Trade*, Publication 2964, Commercial Policy Series 108 (1947).
US Dept. of State, *Analysis of General Agreement on Tariffs and Trade* (1947).
United States Senate, History of The Committee on Environment and Public Works-United States Senate, S. Doc. No. 100-45 (1988).
United States Trade Representative, Bipartisan Agreement on Trade Policy (May 2007).
White House Policy Declaration on Environment and Trade (Nov.16, 1999).
21 Cong. Rec. 4,250-53 (May 7, 1890).
72 Cong. Rec. 8,328 (May 15, 1930).
75 Cong. Rec. 10,639 (May 19, 1932) (statement of Sen. Hull).
115 Cong. Rec. 26,576 (1969) (remarks of Rep. Rogers).
115 Cong. Rec. 29,069 (1969) (remarks of Sen. Jackson).
116 Cong. Rec. 32,918 (1970) (remarks of Sen. Cooper).
116 Cong. Rec. 42,392 (remarks of Sen. Randolph).

Others

League of Nations, *Final Report. The World Economic Conference*, Geneva, May 1927, C.E.I. 44(1).

OECD, *Methodologies for Environmental and Trade Reviews* 5, OECD Doc. OECD/GD(94)103.

Press Release, Address by Secretary General, U Thant, at University of Texas on 14 May: Human Environment and World Order, U.N. Press Release SG/SM/1259 (May 14, 1970).

U.N. ESCOR, Comm'n on Sustainable Dev., 3rd Sess., Supp. No. 12 §69, U.N. Doc. E/CN/.17/1995/36 (1995).

Abbreviations

ADA	*Anti-Dumping Agreement*
APEC	*Asia-Pacific Economic Cooperation*
APTA	*Asia Pacific Trade Agreement*
ASCM	*Agreement on Subsidies and Countervailing Measures*
ASEAN	*Association of South-East Asian Nations*
BTA	*Border Tax Adjustment*
CARIFORUM	*Caribbean Forum*
CBD	*Convention on Biological Diversity*
CBDR	*Common but Differentiated Responsibilities*
CETA	*EU-Canada Comprehensive Economic and Trade Agreement*
CITES	*Convention on International Trade in Endangered Species of Wild Fauna and Flora*
CO_2	*Carbon Dioxide*
COP	*Conference of the Parties*
CSD	*Commission on Sustainable Development*
CTE	*Committee on Trade and Environment*
CTESS	*Committee on Trade and Environment in Special Session*
DSU	*Dispute Settlement Understanding*
EC	*European Community*
ECOSOC	*Economic and Social Council*
ECJ	*European Court of Justice*
EEA	*European Economic Area*
EEC	*European Economic Community*
EFTA	*European Free Trade Association*
EGS	*Environmental Goods and Services*
EIA	*Environmental Impact Assessment*
EIS	*Environmental Impact Statement*
EKC	*Environmental Kuznets Curve*
EMIT Group	*Group on Environmental Measures and International Trade*
EPA	*United States Environmental Protection Agency*
EPP	*Environmentally Preferable Product*
FAO	*Food and Agriculture Organization*
FFSR	*Fossil Fuel Subsidy Reform*
FTA	*Free Trade Agreement*
GATS	*General Agreement on Trade in Services*
GATT	*General Agreement on Tariffs and Trade*
GEO	*Global Environmental Organization*

GPA	*Agreement on Government Procurement*
HS	*Harmonized System*
ICC	*International Chamber of Commerce*
ICCAT	*International Convention for the Conservation of Atlantic Tunas*
ICSID	*International Centre for Settlement of Investment Disputes*
IISD	*International Institute for Sustainable Development*
ITO	*International Trade Organization*
IUCN	*International Union for Conservation of Nature*
IUU	*Illegal, Unreported and Unregulated*
MDGs	*Millennium Development Goals*
MEA	*Multilateral Environmental Agreement*
MFN	*Most Favoured Nation*
MMPA	*Marine Mammal Protection Act*
NAAEC	*North American Agreement on Environmental Cooperation*
NAFTA	*North American Free Trade Agreement*
NRBPs	*Natural Resources Based Products*
NEPA	*National Environmental Policy Act*
NGO	*Non-Governmental Organization*
NGR	*Negotiating Group on Rules*
NT	*National Treatment*
NTB	*Non-Tariff Barrier*
OECD	*Organization for Economic Cooperation and Development*
OSINFOR	*Agency for the Supervision of Forests and Wildlife Resources (Peru)*
PPM	*Process and Production Method*
PTPA	*United States-Peru Trade Promotion Agreement*
RFMO	*Regional Fisheries Management Organization*
RTAA	*Reciprocal Trade Agreement Act*
SADC	*Southern African Development Community*
SDGs	*Sustainable Development Goals*
SEA	*Single European Act*
SIDS	*Small Island Development States*
SPS	*Sanitary and Phytosanitary*
TBT	*Technical Barriers to Trade*
TEPAC	*United States Trade and Environmental Policy Advisory Committee*
TEU	*Treaty of the European Union*
TFEU	*Treaty on the Functioning of the European Union*
TREM	*Trade-Related Environmental Measure*
TRIPS	*Trade-Related Aspects of Intellectual Property Rights*
UK	*United Kingdom*
UN	*United Nations*

UNCLOS	*United Nations Convention on the Law of the Sea*
UNCTAD	*United Nations Conference on Trade and Development*
UNDP	*United Nations Development Programme*
UNEP	*United Nations Environment Programme*
UNESCO	*United Nations Educational, Scientific, and Cultural Organization*
UNFCCC	*United Nations Framework Convention on Climate Change*
US	*United States*
USCFTA	*United States-Canada Free Trade Agreement*
USMCA	*United States-Mexico-Canada Agreement*
USTR	*United States Trade Representative*
VCLT	*Vienna Convention on the Law of Treaties*
WHO	*World Health Organization*
WTO	*World Trade Organization*
WWF	*World Wildlife Fund*

CHAPTER 1

Introduction

Tampico, Mexico
October 2015

The cargo ship *Yacu Kallpa* was scheduled to arrive in Houston from Iquitos, Peru, after riding nearly 2,300 miles down the Amazon River and another 4,000 miles north to Tampico, with lumber harvested from the Amazon rain forest. It was a route that the captain and crew of the *Yacu Kallpa*, just as its predecessors, had run hundreds of times for more than 40 years. This time, however, something was different. Before reaching the United States (US) port, Homeland Security investigators, acting on intelligence from their Peruvian counterparts, seized the entire cargo: 1,770 metric tons of Amazon rainforest wood, almost the entirety of which was found to have been harvested illegally. Most of the shipment belonged to the Peruvian company Inversiones La Oroza SRL (Oroza) and, a few months after these events unfolded, the United States asked Peru to ensure that a particular shipment from that particular company complied with Peru's laws and regulations governing the harvest and trade in timber products. The timber verification process, initiated shortly thereafter, found that significant portions of the wood had been illegally harvested. On October 19, 2017, US Trade Representative Robert Lighthizer directed the US Customs and Border Protection to block all shipments from Oroza for three years or until compliance with Peru's environmental laws was restored. The sanction, just like the US request that Peru verify the company's compliance with Peru's environmental and timber laws, represented a significant step forward in the battle to preserve tropical forests. Yet, they were not triggered or motivated by an environmental treaty, as one might imagine. Rather, they had been adopted within the framework created by the PTPA, the free trade agreement between the United States and Peru.

Buenos Aires, Argentina
13 December 2017

When Susana Malcorra, Argentina's Foreign Minister at the time, took the floor to deliver her statement as Chair of the 11th Ministerial Conference of the World Trade Organization (WTO), she looked back at the three long days that had just passed. Much had been accomplished in those three days, as nearly 4000 ministers, senior trade officials and other delegates had engaged intensively in trying to move forward in numerous areas of the negotiations. With a sense of gratification, she emphasized that, for the first time, negotiators had finally taken a significant step forward with the decision on fisheries subsidies: "Buenos Aires will no doubt be remembered as the Conference at which the fisheries negotiation was launched in earnest."[1] Indeed, on December 13, 2017, WTO Members wrapped up their 11th Ministerial Conference with a commitment to secure a deal on fisheries subsidies by the end of 2019. The plan was to agree on comprehensive disciplines prohibiting certain forms of fisheries subsidies that contribute to overcapacity and overfishing, and eliminating subsidies that contribute to illegal, unreported, and unregulated fishing. In February 2019, at a meeting of the full WTO Membership in Geneva, former WTO Director-General Roberto Azevêdo observed progress in the negotiations and called on all the Members to be ready to engage in discussions at the political level to reach the final agreement by the foreseen 2019 deadline. The importance of such an agreement should not be underestimated, as it reflects the growing consensus within the international community on the need to conserve and sustainably use the ocean's resources, within the framework provided by the United Nations (UN) *2030 Agenda* to achieve the targets set out in Sustainable Development Goal 14.

Strasbourg, France
2 July 2018

Arne Lietz opened the European Parliament debate on the role of climate diplomacy in the context of the Union's External Action, emphasizing the importance that trade agreements can play in achieving the 2030 Sustainable Development Goals and in addressing the negative impacts of climate change. After the votes were cast, the *Resolution on Climate Diplomacy* was adopted with 448 votes in favor. The *Resolution*, among other things, called on the Commission "to integrate the climate change dimension into international trade and investment agreements and to make ratification and implementation of the Paris Agreement a condition for future trade agreements," while recommending the "development and systematic inclusion of a mandatory fundamental climate change clause in international agreements, including trade and investment agreements."[2] In other words, any new comprehensive trade agreement negotiated by the European Union in the future would have to respect these (environmental) conditions. This *Resolution* seems to be in

1 Closing Statement of the Chairperson, Eleventh Ministerial Conference, WT/MIN(17)/67 (Dec. 13, 2017).

2 European Parliament Resolution on Climate Diplomacy, July 3, 2018, 2017/2272(INI) [hereinafter Climate Diplomacy Resolution].

line with an Opinion rendered by the European Court of Justice just a few months before, where the Court had declared that the European Union has the "obligation" to integrate sustainable development objectives into the conduct of its commercial policy.

Geneva, Switzerland
2 October 2018

More than 2000 people—national delegates, leaders of non-governmental organizations (NGOs) and businesses, as well as students—gathered at the WTO headquarters in Geneva for three days of intense discussions on a challenging topic: 'Trade 2030'. The title and theme of the 2018 WTO Public Forum clearly echoed the *2030 Agenda for Sustainable Development* launched in September 2015 in New York. Indeed, former WTO Director-General Roberto Azevêdo emphasized, in his opening speech, that "trade can make a vital contribution to meeting the Sustainable Development Goals."[3] On the very first day of the Public Forum, Azevêdo, joined by then UN Environment Executive Director Erik Solheim, presented the audience with a new publication, which represented the outcome of an almost year-long cooperation between the two organizations. The publication, entitled *Making Trade Work for the Environment, Prosperity, and Resilience,* addressed the thorny question of how to best use trade policies and design trade rules that are conducive to, among others, environmental protection. Some of the findings of this study found their way into another publication presented by Azevêdo on the very same day, entitled *Mainstreaming Trade to Attain the Sustainable Development Goals.* The argument developed in the book—that trade can be used as an instrument to achieve the sustainable development goals—stems from the *2030 Agenda* itself, which describes trade as a 'means of implementations' to attain its 17 goals.

Geneva, Switzerland
17 December 2020

On 17 December 2020, the United States circulated a draft Ministerial Conference Decision aimed at addressing the imbalance in the existence and enforcement of fundamental environmental protection standards among the Members of the WTO.[4] The proposal, entitled *Advancing Sustainability Goals through Trade Rules to Level the Playing Field,* would address the imbalance by making the enactment and enforcement of environmental standards below

3 Roberto Azevêdo, Address at the 2018 WTO Public Forum.

4 Draft Ministerial Decision, *Advancing Sustainability Goals through Trade Rules to Level the Playing Field,* WT/GC/W/814, 17 December 2020.

a certain level of environmental protection an 'actionable subsidy' under the WTO Agreement on Subsidies and Countervailing Measures and allowing other Members to impose duties to offset the benefits received by the subsidized industry. The proposal was presented as part of the *Structured Discussions on Trade and Environmental Sustainability* launched on 20 November 2020 by a group of Members including, among others, the European Union, Australia, Canada, Japan, Mexico, Costa Rica and Senegal. The Discussions are of particular importance in that they seem to convey the idea that the WTO would be the place to deliver progress on issues related to trade and sustainability. The implications of the US proposal, if adopted, could be far-reaching. On the one hand, such a decision could serve as a vehicle to integrate the environmental principle of non-regression in the corpus of WTO law—a principle that has found its way into many recent bilateral and regional trade agreements to avoid regressing in relation to existing levels of environmental protection. On the other, it would introduce the observance of an 'acceptable' standard of environmental protection as a condition for compliance with WTO rules.

1 Vantage Points

These five accounts, although they occurred in different places at different times, and involved different characters, have something in common: they all paint a certain picture of the relationship between trade and the environment, a picture where the environment is portrayed as a value that should be protected, and trade policies, agreements, and institutions as the means to ensure such protection. In other words, these five accounts present the reader with the very same story, seen from five different vantage points:

VP 1. A free trade agreement which led to the creation of an institutional framework devoted to forest and wildlife protection, committed a country to modify and update its environmental laws, and formed the legal basis to block the entry into the US market of illegally-harvested timber when, in the past, these kinds of provisions could only be found in environmental agreements and their consistency with trade rules was often highly contested.

VP 2. A group of WTO negotiators who have made significant efforts to modify trade rules so that they would make sense from an environmental point of view and so that one of the Sustainable Development Goals could be more easily attained, in contrast with decades of discussions on whether environmental policies lined up with the trade agenda.

VP 3. An international institution, the European Parliament, which sees the inclusion of environmental provisions in the text of free trade agreements and being party to certain environmental treaties as a necessary condition to enter into trade negotiations with the European Union while, in the past, the criteria to select partners in trade agreements and to negotiate them were purely economic and not even remotely connected to environmental protection.

VP 4. The heads of the two main international trade and environmental institutions who are shaping their relationship, and that of the underlying international regimes, in terms of mutual coordination and cooperation, in order to design a trade system that is conducive to environmental protection and the realization of the Sustainable Development Goals, after years of reciprocal isolation and reversing once and for all the terms of their relationship.

VP 5. Finally, a proposal to amend WTO rules not simply to carve out some space for the environment but to transform a trade agreement into an instrument that would allow countries to address another country's lack of environmental regulation by equating such a situation to a subsidy, and therefore actively using a trade instrument to advance sustainability goals.

2 The Untold Story of the Trade/Environment Nexus

These five accounts do not certainly represent and exhaust all the current manifestations of the trade/environment nexus. One can surely think of other examples where trade rules are drafted or implemented without the environment in mind, or where trade agreements are negotiated to attain purely economic goals. At the same time, these same five accounts may come as a surprise to all those among us who are well acquainted with the international trade and environmental regimes and with their intricate relationship.[5] They may come as a surprise because they do not depict environmental protection as

5 Regimes are intended in this book as governing arrangements agreed upon by governments to coordinate their expectations and organize aspects of their behavior in various issue-areas. See Stephen Krasner (ed.), *International Regimes* (Cornell University Press, 1983) [defining 'international regimes' as "implicit or explicit principles, norms, rules, and decision-making procedures around which actors' expectations converge in a given area of international relations"]. Robert O. Keohane, *After Hegemony: Cooperation and Discord in the World Political Economy* (Princeton University Press, 1984) and *International Institutions and State Power: Essays in International Relations Theory* (Westview Press, 1989) [defining 'regimes' as "institutions with explicit rules, agreed upon by governments, that pertain to particular sets of issues in international relations" and 'institutions' as "persistent and connected sets of rules (formal and informal) that prescribe behavioral roles, constrain activity, and shape expectations"]. See also Andreas Hasenclever, Peter Mayer and Volker Rittberger, *Theories of International Regimes* (Cambridge University Press, 1997).

antithetical to the overarching purpose of international trade law—interfering with trade and undermining countries' efforts to further liberalize trade and pursue economic growth. Nor do they portray it as a 'non-trade' issue, to be added or accommodated within the trade regime, translated into its economic jargon and subjected to its hard-driving logic. The picture they draw is instead one where environmental protection and sustainable development are part of the very nature and purpose of trade law, and where trade norms and institutions are instrumental to their fulfillment.

2.1 *Transcending the 'Trade and …' Debate*

These five accounts may come as a surprise because the story we have all been told about the so called 'trade/environment nexus' is one of *conflicts*.[6] In this context, the term 'conflict' is defined rather broadly, to refer not only to situations where two or more norms are intrinsically mutually exclusive (normative incompatibilities),[7] but rather situations where "one norm interferes with the intended functioning of another or pursues an objective which is hostile to that of another."[8] The international trade and environmental regimes have been mostly perceived as being in conflict considering that the former is generally regarded as a regime aimed at liberalizing trade and the economy, while the latter as one that seeks to regulate them.[9] As a result, the environmentalists' arguments seem to "sharply challenge the trade regime's *raison d'être*, [which] is to limit the ability of national governments to interfere with trade."[10]

---

6 The literature on norm conflicts in international law is vast. See e.g. Wilfred Jenks, 'The Conflict of Law-Making Treaties' (1953) 30 *British Yearbook of International Law* 400; Hamner Hill, 'A Functional Taxonomy of Normative Conflict' (1987) 6 *Law and Philosophy* 227; Joseph Weiler and Andreas L. Paulus, 'The Structure of Change in International Law or Is There a Hierarchy of Norms in International Law?'(1997) 8 *European Journal of International Law* 545; Joost Pauwelyn, *Conflict of Norms in Public International Law* (Cambridge University Press, 2003); Christopher Borgen, 'Resolving Treaty Conflicts' (2005) 37 *George Washington International Law Review* 573; Erich Vranes, 'The Definition of "Norm Conflict" in International Law and Legal Theory' (2006) 17 *European Journal of International Law* 395.

7 According to Jenks, for instance, a conflict "arises only where a party to two treaties cannot simultaneously comply with its obligations under both treaties." Jenks, 'The Conflict of Law-Making Treaties' (n 6) 426.

8 Mario Prost, *The Concept of Unity in Public International Law* (Hart Publishing, 2012), p. 63. See also Hill, 'A Functional Taxonomy of Normative Conflict' (n 6) 227; Hans Kelsen, *General Theory of Norms* (Clarendon Press, 1991), p. 125.

9 Borgen, 'Resolving Treaty Conflicts' (n 6) 575.

10 Jeffrey L. Dunoff, 'Rethinking International Trade' (1998) 19 *University of Pennsylvania Journal of International Economic Law* 347, 383.

In addition to revolving around conflicts, the story we have been told has been largely approached from the perspective of the trade regime and is therefore one where, whenever the objectives of the two regimes seem to clash, free trade always prevails over protection and market forces always prevail over government intervention;[11] where environmental protection, because it cannot be realized through trade liberalization and market mechanisms alone, but requires some form of government intervention, is regarded with suspicion and even hostility, as it may hide protectionist intents. All efforts to reconcile what appears to be an irreconcilable conflict and to ensure the peaceful coexistence of trade and environmental rules at an international level have been anchored to a trade-centred perspective. In fact, the focus has been on mapping the objectives, values, and rules of the international environmental regime, comparing them with those of the international trade regime, identifying conflicts and incompatibilities, and then coming up with solutions to aid in the resolution or prevention of those conflicts.[12] And, in designing these solutions, trade norms have served as the relevant framework against which any environmental measure or policy needs to be evaluated and assessed, and have provided the language needed to describe them and the parameters used to assess their trade restrictiveness.

Despite internal differences,[13] these efforts share one important common denominator, as they all tend to frame the relationship between the trade and environmental regimes as part of the broader 'trade and …' debate.[14] The latter

11 While in the 1940s, when the multilateral trading system was first created, neoliberal ideas coexisted with the theory of embedded liberalism, in the 1970s, neoliberalism emerged as a salient political force and began to provide the shared normative narrative supporting the trading system ever since. See e.g. John G. Ruggie, 'International Regimes, Transactions and Change: Embedded Liberalism in the Postwar Economic Order' (1982) 36 *International Organization* 379; Robert Howse, 'From Politics to Technocracy—And Back Again: The Fate of the Multilateral Trading Regime' (2002) 96 *American Journal of International Law* 94; Andrew Lang, *World Trade Law After Neoliberalism. Re-Imagining the Global Economic Order* (Oxford University Press, 2013); Harlan Grant Cohen, 'What is International Trade Law For?' (2019) 113(2) *American Journal of International Law* 326.

12 This has been the approach vis-à-vis other non-trade concerns as well, such as human rights or labor issues. See Andrew Lang, 'The Role of the Human Rights Movement in Trade Policy-Making: Human Rights as a Trigger for Policy Learning' (2007) 5 *New Zealand Journal of Public International Law* 77, 91.

13 Scholars have been rather divided as to how to achieve convergence between trade liberalization and environmental protection. Some have argued that existing trade rules do not require any amendment, as they already allow countries to adopt environmental measures, as long as they are not discriminatory, while others have been holding that improvement would be necessary. And many different views exist with regards to what form these improvements should take.

14 See e.g. the 2002 AJIL Symposium on *The Boundaries of the WTO*.

addresses the question of how the trade regime should best deal with a variety of 'non-trade' objectives, including environmental protection, and therefore presupposes a certain perspective on the issue. Constructing certain values as 'trade values' and others as 'non-trade values' necessarily favours the former over the latter when it comes to defining their relationship.[15] Moreover, this approach assumes that the purpose and *raison d'être* of the two regimes are inherently antithetical, so that their relationship can only be framed as a conflict to be more or less successfully reconciled. As long as the trading system is understood as a system aimed solely at liberalizing trade and limiting national governments' interference with it, environmental protection will always be labelled as a 'non-trade' issue, to be translated in economic terms, and the relationship between the two legal regimes will always be framed as in conflict. And even those who argue that the trade regime should be 'greened' do not seem to question these assumptions, and rather continue to operate within this traditional framework.

This is the traditional story of the relationship between trade and the environment: a conflicting relationship between what is and what is not—technically—trade; a relationship addressed from a free trade perspective, where trade liberalization is portrayed as the overarching goal of the trade regime and non-discrimination represents the rule, while environmental protection is nothing more than an exception. The result is that even when states are allowed to discriminate or otherwise restrict trade to pursue legitimate (environmental) policy goals, strict requirements are imposed.

This book tells a different story of the relationship between international trade and environmental law, one where the five accounts described at the beginning of this chapter do not come as a surprise but rather as the natural culmination of a long and intricate story. A story where the keyword is no longer *conflict*; where the international trade and environmental regimes were never meant to be pitted against one another; and the environment was never intended to be simply a footnote in the history of international trade cooperation, cornered in a narrow exception, but rather an integral part of its evolving purpose.

The perception of the relationship between the two regimes as a conflicting one rests on the assumption that they pursue very different—nearly diametrically opposite—objectives and their norms end up interfering with their reciprocal intended functioning. The assumption, in other words, is that trade norms are designed to liberalize trade, while environmental norms are

---

15 Dunoff, 'Rethinking International Trade' (n 10) 383.

designed to regulate it. It is a perception that is equally based on the assumption that trade and the environment belong to two separate issue areas, and whenever attempts are made to 'link' the environment to the trade regime, a hierarchy is almost instantaneously established between what is and what is not, technically, 'trade'. To the contrary, this book intends to challenge the architecture on which the existing debate rests, questioning the very meaning given to its different terms and challenging the idea of trade liberalization as the sole *raison d'être* of the trade regime.

In doing so, the following chapters will argue that the trade regime was always meant for something greater than simply trade liberalization. In the first half of the twentieth century, this 'something greater' was international peace and stability, to avoid the horrors of the two world wars. Over time, as the spectre of war became just a long-distant memory, the trade regime was retooled for other ultimate goals, as part of different grand visions. Today, environmental degradation, lack of access to clean and affordable water, and spreading hunger and poverty have become as pressing as ensuring peaceful inter-state relations was in the 1940s. As a result, environmental protection and sustainable development, rather than antithetical to the overarching purpose of the trading system or simply labeled as 'non-trade' issues to be accommodated within the hard-driving logic of trade, should be seen as part of the very nature and purpose of the trade regime.

2.2 *The Importance of Historical Inquiry*

To tell this story adequately and convincingly, it will be necessary to unpack the historical evolution of the trade and environmental regimes and dig deep into the motivations of their respective founders: to closely follow the development of certain ideas within the two regimes, and see them draw near, get tangled, and grow together as the respective communities begin interacting and the two regimes begin intersecting. Above all, it will be necessary to stop wearing the lenses provided by the international trade law framework and start questioning and challenging the very meaning of 'trade liberalization' and the *raison d'être* of the international trade regime.

Tracing the chronological unfolding of the two regimes forces us to look at history, and it is precisely this newly-acquired historical awareness that will allow the reader to recognize that the meaning of both 'free trade' and 'trade liberalization' is far from fixed, and the motivations and rationales underlying the trade regime itself are anything but timeless. It is only by tracing the historical evolution of the two regimes that one can fully appreciate and properly understand the nature of their relationship. Overlooking history, on the other hand, can contribute to a distorted vision of the trading system, and of the relationship between the two regimes, which, nevertheless, has become dominant over the years. This vision seems to forget the instrumental role of trade liberalization and to ignore the evolving nature of the underlying rationale and purpose of the trade regime, focusing instead on the potential for conflict between international trade and environmental law.

Moreover, it is a vision that seems to forget that environmental protection has been limited to an exception for many years simply as a result of a series of 'concurring circumstances', and not as part of some grand scheme of the founders of the General Agreement on Tariffs and Trade (GATT). The subsequent appearance of the 'environment issue' on the international agenda forced the latter to fit within the already existing (economic) legal framework. Efficiency considerations motivated the preference for relying on existing instruments, provisions, and institutions rather than creating new ones to accommodate the environment. Added to this was the profound transformation of the trading system after the 1970s, which became more formalized and 'technicalized', as well as motivated by economic and ideological concerns rather than the political ones that had inspired the founders of the regime. By the time the environment had become an issue worthy of international cooperation, embedded liberalism, which depicted the market as 'embedded' in a broader social fabric, and multilateralism, as predicated upon domestic interventionism, had given way to neoliberal thought. The latter upheld the indisputable superiority of free trade over protection and of market forces over government intervention, and had subtly become the prevailing normative narrative underlying the trade regime.

Only by unpacking the historical evolution of the trade and environmental regimes, digging deep into the motivations of their respective founders, and following closely the development of certain ideas, one can truly part from this traditional narrative and tell the story of a trade regime that was always meant to be for something greater than simply trade liberalization, and where environmental protection was never truly in irreconcilable conflict with the purposes of the trading system, but rather an integral part of those purposes. The complete isolation in which the trade and environmental communities had been working for years, together with these communities' deep cultural differences, undermined any attempt of communication or interaction, contributing to an environment entirely non-conducive to normative development and change. In fact, to develop and disseminate, *ideas* require a process of *learning,* which can only take place under certain conditions and in the context of policy-making environments conducive to change.[16] As aptly explained by Ruggie, "actors not only reproduce normative structures, they also change them … as underlying conditions change, as new constraints or possibilities emerge, or as new claimants make their presence felt."[17] After years of reciprocal isolation, conditions have changed and new actors have come along, encouraging new discourses and disseminating new ideas. This book tells the story of these ideas, of these changed conditions and new actors. It tells the story of a trading system where it is precisely certain *changes in conditions* (i.e. the gradual openness of trade institutions) and the *presence of new claimants* (i.e. the growing environmental community) that have facilitated the development of certain ideas and allowed the inherently complementary and synergetic nature of the trade and environmental regimes to come to the surface, giving rise to trade norms and institutions that are increasingly working for the protection of the environment and the promotion of sustainable development goals.

By telling this 'untold' story, this book intends to raise historical awareness, stimulate questions regarding the relationship and the purpose of the trade and environmental regimes, as well as explore the future of international economic law governance. It is also meant to part ways from the

16 The role of ideas and learning as conducive to normative change has been studied far and wide by international relations theorists. See e.g. Bo Hedberg, 'How Organizations Learn and Unlearn', in Paul C. Nystrom and William H. Starbuck (eds.), *Handbook of Organizational Design* (Oxford University Press, 1981); Judith Goldstein, 'Ideas, Institutions and American Trade Policy'(1988) 42(1) *International Organization* 179; William J. Drake and Kalypso Nicolaïdis, 'Ideas, Interests, and Institutionalization: "Trade in Services" and the Uruguay Round' (1992) 46(1) *International Organization* 37; Judith Goldstein and Robert O. Keohane (eds.), *Ideas and Foreign Policy, Ideas, Institutions, and Political Change* (Cornell University Press, 1993); Kathryn Sikkink, 'Transnational Advocacy Networks and the Social Construction of Legal Rules', in Yves Dezalay and Bryant G. Garth (eds.), *Global Prescriptions: The Production, Exportation, and Importation of a New Legal Orthodoxy* (Ann Arbor, 2002), p. 37; Mark Blyth, *Great Transformations: Economic Ideas and Institutional Change in the Twentieth Century* (Cambridge University Press, 2002); Diana Tussie (ed.), *The Politics of Trade: The Role of Research in Trade Policy and Negotiation* (Brill Academic Publishers, 2009); Lang, *World Trade Law After Neoliberalism* (n 11) and 'The Role of the Human Rights Movement' (n 12).

17 John G. Ruggie, 'Epistemology, Ontology, and the Study of International Regimes', in John G. Ruggie (ed.), *Constructing the World Polity: Essays on International Institutionalization* (Routledge, 1998), p. 85. Sociologists call this process "structuration." See Anthony Giddens, *A Contemporary Critique of Historical Materialism* (University of California Press, 1981).

prevailing—neoliberal—narrative of the trading system. A narrative that, oblivious to the historical, economic, and political changes that have occurred over the years, remains deeply rooted in the belief of the timelessness of the international trade regime. One should not forget that learning can influence a given regime at different levels:[18] at a first, shallower level, learning can influence the prevailing view about the best technical means to achieve certain policy goals—in other words, the rules and procedures of the regime;[19] at a deeper level, it can influence the way in which the nature of the regimes' goals is perceived, requiring a re-evaluation of the normative narrative underlying and justifying the regime itself.[20] And this narrative, just as any other, is not eternal: "over time, other stories have been told about trade's purpose, producing different policies and encouraging different politics"[21] and the time may be ripe to tell a new story.

What follows is an invitation to suspend the mainstream discourse on the relationship between trade and the environment in terms of conflicts and to call the notion of trade liberalization as the *raison d'être* of the trade regime into question. This means questioning the use of trade liberalization as an undisputed assumption, showing that it is not self-evident and can—or should—instead be challenged.

---

18 Andrew Lang discusses this process of ideational change, which he refers to as 'policy learning' in the context of trade and human rights. See Lang, 'The Role of the Human Rights Movement' (n 12).

19 As explained by Krasner, regimes are a composite of four analytical components: *principles* ("beliefs of fact, causation, and rectitude"), *norms* ("standards of behavior defined in terms of rights and obligations"), *rules* ("specific prescriptions and proscriptions for action"), and *decision-making procedures* ("prevailing practices for making and implementing collective choice"). Krasner (ed.), *International Regimes* (n 5). Ruggie and Kratochwil apply these four analytical components to the GATT, as an example: "The principle that liberalized trade is good for global welfare and international peace was readily translated by states into such norms as nondiscrimination, which in turn suggested the most-favored-nation rule, all of which led to negotiated tariff reductions based on reciprocal concessions." John G. Ruggie and Friederich Kratochwil, 'International Organization: A State of the Art on an Art of the State' (1986) 40(4) *International Organization* 753, 769. Moreover, these four components are not always necessarily coherent, and changes can take place in some components and not in others. Ruggie argues that "only under extremely unusual circumstances could we imagine parallel and simultaneous changes having taken place in each of the four component parts of regimes such that they remained coherent." Ruggie, 'Epistemology' (n 17) 99.

20 Lang, 'The Role of the Human Rights Movement' (n 12).

21 Cohen, 'What is International Trade Law For?' (n 11) 327.

3 The Hidden Thread

This untold story relies on three simple ideas. First, trade is a means to an end rather than an end in itself. Second, the trade regime and its underlying rationales are historically contingent. And third, individuals and communities contribute to the development of new ideas and learning. Trite as this may sound, these three ideas have significant implications for the way we think about the relationship between international trade and environmental law and, more broadly, about the international trading system as a whole.

3.1 *Trade Is a Means to an End*

The starting point of this inquiry is the acknowledgement that *trade is a means to an end*, rather than an end in itself. In other words, it is necessary to move away from the temptation of attaching normative significance to trade itself.[22] When the idea of free trade first gained ground in the 1850s, liberalized trade among sovereign nations was praised because it was believed to increase the wealth of the nations that took part in it. A century later, the preamble of the GATT emphasized that trade was useful only insofar as it served broader goals, namely "raising standards of living, ensuring full employment and a large and steadily growing volume of real income and effective demand, developing the full use of the resources of the world and expanding the production and exchange of goods."[23] Although this may appear to some readers as a truism, it is often forgotten. Trade officials, in particular, can sometimes "lose sight of these goals by narrowing the operational goal of trade agreements to that of trade liberalization."[24] This narrow understanding of the trade regime can be explained with the strong influence of the 'bicycle theory' of trade liberalization on the trade community. The theory, generally attributed to Fred Bergsten, of the 'neo-liberal-oriented' Institute for International Economics,[25]

---

22 See e.g. Dani Rodrik, *One Economics, Many Recipes: Globalization, Institutions, and Economic Growth* (Princeton University Press, 2008), p. 227.

23 General Agreement on Tariffs and Trade, Oct. 30, 1947, 61 Stat. A-11, 55 U.N.T.S. 194 [hereinafter GATT], Preamble.

24 Gregory Shaffer, 'Retooling Trade Agreements for Social Inclusion' (2019) 1 *University of Illinois Law Review* 1, 5.

25 Fred Bergsten, *Toward a New International Economic* Order (Lexington Books, 1975). See also Jagdish Bhagwati, *Protectionism* (MIT Press, 1988). The description of the Institute for International Economics as "neo-liberal-oriented" is borrowed from Robert Howse, 'The World Trade Organization 20 Years On: Global Governance by Judiciary' (2016) 27(1) *European Journal of International Law* 9, 22.

states that an open trading system will be maintained only if forward momentum for trade liberalization continues, so to avoid that the bicycle might fall over. Despite lacking any rigorous explanation or justification,[26] this theory has been guiding the trade community for decades, explaining the frequent unidirectional focus of trade negotiations.

Similar to the GATT, the preamble to the Agreement establishing the World Trade Organization—generally known as WTO Agreement—lists all the goals that multilateral trade liberalization should serve. If one were to compare the two preambles, as many have done over the years,[27] a corollary of the idea that "trade is a means to an end" would immediately stand out, namely that these ends tend to change over time. In 1947, trade was instrumental to economic growth—in the narrow sense of increasing per capita income and raising standards of living and employment opportunities—and indirectly to ensuring more peaceful relations among states as a result of each country being better off economically. In 1995, instead, trade was seen as serving much broader social and developmental goals, as evidenced by the new addition to the preamble of the WTO Agreement:

> Recognizing that their relations in the field of trade and economic endeavor should be conducted with a view to raising standards of living, ensuring full employment and a large and steadily growing volume of real income and effective demand, and expanding the production of and trade in goods and services, while allowing for the optimal use of the world's resources *in accordance with the objective of sustainable development, seeking both to protect and preserve the environment* and to enhance the means for doing so in a manner consistent with their respective needs and concerns at different levels of economic development.[28]

In the 1995 preamble, the notion of 'sustainable development' replaced that of 'economic growth', pure and simple. *Development,* on the one hand, refers to a process of transformation, which is not limited to economic growth but rather combines it with broader social and cultural changes, to enable individuals to achieve a certain 'quality of life' and realize their full potential.[29] *Sustainability,*

---

26 See e.g. Dani Rodrik, 'Trade Policy as Riding Bicycles' (July 20, 2007).

27 See e.g. Steve Charnovitz, 'The WTO's Environmental Progress' (2007) 10(3) *Journal of International Economic Law* 685.

28 Marrakesh Agreement Establishing the World Trade Organization, April 15, 1994, 1867 U.N.T.S. 154 [hereinafter WTO Agreement], Preamble (emphasis added).

29 Neil Carter, *The Politics of the Environment: Ideas, Activism, Policy* (Cambridge University Press, 2018), p. 211.

on the other, brings the recognition that growth and development "must … adhere to the physical constraints imposed by ecosystems, so that environmental considerations have to be embedded in all sectors and policy areas."[30] This dynamic nature of the goals trade is asked to serve points to the historical contingency of the meaning of 'free trade' and of the purpose of the international trade regime itself.

3.2 *The International Trade Regime Is Historically Contingent*

As clearly stated by Andrew Lang, "different epochs in the history of international trade are characterized by differences in the prevailing meaning of free trade"[31] and in the prevailing understanding of what the trade regime is for. The socio-economic and political environment of a specific time period influences the rationales and the motivations behind the regime's existence, as they are themselves historically contingent. Were the motivations behind trade liberalization and international cooperation on trade matters in 1850 the same as in 1947, in 1994, or today? There is hardly any doubt that this question should be answered in the negative. In turn, these different motivations, just as the different meanings given to free trade, influence the principles, norms, rules, and procedures of the regime.[32] As noted by Robert Baldwin, while economists tend to judge the rules of agreements such as the GATT "on the basis of whether they promote economic efficiency, growth and stability,"[33] their primary purpose is rather to protect certain political goals of nation states. Economic factors, although important, simply influence such political goals. It follows that the prevailing meanings of free trade did not change over time because of different economic considerations alone, but most importantly because they responded to certain ideologies and were embedded in certain political and historical environments.

---

30 Ibid., p. 212.

31 Andrew Lang, 'Reflecting on "Linkage:" Cognitive and Institutional Change in the International Trading System' (2007) 70(4) *Modern Law Review* 523, 529. The lack of one single definition of free trade is addressed extensively by David Driesen, who argues that, because the term has never been defined, ever since it emerged in the works of Smith and Ricardo, it is characterized by a certain ambiguity. The same agreement, as Driesen explains, can contain provisions that reflect different meanings of 'free trade'. Article III of the GATT, for instance, reflects a definition of 'free trade' as "trade free from discrimination against foreign goods as a tool of economic policy." Article XI, on the other hand, defines 'free trade' more broadly than trade free from discrimination, as trade free of burdens. David M. Driesen, 'What is Free Trade? The Real Issue Lurking Behind the Trade and Environment Debate' (2001) 41 *Virginia Journal of International Law* 279.

32 Lang, 'Reflecting on "Linkage"' (n 31) 529.

33 Robert E. Baldwin, 'The Economics of the GATT', in Peter Oppenheimer (ed.), *Issues in International Economics* (Oriel Press, 1978), p. 83.

3.2.1 The Emergence of Free Trade thought—The 1850s

Free trade, defined as the "absence of protectionist trade policies that discriminated against foreign goods,"[34] emerged in Europe in the 1850s, in several ways in reaction to the mercantilist doctrine. The latter had been shaped by the international economic environment of the time—in particular by the vast expansion of world trade overseas and the rise of nation-states as political entities—and proposed government regulation of foreign trade to achieve various objectives.[35] Starting from the assumption that the private interests of the merchants could differ from the broader interest of the nation, "state oversight, guidance, and intervention" was seen as necessary to ensure "that trade was carried on for the enrichment of the country rather than for the merchants alone."[36] In the 1850s, a new idea gained ground, generally associated with the earlier work of Adam Smith and David Ricardo, which argued that "a policy of liberalizing restrictions on imports would maximize the wealth of the sovereign."[37] This new idea emerged in reaction to the mercantilist view that wealth was reduced by free trade and, at the same time, cast doubt "on the ability of government to administer regulations in a way that would improve national welfare."[38] In fact, Smith's theory was based on a strong separation between the public and the private sphere: "the market, domestic or international, is an independent category of activity that should be insulated from governmental interference, even to further other values."[39] This private/public separation and

34 Douglas A. Irwin, *Against The Tide* (Princeton University Press, 1996), p. 48. 'Free trade', in its original meaning, referred to "a commercial activity in which entry was unrestricted, where the liberty of the merchant to participate in trade was unhindered by exclusionary guild regulations or government grants of monopoly rights and privileges." In other words, it had nothing to do with the abolition of import tariffs and the like. See p. 46.

35 Ibid., p. 28.

36 Ibid., p. 32. The point of state regulation of trade was to promote so-called 'good channels' and discourage 'bad channels', keeping in mind a twofold objective: to achieve a favorable balance of trade and to promote economic development and employment in manufacturing. To this end, imports were highly regulated, while exports were favored.

37 Howse, 'From Politics to Technocracy' (n 11) 94.

38 Irwin, *Against The Tide* (n 34) 50.

39 Adam Smith, *An Inquiry into the Nature and Causes of the Wealth of Nations* (1776). On the other hand, Smith did not deny that governments could have an important role, but in his visions this role was restricted to national defense, protection of property rights, and administration of justice. See Dani Rodrik, *The Globalization Paradox* (Norton & Company Inc., 2011), p. 9. Kenneth W. Abbott, '"Economic" issues and Political Participation: The Evolving Boundaries of International Federalism' (1996) 18 *Cardozo Law Review* 971, 977. As explained by Ruggie, "the image of the market became an increasingly captivating social metaphor and served to focus diverse responses on the outcome of free trade ... The role of the state became to institute and safeguard the self-regulating market." Ruggie, 'International Regimes' (n 11) 386.

the rigid independence of markets from governments were seen in those years as fundamental to remove economic rivalries and conflicts that may derive from the coexistence of sovereign states.[40] Another reaction to the mercantilist doctrine was the unilateral nature of free trade, which can also be explained by the leading role played by Great Britain in that epoch, as British classical economists were skeptical of multilateralism. Commercial treaties were seen as diverting "trade into channels where it would not naturally flow,"[41] and as producing "international tension and suspicion."[42]

3.2.2 Post-War Economic Reconstruction and the GATT

The political reality of the post-war period contributed to the creation of a notion of free trade which differed in many ways from the one embraced by Europe in the nineteenth century, as well as of a precise understanding of what post-war trade cooperation should look like. As has been pointed out, "the collective historical memory of the resurgence of protectionism in the interwar years, and the subsequent descent into world war, were at the heart of the reconstitution of free trade in the aftermath of World War II."[43] In those years, the paramount goal was the avoidance of a protectionist *summum malum*,[44] embodied in the Smoot-Hawley Tariff Act of 1930 and soon associated in the public eye with the Great Depression and World War II. Multilateral cooperation to reduce tariffs, on the other hand, was identified with expanding trade and increasing peaceful relations among nations. As a result, the case for protectionism was significantly weakened and free trade principles slowly gained ground once again.[45]

However, it was a different kind of 'free trade' than the one that had emerged in Great Britain in the 1850s. First, there had been a shift in political power, and it was the United States, rather than Britain, who provided international economic leadership during the 1940s, and for at least two decades. The

40 Wilhelm Röpke, 'Economic Order and International Law', in *Collected Courses of the Hague Academy of International Law* (The Hague Academy of International Law, 1954), p. 224.

41 Denis O'Brien, 'Customs Unions: Trade Creation and Trade Diversion in Historical Perspective' (1976) 8(4) *History of Political Economy* 540, 547. See Smith, *The Wealth of Nations* (n 39).

42 O'Brien, 'Customs Unions' (n 41) 554. See *Speech Delivered by Lord Overstone in the House of Lords 1.5 March 1860 on the Address on the Treaty of Commerce with France; with an Appendix* (London, 1860), p. 9.

43 Lang, 'Reflecting on "Linkage"' (n 31) 528.

44 Howse, 'From Politics to Technocracy' (n 11) 94–5.

45 Douglas A. Irwin, *Clashing Over Commerce* (The University of Chicago Press, 2017), p. 26.

extraordinary power and perseverance of the United States contributed greatly to the particular shape taken by post-war economic reconstruction and trade cooperation. It was for instance the United States who pushed for a *multilateral* trade order,[46] in contrast to the traditional British preference for unilateral trade liberalization.[47] Despite its leading role, however, the United States proved to be prepared to make economic concessions and accommodate both British and developing countries' demands, precisely because non-economic concerns underlay post-war trade negotiations, and international cooperation on economic matters was seen as fundamental to facilitate the abandonment of dangerous unilateral policies and to increase the chances for world peace:

> The hegemon's willingness to accept asymmetric trade agreements is not a function of economic interests alone. Both trade agreements and trade disputes have inherently international political underpinnings; their foundations are not solely economic: Great Britain and the United States had important political objectives for which they were prepared to make economic concessions.[48]

Second, during the inter-war period, state-society relations had undergone a profound transformation.[49] As a result of industrialization, democratization,

46 Ruggie, 'International Regimes' (n 11) 397.

47 The leading role played by Great Britain in the late XIX century and the United States after World War II, has fueled the *hegemonic stability theory*, which argues, as explained by Charles Kindleberger, that "only a single, strong and dominant actor in international politics can provide and maintain a stable international economic order." Douglas A. Irwin, Petros C. Mavroidis, and Alan O. Sykes, *The Genesis of the GATT* (Cambridge University Press, 2008), p. 189. As explained by Kindleberger, "[f]or the world economy to be stable, it needs a stabilizer." Charles P. Kindleberger, 'Dominance and Leadership in the International Economy' (1981) 25(2) *International Studies Quarterly* 242, 247. He argues that "Britain, with frequent assistance from France, furnished coherence to the world economy along these lines during the nineteenth century and through the 'belle epoque.' The United States did so from 1945 (or perhaps 1936) to 1968 (or 1963 or 1971). From 1919 to 1939, Britain could not, and the United States would not, act in the capacity of world leader." See also Röpke, 'Economic Order and International Law' (n 40) 223: "every workable international order seems to require the guiding and controlling hand of a *dominant power* which, by its political force, economic weight, diplomatic experience and firmness of principles, is able to set the tone, to give the example and to assume responsibilities of the first order ... Great Britain lost this position after two world wars [and] the United States ... step[ped] into her place" (emphasis added).

48 Arthur A. Stein, 'The Hegemon's Dilemma: Great Britain, the United States, and the International Economic Order' (1984) 38 *International Organization* 355, 395.

49 Ruggie, 'International Regimes' (n 11) 387.

and World War I, society had become more politically active and empowered, and had begun demanding greater economic protection from the government, together with greater control over the market forces, in the face of extreme adversity.[50] And the post-war international economic order reflected these changes: the world economy had outgrown the classical 'liberal' economic order and, to avoid the inter-war economic and political calamities, "any future international economic order would have to strike a better balance between the demands of international economy and those of domestic social groups."[51] The GATT founders, as explained by Ruggie, saw the market, as 'embedded' in a broader social fabric, and multilateralism would be predicated upon domestic interventionism.[52] History had demonstrated that, whenever domestic needs clashed with the requirements of the global economy, the former generally prevailed, and the drafters of the GATT "realized that it was better to accept this and build safety valves into the system than to ignore it and risk total collapse."[53] As a result, on the list of Anglo-American postwar economic objectives, multilateralism was joined by collaboration to assure domestic economic growth and social security. This 'compromise' explains many provisions of the GATT: while "the principles of multilateralism and tariff reductions were affirmed" so were safeguards and exceptions, "designed to protect the balance of payments and a variety of social policies."[54]

3.2.3 The 1980s and the WTO Project

In the 1980s, trade cooperation was moved by yet other factors. The political landscape had changed once again: by then, the specter of the war was a long-distant memory and the need to guarantee social stability and cohesion was no longer such a pressing concern. At the same time, global recessions and stagflation revealed the inadequacy of the postwar accommodation of trade and social welfare policies.[55] The collapse of the gold standard combined with the economic pressures of the 1970s led to new kinds of interventions and trade restrictions. The 1980s were the decade of the Reagan-Thatcher revolutions, of the Washington Consensus, of market fundamentalism and neoliberalism.[56]

---

50 Ibid., 387; Rodrik, *The Globalization Paradox* (n 39) 45.

51 Rodrik, *The Globalization Paradox* (n 39) 46.

52 See Ruggie, 'International Regimes' (n 11) and Karl Polanyi, *The Great Transformation: The Political and Economic Origins of Our Time* (Amereon Limited, 1996).

53 Rodrik, *The Globalization Paradox* (n 39) 68.

54 Ruggie, 'International Regimes' (n 11) 396.

55 Cohen, 'What is International Trade Law For?' (n 11) 336.

56 Rodrik, *The Globalization Paradox* (n 39) 77.

The trade community saw all industrial policies as a "beggar-thy-neighbor approach to declining industries or declining demand"[57] and governments, rather than complementary and indispensable for the correct functioning of the market, were suddenly regarded as a cumbersome presence standing in the way. The definition of 'free trade' changed as well, as it started being defined more broadly than 'trade free from discrimination', but rather as 'trade free of burdens', in other words, a broad laissez-faire principle.[58] The result was the abandonment of the Bretton Woods system for a far more ambitious agenda of trade liberalization and deep integration, perfectly embodied by the Uruguay Round of negotiations, which resulted in the creation of a legal framework with much broader coverage than anything else ever accomplished under the GATT.[59] The same foreseeable outcome that got the US Congress worried in 1947 and pushed it to vote against the establishment of the International Trade Organization (ITO)—that it would encroach too much on domestic prerogatives—suddenly became the very goal of the Uruguay Round.

At the same time, the changed economic and political circumstances determined a change in membership: while the 1947 GATT was dominated by the United States, the United Kingdom, and their post-war partners, as decolonization increased, developing countries began to join the GATT. To effectively remove all governmental interferences, the system needed to not only expand in scope but become universal as well. And it did, by gathering 123 countries in the Uruguay Round negotiations, as opposed to the 23 founding members of the GATT.

Finally, the political concerns that had originally motivated the drafting of the GATT, as well as the very first years of multilateral trade cooperation and negotiations, had been replaced by concerns of a rather economic and ideological nature, aptly embodied by the neoliberal economic thought.

3.2.4 A New Rationale?

This brief historical excursus has exemplified how different epochs in recent history, because of their specific economic and political circumstances, have contributed to the development of differences in the prevailing rationales underlying the international trade regime and its features. The five stories introduced at the beginning of this chapter, however, present us with yet a

57 Howse, 'The World Trade Organization 20 Years On' (n 25) 16.

58 Driesen argues that this broader definition of 'free trade' was already present in the text of the GATT at Article XI. Driesen, 'What is Free Trade?' (n 31) 293.

59 Dani Rodrik introduced the expression 'deep integration' as opposed to the 'shallow integration' of the GATT years.

different picture. The rationales and motivations behind the liberal trade project in nineteenth century Britain, in the 1947 GATT negotiations, or even in the context of the Uruguay Round, cannot possibly be the sole reasons underlying these more recent developments. Can the reasons behind trade cooperation after World War II or in the 1980s explain the European Parliament's decision to subordinate the negotiation of any comprehensive trade agreement to the condition that all the parties be signatories of the Paris Agreement or that strong climate change provisions be included in the text of the agreement? Can they explain why states are negotiating an agreement within the WTO where the ultimate goal is the conservation and sustainable use of the oceans, seas and marine resources, or why recent free trade agreements (FTAs) contain environmental *rules* and not just exceptions? To the contrary, as the next chapters will describe, new rationales are hiding beneath the surface.

3.3 *Individuals and Communities Contribute to Changes in Collective Ideas*

This brief sketch shows that the historical contingency of the notion of free trade and of the *raison d'être* of the international trading system is closely linked to the emergence and gaining ground of certain ideas.[60] The actual contribution of new ideas to the design of a given rule or even to the prevailing understanding of the purpose and goal of a given regime requires a process of *learning*, which Adler defines as

> the adoption by policy-makers of new interpretations of reality, as they are created and introduced to the political system by individuals and institutions. This implies that national policy-makers are subject to absorbing new meanings and interpretations of reality, as generated in intellectual, bureaucratic, and political circles, and therefore are subject to changing their interests and ability and/or willingness to consider new courses of action.[61]

60 In this context, the definition of 'collective ideas' provided by Legro can be used as a point of reference: " 'Collective ideas' refers to concepts or beliefs held by groups (i.e. states). These ideas are social and holistic—they are not simply individual conceptions that are shared or added together. Collective ideas have an intersubjective existence that stands above individual minds and is typically embodied in symbols, discourse, and institutions. Individuals and their interaction naturally influence collective ideas, but they also must confront them as 'fact'." Jeffrey W. Legro, 'The Transformation of Policy Ideas' (2000) 44 *American Journal of Political Science* 419, 420.

61 Emanuel Adler, 'Cognitive Evolution: A Dynamic Approach for the Study of International Relations and their Progress', in Emanuel Adler and Beverly Crawford (eds.), *Progress in Postwar International Relations* (Columbia University Press, 1991), p. 54.

Moreover, ideational and normative change can only occur under certain conditions and in the context of certain policy-making environments.

3.3.1 Right Conditions, Right Environment

Often, it can take a long time for an idea to have any concrete influence on policy-making, because the right conditions do not materialize, or the environment is not conducive to learning. For instance, although Adam Smith wrote his seminal book *The Wealth of Nations* in 1776, it was only after the 1850s that his ideas finally got some traction. Until then, mercantilism reigned supreme. This change of economic narrative has been ascribed by economic historians to a number of factors, including the development of new technologies, such as the steamship, railroads, and the telegraph, which revolutionized international transport and communication and reduced trade costs greatly, and the widespread adoption of the gold standard, which allowed capital to move internationally more easily.[62] This example illustrates the importance of a certain environment for ideas to be able to develop and disseminate.

At the same time, if it is true that normative changes are the result of a wide variety of external factors, they also have an indispensable ideational basis, and individuals and communities play a crucial role in creating environments that are more or less conducive to ideational change. As stated by Jacob Bronoski and Bruce Mazlish in their seminal work *The Western Intellectual Tradition*, "the history of ... ideas ... is necessarily a history of movement. The movement is created by that which gives life to ideas: by the interplay of all the interests of the mind, by the pressure of events, and by the expression of personalities."[63] The history of the trade and environmental regimes, just as any intellectual history, needs to be read as the history of the relevant movements (free trade, environment, and development), and of the communities and individuals behind them.

As a matter of fact, technological developments and the widespread adoption of the gold standard were not the only reasons why free trade principles gained traction after the 1850s. Another important factor that enabled the change of narrative was a "convergence in belief systems" among the key economic decision-makers of that period.[64] Similarly, it was not just the adoption

62 See e.g. Rodrik, *The Globalization Paradox* (n 39) 9.

63 Jacob Bronowski and Bruce Mazlish, *The Western Intellectual Tradition* (Harper Collins, 1962), p. xiii.

64 Rodrik, *The Globalization Paradox* (n 39) 25. And these new ideas found a vehicle to spread and reach the most extreme corners of the population. The opponents of Napoleonic Wars-era tariffs on imports of grain—the so-called 'Corn Laws'—which Britain abolished

of the Smoot-Hawley Tariff Act, the beginning of the Great Depression, or the outbreak of the two World Wars that fueled multilateral trade cooperation in the 1940s. It was the impact that these events had on certain individuals, such as Cordell Hull and James Meade, who learnt from them and managed to bring a change in collective ideas.[65] Again, the diversity of the membership of the trade regime, the globalization of the economy, and the increasing commercial significance of domestic regulations explain only in part the expansion of the scope of the trade regime as well as its normative content, which began with the Tokyo Round of trade negotiations in 1973. The redefinition of the trade regime as a 'marketplace'—and the idea that 'free trade' equals a trade free from burdens and the consequent convergence of the idea of trade barriers and that of trade distortions—have also contributed to creating the conceptual framework underlying this expansion.[66]

Precisely because learning implies "actors' improved understanding of alternative ideas,"[67] the interaction between two or more communities is here seen as conducive to change.[68] Accordingly, the following chapters will explore the developments and interactions of the trade and environmental communities over the years.[69] In order to do so, this book employs a narrative form of explanation, which links diverse events along a temporal dimension, organizing them into an "interpretive coherence structure."[70] Polkinghorne uses the

---

in 1846, founded the well-known magazine *The Economist*, which began to popularize and spread free trade views across the country and beyond.

65 Describing the role that Cordell Hull played in the process of post-war economic reconstruction, Douglas Irwin makes the point that "[h]is success demonstrates that individuals, not just impersonal economic and political forces acting through Congress, can shape policy at critical moments." Irwin, *Clashing Over Commerce* (n 45) 420. Describing instead the role played by James Meade, Ernest Penrose wrote that "if any one person can be described as the originator of the movement for an International Trade Organization it is James Meade." Ernest F. Penrose, *Economic Planning for the Peace* (Princeton University Press, 1953), pp. 89–90.

66 Lang, *World Trade Law After Neoliberalism* (n 11) 238.

67 See Donald A. Schon and Martin Rein, *Frame Reflection: Toward the Resolution of Intractable Policy Controversies* (Basic Books, 1994); Alexander Wendt, *Social Theory of International Politics* (Cambridge University Press, 1999).

68 It should be noted that learning can also occur within a single policy community.

69 This analysis is based on the study of the record of interactions between the two communities (paying particular attention to the activities of the WTO Committee on Trade and Environment) and on a body of international relations literature that has been exploring and studying these interactions.

70 Donald Polkinghorne calls this interpretive coherence structure "gestalt." See Donald Polkinghorne, *Narrative Knowing and the Human Sciences* (State University of New York Press, 1988), p. 18. See also Ruggie, 'Epistemology' (n 17) 86.

literary term "emplotment" to describe this process, which is a "dialectic process" that takes place between a series of events, that would otherwise appear as discontinuous and separate, and a theme, or plot, "which discloses their significance and allows them to be grasped together as part of one story."[71] Because causalities per se are unobservable[72] and it is "generally accepted that the social world is inherently indeterminate,"[73] this book does not claim to provide definitive answers as to the reasons underlying the development and dissemination of certain ideas and the subsequent evolution of the two regimes. Rather, as aptly put by Peirce, this "method of interrogative reasoning" necessarily involves "a certain element of guess work,"[74] whose aim is to produce results that are "verisimilar and believable."[75]

3.3.2 The Trade Policy Elite: The Creation of an Environment Un-Conducive to Learning and Change

The years after World War II represent a time when trade policies were deeply entangled in much broader political contexts, and when a few political figures had a strong influence on political developments, which meant on economic policy as well.[76] In the years after the adoption of the GATT, on the contrary, trade policy became insulated from national politics and became the province of a technocracy, and the same was reproduced at the international level, within the GATT Secretariat. What had developed in those years has been defined as a *trade policy elite,* which encompassed a large group of 'experts' who, although formally *outside* of the GATT/WTO system, were, for all purposes, *insiders.*[77] Despite their differences in terms of national or personal

---

71 Polkinghorne, *Narrative* Knowing (n 70) 19–20.

72 Richard A. Berk, 'Causal Inference for Sociological Data', in Neil J. Smelser (ed.), *Handbook of Sociology* (Sage, 1988).

73 Ruggie, 'Epistemology' (n 17) 92.

74 C.S. Peirce, *Philosophical Writings* (Justus Buchler ed., 1955), pp. 151–52.

75 Ruggie, 'Epistemology' (n 17) 94.

76 While in XIX-century Britain, "the fight over the Corn Laws illustrates that because trade policies have important consequences for income distribution, they get entangled in much broader political contests," in the United States, "trade policies fed directly into the most important social and political cleavage in the country, between South and North." Rodrik, *The Globalization Paradox* (n 39) 28–9.

77 They included, among others, "former or current governmental trade officials, GATT-friendly academics who often sat on GATT/WTO dispute settlement panels and were invited to various conferences and meetings of the GATT/WTO, international civil servants in other organizations preoccupied with trade matters, and a few private attorneys, consultants, and former politicians." Howse, 'From Politics to Technocracy' (n 11) 98.

interests, these *insiders* formed a network that tended to understand the system in terms of "the policy science of economics [rather than] a grand normative political vision."[78]

This network can be understood as an *epistemic community*, a concept borrowed from international relations theory and used to refer to "a network of professionals with recognized expertise and competence in a particular domain and an authoritative claim to policy-relevant knowledge within that domain or issue-area."[79] Although they may belong to different disciplines and work in different institutions, all members of a given community share what Ruggie calls an *episteme*, meaning a "dominant way of looking at social reality, a set of shared symbols and references, mutual expectations and a mutual predictability of intention."[80]

In constructivist terms, this model of multilateral cooperation is referred to as a 'club model'.[81] Under this model, each club is responsible for a specific 'issue-area' and is able to keep outsiders out by excluding from the negotiations officials in other government bureaucracies and international organizations working on other issue-areas (for instance environmental protection). As a

78 Ibid.

79 Peter M. Haas, 'Introduction: Epistemic Communities and International Policy Coordination' (1992) 46 *International Organization* 1, 3; Emanuel Adler, 'The Emergence of Cooperation: National Epistemic Communities and the International Evolution of the Idea of Nuclear Arms Control' (1992) 46 *International Organization* 101; Emanuel Adler and Peter M. Haas, 'Conclusion: Epistemic Communities, World Order, and the Creation of a Reflective Research Program' (1992) 46 *International Organization* 367.

80 John G. Ruggie, 'The New Institutionalism in International Relations', in *Constructing the World Polity: Essays on International Institutionalization* (Routledge, 1998), pp. 45, 55. As explained by Adler, epistemic communities "can play an important role in the process of intellectual innovation and political selection of ideas and understandings ... can provide decision-makers with new answers to old questions and can help them redefine and reconceptualize problems." See Adler, 'Cognitive Evolution' (n 61) 64.

81 See Robert O. Keohane and Joseph S. Nye Jr., 'The Club Model of Multilateral Cooperation and Problems of Democratic Legitimacy', in Roger B. Porter et al. (eds.), *Efficiency, Equity, and Legitimacy: The Multilateral Trading System at the Millennium* (Brookings Institution Press, 2001), pp. 264–291. See also Robert E. Hudec, 'The GATT Legal System: A Diplomat's Jurisprudence' (1970) 4 *Journal of World Trade Law* 615, 635 (1970); Gerard Curzon, *Multilateral Commercial Diplomacy: the General Agreement on Tariffs and Trade and its Impact on National Commercial Policies and Techniques* (Praeger, 1965); Gerard Curzon and Victoria Curzon, 'GATT: Traders' Club', in Robert W. Cox and Harold K. Jacobson (eds.), *The Anatomy of Influence: Decision Making in International Organizations* (Yale University Press, 1973); John H. Jackson, 'The WTO "Constitution" and Proposed Reforms: Seven "Mantras" Revisited' (2001) 4(1) *Journal of International Economic Law* 67.

result, the newly formed environmental community was kept at bay and was not able to influence the prevailing discourse in any meaningful way.

3.3.3 Making Learning Possible

As time passed, conditions began to change, paving the way for the development of new ideas and allowing the inherently complementary nature of the two regimes to emerge. Gradually, the conditions that had allowed the trade community to remain an exclusive club, which included the "relatively restricted and homogenous membership of GATT" and the "supposedly technical and professional nature of the subject matter and the consequent media indifference,"[82] began to vanish. Three factors, in particular, can be seen as having played a central role in creating conditions more suitable to change: the creation of the Appellate Body, as detached from the *trade elite*; the greater openness of the trade community towards external constituencies and values; and the convergence, in certain contexts, of the environment and development agendas.

First, the creation of a dispute settlement mechanism—and of the Appellate Body in particular—as a result of the Uruguay Round, allowed for the adoption of decisions independent of the *trade elite* and therefore detached from the prevailing narrative. While there was essentially no distance or independence of the GATT ad-hoc panels—and of WTO panels later—from the insider community, precisely because their members belonged to that community, Appellate Members were largely disconnected from the *trade elite*, at least at the beginning.[83] The different composition of GATT and WTO panels on the one hand, and the Appellate Body on the other, can partially explain the 'greener' evolution of the WTO jurisprudence.[84]

---

82 Joseph Weiler, 'The Rule of Lawyers and the Ethos of Diplomats: Reflections on the Internal and External Legitimacy of Dispute Settlement', in Porter et al. (eds.), *Efficiency, Equity, and Legitimacy* (n 81) 337.

83 While panels, were "made up of various members of the insider network ... closely associated with the GATT 'community'[and] supported by the GATT bureaucracy," Appellate Body Members are chosen among "distinguished generalist jurists, not eminent experts in GATT/WTO law." Howse, 'The World Trade Organization 20 Years On' (n 25) 15, 27. Howse underlines that only "one insider, the late Julio Lacarte-Muro, was appointed to the founding membership of the Appellate Body."

84 Howse, in particular, makes the case that the independence of the Appellate Body from the trade elite allowed this judicial body to deviate from some of the basic tenets of the trade insiders in what he calls a *Declaration of Independence*, which in turns formed the basis of its effectiveness and legitimacy. Pauwelyn, on the other hand, argues that the effectiveness and legitimacy of the system cannot be ascribed to the Appellate Body distancing itself from the trade elite, but rather to its ability to respond to the underlying WTO member preferences. See Howse, 'The World Trade Organization 20 Years

Second, the trade community has increasingly been opening its doors to outside constituencies, in particular to (environmental) non-state actors. This process of 'institutional integration' has occurred both at the domestic and international level. Domestically, it has allowed certain ideas to develop and ultimately shape the positions adopted by certain countries in regional and multilateral discussions and negotiations. At the international level, it has taken several different forms. On the one hand, the Appellate Body has allowed the submission of *amicus* briefs from non-governmental actors, including environmental NGOs.[85] On the other, environmental international organizations have been allowed to take part in the meetings of several WTO committees, and environmental NGOs and experts have been actively contributing to trade negotiations, both at the multilateral and the regional/bilateral level.[86] The increasing engagement of environmental law voices and actors in trade debates has provided an impetus for the evolution of ideas regarding rational and desirable trade policies. By addressing the relationship between trade and the environment from an environmental standpoint, the environmental community has prompted reflection on the broader goals and values that the trading system is designed to achieve, opening discussions on the very meaning of the ideas of 'free trade' and 'trade liberalization'.

Third, the mainstreaming of the notion of a "green economy" as a fundamental component of sustainable development has led to a gradual convergence

On' (n 25), Joost Pauwelyn, 'The WTO 20 Years On: "Global Governance by Judiciary" or, Rather, Member-Driven Settlement of (Some) Trade Disputes between (Some) WTO Members?' (2016) 27(4) *European Journal of International Law* 1119. In Pauwelyn's view, in particular, the composition of the Appellate Body is not so far from that of the panels, and only the founding membership reflected the description provided by Howse. See also Joost Pauwelyn, 'The Rule of Law Without the Rule of Lawyers? Why Investment Arbitrators Are from Mars, Trade Adjudicators from Venus' (2015) 109 *American Journal of International Law* 761, 799–800. For an overall assessment of the Appellate Body approach to the trade/environment nexus, see Joel P. Trachtman, 'WTO Trade and Environment Jurisprudence: Avoiding Environmental Catastrophe' (2017) 58(2) *Harvard Journal of International Law* 273.

85 Appellate Body Report, *United States—Import Prohibition of Certain Shrimp and Shrimp Products*, WT/DS58/AB/R (Oct. 12, 1998); *United States—Countervailing Duties on Certain Corrosion-Resistant Carbon Steel Flat Products from Germany*, WT/DS213/AB/R (Dec. 19, 2002); *European Communities—Measures Affecting Asbestos and Products Containing Asbestos*, WT/DS135/AB/R (Mar. 12, 2001).

86 This greater openness is not unique to the environmental field, but has a much broader spectrum, as evidenced by the manner in which the declaration on Trade-Related Aspects of Intellectual Property Rights (TRIPS) and access to medicines came about in Doha, the way in which NGOs are intervening in the ongoing services negotiations, as well as the outcome of the negotiations for a Trade Facilitation Agreement.

of the environmental and development agendas. Going 'green' has become a necessary step to development, reclassifying the whole idea of environmental protection in the eyes of the strenuous promoters of the development agenda. The drafters of the *2030 Agenda* made sure to emphasize that all 17 goals are of equal importance and should be accorded equal priority. At the same time, the need to assist developing and least-developed countries underlies all the Goals and has to be necessarily factored in the design of the means of implementation thereof. In other words, as long as development is factored into the equation, discussions can move forward.

4 What Lies Ahead

4.1 *Choices*

These three ideas—trade as a means to an end, historical contingency of the regimes, and the role played by individuals and communities in inducing learning and changes in collective ideas—underlie the main arguments developed in the next chapters. As the goal of this book is to show the evolution of the trade/environment nexus, to explore the reasons behind it, and to call into question the traditional and prevailing way of approaching the nexus itself, specific aspects of the nexus have been selected to serve the three prongs of the argument. Inevitably, in telling this controversial story, choices had to be made in selecting the aspects of the trade/environment nexus to be included in this volume. The reader will not find here an exhaustive account of all the intersections between international trade and environmental law. Instead, omissions will certainly be noticed. There is no chapter on TRIPS and biodiversity or on environmental services, for instance. Nor are there chapters providing a systematic analysis of all the WTO provisions and case law on the subject. The literature on all these issues is already extremely rich and the present monograph has greatly benefitted from it. Ultimately, the aspects of the nexus, the rules, and the cases that the reader will find in the following pages have been selected because, in the opinion of the author, they are particularly important and exemplary.

Moreover, it is important to clarify that this is not a book on international relations, although it does rely on certain theories and methodologies borrowed from this discipline when investigating the reasons behind the evolution of the two regimes. Finally, it should be kept in mind that this is not solely an international story. Throughout the book, it will appear clear to the reader the relevance of domestic politics in the evolution of the two regimes, as many of the key drivers of transformation and normative change are found in domestic systems, with significant implications that are felt both at the national and international level. It is in fact impossible to fully understand the origins of international cooperation on trade matters without first considering the characteristics and evolution of US and British trade policy in the crucial years before and after the World Wars, just as it would be difficult to entirely comprehend the way in which international environmental law emerged without taking into due account the role of domestic environmental movements as well as the development of environmental law as a legal discipline within individual countries.

4.2 *A Cartography*

To help the reader navigate the complex evolution of the relationship between international trade and environmental law over time, the book presents it as the evolution from an *exception-based* to a *promotion-based* model, intended to describe the two main stages of the evolution itself. The *exception-based* model reflects the traditional approach to the relationship between trade and the environment, which was in many ways shaped by the history of the two regimes. It is an approach that looks at environmental concerns with mistrust and skepticism, as they could always hide protectionist motives, and ends up relegating the environment to narrow exceptions to the free trade rule. As a result, even when trade agreements allow states to discriminate to pursue legitimate (environmental) policy goals, strict requirements are imposed: in other words, non-discrimination remains the rule, and environmental protection merely the exception. Throughout the years, the trading system has proven to be increasingly open to environmental concerns. New provisions have been introduced in the text of free trade agreements and existing WTO exception clauses have been given increasingly expansive interpretations. Yet, the underlying *rule-exception* scheme has not changed: no matter how broadly we draft or interpret Article XX of the GATT, it remains a mere exception, just like protecting the environment remains an exception to the general non-discrimination rule. In other words, these developments continued to be perfectly captured by the *exception-based* model. Only more recent examples—just like the five stories at the outset of this chapter—are beginning to show a more radical change in the relationship between the trade and environmental regimes. A relationship which can no longer be described solely in terms of rule v. exception, as it is framed in the *exception-based* model. And yet, the underlying narrative which justifies this model seems hard to shake off: the reality is changing but the language used to describe it is not. To better capture these new developments, a new model, called *promotion-based* model, is used. This model explains a new phase where rather than assessing environmental measures based on their compatibility with the international trade law framework, trade rules and institutions are designed to forward and, precisely, *promote* sustainable development and environmental goals.

4.3 *Structure of the Book*

With these clarifications in mind, the next chapters will tell the untold story of the emergence, development, and interaction of the international trade and environmental regimes. They will attempt to weave together a complex series of events to make a single story, taking into account the historical context in which these events took place. The three ideas laid out in the first part of this chapter constitute the thread, the *fil rouge* underlying all subsequent chapters and supporting the arguments this book puts forth. Chapter after chapter, it will unveil the evolution of two regimes, explore the reasons behind this evolution, and attempt to show the inadequacy of the prevailing narrative to account for new developments. What follows is a succinct overview of the content of the book, which can be used as a roadmap to navigate the pages that follow.

Chapter 2 provides an historical account of the origin of the two regimes. The purpose of this chapter is threefold. First, to remind the reader of the chronological order in which events unfolded, with the environmental regime surfacing once the trade regime had already been in place for several decades, thus constraining countries' efforts to protect the environment at the international level within the boundaries set by the already existing international (economic) law framework. This chronological sequence and the different maturity of the two regimes will help the reader understand the trade-centered approach that has characterized the debate since its inception, as Chapter 3 will show in greater detail. The second purpose of the chapter is to emphasize the historical contingency of the international trade regime: the post-war economic reconstruction which ultimately led to the adoption of the GATT took place against the backdrop of a very specific socio-economic and political environment, different from the one that had witnessed the emergence of free trade in the late nineteenth-century Europe, and from the one characterizing the world today. Third, to show the role that ideas and individuals can play in defining a certain understanding of the trade regime, at a certain moment in time.

Chapter 3 takes the reader to the years that followed the Stockholm Conference and the emergence of the 'environment' as an international law issue. If one looks at the GATT through the lenses of the 'embedded liberalism theory' pioneered by Ruggie, governments' efforts to protect the environment and international regulation of trade should be able to peacefully coexist, as the GATT founders, seeing the market, as 'embedded' in a broader social fabric, reached a compromise between multilateralism and domestic interventionism. This would explain why, next to the principles of multilateralism and tariff reductions, the agreement contained exceptions designed to protect a variety of social policies. However, the embedded liberalism theory coexisted for many years with the neoliberal view of the trading system which, once the first trade/environment questions presented themselves, seemed to be prevailing: as a consequence, any government intervention to protect the environment was portrayed as a potential 'interference' in the market, as a barrier to trade, and therefore has been constrained into narrow exceptions, interpreted restrictively by men with no environmental expertise. There goes the choice to call this very first approach to the trade/environment nexus *exception-based* model. The complete isolation of the communities and their different cultures are here portrayed as important factors contributing to maintaining the centrality of such model.

Chapter 4 opens with two milestones for both the trade and environmental regimes: the establishment of the WTO and the convening of the Rio Conference, which introduced the world to the notion of sustainable development. This notion has begun to affect both regimes: on the one hand, 'sustainable development' replaced 'economic growth' as the stated purpose of the trading system, while, on the other, it triggered a paradigm shift from traditional environmentalism with its primary focus on environmental protection to the notion of sustainability "which requires a much more complex process of trading off social, economic, and environmental priorities."[87] Starting from these premises, the chapter describes how the greater openness of the trade community and its growing interactions with the environmental community have allowed the *exception-based* model to evolve, an evolution that has been constantly characterized by the tension between this new stated purpose of the trade regime and the still prevailing neoliberal thought. While this tension allowed for an expanded interpretation and application of the well-known exceptions, it prevented the trade regime from being genuinely true to its preamble and to pursue sustainable development as its ultimate objective.

Chapter 5 further develops the five stories told at the outset of this introductory chapter, portraying trade rules, agreements, and institutions as positively contributing to the achievement of sustainable development goals, including environmental protection, thus fitting under what the author has labeled a *promotion-based* model. These stories are framed against the backdrop of the

---

87 Carter, *The Politics of the Environment* (n 29) 215.

2030 Agenda and the emergence of new notions, such as that of 'green economy', which have allowed the sustainable development principle to finally penetrate the trade regime, thus beginning to change its instruments. At the same time, it has changed the terms of the discussion for the environment as well, now nothing more than one component of the sustainable development goals. That is to say that, when pursuing sustainable development goals, environmental protection is only one of its dimensions, which can be limited by the others. These visible changes, which can be detected in trade rules when dealing with sustainable development, seem hard to frame within the prevailing narrative, which sees trade and environment as mostly conflicting, and still looks at environmental measures with suspicion, as evidenced by the treatment of process and production methods. The prevailing narrative of the trade regime is still centered around the neoliberal thought, oblivious of the historical, economic, and political changes that have occurred throughout the years. These new developments, on the other hand, question the accuracy and appropriateness of the dominant narrative and of its underlying assumptions, opening the door to a question that has been addressed by many trade scholars over the years: whether the prevailing narrative is still viable or should be 'rethought'.

Chapter 6 concludes briefly by picking up on this invitation to rethink the nature and purpose of trade law, advancing some ideas in terms of the way forward. In fact, although the prevailing narrative has come to be seen, over the past few decades, almost as a truism, it has not remained uncontested. Since the 1990s, scholars and commentators have shown the flaws and shortcomings of this narrative, its inability to keep up with new issues, and address the current criticisms of the WTO and the overall international trade regime. Several alternative theories and approaches have been proposed, in an attempt to compensate for these shortcomings. While an exhaustive treatment of all these new issues, criticisms, and proposals is far beyond the scope of this research, this book intends to contribute to the discussion by relying on the evolution of the trade/environment nexus to propose an alternative narrative. Relying on the recent developments described in Chapter 5, which show trade rules that do not simply *allow* domestic (environmental) policies but rather *facilitate* them, trade liberalization and cooperation is seen neither *conflicting* with nor *embedded* in domestic policy-making but rather *instrumental* to the achievement of certain legitimate policy goals: the question becomes how trade instruments can serve broader social and environmental goals, rather than how those goals might be simply accommodated within the hard-driving logic of trade. And in calling into question the purpose of trade law, the arguments made in this book are relevant beyond the confines of the trade and environment debate.

CHAPTER 2

First Came Economic Cooperation

The Genesis of the Nexus

To appreciate the relationship between the international trade and environmental regimes and to understand why it took the particular shape and form that it did, it is important to explore the original goals and intentions of their respective founders. The multilateral trading system grew out of the traumatic events that unfolded during the period between World War I and World War II. A strong desire for peaceful relations among states, and the United States (US)' abandonment of its previous isolationism in favor of a leadership role in global affairs[1] fostered support all around the world for international economic cooperation, which was seen as fundamentally linked to international peace and stability. Only after the creation of this very first form of cooperation, when large numbers of people were finally free from the immediate obligation of protecting themselves and their families from wars and finding food and shelter, the international community could begin to consider new issues worthy of cooperation. It was against this backdrop that delegates from 113 countries gathered in Stockholm in June 1972 to discuss, for the very first time, what to do with the world's rapidly deteriorating environment, and to lay the foundations for the future development of international law in this area.

The Anglo-American discussions on economic cooperation, which led after only a handful of years to the signing of the General Agreement on Tariffs and Trade (GATT), as well as the early years of the environmental movement, took place in a unique period in history, when a few individuals had enormous influence over the shape of international relations and international law. Men like Cordell Hull, Woodrow Wilson, Theodore Roosevelt, and Clair Wilcox, on one side of the Atlantic, and Winston Churchill, James Meade, and Lionel Robbins, on the other, played a crucial role in shaping the international trade regime.[2]

1 Douglas A. Irwin, Petros C. Mavroidis, and Alan O. Sykes, *The Genesis of the GATT* (Cambridge University Press, 2008), p. 5.

2 The focus on the United States is explained by its unique economic power, which "created an inevitable leadership role" so that "the trade system set up under the GATT was no exception, for it incorporated many of the ideas for post-war trading relations generated in the US government during the war." Gilbert R. Winham, *International Trade and the Tokyo Round Negotiations* (Princeton University Press, 1985), p. 30. Indeed, as already pointed out in the introductory chapter, the US did provide unique economic leadership during the 1940s.

Similarly, individuals like Maurice Strong, Barbara Ward, Edmund Muskie, and Stewart Udall, among many others, can be seen as the founders of environmental law and cooperation. Their leadership, foresight, and willingness to look to the future when offered the opportunity to make seminal change, proved critical to the development of international law and cooperation in these areas.

The chronological unfolding of these events is at the root of the particular shape that the relationship between trade and environmental law took at its very beginning. When the protection of the environment became an issue worthy of international cooperation and regulation, the multilateral trading system was already well established: as a late-comer, the 'environment issue' had to be framed and further developed within an already existing legal framework and well-oiled institutional machinery, originally thought of and designed to deal with peace and economic relations alone.

1 The Moral Value of Trade and the Need for International Trade Cooperation

> All the nations of the world are afflicted with many conditions in common. … All the nations are equally interested in restoring the structure of international trade, now prostrate. … The necessity for some degree of cooperation is patent to every intelligent person, if we are to make satisfactory progress back to a stable and sound business recovery.[3]
>
> CORDELL HULL, Address to the Senate, May 19, 1932

The conditions that afflicted "all the nations of the world" when Senator Hull made this statement on the floor of the Senate on May 19, 1932, included, among others, the disruption of world trade that had followed the Great Depression. The epidemic wave of protectionism, isolationism, and beggar-thy-neighbor policies that were at the very root of the contraction of world trade had been set in motion by the adoption in 1930 in the United States of the Smoot-Hawley Tariff Act,[4] which had pushed the average US import tariff to near-record levels, spurring retaliatory trade actions in a number of other countries. In France, the tariff was compared to a declaration of war, while a British newspaper compared it to the German attack of 1914.[5] A statement

3 75 Cong. Rec. 10, 10,639 (May 19, 1932) (statement of Sen. Hull).

4 Tariff Act of 1930, 19. U.S.C. 4.

5 Percy W. Bidwell, 'The New American Tariff: Europe's Answer' (1930) 9(1) *Foreign Affairs* 13–26. Bidwell describes the general European reaction to the Smoot-Hawley tariff as "disapproval, immediate, undisguised, and unanimous."

signed by 1,028 economists featured on the front page of the New York Times asking President Hoover to veto the bill, protested that higher tariffs "would inevitably inject [bitterness] into our international relations [as they] plainly invite other nations to compete with us in raising further barriers to trade."[6] Nevertheless, the tariff came, and it did so at a critical juncture, helping undermine the first fragile multilateral efforts to reduce trade barriers.

Not only had the United States refused to join the League of Nations, but was now actively undermining the League's efforts to negotiate a multilateral tariff truce: "America had brought the world to the brink of international commercial collapse," and it was now the turn for "an American to reverse the process."[7] The American in question was one of the few individuals who had enormous influence over the shape of US postwar policy and who, having witnessed the interwar debacle, made it his lifetime mission to reduce trade barriers through negotiations and restore world trade to its previous flourishing condition.[8] The American in question was a Congressman from Tennessee who, just one year after his statement on the floor of the Senate, became America's longest-serving Secretary of State, holding that office from 1933 to 1944. The American in question was Senator Cordell Hull.

1.1 *The Senator from Tennessee and the International Dimension of Trade Policy*

Born on October 2, 1871 in Overton County, Tennessee, on the border line between the North and the South during the Civil War, and son of a Democrat "of the strictest sect," Hull was always a low tariff proponent.[9] He perfectly fit the pattern for Democrats not just at that time but from the earliest days of the Republic, when Democrats advocated low tariffs, drawing their support from the agrarian South where farmers produced staple crops for export, and Republicans defended high protective tariffs, drawing theirs from the industrial North where manufacturers faced foreign competition.[10] Despite being

6 72 Cong. Rec. 8,328 (May 15, 1930). See Douglas A. Irwin, *Clashing Over Commerce* (The University of Chicago Press, 2017), p. 387.

7 William J. Bernstein, *A Splendid Exchange. How Trade Shaped the World* (Atlantic Monthly Press, 2008), p. 352.

8 Irwin, *Clashing Over Commerce* (n 6) 420; Irwin, Mavroidis, and Sykes, *The Genesis of the GATT* (n 1) 27.

9 Cordell Hull, *The Memoirs of Cordell Hull* (Macmillan, 1948), pp. 3, 7.

10 Irwin, *Clashing Over Commerce* (n 6) 21–22. The existence of different economic interests within a given society and their influence on government policy had been observed by James Madison in *Federalist 10*, where he prophetically noted that "[a] landed interest, a manufacturing interest, a mercantile interest, a moneyed interest, with many lesser interests, grow up of necessity in civilized nations, and divide them into different classes,

a pro-trade Southern Democrat, Hull was not simply acting on behalf of economic interests. It was rather his attachment to certain ideas that became critical to moving trade policy in a new direction. He soon became a firm believer in the importance of low tariffs for the growth of world peace and, insisting on the international reach of domestic trade policies, a vocal advocate of international cooperation on trade and tariff matters.

Trained as a lawyer, Hull started studying tariffs in 1888, when the Mills Bill was pending in Congress.[11] As a young congressman, he had been advised by more experienced politicians that without a specialization he would get nowhere in the Capitol. He then soon decided to specialize in "revenue, tariff, and other forms of taxation, economics and finance,"[12] following the steps of his political mentor and fellow Tennessean, Congressman Benton McMillin, who fought excessive high tariffs on the Ways and Means Committee for many years.

Even before becoming a congressman, Hull had "breathed in the fire of great tariff battles,"[13] such as those surrounding the Mills, McKinley, Wilson, and Dingley Bills. In those years, tariffs were treated as a purely domestic matter. The objective of tariff policies was raising revenue for the government or restricting imports to protect domestic producers from foreign competition,[14] and Congressional debates boiled down to what policy was more beneficial for *American* producers and *American* workers, depending on what domestic interests one was defending.[15]

---

actuated by different sentiments and views ... The regulation of these various and interfering interests forms the principal task of modern legislation, and involves the spirit of party and faction in the necessary and ordinary operations of the government." The Federalist No. 10 (James Madison).

11 The Bill, which proposed a downward revision of existing tariff rates, after passing in the House in July 1888, was eventually rejected by the Republican-controlled Senate.

12 Hull, *Memoirs* (n 9) 46.

13 Ibid., p. 83.

14 Douglas Irwin identifies three principal objectives pursued by US trade policy. The first two objectives—raising revenue for the government and restricting imports to protect domestic producers from foreign competition—have been pursued respectively until the Civil War and until the Great Depression. It was only after 1929, that he finds the objective to have become 'international': concluding reciprocity agreements to reduce trade barriers and expand exports. Irwin, *Clashing Over Commerce* (n 6) 2.

15 Grover Cleveland precisely referred to 'our people' as the beneficiaries of lower tariffs, as quoted in Tom E. Terrill, *The Tariff, Politics, and American Foreign Policy* (Greenwood Press, 1973), pp. 196–97, and in Carolyn Rhodes, *Reciprocity, U.S. Trade Policy, and the GATT Regime* (Cornell University Press, 1993), p. 27. See also 21 Cong. Rec. 4,250–53 (May 7, 1890), as quoted in Alfred E. Jr. Eckes, *Opening America's Market: U.S. Foreign Trade Policy Since 1776* (University of North Carolina Press, 2000), pp. 71, 73.

The method of tariff-setting itself reflected the domestic dimension of tariff policy. Tariff bills were largely the result of the pressure of special interest lobbyists,[16] as it had been from the earlier times of the Republic. Even the ferocious attacks against high tariffs and the corrupt politics and special interests that operated behind the scenes were based on their domestic impacts. One of the strongest attacks came from the well-renowned journalist Ida Minerva Tarbell, who had already established herself as America's first great woman journalist. Tarbell, who had a few years earlier exposed the 'Mother of all Trusts', Rockefeller's Standard Oil,[17] set upon the mission to expose the negative impact of protection on American working families. In her article *Where Every Penny Counts*, Tarbell "popularized the notion that protection inflated the profits of manufacturers while raising the cost of living and reducing the standard of living of working families."[18]

The domestic dimension of trade policy permeated every aspect of US society, from Congressional debates, to newspapers' headlines and public opinion, while there was "little or no thought of their effect on other countries."[19] Of course, whenever Congress introduced higher tariffs, Europe would not sit still. Rather, such high tariffs would make Europe, and particularly Britain and France, "deeply indignant."[20] Britain's decision to establish a trade bloc with tariff preferences with the British Empire, for instance, was the result of the high tariff rates provided for by the McKinley Bill.[21] Yet, no one in the United States seemed to give credit to the significant international consequences of American trade policies.[22]

---

16 In his 1909 scathing article, *The Tariff Make-Believe*, Wilson argued that "the process by which such a bill is made is private, not public; because the reasons that underlie many of the rates imposed are private" (at 536). See also Raymond Leslie Buell, 'The Hull Trade Program and the American System' (1938) New York, N.Y., Foreign policy Association, in cooperation with National peace conference, 13.

17 Ida M. Tarbell, *The History of the Standard Oil Company* (McClure, 1904).

18 Irwin, *Clashing Over Commerce* (n 6) 312.

19 Hull, *Memoirs* (n 9) 83.

20 Ida Tarbell, *The Tariff in Our Times* (MacMillan, 1911), p. 7.

21 Irwin, *Clashing Over Commerce* (n 6) 269.

22 Exceptional in this sense had been the efforts of James Blaine. Once an ardent protectionist, this Republican from Maine soon became aware of the link between domestic and international trade and began advocating reciprocity as a new approach to trade policy, in particular when negotiating trade agreements with Latin America. For instance, in a letter he wrote to McKinley during the drafting of the McKinley Act, Blaine stressed that certain elements of the tariff should be reconsidered as they would be "a slap in the face of the South Americans, with whom we are trying to enlarge our trade." As quoted in Tarbell, *The Tariff in Our Times* (n 20) 204.

Even Hull's strenuous fight for lower tariffs in his early years in Congress[23] was largely driven by their immediate domestic effects—mainly higher costs of living for American citizens. Hull's drive to study the interrelation of trade throughout the world was first inspired by his long Sunday afternoon discussions with Connecticut Republican, Ebenezer J. Hill, whom he met when he first moved to Washington and settled for a long period of time at the Cochran Hotel. At the corner between Fourteenth and K Streets, the Cochran was very popular among Senators and Representatives, and Hill was one of them.[24] He and Hull would sit for hours on one side of the hotel lobby discussing all kinds of legislative questions, including tariffs. Hill had traveled the world between 1907 and 1910 to study tariffs, bringing back with him endless reports of economic conditions overseas. Inspired by these discussions, and later by the outbreak of World War I, Hull continued studying tariffs and trade questions abroad, and became the most vocal advocate of international cooperation on trade matters. Yet, *his* remained for many years an isolated voice, as President Hoover, in the 1930s, still referred to tariff policy as "solely a domestic question."[25]

1.2 *'When Goods Don't Cross Borders, Soldiers Will'*[26]

World War I was the event that most significantly enlarged Hull's views on trade and tariffs from the national to the international theatre. The 'Great' War played a dual role in Hull's life: as he confessed in his *Memoirs*, "disastrous as it was in all aspects, [it] offered both tragedy and a springboard for constructive legislation"[27]:

> When the war came in 1914, I was very soon impressed with two points. The first was its terrific commercial impact on the United States. I saw that you could not separate the idea of commerce from the idea of war and peace ... And the second was that wars were often largely caused by economic rivalry conducted unfairly. I thereupon came to believe that if we could eliminate this bitter economic rivalry, if we could increase

---

23 Already in his maiden speech in March 1908, Hull "made a vigorous attack on the high tariff and the monopolies and trusts that grow up behind it ... the protective tariff ... the king of evils, our present tariff, should be given a place near the center of the stage." Hull, *Memoirs* (n 9) 52.

24 Ibid., p. 47.

25 Pub. Papers 1932, 2015–7, as quoted in Irwin, *Clashing Over Commerce* (n 6) 409.

26 This phrase, commonly attributed to Bastiat, was most likely coined by Otto T. Mallery in his book *Economic Union and Durable Peace*.

27 Hull, *Memoirs* (n 9) 75.

> commercial exchanges among nations over lowered trade and tariff barriers and remove unnatural obstructions to trade, we would go a long way toward eliminating war itself.[28]

As a matter of fact, after the outbreak of the war, Hull embraced the philosophy he ended up carrying throughout his 12 years as Secretary of State that trade had a fundamental international dimension, and that "unhampered trade dovetailed with peace [while] high tariffs, trade barriers, and unfair economic conditions, with war."[29] In his memoirs, Hull explained:

> Though realizing that many other factors were involved, I reasoned that, if we could get a freer flow of trade—freer in the sense of fewer discriminations and obstructions—so that one country would not be deadly jealous of another and the living standards of all countries might rise, thereby eliminating the economic dissatisfaction that breeds war, we might have a reasonable chance for lasting peace.[30]

The idea of a positive link between free(er) trade and peace had a long intellectual lineage. In his seminal piece, *De l'esprit de lois*, Montesquieu had, already in 1748, expressed very clearly the idea that the natural effect of commerce is to lead to peace: "deux nations qui négocient ensemble se rendent réciproquement dépendantes: si l'une a intérêt d'acheter, l'autre a intérêt de vendre; et toutes les unions sont fondées sur des besoins mutuels."[31] As the most influential exponent of the doctrine of the *doux commerce*, he firmly believed that commerce polishes and softens barbarian ways: "c'est presque une règle générale que, partout où il y a des mœurs douces, il y a du commerce; et que partout où il y a du commerce, il y a des mœurs douces."[32] A century later, John Stuart Mill expressed the very same idea defining "the great extent and rapid increase of international trade" as "the principal guarantee of the peace of the world,"[33] while Richard Cobden argued, in his *Political Writings*, that "the more

---

28 Ibid., p. 84.

29 Ibid., p. 81.

30 Ibid.

31 Montesquieu, *De l'esprit de lois* (1748), XX, II. See also Albert O. Hirschman, *The Passions and Interests* (Princeton University Press, 1977), p. 80; and Robert Howse, 'Montesquieu on Commerce, Conquest, War, and Peace' (2006) 31(3) *Brooklyn Journal of International Law* 1.

32 Montesquieu, *De l'esprit de lois* (n 31) XX, I.

33 John S. Mill, *Principles of Political Economy* (Longman Green, 1909), p. 582. See Douglas A. Irwin, 'Trade Liberalization: Cordell Hull and the Case for Optimism' (2008) *Council on Foreign Relations*, 6.

any nation traffics abroad upon free and honest principles, the less it will be in danger of wars."[34]

Hull was well acquainted with the work and ideas of these intellectuals. The experience of the War brought all these ideas to the surface and fortified a wheel that was already in motion. More importantly, he had found someone who shared his vision. The Presidential victory of the Democrat Woodrow Wilson in 1913, right before the outbreak of the War, represented the opening of a new era for Hull. Although he had never met him during the campaign, he had been following Wilson's career for many years, and welcomed his election with contentment as, in his own words, "there was no doubt that Wilson's principles were mine."[35]

One of the principles they shared was precisely the moral value of low tariffs and free trade and their role in pursuing peaceful international relations. The *Third Point* of the famous *Fourteen Points* delivered by Wilson in 1918 before a joint session of Congress as a statement of principles of post-war peace, proposed "the removal, so far as possible, of all economic barriers and the establishment of an equality of trade conditions among all the nations consenting to the peace and associating themselves for its maintenance."[36] According to Wilson, this not only made economic sense, but it would contribute to reducing commercial tensions that bred political frictions leading to war:

> The experiences of the past among nations have taught us that the attempt by one nation to punish another by exclusive and discriminatory trade agreements has been a prolific breeder of that kind of antagonism which oftentimes results in war, and that if a permanent peace is to be established among nations, every obstacle that has stood in the way of international friendship should be cast aside.[37]

After studying the 'peacemaking' role of free trade during World War I and in his relationship with Wilson, Hull continued to vocally advocate for it during all his years as Secretary of State,[38] and this idea later became the manifesto of

34 Richard Cobden, *The Political Writings of Richard Cobden* (1903), p. 222 (emphasis in original).

35 Hull, *Memoirs* (n 9) 69.

36 Woodrow Wilson's Fourteen Points (Jan. 8, 1918).

37 Woodrow Wilson and Arthur S. Link, *The Papers of Woodrow Wilson* (Princeton University Press, 1966), p. 51:476.

38 In his first address as Secretary of State, Hull declared that "most modern military conflicts and other serious international controversies are rooted in economic conditions, and that economic rivalries are in most modern instances the prelude to the actual wars that have occurred." *N.Y. Times*, Apr. 30, 1933.

his tireless campaign in favor of a reciprocal trade agreements program, which he saw as a necessary instrument to peaceful inter-state relations.[39]

1.3 *The Call for an International Trade Conference*

In his famous 1918 speech, President Wilson did more than just advocate for lower tariffs. He set out his vision for a new postwar world based on "national self-determination and international cooperation, bringing secret diplomacy to an end and making World War I 'the war to end all wars'."[40] The centerpiece of his proposal was the creation of a general association of nations, for the purpose of guaranteeing political independence and territorial integrity, thereby preventing future wars. However, while Wilson's vision for the creation of the League of Nations was clear, he did not have an equally concrete plan for the postwar *economic* order.[41]

Hull, on the other hand, did. On July 8, 1916, speaking of high tariffs to the House of Representatives, he suggested that governments of all commercial nations should convene, after the end of the war, at an international trade conference to "be held in the city of Washington for the purpose of establishing a permanent international trade congress."[42] According to his speech, the functions of this congress should be to consider

> all international trade methods, practices, and policies which in their effects are calculated to create destructive commercial controversies or bitter economic wars, and to formulate agreements with respect thereto, designed to eliminate and avoid the injurious results and dangerous

39 In 1934, he wrote that "the trade agreements program is the first step in a broad movement to increase world trade. Upon this program rests largely my hope of insured peace and the fullest measure of prosperity." *Foreign Relations of the United States*, 1937, Vol. 1, at 841–45. In late 1939, Hull delivered a widely noted address in which he stated that "the trade agreements program should be retained intact to serve as a cornerstone around which the nations could rebuild their commerce on liberal lines when the war ended ... [The trade agreements program] offers a solid basis for the hope that, with peace regained, there will be a good opportunity for completing the work of trade restoration." Hull, *Memoirs* (n 9) 746–47. In 1941, when it was the time to renew the program a few years later, Hull argued that "a revival of world trade was an essential element in the maintenance of world peace ... without prosperous trade among nations any foundation for enduring peace becomes precarious and is ultimately destroyed." *State Department Bulletin*, 1943, at 329, 333.

40 Irwin, *Clashing Over Commerce* (n 6) 344.

41 Ibid., p. 344–5.

42 Hull, *Memoirs* (n 9) 82.

> possibilities of economic warfare, and to promote fair and friendly trade relations among all the nations of the world.[43]

For that matter, Hull did more than make a suggestion. A few months before delivering this speech, he had already prepared a resolution calling for an international trade conference and was ready to introduce it to Congress. Before doing so, he asked Secretary of State Robert Lansing for his opinion on the matter and, to Hull's surprise and disappointment, Lansing replied that some of its features risked producing friction with some other countries and asked him to defer its introduction. In the end, the proposal was never introduced to Congress, but Hull never faltered in his belief that an international trade conference—and subsequent agreement—were essential to restoring the structure of international trade.

As he watched with frustration the failure of domestic efforts to convene an international trade conference, Hull carried his vision to the London Economic Conference in 1933. This was the second of a series of conferences sponsored by the League of Nations to discuss trade restrictions and propose concrete solutions for their removal.[44] The first one had taken place a few years earlier, in 1927, in Geneva, where, despite the call for international cooperation on trade, no concrete steps were taken.[45] Similarly, despite Hull's hopes and expectations, the 1933 London Conference did not succeed in securing

43 Ibid.

44 Interestingly, the Covenant makes no mention of reducing trade barriers. Article 23(e) of the League of Nations Charter merely stated: "Subject to and in accordance with the provisions of international conventions existing or hereafter to be agreed upon, the Members of the League ... will make provision to secure and maintain freedom of communications and of transit and equitable treatment for the commerce of all Members of the League." League of Nations, *Covenant of the League of Nations*, Apr. 28, 1919, Art. 23(e).

45 One of the core documents prepared for the Conference, the *Report of the Trade Barriers Committee of the International Chamber of Commerce* (ICC), recommended "the creation, under the auspices of the League of Nations, of a permanent conference in which representatives of the Governments would have the opportunity of meeting regularly, of constantly studying the condition and needs of international trade, as well as the best remedies for existing difficulties; in which the representatives of Governments would be able to draft treaties to satisfy these needs, and arbitrate disputes arising out of the interpretation of treaties already in force." ICC, *Report of the Trade Barriers Committee of the International Chamber of Commerce*, at 400. The final report of the Conference, however, merely recognized the importance of the principle of "parallel and concerted action by the different nations," without any further details or concrete plans. League of Nations, *Final Report. The World Economic Conference*, Geneva, May 1927, C.E.I. 44(1), p. 178. See also Leslie Runciman, 'Note and Memoranda. The World Economic Conference at Geneva' (1972) *Economics Journal* 465–472.

international cooperation on trade matters, nor in agreeing on an acceptable method of reducing trade barriers. Once back in Washington, having learned his lesson, Hull provisionally set aside his original proposal for an international trade conference and for multilateral tariff reduction and decided it would be best to try to secure the enactment of a reciprocal trade agreement program in the US, which would allow the bilateral reduction of tariffs on the basis of reciprocity and without having to be submitted to the Senate. On June 4, 1934, the Senate approved the Reciprocal Trade Agreement Act (RTAA)[46] by a vote of 57-33, and Roosevelt signed it the following week:

> At 9:15 on the night of June 12, I watched the President sign our bill in the White House. Each stroke of the pen seemed to write a message of gladness on my heart. My fight of many long years for the reciprocal trade policy and the lowering of trade barriers was won. To say I was delighted is a bald understatement.[47]

On that occasion, Hull reiterated his firm belief in the peace-making qualities of trade, arguing that the trade agreements program was the first step in a broad movement to increase world trade: "upon this program rests largely my hope of insured peace and the fullest measure of prosperity."[48] Despite everything, the program, which the League of Nations defined as the "most practical method of curing the world's economic illness,"[49] could not prevent the outbreak of a new, much bloodier war in 1939. As World War II raged, Hull worked toward expanding the RTAA into a full-fledged, multilateral system of world trade.[50] Although he retired as Secretary of State in 1944 and was not directly

46 The RTAA introduced three novel features: tariffs could be reduced by as much as one-half, but only if the United States gained corresponding concessions from other countries; reductions applied to all countries that did not discriminate against the United States; and agreements could be negotiated without their having to be submitted to the Senate. On the RTAA and its impact on US trade policy, see e.g. Stephan Haggard, 'The Institutional Foundations of Hegemony: Explaining the Reciprocal Trade Agreement Act of 1934' (1988) 42(1) *International Organization* 91; Douglas A. Irwin, 'From Smoot-Hawley to Reciprocal Trade Agreements: Changing the Course of U.S. Trade Policy in the 1930s', in Michael D. Bordo et al. (eds.), *The Defining Moment. The Great Depression and the American Economy in the Twentieth Century* (NBER, 1997) p. 325; Kenneth W. Dam, 'Cordell Hull, the Reciprocal Trade Agreement Act, and the WTO: An Essay on the Concept of Rights in International Trade' (2005) 1 *New York University Journal of Law and Business* 709.

47 Hull, *Memoirs* (n 9) 357.

48 Irwin, *Clashing Over Commerce* (n 6) 447.

49 Hull, *Memoirs* (n 9) 518.

50 Irwin, 'Trade Liberalization' (n 33) 7–8.

involved in the GATT negotiations, he was able to give "the State Department a strong and lasting intellectual direction,"[51] which contributed greatly to the success of the subsequent trade negotiations. After retiring, he watched with "profound gratification" the successful conclusion of the Geneva Conference that led to the adoption of the GATT, noting that "the nations which participated in the negotiations have made a long stride toward the goal of economic betterment and world peace."[52]

1.4 *Anglo-American Trade Collaboration: The Atlantic Conference*

For Hull's vision of a multilateral trading system to get one step closer to reality, one has to look across the Atlantic, to the Economic Section of the United Kingdom (UK) War Cabinet Secretariat. Here, the Oxford economics professor James Meade started drafting the first concrete proposals for a post-war trading system. As Ernest Penrose, an economic adviser at the American Embassy in London at the time, wrote, "if any one event can be designated as marking the origin of the International Trade Organization proposed at Havana in 1947, it took place in Whitehall in the latter part of 1942" and "if any one person can be described as the originator of the movement for an International Trade Organization it is James Meade."[53] Of course, Meade was not alone in these efforts. In London he was surrounded by other economists of the Economic Section of the War Cabinet, in particular Lionel Robbins, Sir John Anderson, and Sir Percival Liesching, and worked alongside Will Clayton, Dean Acheson, Harry Hawkins, Clair Wilcox, and others working in the US State Department.

Despite many challenges, this handful of men succeeded in creating a 'charter for world trade',[54] which would mark the beginning of a long era of cooperation on trade and economic matters not just between the US and the UK but

---

51 Irwin, Mavroidis, and Sykes, *Genesis of the GATT* (n 1) 11. James N. Miller, *Wartime Origins of Multilateralism, 1939–1945: The Impact of the Anglo-American Trade Policy Negotiations*. Ph.D. thesis, Emmanuel College, University of Cambridge (2003), as quoted in Irwin, Mavroidis, and Sykes, *Genesis of the GATT* (n 1). As Miller put it, "[Hull] carefully chose a group of men, based upon their views about trade, to formulate his favored policies: if the officials arrived in the Department without decided views, then senior officials quickly inculcated them. Never before had trade policy originated in such a centralized, small, and carefully controlled location. More than any of their predecessors or successors, Hull's men shared several advantages: tremendous power relative to other branches of government, uniformity of opinion and purpose, and the Secretary's passionate commitment to their work and results."

52 *N.Y. Times*, Oct. 31, 1947, 99.

53 Ernest F. Penrose, *Economic Planning for the Peace* (Princeton University Press, 1953), pp. 89–90.

54 The phrase is borrowed from Clair Wilcox, *A Charter for World Trade* (Macmillan, 1949).

among many countries all over the world. This success was possible because it was accomplished at the end of a war, which provided a favorable atmosphere for multilateral action as public opinion could be more easily mobilized.[55] But the time factor was not the only reason behind this success. The latter was also made possible because the two countries involved in this collaboration were led by men of vision, who were able to surround themselves with a relatively small group of individuals of great intellectual ability, united by a common commitment to international cooperation.[56] They envisioned the post-war economic system as "a universal system [or] at least a single multilateral system ... rather than a collection of trading blocs. They wanted permanent international institutions to promote cooperation on monetary, trade and development problems."[57]

The story of the Anglo-American collaboration on trade matters began precisely with the encounter of two such 'men of vision', a meeting held in complete secrecy in August 1941, on an American cruiser off the coast of one of the bases recently secured by the United States in Newfoundland. The two 'men of vision' in question were the American President F.D. Roosevelt, and the British Prime Minister Winston Churchill, and their secret meeting became later known as the 'Atlantic Conference'.[58]

The Atlantic Conference, which resulted in the Charter of the same name, had begun on August 9, 1941, when Churchill arrived in Placentia Bay, Newfoundland, aboard the new battleship *Prince of Wales* after five days crossing the Atlantic.[59] A few weeks earlier, his trusted personal adviser, Harry Hopkins, had met with the Prime Minister in the garden of Downing Street to inform him that Roosevelt had expressed the desire to arrange a meeting.[60] Churchill, having corresponded with the President with increasing intimacy for nearly two years, accepted without hesitation. When he reached Placentia Bay, he was greeted by the impressive sight of several American warships. Roosevelt, who had arrived two days prior, was waiting aboard the cruiser

55 John B. Condliffe, *The Reconstruction of World Trade* (Norton, 1940), p. 355; Richard N. Gardner, 'Sterling-Dollar Diplomacy in Current Perspective' (1985) 62 *International Affairs*, 24–5. Jay Culbert, 'War-time Anglo-American Talks and the Making of the GATT' (1987) 10 *World Economy* 381, 393.

56 Gardner, 'Sterling-Dollar Diplomacy' (n 55) 24–5.

57 Ibid., 22.

58 For an account of the meeting, see Winston S. Churchill, *The Grand Alliance* (Houghton Mifflin, 1985), pp. 385–400, and Sumner Welles, *The Time for Decision* (Harper & Brothers Publishers, 1944), p. 174.

59 Welles, *The Time for Decision* (n 58) 174.

60 Churchill, *The Grand Alliance* (n 58) 381.

Augusta. All arrangements had been made in deepest secrecy: officially, Roosevelt was on a mid-summer fishing trip on the *Potomac* and very few knew he had been transferred to the *Augusta* and was now about to begin one of the most memorable personal encounters of the War.[61]

This meeting was the realization of Roosevelt's long-standing desire to discuss a number of pressing political issues with the British Prime Minister, in particular the question of future policy regarding Japan.[62] Although the Conference was supposed to be focused on political and war-related matters rather than post-war plans—considering in particular that on the British side, everything was focused on winning the war—it was "none too early to lay down at least some of the principles by which policies must be guided at the conclusion of the war, to press for a broad program of world economic reconstruction and to consider tentative plans for the application of those policies."[63]

As a result, during one of their first conversations on board of the *Augusta*, Roosevelt proposed to Churchill to "draw up a joint declaration laying down broad principles which should guide our policies along the same road."[64] Yet, nothing was said on economic policies at the time and the first draft prepared by Churchill's party contained five general principles, none of which mentioned economic reconstruction or trade.[65] Only later, as a result of negotiations that were under way during the very same days in Washington concerning the Mutual Aid Agreement, economic considerations crept in: the *Fourth Point* was added to the Charter, which laid out the foundations of the imminent Anglo-American talks:

> *Fourth*, they will strive to bring about a fair and equitable distribution of essential produce, not only within their territorial boundaries, but between the nations of the world, *without discrimination and on equal terms*. [66]

61 William L. Langer and S. Everett Gleason, *The Undeclared War, 1940–1941* (Harper and Brothers Publishers, 1953), p. 664.

62 Ibid., pp. 663, 670. Stewart Patrick, *The Best Laid Plans* (Rowman & Littlefield Publishers, 2008), p. 48; Sumner Welles, *Where Are We Heading?* (Harper & Brothers, 1946).

63 This statement has been delivered by Cordell Hull in a radio address, conveying the US government line, as quoted in Harley A. Notter, *Postwar Foreign Policy Preparation, 1939–1945* (Greenwood Press, 1949), pp. 45–46. The Charter was merely a by-product of the Conference. See Richard N. Gardner, *Sterling-Dollar Diplomacy in Current Perspective: The Origins and the Prospects of Our International Economic Order* (Columbia University Press, 1980), p. 40; Langer and Gleason, *The Undeclared War* (n 61) 677.

64 Churchill, *The Grand Alliance* (n 58) 385.

65 For the full text of the first draft of the Charter, see Ibid., pp. 385–6.

66 Ibid., Fourth Point.

The phrase "without discrimination and on equal terms" implied the abolition of all Imperial Preferences, and therefore could not be accepted by Churchill. Although a convinced free trader and himself not in favor of Preferences, he did not have the constitutional power to agree to such a commitment on his own.[67] Under his suggestion, the tone of the fourth point was softened with the addition of the caveat "with due respect for their existing obligations."[68] This formulation eventually found its way in the final draft of the Charter, which was announced to the world on August 14 as a joint declaration of the two Statesmen.

While the British were relieved, this caveat left Cordell Hull "keenly disappointed", as it seemed to deprive "the article of virtually all significance."[69] Nevertheless, the article did contain "a statement of basic principles and fundamental ideas and policies that are universal in their practical application,"[70] and it did start an impressive pyramid of collaboration on post-war economic policy between the two powers. The next few years saw a small number of men, on both sides of the Atlantic, build upon the Charter to answer Hull's call for international cooperation on trade. One of these men, the Oxford economics professor James Meade, had just completed a short book entitled *The Economic Basis of a Durable Peace,* profoundly inspired by Hull's ideas and vision, and was about to embark on a much more challenging project which ended up being the precursor of what would eventually become the GATT.

1.5 *Anderson's Circus*

Meade's colleagues at the Economic Section of the War Cabinet described him as a natural government economist: "he brought a rare clarity of mind, a systematic economic philosophy ... He had a vision of how economics should work and a clear understanding of what made it work as it did."[71] However, Meade had not begun his education with a focus on economics and was never passionate about economics per se, but rather about what economics could do.

Born on June 23, 1907 in Dorset, he was brought up in the city of Bath in England. His College education at Oxford was concentrated on classics. His

---

67 Welles, *The Time for Decision* (n 58) 176; Langer and Gleason, *The Undeclared War* (n 61) 684.

68 Churchill, *The Grand Alliance* (n 58) 388; Irwin, Mavroidis, and Sykes, *Genesis of the GATT* (n 1) 16.

69 Hull, *Memoirs* (n 9) 975.

70 Ibid.

71 Alec Cairncross and Nita G.M. Watts, *The Economic Section, 1939–1961* (Routledge, 1989), pp. 54, 113.

interest for economics and the decision to move to the newly started School of Philosophy, Politics and Economics found their roots in the Great Depression:[72] like many others of his generation, he thought that the phenomenon of heavy unemployment in the United Kingdom in the inter-war period was "both foolish and wicked."[73] He started pursuing economic theory not as an end in itself but rather as a means for "improving the economic and social organization of the country,"[74] in other words, as a means to "do good."[75]

After a short period at Cambridge, in 1931 he returned to Oxford, where he taught until 1937. During those years, he worked alongside a number of brilliant economists, but one in particular, with whom he was going to cross paths for many years, had a special intellectual influence on him: Lionel Robbins. Robbins, nine years older than Meade, ran the Adam Smith Society at Oxford, which Meade attended regularly.[76] Despite their political differences—Meade was more to the Left and Robbins more to the Right—they had a lot in common. Just like Meade, Robbins had not always intended to be an economist. His first love was English literature and his ambition in life was to become a poet.[77] The Great Depression and the disillusionment that surrounded the immediate post-war period pushed him to study economics.[78] Meade and Robbins even had the same mentor, Major C.H. Douglas, who helped shape their conviction that economic theory could be used as a cure for the evil they saw in society, by contributing to the formulation of wise and effective policies.

A few years after their first encounter in Oxford, they found themselves working together in the Economic Section of the War Cabinet. The Section, which became known as 'Anderson's Circus' after the cabinet minister who was in charge, Sir John Anderson,[79] gathered professional economists, in charge not only of the war economy but, even more importantly, of the preparation of plans for what should happen after the end of the war.[80] Under Anderson, and thanks to the high-level briefs prepared by its members, the Section became

72 Susan Howson (ed.), *Collected Papers James Meade V1* (1st ed., Routledge, 2016), p. 1; David A. Reisman, *James Edward Meade, Great Thinkers in Economics* (Palgrave Macmillan, 2018), p. 5.

73 James Meade, *Wage-Fixing: Stagflation, Vol. I* (Allen and Unwin, 1982), p. 53.

74 Alec Cairncross, 'Economic Forces in a Social Context: James Meade: Obituary', *Guardian*, Dec. 28, 1995, 12.

75 Reisman, *James Edward Meade* (n 72) 2.

76 Ibid., p. 10.

77 Susan Howson, *Lionel Robbins* (Cambridge University Press, 2011), p. 2.

78 Ibid., p. 51.

79 Culbert, 'War-time Anglo-American Talks' (n 55) 388.

80 Lionel Robbins, *Autobiography of an Economist* (Macmillan, 1971), p. 186.

an integrated part of the Whitehall machine.[81] It comprised seven main areas of work and Meade, who had just been pulled from the League of Nations Secretariat where he had been writing their economic survey, was in charge of "finance, exchange and export policy."[82]

Robbins and Meade served consecutive terms as directors of the Section, both actively committed to a better post-war world. Mindful of the lessons of their teacher and mentor Douglas, they were both committed to practical and constructive internationalism, convinced that post-war reconstruction could only be built on universal, or at least multilateral economic cooperation.

1.6 *Meade's Multilateral Approach to Trade Agreements*

Just like Cordell Hull, Meade believed that "the causes of international conflicts are economic in character and for this reason only an International Organization which is based upon a stable, just, and efficient economic foundation can hope to succeed in its primary political tasks."[83] In his short volume *The Economic Basis of a Durable Peace*, Meade advocated for some form of international organization as a necessary prerequisite for the international regulation of economic affairs, which should be based on the principle of free trade. More precisely, he argued for a "gradual approach to free trade," to reduce trade barriers over a series of years rather than removing them altogether.[84] The arrangement of this gradual reduction of barriers to trade would constitute one of the priorities of the international organization in question.[85]

After joining the Economic Section in 1941, Meade had the opportunity to further develop and polish his ideas, which he eventually fine-tuned in his famous piece *Proposal for a Commercial Union*.[86] The *Proposal*—which envisaged a system where tariffs would be reduced, discrimination removed, and an international institution created to administer disputes—built on the long and rich history of bilateral treaties of commerce whose origin dates back to the middle ages. Treaties of commerce between states made their first appearance in the fourteenth century, thanks to the efforts of the King of England,

81 Howson, *Lionel Robbins* (n 77) 387–8.

82 Robbins was in charge of "price and wages;" John Jewkes of "manpower;" Joan Robinson of "production and supply;" P.K. Debenham of "food and consumption;" Alec Cairncross of "shipping and transport;" and Harry Campion of "general statistics." See Alan Booth, 'Economic Advice at the Centre of British Government, 1939–1941' (1986) 29 *History Journal* 655, 659, 664.

83 James E. Meade, *The Economic Basis of a Durable Peace* (Allen & Unwin, 1940), p. 11.

84 Ibid., p. 85.

85 Ibid., p. 180.

86 James E. Meade, *Proposal for a Commercial Union* (1943).

Edward III.[87] Before this time, they simply took the form of unilateral privileges accorded by the sovereign to foreign merchants to ensure their safety on their territory.[88] As time went by, more and more states followed England's example and treaties gradually became increasingly detailed and the legal technique equally improved. More importantly, they crystallized a few essential principles and clauses that became customary in almost all treaties and that came to constitute the core of bilateral regulation of trade. These same principles and clauses found their way in Meade's *Proposal* many centuries later.

The whole document was centered around the notion of tariff reduction and the prohibition of quantitative restrictions.[89] These notions clearly recalled the principle of "freedom of commerce" (*liberté du commerce*), which had characterized treaties of commerce since their inception:

> Les parties contractantes s'engagent à n'empêcher les échanges mutuels ou citoyens de chacune des deux parties auront la faculté de venir par aucune interdiction d'importation, d'exportation ou de transit ...[90]

The *Proposal* further embodied the two traditional guarantees of the principle of free trade, the Most-Favored Nation (MFN) and the National Treatment principles, by forbidding parties to discriminate between foreign products and between foreign and domestic products,[91] representing two of the traditional

87 The most ancient of such treaties was signed between Edward III, King of England and France, and the maritime cities of the Kingdom of Castilla and the Lordship of Biscay. Boris Nolde, 'Droit et technique des traités de commerce (Volume 003)', in *Collected Courses of the Hague Academy of International Law* (The Hague Academy of International Law, 1924), p. 301.

88 An example is provided by the promise made by Henry III of England to the merchants coming from Gotland, Sweden: "quod ... salus et secure veniant in Angliam cum relus et mercandisis suis quas decent de partibus suis Gothlandiae et quod saluo ibi morentur et saluo inde recéedant." Ibid., p. 299.

89 The third principle on which the *Proposal* was based called Members to "remove altogether certain protective devices against the commerce of other members of the Union and to reduce to a defined maximum the degree of protection which they would afford to their own home producers." Along the same lines, the *Proposal* forbade Members from imposing quantitative restrictions or prohibitions (clause v).

90 Treaty of Commerce and Navigation, Sweden-Germany, 1911, Martens, N.R.G., 3rd Ser. VIII, 435, as quoted in Nolde, 'Droit et technique' (n 87) 373.

91 Meade, *Proposal* (n 86). According to clause (ii), "Members would be bound to give other members of the Union as favourable prices for their produce as they gave for the similar produce from any non-member state." Clause (iv) instead read: "Members would be forbidden to give a preference (whether by tax, subsidy, price offered by state trading body or other means) in price to their home producers which was more than, say, 25 per cent greater than the price offered to similar goods produced by other members of the Union."

and essential clauses of all modern trade treaties. The MFN clause was introduced for the first time in its modern form in the 1486 Treaty between England and Brittany,[92] while the National Treatment clause started being introduced during the eighteenth century to put an end to the rapidly spreading mercantilist wars.[93]

Despite being very much imbued with tradition, Meade's *Proposal* introduced an important innovation, which was immediately endorsed by the Economic Section and later by the Board of Trade: it emphasized the need for a post-war regime of *multilateral* international trade, rather than one based upon "bilateral barter and preferential trade treatment between particular countries."[94] Treaties of commerce, up until 1943, had been bilateral in nature: although they shared some core principles and clauses, they all differed from one another, sometimes even in the treatment accorded to the parties to the same treaty.[95] Instead, Meade's underlying idea was to have one single treaty signed by all, or at least a vast majority of states: only then could one talk about a truly international trade regime.

Moreover, this international trade regime would be 'managed' by an International Commerce Commission, an international body with the competence "to interpret the Charter of the Commercial Union, and to arbitrate or to give decisions in case of disputes among its members."[96] The *Proposal* covered most of the main points that would become, five years later, the GATT,[97] while

92 The MFN clause in the 1486 Treaty between England and Brittany read: "Item, que les marchans d'Angleterre auront et pourront avoir et tenir es villes de Bretagne [sauf les villes de Saint-Malo, Brest et Toucq] et joyront illecques de toutes et pareilles franchises comme les autres marchans estrangiers qui ont entrecours et communication de marchans en Bretagne, et seront traictez aussi doulcement et gracieusement comme les autres nations frécantans en icelui Paiis, villes et lieux d'icelui; et pareillement les marchans de Bretagne auront et pourront avoir et tenir es villes du dit royaume d'Angle- terre, Irland, ville et marche de Calays [sauf les places exceptées par lettres royales] et joyront des dites franchises et aussi seront traités comme dessus est dit des dites marchans d'Angleterre." Nolde, 'Droit et technique' (n 87) 304.

93 States had begun increasing their wealth by reducing imports and increasing exports, adopting protectionist tariffs to protect domestic production and hampering the entry of foreign products. This tariff war gave a whole new meaning to the concept of 'equality' and contributed to the drafting, in all subsequent treaties, of a National Treatment clause. Ibid., p. 306.

94 Irwin, Mavroidis, and Sykes, *Genesis of the GATT* (n 1) 28.

95 There had been a few attempts to 'internationalize' treaties of commerce, but they have all been sectoral, including the sugar conventions of 1902 and 1907, the 1921 Barcelona Convention and Statute on Freedom of Transit, and the 1923 Geneva Convention relating to the Simplification of Customs Formalities.

96 Meade, *Proposal* (n 86) para. 18.

97 Penrose, *Economic Planning* (n 53) 94–5.

the International Commerce Commission was nothing but a precursor of the World Trade Organization.

1.7 *Havana*

Meade's *Proposal* soon caught the attention of Hugh Dalton, the President of the Board of Trade in the British Government, who saw it as a possible basis for international negotiations. In September 1943, with the *Proposal* in his pocket, Meade traveled to Washington as part of the Law Commission in charge of discussing trade policy with the Americans. The 'Washington talks on commercial policy' proceeded relentlessly until the summer of 1945. During these two years, Meade, Robbins, and Liesching, the senior civil servant responsible for the Commercial Union in the Board of Trade, discussed trade and commercial-policy issues with Harry Hawkins, Dean Acheson, and other American officials.

The talks proceeded smoothly and cordially.[98] Little did Meade know, when he first penned the words 'Commercial Union', that he would be present "on the occasion when they were handed over by the British to the Americans ... or that the Americans would receive them with such welcome."[99] By October he reported that

> The Americans are drafting a report on Commercial Policy, rather on the lines of our Commercial Union proposals, which is to be jointly agreed with us. Where there are unresolved differences, both views will be expressed. There could not be a more desirable outcome to our deliberations ... Ten years ago at Oxford I should never have dreamed that an economist could live in such a heaven of practical application of *real* economic analysis![100]

The idea of liberalizing trade on a multilateral basis, in particular, marked a stark departure from British tradition and was welcomed with enthusiasm by the American delegation. Both countries agreed, without the slightest doubt or hesitation, on the necessity of international cooperation on a greater scale than ever before in the area of trade regulation and policy. This agreement led to the publication, at the conclusion of the two years of talks, of the *Proposals for Expansion of World Trade and Employment*, as a joint United States-United

98 Lionel Robbins et al., *The Wartime Diaries of Lionel Robbins and James Meade, 1943–45* (Palgrave Macmillan Springer, 2014), p. 133.

99 Ibid., p. 111.

100 Ibid., pp. 124, 130 (emphasis in original). See also Irwin, Mavroidis, Sykes, *Genesis of the GATT* (n 1) 41.

Kingdom document, which built on Meade's *Proposal* and called for an International Conference on Trade and Employment to be convened by the United Nations not later than the summer of 1946.[101] As a result, GATT negotiations officially kicked off at Church House in London in October 1946.

In London, the US delegation was headed by Clair Wilcox who, nearly 20 years earlier, had organized the famous statement signed by 1,028 economists and featured on the front page of the New York Times asking President Hoover to veto the Smoot-Hawley Tariff Act, and had later become Director of the State Department's Office on International Trade Policy. The UK delegation, headed by H.A. Marquand, a member of Parliament, included, among others, none less than James Meade. This was also the first time that countries other than the United States and the United Kingdom joined in the discussion, submitting drafts and proposals. At the end of the London round, most of the provisions of a draft charter for an International Trade Organization (ITO) were agreed on. It was also agreed that a provisional agreement on international commercial policy, the GATT, would be concluded before the approval of the charter.

After London, negotiators from the participating countries met again in Lake Success, the temporary location of the UN headquarters just outside of New York City on Long Island, and then in Geneva. After a total of 626 meetings, by mid-August 1947 the final text of the GATT and the draft of the charter for an International Trade Organization had been finalized.[102] These two documents, whose overall objective was to facilitate the flow of international commerce,[103] represented the "greatest step ever taken toward the establishment, by mutual agreement between governments, of the rules which nations will follow in their conduct of world trade and commerce."[104] As President Truman hailed the completion of the General Agreement on Tariffs and Trade, on October 29, 1947, he observed that "never before have so many nations combined in such a sustained effort to lower barriers to trade. Never before have

---

101 U.S. Dept. of State, *Proposals for Expansion of World Trade and Employment*, State Department Publication No. 2411, Dec. 1945. See also US Dept. of State, *Suggested Charter for an International Trade Organization of the United Nations*, State Department Publication No. 2598, Sept. 1946.

102 For a detailed account of the meetings and corresponding drafts, see Irwin, Mavroidis, and Sykes, *Genesis of the GATT* (n 1). The ITO never materialized in the end. See John Jackson, *World Trade and the Law of the GATT* (Bobbs-Merrill Company, 1969).

103 Woodbury Willoughby, 'American Trade Policy', U.S. Dept. of State Publication 3091, Commercial Policy Series 110 (1948).

104 U.S. Dept. of State, 'A Constitution for World Trade', Publication 2964, Commercial Policy Series 108 (1947).

nations agreed upon action, on tariffs and preferences, so extensive in its coverage and so far-reaching in its effects …"[105]

2 International Cooperation to Protect Our Spaceship Earth

Approaching 56 hours into their mission, Captain James A. Lovell Jr., Fred W. Haise Jr., and John L. Swigert were only a few hundred thousand miles away from the moon. A massive power failure aboard the spacecraft forced the astronauts to make a drastic change of plans: after swinging around the moon, the crippled Apollo 13 rocketed towards an emergency splash down in the Pacific Ocean on Friday April 17, 1970. As they turned their backs on the moon, the three astronauts were racing against time, trying to reach the Earth before their severely limited reserves of oxygen, electricity, and water ran out.[106]

The crucial problem in those agonizing days of Apollo 13's return from the moon was the uncertain balance between the capacity of the spaceship to support life and the demands made on it by its inhabitants. A month later, then Secretary General of the United Nations, U Thant, told this very same story to the students of the University of Texas. His goal was to spur in them a certain interest and concern for the protection and preservation of the global environment. To this end, he compared the problem faced by Apollo 13 during those last few days to the one faced by our planet Earth—though vaster and more complex. Just like the spaceship, the Earth was struggling to meet the needs of its passengers and to absorb the various waste products they produced: the balance between the life-sustaining systems of the Earth and the industrial, agricultural, technological, and demographic demands of its inhabitants had been lost.[107]

In 1970, when U Thant gave this speech at the University of Texas, the environment was becoming "the most international of all the great issues which have confronted, or are likely to confront, the human race"[108] which would give the East and West a new reason to cooperate. Of course, the East and West had

105 Harry S. Truman, *Proclamation 2761: Carrying Out General Agreement on Tariffs and Trade Concluded at Geneva* (Oct. 30, 1947).

106 John Noble Wilford, 'Crew of Crippled Apollo 13 Starts Back After Rounding Moon and Firing Rocket; Men Appear Calm Despite Low Reserves', *N.Y. Times*, Apr. 15, 1970.

107 Press Release, Address by Secretary General, U Thant, at University of Texas on 14 May: Human Environment and World Order, UN Press Release SG/SM/1259 (May 14, 1970).

108 Maurice F. Strong, Opening Remarks at Informal Meeting of Preparatory Committee for the Conference (Nov. 9, 1970) (on file with the Environmental Science and Public Policy Archives at Harvard University, Maurice F. Strong Papers, Box 28[283]).

already been cooperating for nearly 30 years on matters of war, peace, national security, and trade. Before 1968, when the UN first decided to call the very first Conference on the Human Environment, the environment was not considered as a global issue except by a few people in a small number of countries, primarily in the industrialized world.[109] The term 'environment' itself was entirely new to the jargon of public affairs. 'Pollution' was more frequently used, and it was treated as a purely local concern.[110] The truth is that the 'environment issue' had just been put on the table of national and international decision-makers, catching them entirely unprepared.

2.1 *The Utilitarian Approach to Environmental Protection*

Of course, man had always interacted with nature: from the time primitive man discovered fire and fashioned his first tools and weapons, his technologies have significantly been affecting the natural environment.[111] Nature represented both a threat and a resource, and throughout history man has used his technologies and inventions to tame and exploit it. For years, almost all the nations of the world have been preoccupied with economic growth. On the one hand, science and technology seemed to offer the key to ever-expanding material well-being, while on the other, nature seemed to offer unlimited abundance of resources to be exploited.

Accordingly, international treaties signed during the end of the nineteenth and the beginning of the twentieth century were not devoted to the protection of the environment *per se*, but rather to the exploitation of certain resources, the control of transboundary damage, and the use of shared watercourses, always with economic growth in mind.[112] In 1902, for instance, eight countries

109 'The Environment: A Global Issue'. Maurice Strong Interviewed by Kurt R. Swinton and 'Maurice Strong: Can Savages Learn Self-Reliance?' Interview for *Populi* (1972–75) (both documents on file with the Environmental Science and Public Policy Archives at Harvard University, Maurice F. Strong Papers, Box 27[268]).

110 See e.g. United States Senate, *History of The Committee on Environment and Public Works-United States Senate*, S. Doc. No. 100–45 (1988), 11.

111 Maurice F. Strong, Statement to the Economic Commission for Latin America in Santiago, Chile (May 3, 1971) (on file with the Environmental Science and Public Policy Archives at Harvard University, Maurice F. Strong Papers, Box 28[282]).

112 See e.g., London Convention Designed to Ensure Conservation of Various Species of Wild Animals in Africa Which Are Useful to Man or Inoffensive, 1900 C.d. 101, Vol. 56, pp. 825–837; Convention for the Protection of Birds Useful to Agriculture, March 19, 1902, 191 C.T.S.; Treaty for the Preservation and Protection of Fur Seals, June 7, 1911, 37 Stat. 1542; London Convention relative to the Preservation of Fauna and Flora in their Natural State, November 8, 1933, 172 U.N.T.S. 241; Washington Convention on Nature Protection and Wildlife Preservation in the Western Hemisphere, October 12, 1940, 161 U.N.T.S. 193; Washington International Convention for the Regulation of Whaling, December 2,

signed a convention aimed at protecting certain species of birds. Their protection, however, was only instrumental for the ultimate goal of the convention, which was to foster the countries' agricultural sector, explaining the full title of the document—Convention for the Protection of Birds *Useful to Agriculture*. Along these very same lines, the United States had a few years prior defended its decision to prevent British vessels from sealing in the Bering Sea in order to prevent over-exploitation of fur seals.[113] In its argument, the United States explained that the US Government had "an interest, an industry, and a commerce derived from the legitimate and proper use of the produce of the seal herd on its territory, which it is entitled … to protect against wanton destruction by individuals."[114]

Even the notion of 'conservation', which developed in the nineteenth century in the United States through the work of a small number of naturalists and philosophers,[115] carried with it a certain utilitarian flavor: in his first message to Congress on December 3, 1901, on the question of resource development, Roosevelt had proclaimed that "[f]orest protection is not an end in itself; it is a means to increase and sustain the resources of our country and the industries which depend upon them. The preservation of our forests is an imperative *business* necessity."[116] Along the very same lines, 40 years later, the Atlantic Charter reiterated the importance of equal access to raw materials and natural resources *solely* to ensure states' economic prosperity.

And the same utilitarian vision characterized those international cooperation efforts, which had their origin precisely in the Atlantic Charter and had

---

1946, 161 U.N.T.S. 72; Washington International Convention for the North-West Atlantic Fisheries, February 8, 1949, 157 U.N.T.S. 157; Tokyo International Convention for the High Seas Fisheries of the North Pacific Ocean, May 9, 1952, 205 U.N.T.S. 65; International Convention for the Prevention of Pollution of the Sea by Oil, May 12, 1954, 327 U.N.T.S. 3. See Edith Brown Weiss, 'The Evolution of International Environmental Law' (2011) 54 *Japanese Yearbook of International Law* 1; Pierre M. Dupuy and Jorge E Viñuales, *International Environmental Law* (Cambridge University Press, 2015), p. 6.

113 Arbitration between the United States and the United Kingdom related to the Rights of Jurisdiction of United States in the Bering's Sea and the Preservation of Fur Seals, August 15, 1983, XXVIII R.I.A.A. 1.002 [hereinafter Bering Sea Arbitration], Argument for the United States before the Tribunal of Arbitration convened at Paris under the provisions of the treaty between the United States of America and Great Britain, concluded February 29, 1892.

114 See Bering Sea Arbitration. See also Lake Lanoux Case (France v. Spain), November 16, 1957, 12 R.I.A.A. 281; 24 I.L.R. 101; Trail Smelter Case (US v. Canada), March 11, 1941, 3 R.I.A.A. 1938.

115 For a historical overview of the conservation movement in the US, see Stewart P. Udall, *The Quiet Crisis* (Avon Books, 1964).

116 Theodore Roosevelt, First Annual Message, Dec. 3, 1901 (emphasis added).

led, only a few years later, to the creation of the United Nations. Such efforts were aimed at uniting the nations of the world in the common effort to end wars and resource conservation was seen merely as instrumental in the struggle for peace that motivated the international economic conferences of the 1940s. Precisely because national and international attention was focused on matters of peace, and on the economic integration that made it possible, the protection of the natural environment remained a far less prominent political issue for many years.

2.2 *"We Have Met the Enemy and He Is Us"*[117]

Then the 1960s came, and things began to change. After World War II, while working for the US government, the popular author and biologist Rachel Carson had tried to interest some magazines in an article on the dangers of the pesticide DDT, but all her efforts seemed to be in vain. Ten years later, in 1958, she tried once again to reach out to publishers but, just like before, each and every one of them turned her down. The only exception was the *New Yorker*, which, in 1962, agreed to publish a series of articles exposing the hazards of DDT.[118] The pesticide, which had long been regarded as some sort of miracle drug, destroying pests and reducing insects-borne diseases, had been found to do more harm than good, causing wholesale destruction of wildlife and its habitat, and clearly endangering human life.[119] The articles were later gathered in what became one of the landmark books of the twentieth century, *Silent Spring*, opening the door to the birth of the environmental movement and helping launch a new decade of rebellion and protest.[120]

---

117 This quote was printed on a poster to promote Earth Day in 1970 and was later used by Walk Kelly in a famous cartoon strip that caught the collective imagination of Americans and is still used in public discourse to describe negative impacts of human activity on our planet (i.e. global warming). The phrase is deemed to derive from braggadocio during the War of 1812 in which commodore Oliver Hazard Perry reported "we have met the enemy and they are ours" to William Henry Harrison after the Battle of Lake Erie.

118 Rachel Carson, 'Silent Spring—I', *New Yorker* (June 16, 1962).

119 The example of DDT is just one of many instances where technology introduced to address certain concerns has backlashed and in turn created a whole array of other—more serious—environmental problems. Some of the most striking examples have been gathered in a Special Supplement of Natural History in 1969 and later a book: M. Taghi Farvar and John Milton (eds.), *The Unforeseen International Ecologic Boomerang* (American Museum of National History, 1969).

120 Rachel Carson, *Silent Spring* (Houghton Mifflin, 1962). This book was the first of several publications on the adverse impact of human activities on the environment. Other examples include *Our Synthetic Environment*, published by Murray Bookchin under the pseudonym 'Lewis Herber' in 1962 and *The Population Bomb* by Stanford professor Paul Ehrlich in 1970.

With increasing frequency, television brought images of environmental disasters—such as the 1967 Torrey Canyon oil spill off the British coast and the 1969 Santa Barbara oil spill—into homes all over the world. These catastrophic events created a sense of vulnerability and showed the potentially destructive impact of man's interaction with nature:[121] while for most human history, the principal threats to man had come from nature, in those years it became increasingly clear that the principal threats to both man and nature were coming from man himself.[122]

From being the concern of a small group of conservationists for the protection of species of wildlife and the natural landscape, the environment had become the concern of many individuals and communities, mostly in industrialized countries, with the local and visible problems of air and water pollution.[123] Yet, the 'environment issue' was still perceived only as a local problem, to be dealt with nationally. We are still a few years away from the image of 'Spaceship Earth' and the awareness of the 'environment issue' as a truly and intrinsically global issue. It would still be a few years before we would begin to grasp "the complexity of the ecological relationships through which man interacts with his natural environment and the magnitude of the problem he is creating by his interventions in the ecosystems which are vital to his own well-being—indeed his very survival."[124]

2.3 *Spaceship Earth*

In 1972, the crew of the Apollo 17 mission provided us with 'The Blue Marble', the most powerful image of the Earth seen from outer space—an incredibly beautiful, yet finite and vulnerable, planet which provides the home and safeguards the hopes of humankind. This and other photographs of our blue planet, coming from even earlier Apollo missions, dramatized the unity and

---

121 The earliest known comprehensive scientific examination of human activity degrading the earth's ecosystems is George Perkins March's classic work *Man and Nature: Or Physical Geography as Modified by Human Action,* published in 1864.

122 Maurice F. Strong, Address at the National Foreign Trade Convention, The Waldorf Astoria NY: The Crisis of Our Environment and the Quality of Life (Nov. 17, 1971) (on file with the Environmental Science and Public Policy Archives at Harvard University, Maurice F. Strong Papers, Box 28[281]). See also Stewart P. Udall, 'We Must Save the Beauty of Our Land', *The Carpenter*, Apr. 1964, 2: "Like little gods, we manipulate and mold our natural and physical environment to suit our designs. But, in exercising dominance over nature, we have too often ignored our dependence on nature. The pressures of overpopulation, the sense of rootlessness that accompanies a wheel-happy nation, and the soft-confidence that follows prosperity have all taken their toll on nature."

123 Strong, Address at the National Foreign Trade Convention (n 122).

124 Ibid.

fragility of the biosphere and contributed to the analogy of the Earth as the planetary life-support system.[125]

At the same time, these photographs conveyed a decisive image of the Earth as spherical and 'closed', signaling a long process of transition in the "nature of the image which man has of himself and his environment."[126] Largely regarded as the father of the idea of 'spaceship Earth', Kenneth Boulding described this transition as pressing and inevitable.[127] According to Boulding, the man of the past was unaware of the inherent limits of the world he inhabited. Rather, he imagined himself living in a 'virtually illimitable plane': "[t]here was almost always somewhere beyond the known limits of human habitation ... there was always someplace else to go when things got too difficult."[128] If a piece of land suddenly became barren, a forest burned to the ground, or a lake dried up completely, there was always the possibility to find new fertile soil, lush vegetation, and rich bodies of water. This kind of 'open' Earth was picturesquely defined by Boulding as 'cowboy economy', characterized by illimitable plains and countless frontiers man could constantly push back. The 'closed' spherical Earth that photographs of the 'Blue Marble' were showing could instead be better explained by the idea of a 'spaceman economy', "in which the Earth had become a single spaceship, without unlimited reservoirs of anything, either for extraction or for pollution, and in which, therefore, man must find his place in a cyclical ecological system ...".[129]

Despite the rather 'esoteric' nature of Boulding's thinking,[130] his ideas of a 'spaceship Earth' rapidly gained traction and soon began to inform all subsequent discussions on the environment. In his last speech before the Economic and Social Council in Geneva, US Ambassador Adlai Stevenson referred to the Earth as a little spaceship on which we travel together, "dependent on its vulnerable supplies of air and soil."[131] The same analogy was later recalled by the biologist and philosopher René Dubos and the economist Lady Barbara Ward Jackson, who co-authored a report on the state of the global

---

125 Lynton K. Caldwell, 'A World Policy for the Environment', *The Unesco Courier* (Jan. 1973), 5.

126 Kenneth E. Boulding, 'The Economics of the Coming Spaceship Earth', in H. Jarrett (ed.), *Environmental Quality in a Growing Economy* 3–14 (John Hopkins University Press, 1966).

127 See Robert F. Blomquist, '"Clean New World": Toward an Intellectual History of American Environmental Law, 1961–1990' (1990) 25(1) *Valparaiso University Law Review* 1, 27.

128 Boulding, 'The Economics of the Coming Spaceship Earth' (n 126) 3.

129 Ibid.

130 Blomquist, '"Clean New World"' (n 127) 27.

131 Adlai Stevenson, 1965, extract from his last speech, as quoted in John McHale, 'The Changing Pattern of Futures Research in the USA', *Futures* (1973), 258.

environment—entitled *Only One Earth*—which served as the scientific basis and conceptual framework for the Stockholm Conference. In their words,

> We are indeed travelers bound to the earth's crust, drawing life from the air and water of its thin and fragile envelope, using and reusing its very limited supply of natural resources. Now that all habitable parts of the globe are occupied, the careful husbandry of the earth is a *sine qua non* for the survival of the human species, and for the creation of decent ways of life for all the people of the world.[132]

At the same time, the closed nature of the Earth triggered heated discussions on the impact of the growth of the world's population on its limited resources. In 1968, a small international group of scientists, industrialists, and bankers had formed an organization, named the Club of Rome after the *Accademia dei Lincei* of Rome, where they held their first meeting.[133] In 1972, united in their conviction of the gravity of the situation facing mankind, these men produced a report titled *Limits to Growth*, which addressed the issue of a growing population on the Earth's limited resources, pointing out that this was a global concern.[134] The scale of the present human population, of its intervention in the natural system, and of the impact of those interventions on that system had grown at such a rate that the historical man-nature relationship had been turned on its head.[135]

A natural consequence of the 'spaceship Earth' idea was the realization that international cooperation was crucial if one were to guarantee its protection and preservation. Environmental problems were finally seen as transcending

---

132 Barbara Ward and René Dubos, *Only One Earth* (W.W. Norton & Company, 1972), pp. xvii-xviii.

133 Alexander King, 'New Ethic for Survival', in Clifton Fadiman and Jean White (eds.), *Ecocide—And Thoughts Toward Survival* (Center for Study of Democratic Institutions, 1971).

134 Donella H. Meadows, *The Limits to Growth: A Report for the Club of Rome's Project on the Predicament of Mankind* (Penguin, 1972). For earlier examples of studies on the impact of population growth on the environment and natural resources, see William Vogt, *The Road to Survival* (W. Sloane Associates, 1948); Fairfield Osborn, *Our Plundered Planet* (Little Brown, 1948); and Paul Ehlrich, *The Population Bomb* (Ballantine Books, 1970).

135 Maurice F. Strong, Montague Burton Lecture: The United Nations Conference on the Human Environment at Stockholm (Jan. 19, 1973) (on file with the Environmental Science and Public Policy Archives at Harvard University, Maurice F. Strong Papers, Box 28[283]). See also Udall, *The Quiet Crisis* (n 115) 190. As to the numbers related to the increase in population, see United Nations Conference on the Human Environment, An Action Plan for the Human Environment, A/CONF.48/5 (Feb. 9, 1972) [hereinafter Stockholm Action Plan], 10.

national boundaries, together with the acceptance of the concept of the environment as embracing the whole series of cause and effect relationships by which man interacts with nature and in doing so affects himself:[136]

> The simple truth is that no place on our planet lives alone and no place can deal alone with the pollution of the planet. We are far from one world politically—but by necessity if not by choice, we are one world environmentally. And the crisis of the environment has made us common victims of a common adversity.[137]

In only a few decades, the environment—the most local of all issues—had suddenly become one of the most international of all issues: if it is true that environmental problems can and should be addressed by national jurisdictions, effective action to cope with the environmental crisis would require an unprecedented level of international cooperation.[138] To paraphrase what Adlai E. Stevenson once said about making peace, "protecting our environment is not merely a matter of nations looking at each other, but of their looking together in the same direction."[139] The first steps towards this new kind of cooperation were taken by the man who was put in charge of the Stockholm Conference on the Human Environment, a Canadian self-made man involved both in business and in politics. This man was Maurice Strong, and his inspiring and forceful leadership played a crucial role in the success of the Conference,[140] which has been often referred to as "one of the boldest adventures in international

---

136 *Maurice Strong Defines Many Environment Problems and Seeks Solutions*, Delegates World Bulletin, June 2, 1975, 1084.

137 Edmund Muskie, Address at the Conference on International Organization and the Human Environment, New York: An Alliance for Survival (1971) (on file with the Environmental Science and Public Policy Archives at Harvard University, Maurice F. Strong Papers, Box 28[283]). See also Senator Muskie's address at the opening session in Rensselaerville, as quoted in Richard N. Gardner, 'Global Pollution III: U.N. as Policeman, in Environment and the Quality of Life', 54 *Saturday Review*, Aug. 7, 1971, 50.

138 Maurice F. Strong, Address at the University of Toronto Study Conference on The Crisis of the Human Environment and International Action (May 27, 1971) (on file with the Environmental Science and Public Policy Archives at Harvard University, Maurice F. Strong Papers, Box 28[283]).

139 Maurice F. Strong, Address at the International Youth Conference on the Human Environment, McMaster University (Aug. 27, 1971) (on file with the Environmental Science and Public Policy Archives at Harvard University, Maurice F. Strong Papers, Box 28[281]), quoting Adlai E. Stevenson, *Looking Outward Years of Crisis at the United Nations.*

140 With these words, Swedish Prime Minister Olof Palme described the character of Maurice Strong, an opinion shared by many members of the UN preparatory staff. 'Canadian Praised as Ecologists Meet', *The Gazette*, Montreal, June 5, 1972, 45 (on file with the Environmental

cooperation ever attempted,"[141] and which represented the first step in what have been now nearly 50 years of international environmental cooperation.

2.4 *The 'Internationalist' from Oak Lake*

Born in April 1929 in the small town of Oak Lake in rural Manitoba, Maurice Strong was yet another man deeply affected by the events of that year. The Great Depression was indeed one of the great shaping forces in his life, "a calamity visited not just on [his] family but on [his] community and [his] country and on many millions of people around the globe," as he would later describe it.[142] A very private child, he would mostly keep to himself, finding refuge in nature to the point of creating an emotional connection with the natural environment that never left him.[143] In school, thanks to the support and encouragement of his teacher and school's principal Clarence 'Curly' Heapy, Strong eagerly devoured books on science to better understand the mysterious processes of nature that so excited and challenged him.[144] He counted Curly Heapy as one of the two main influences in his life. The other was his mother, who taught him life's true values and left him with a single overriding message: "never hold yourself back from trying to achieve what you want. Always press to the limit."[145]

Despite his strong interest in natural science, which Strong further pursued when he left Oak Lake to live with the Eskimos looking for adventure, travel, and a closer connection with nature, he never called himself an 'environmentalist'. The word did not even exist at that time, and would not exist for two more decades. What he has always considered himself, though, was a committed 'internationalist'.[146] When he left home in 1941, while crossing the country to join the merchant marine, Strong picked up a discarded newspaper rustled by the light breeze in a Saskatchewan freight yard and learned about the meeting between Roosevelt and Churchill in the Atlantic. Though still a boy, Strong could barely contain his excitement, as international affairs had long impinged on his consciousness. As soon as he read that Churchill and Roosevelt had met

Science and Public Policy Archives at Harvard University, Maurice F. Strong Papers, Box 42[418]).

141 Gardner, 'Global Pollution III' (n 137) 47–50.

142 Maurice F. Strong, *Where On Earth Are We Going?* (Knopf Canada, 2010).

143 Ibid.

144 Ibid.

145 Ibid.

146 John Hess, 'What We Hope to Accomplish at Stockholm', *International Wildlife* (March-April 1972), 20 (on file with the Environmental Science and Public Policy Archives at Harvard University, Maurice F. Strong Papers, Box 27[268]).

and had declared that the world was going to be a different place, he knew at once that he had to be part of that endeavor. This single event gave him a whole new purpose in life: he started learning all he could about the League of Nations and followed with great attention the San Francisco Conference and the formation of the United Nations.[147]

It is no surprise that when in February 1970, almost 30 years later, then UN Secretary General U Thant asked him to serve as Secretary General of the UN Conference on the Human Environment, Strong, who at that time was running Canada's foreign aid program, could not refuse.[148] He saw immediately that the Conference would give him the opportunity to merge his two great passions: international affairs and nature. Moreover, he was a firm believer that the environment was "the most international of all the great issues which have confronted, or are likely to confront, the human race."[149] The 1945 San Francisco Conference and the economic conferences of the late 1940s had ensured international cooperation to maintain and nurture peaceful relations between states and economic stability. The stage was set for a new kind of international discussion, and the first step in this direction was taken by Sweden.

2.5 *On the Road to Stockholm*

The busy corridors of the UN headquarters in New York were constantly bubbling and overflowing with all kinds of political murmuring. In 1967, some voices were unquestionably louder than the others: the Swedish delegates were trying to convince other delegations, in particular the US delegates, about the necessity for protective action towards the environment. They had been sent to New York by the Social Democratic Party, while the country was in political ferment.[150] Back in 1950, the Swedes had noticed that wild birds were dying in unprecedented number, and their death was soon traced to the seeds the birds ate, which were coated in methylmercury compounds. A few years later, a dangerous amount of this same substance was found in eggs and fish and, as a result, 40 lakes in Sweden were closed to fishing.[151] After organizing an international conference on the methylmercury threat to the natural environment

147 Strong, *Where On Earth* (n 142).

148 Hess, 'What We Hope' (n 146).

149 Strong, Opening Remarks (n 108).

150 John Lear, 'Global Pollution I: The Chinese Influence, in Environment and the Quality of Life', 54 *Saturday Review*, Aug. 7, 1971, 41–2.

151 By that time, methylmercury spilled from a petrochemical company during the 1950s in the Japanese village of Minamata had poisoned and caused an epidemic among those who ate fish caught in Minamata Bay. Ibid., 1–2.

and human health, the Swedes took it to the UN, as they felt it would be the best forum to deal with the issue.[152]

After negative responses from other delegations,[153] the Swedish requests found their way into the text of a resolution presented by the Economic and Social Council (ECOSOC),[154] which was then endorsed by the General Assembly at its 23rd Session, culminating in the decision to convene, four years later, a United Nations Conference on the Human Environment[155]

The Conference, which took place in Stockholm between the 5 and the 16 of June 1972, was one of a kind. It was the first time in history that the "leaders of the nations had gathered together specifically to look at the evidence that had come from the scientific community as to the effects of man's own activities on the future of the human species and to determine what actions were required by the leaders of the governments of the world to deal with the situation."[156] It was the first time the environment, in its newly acquired meaning, was being discussed at the international level: environmental problems *per se* were not new, but awareness of the problems was, and Maurice Strong, as the man in charge with organizing the Conference, had to start everything from square one.

He knew the first fundamental step was to gather all the relevant information and documentation on the current state of the environment. In order to do so, it was necessary to obtain the active participation of most—if not all—governments. Although Strong's goal was to start an international discussion on the 'environment issue', environmental problems were, first and foremost,

---

152 Lars-Goran Engfeldt, 'The United Nations and the Human Environment—Some Experiences' (1973) 27(3) *International Organization*, 394.

153 In particular, strong opposition came from the US delegation. The State Department was against spending USD 2 million on "8 concurrent long-winded discussions on the environment." The attitude of the United Kingdom and France was also initially rather skeptical of the idea of a United Nations Environment Conference, as they rather favored a continuation of sectoral activities within the specialized agencies, fearing developing countries would use "the environmental bandwagon" as a vehicle for more financial assistance from the industrialized countries. The Soviet delegation, instead, supported the initiative since the beginning, stressing the need for international cooperation to successfully solve environmental problems. Similarly, Belgium, Czechoslovakia, Canada, Iceland, New Zealand, Austria, Uganda, Italy and China, among many others, immediately supported the Swedish initiative. See Lear, 'Global Pollution I' (n 150)41–2; Engfeldt, 'The United Nations and the Human Environment' (n 152) 397; Report of the United Nations Conference on the Human Environment, Stockholm, 5–16 June 1972, A/CONF.48/Rev.1.

154 E.S.C. Res. 1346 (XLV) (July 30, 1968).

155 G.A. Res. 2398 (XXIII) (Dec. 3, 1968).

156 'The Environment: A Global Issue' (n 109).

of a local nature, and the experience of each nation was an essential ingredient to identify environmental problems and provide guidelines for action.[157] To this end, more than 12,000 pages of documentation were collected by the Conference secretariat, representing "the first global survey of environmental issues and concerns" ever made.[158]

Second, he needed scientists. For years, politicians had been ignoring warnings from scientific circles about the global significance of the threat to the environment caused by man's activities.[159] Although the Conference was, of course, a conference of political leaders and not a scientific conference, it was almost entirely based on the best possible evidence gathered from the scientific community and it operated at the critical interface between science and politics.[160] This was indeed the very first time that the scientific community and that of politicians and decision-makers came together in a constructive manner.[161]

Third, he needed to be prepared. And he was. Thoroughly. At that time, it was indeed difficult to think of another UN meeting so meticulously prepared in advance, to the point that one UN official aptly compared the Conference to a marriage ceremony, where most things had been arranged beforehand, and as little as possible was left to change on the date.[162] When he was appointed Secretary-General of the Conference in September 1970, Strong began an uphill battle, which would last 20 long months. During this time, he worked 18 hours

157 G.A. Res. 2398 (XXIII) and G.A. Res. 2581 (XXIV) (Dec. 15, 1969). A total of 86 Governments submitted national reports outlining their environmental experience and concerns. Besides the national reports, the Conference secretariat received contributions from the United Nations system, intergovernmental organizations, non-governmental organizations, and individual experts.

158 Stockholm Action Plan.

159 Engfeldt, 'The United Nations and the Human Environment' (n 152)394.

160 The political character of the Conference was underlined by its mandate to serve as a practical means to encourage—and provide guidelines for—action by governments and international organizations in the environmental field. Ibid., 395. See Maurice F. Strong, Address before the 24th Session of the International Geological Congress: Science and Society in the Environment Age (Aug. 21, 1972) (on file with the Environmental Science and Public Policy Archives at Harvard University, Maurice F. Strong Papers, Box 29[296]).

161 One might consider the Paris Biosphere Conference of 1968, sponsored by Unesco (in cooperation with the UN, the WHO, FAO, IUCN, and the International Biological Program of the International Council of Scientific Unions) to mark the arrival of international political awareness of the world environmental issue. However, the Biosphere Conference was still technically a meeting of just scientific experts, while the Stockholm Conference, gathered, next to scientists, political representatives of governments. See Caldwell, 'A World Policy' (n 125) 4.

162 Gardner, 'Global Pollution III' (n 137) 47–50.

a day, rising each day at 5:30 a.m. and placing his own family on 'a war footing,' as he himself described it.[163] Among the main obstacles he encountered was the great gap in the knowledge about the global ecosystem: there was so much uncertainty around the complex interactions between the natural order and the manifold activities of man that Maurice Strong once referred to the little that was known as "islands of knowledge in a sea of ignorance."[164] Even within the scientific community there was not always common consensus on many environmental problems, although more often than not, the discrepancy of opinions originated not from uncertainties about scientific facts, but from differences in attitudes towards social values.[165] Indeed, each country perceived environmental issues differently, depending on its level of environmental sensitivity, as well as on its specific stage of social and economic development. In particular, the disparity in the weight placed on environmental issues was especially pronounced between industrialized and developing countries.[166]

As a result, a second difficulty lay in ensuring the participation of the developing world. In 1969, developing nations still viewed the 'environment issue' in relatively narrow terms: as a disease of the rich, mostly limited to problems of air and water pollution and other associated ills stemming from the processes of industrialization and urbanization.[167] As he traveled to many of these countries during the preparatory process of the Conference, Strong found that the word 'environment' had not yet acquired the weight it already had in more industrialized nations. Yet, he was able to show that the issues the word embraced were of equally real and growing concern for the developing world.[168] Understanding its importance and sensitivity, Strong made sure that

163 'Strong Confident Environment Talks Will Be a Success', *The Intelligencer*, June 12, 1972.

164 Press Release, Statement by the Secretary General of the Conference on the Human Environment at the 2nd Session of the Preparatory Committee for the Conference, Geneva, 8 February 1971, HE/2 (Feb. 9, 1971) (on file with the Environmental Science and Public Policy Archives at Harvard University, Maurice F. Strong Papers, Box 28[283]). Precisely for this reason, the *Action Plan for the Human Environment*, one of the core documents prepared by the Preparatory Committee and submitted to the Conference as a basis to work on, stressed the importance, in parallel with immediate measures, of ensuring new knowledge on a wide array of environmental problems.

165 Ward and Dubos, *Only One Earth* (n 132) xvii.

166 Mark Edward Foster, 'Trade and Environment: Making Room for Environmental Trade Measures within the GATT' (1998) 71 *Southern California Law Review* 393, 407–8.

167 Policy-makers in developing countries were not sidetracked by "dreams of landscapes innocent of chimney stacks" when they were stressing the importance of their development agenda, but rather they were prepared to accept some environmental cost to be able to develop. Ward and Dubos, *Only One Earth* (n 132) xiii.

168 These issues included, for example, "polluted water supplies, degradation of agricultural lands, depletion of wildlife and fisheries and, perhaps most urgent, the problems

the development-environment issue received a prominent place both in the preparatory work and on the agenda of the Conference itself. He organized a meeting of experts on the topic in Founex, near Geneva, from 4–12 June 1971, and he was able to reconcile seemingly irreconcilable opposing views by emphasizing that the labels 'development' and 'environment' had obscured the essential common nature of the ultimate goals of both, namely the well-being of man.[169]

Finally, there was the question of the organizational arrangements for the years after Stockholm: how could the international community be organized most effectively for environmental action? Was relying on the existing UN agencies the best solution? Or did the world need a new framework?[170]

Grappling with these extremely complex and entirely new questions, after 20 months of extenuating work, everything was ready.[171] On the night of June 5, 1972, The Swedish Prime Minister Olof Palme and then UN Secretary General Kurt Waldheim officially opened the environment conference with a ceremony at the Opera House.[172] During the following two weeks, the Conference was held in three places—the Old and the New Parliament Buildings and the Folkets Hus, the modern headquarters of the Swedish Labor Movement—each a few minutes' walk apart in the center of Stockholm. Sitting concurrently

---

of cities which are growing at rates unprecedented in human history." Maurice F. Strong, Address at the Man and Science Institute, Rensselaerville (May 23, 1971) (on file with the Environmental Science and Public Policy Archives at Harvard University, Peter S. Thacher Papers, Box 32[279]). See also, on specific environmental problems affecting developing countries, Erik P. Eckholm, 'Cheaper Than Oil but More Scarce', *The Washington Post*, July 27, 1975, and 'The Deterioration of Mountain Environments' (1975) 189 *Science* 764; Henry Pelham Burn, 'Packaging Paradise' (1975) 60 *Sierra Club Bulletin* 25.

169 Conflicts might instead arise at the level of decisions on individual questions. The success of Strong's efforts to include developing countries in the process was later proven by the high participation in the Conference, as well as the fact that they pushed to get UNEP to Nairobi. Engfeldt, 'The United Nations and the Human Environment' (n 152) 402; Delegates World Bulletin (n 136) 1084.

170 See Phillip C. Jessup, 'Do New Problems Need New Courts?' (unpublished paper on file with the Environmental Science and Public Policy Archives at Harvard University, Peter S. Thacher Papers, Box 32[279]).

171 The Preparatory Committee, composed of 27 governments, held four consecutive sessions, the first one in New York from 10 to 20 March 1970; the second one in Geneva from 8 to 19 February 1971; the third one in New York from 13 to 24 September 1971; and the fourth one again in New York from 6 to 17 March 1972. The results of the preparatory process, spread in the four sessions, are reflected in documents A/CONF.48/6 to A/CONF.48/11 which constitute individual reports and recommendations in each of the six subject areas of the Conference.

172 'Canadian Praised as Ecologists Meet' (n 140) 45.

were three committees, dealing respectively with marine pollution, natural resources and the development-environment issue, and the problems arising from the spread of human settlement.

The main goal of the conference was the development of international consensus on certain new principles to guide governments' action.[173] The Declaration on the Human Environment, circulated after the end of the preparatory process and endorsed in Stockholm on the very last day, represented the first attempt in this direction. Its preparation had been extremely lengthy and difficult, precisely because the members of the Preparatory Committee did not want a mere exercise in rhetoric, a pious statement of goals. They wanted it to mean something, to establish the first strong principles that would ultimately form the basis of international law in this area.[174] Being the first document of this kind, everything was open for discussion and every suggestion was duly taken into account. Much of the second week of the Conference was devoted to finalizing the drafting of the Declaration and, after five long days of arguing over nearly every single word of the draft, on the last day of the Conference, just before midnight, Strong emerged to announce: "There will definitely be a declaration."[175]

Although the Conference did not resolve all the major environmental issues—and no one would have expected it to—it did provide world governments "with the first opportunity to consider on a global basis the important implications of environmental problems for their own people."[176] Thanks to Stockholm, "to defend and improve the human environment for present and future generations [had] become an imperative goal to be pursued together with, and in harmony with, the established and fundamental goals of peace and of world-wide economic and social

173 Hess, 'What We Hope' (n 146).

174 Maurice Strong ventured the idea of a Declaration that would go beyond a mere inspirational document: "I think we should consider if it might also go beyond this to include the commitment of governments to certain fundamental principles which would provide the basis for their individual and collective approaches to the challenges of the human environment." Strong, Opening Remarks (n 108).

175 'Strong Breaks Back-Stage Deadlock Over UN Declaration on Pollution', *Toronto Star*, June 15, 1972, 3; 'Canadian Praised as Ecologists Meet' (n 140). See e.g. Louis B. Sohn, 'The Stockholm Declaration on the Human Environment' (1973) 14 *Harvard International Law Journal* 423; Alexandre Kiss and Jean-Didier Sicault, 'La Conférence des Nations Unies sur l'environnement (Stockholm, 5–16 juin 1972)' (1972) 18 *Annuaire Français de droit international* 603 ; Jutta Brunnée, 'The Stockholm Declaration and the Structure and Process of International Environmental Law', in Aldo Chircop (ed.), *The Future of Ocean Regime-Building: Essays in Tribute to Douglas M. Johnston* (Martinus Nijhoff, 2009), pp. 41–62.

176 Strong, Address at the University of Toronto (n 138).

development."[177] After many years, the protection of the environment had finally caught up, and had become one of the goals to be pursued through international law and cooperation.

3 The Environment as a Late-Comer

In 1975, in his first address to the Governing Council of the United Nations Environment Program (UNEP), Maurice Strong declared that "almost all governments had recognized the importance of the environment to their national interests and had taken steps to establish national environmental policies and administrations, most as a direct result of the Stockholm Conference."[178] In a number of instances, the establishment of Ministries of the Environment or of similar government authorities, and the enactment of environmental laws and regulations, owed much to internationally generated concerns.[179] This was for example the case of the European Union (EU) (then the European Economic Community or EEC), as it was only after Stockholm that environmental problems started receiving increasing attention at the Community level. In other countries, such as the United States, national environmental movements in the 1960s had already planted the seeds for reform, and the international events that took place in the early 1970s simply gave a final push to a wheel that was already in motion.

Either way, legislators quickly had to face the fact that the 'environment issue' was a late-comer on the political and legal arenas: it required the development of new principles and the enactment of entirely new laws, which had to be built within a well-oiled legal framework, and respect the limits imposed by the already existing regulation of economic matters. In the United States, Congress' power to regulate commerce had been an integral part of the Constitution since its adoption in 1787, while federal environmental law-making, lacking a constitutional foundation, started off as entirely dependent and conditional to the Commerce Clause. In the context of the European

177 United Nations Conference on the Human Environment, Stockholm, Sweden, June 5–16, 1972, *Stockholm Declaration on the Human Environment*, U.N. Doc. A/CONF.48/14/Rev.1 [hereinafter Stockholm Declaration].

178 'Concept of UNEP as Leader and Catalyst Becoming Reality; Director Reports Progress', Excerpts of Maurice Strong's address to the UNEP Governing Council on 17 April 1975 and of the accompanying report, UN Chronicle (May 1975).

179 Maurice F. Strong, 'The Institutional Aspects of the Environment', May 20, 1972 (unpublished outline on file with the Environmental Science and Public Policy Archives at Harvard University, Maurice F. Strong Papers, Box 28[282]).

Union, which had been created precisely to cooperate on trade and customs matters, the introduction of environmental regulation faced similar challenges. And at the international level as well, the efforts of Maurice Strong and all the other negotiators in Stockholm had to face the harsh reality: the GATT, and all the bilateral trade agreements signed by countries until then, had been negotiated at a time when the environment was not a public policy issue, and had been drafted completely ignoring it. As a late-comer, the environment was simply 'added' to the already existing legal framework and could only be regulated and protected within the limits and constraints provided by it.

3.1 *Mr. Clean—The Senator from Maine*

Already in 1963, then US Secretary of the Interior Stewart Udall had called for new forms of international cooperation to realize the full potential of natural resources: "geography has always been a global science and conservation must now become a truly global concept if the optimum use of resources is to be achieved."[180] One of the most eloquent environmental leaders of his time, Udall spoke early on about a 'quiet crisis' that required strong and global preservation efforts. A quiet, yet urgent, crisis, as clarified by John F. Kennedy,[181] which reached a dramatic climax on April 22, 1970, better known as the first Earth Day. On that occasion, millions of Americans took to the streets of major cities all around the country, marching, listening to folk singers and speeches by environmental activists, and waving 'Save the Earth' banners on crowded streets.[182]

The idea for Earth Day had been developed two years earlier by Wisconsin senator Gaylord Nelson, who had casually suggested a national teach-in on the crisis of the environment, drawing on the tactics of the anti-Vietnam War movements. Nelson was convinced that the environmental crisis was "the most critical issue facing mankind, [making] Vietnam, nuclear war, hunger, decaying cities, and all the other major problems one could name ... relatively insignificant by comparison."[183]

---

180 Udall, *The Quiet Crisis* (n 115) 196, 199. He also pointed out that although "the atmosphere and the oceans are the two resources that are owned by all of the people of the world ... save for a few farsighted treaties, we have no plan of management for these common resources ...".

181 Ibid., p. xii (preface by John F. Kennedy).

182 David Vogel, 'A Big Agenda' (1987) *Wilson Quarterly*, 51.

183 See 'Environment. The Downing of Earth Day', *Time* (Apr. 27, 1970). Robert Gottlieb, *Forcing the Spring: The Transformation of the American Environmental Movement* (Island Press, 2005), pp. 148–9. See also Edward E. C. Clebsch, 'The Campus Teach-in on the Environmental Crisis: 1970' (1970) 34(109) *The Living Wilderness*, 10.

Earth Day represented a turning point in American history, marking a radical upsurge in public anxiety about the environment.[184] It is also commonly regarded as the beginning of American environmental politics.[185] Just 18 months prior, during the 1968 presidential campaign, environmental issues had received virtually no attention in either party's platform.[186] But by 1970, a Harris poll found that Americans regarded pollution as "the most serious problem facing their communities"[187] and *TIME* magazine named protection of the environment the "issue of the year," ahead of the Vietnam War.[188] By 1970, both the Nixon White House and the Democratic-controlled Congress were stressing the need to safeguard the national environment for future generations,[189] and by 1972, Congress had passed half a dozen sweeping new environmental laws—starting with the National Environmental Policy Act (NEPA)—making the 92nd Congress "the most productive record for environmental protection in the nation's history."[190]

Immediately after the singing into law of NEPA, Nixon dramatically proclaimed that "the 1970s absolutely must be the years when America pays its debt to the past by reclaiming the purity of its air, its waters, and our living environment. It is literally now or never." This, he declared, would be "the environmental decade."[191] Nixon's zeal for the environment, however, was short-lived

184 Vogel, 'A Big Agenda' (n 182) 53.

185 Samuel P. Hays, Beauty, *Health, and Performance. Environmental Politics in the United States, 1955–1985* (Cambridge University Press, 1989), p. 52. Others rather emphasize the publication of Carson's *Silent Spring*, the Santa Barbara oil spill, or even the controversy over the proposed construction of the Storm King pumped-storage power plant on the Hudson River.

186 Richard Lazarus, *The Making of Environmental Law* (The University of Chicago Press, 2006), pp. 53–4.

187 Vogel, 'A Big Agenda' (n 182) 53.

188 *Time* Vol. 97(1), Jan. 4, 1971. See also Gladwin Hill, 'Environment May Eclipse Vietnam as College Issue', *N.Y. Times* (Nov. 29, 1970), A1:2; James McEvoy, 'The American Concern with the Environment', in William Burch et al. (eds.), *Social Behavior, Natural Resources and the Environment* (1972), pp. 214–36.

189 See e.g., 115 Cong. Rec. 26,576 (1969) (remarks of Rep. Rogers); 115 Cong. Rec. 29,069 (1969) (remarks of Sen. Jackson); 116 Cong. Rec. 32,918 (1970) (remarks of Sen. Cooper); 116 Cong. Rec. 42,392 (remarks of Sen. Randolph); Remarks of President Nixon on Signing Public Law 91–604, Dec. 31, 1970, 7 Weekly Comp. Pres. Docs. 11–12 (1971); Environmental Quality: The President's Message to the Congress Recommending a 37-Point Administrative and Legislative Program, 6 Weekly Comp. Pres. Docs. 160 (1970).

190 National Environmental Policy Act of 1969 § 102, 42 U.S.C. § 4332 (2006) [hereinafter NEPA].

191 Richard Nixon, 'Statement about the Environmental Policy Act of 1969', Jan. 1, 1970. The adoption of NEPA is considered one of the most creative moments in the history of environmental law. See William H. Jr. Rodgers, 'The Most Creative Moments in the History of Environmental Law: "The Whats" ' (2000) *University of Illinois Law Review* 1.

(lasting less than two years) and largely stemmed from political calculation rather than personal ideology.[192] His environmentalism might have even been a strategy to steal the spotlight from his likely opponent in the 1972 presidential election, a man that has often been defined as America's most important environmental leader and champion, Senator Edmund S. Muskie.[193]

Edmund Muskie was born in Rumford, Maine, on March 28, 1914. For him, being born and raised in Maine played a crucial role in his early interest and later involvement in American environmental law. He described his native state as "a place of great natural beauty, marred by intermittent ugliness."[194] The dichotomy between evergreen forests, trout streams, and abundant fields on the one hand, and the "ugly reality" of pollution and despoliation of nature on the other, was set in his mind since he was just a child. As a son of Maine, he was, viscerally, a conservationist, and whenever that natural beauty was threatened, he felt the need to do something about it. Yet, he recalls the 'environment' not being an issue back then:

> When I was a boy, we didn't think about 'pollution'. The word wasn't part of our everyday vocabulary, and it was hardly in the public dialogue. If we thought at all about such matters, what we saw appeared to be a necessary balance between jobs and some pollution of rivers; between wide, open, clean spaces, streams, lakes, forests, mountains, and a few less than lovely factories or plants. The beauties of nature were around us [in Maine] in almost pristine form. What development we had [we thought back then] was the price we paid for the economic benefits, even if it defiled the river some.[195]

192 Already in 1972, he vetoed the amendments to the Federal Water Pollution Control Act. Richard Lazarus, 'Senator Edmund Muskie's Enduring Legacy in the Courts' (2015) 67(2) *Maine Law Review* 240, 240–1. For an account of Nixon's role in these formative years of American environmental law, see J. Brooks Flippen, *The Nixon Administration, Politics and the Environment* (UNM Press, 1994) and *Nixon and the Environment* (UNM Press, 2000).

193 Leon G. Billings, 'Edmund Muskie: A Man with a Vision' (2015) 67(2) *Maine Law Review* 234. Muskie's role in shaping modern American environmental law has been consistently acknowledged by US courts: according to Lazarus, "[f]ederal courts in their opinions have cited the views of Senator Muskie in the enactment of federal environmental statutes in at least 293 separate cases" while the Justices of the US Supreme Court "have cited to Muskie in 22 different cases." Lazarus, 'Senator Edmund Muskie's Enduring Legacy' (n 192) 242.

194 Edmund S. Muskie, *Journeys* (Doubleday, 1972), p. 79, as quoted in Robert F. Blomquist, 'What is Past is Prologue: Senator Edmund S. Muskie's Environmental Policymaking Roots as Governor of Maine, 1955–58' (1999) 51(1) *Maine Law Review* 88, 89.

195 Muskie, *Journeys* (n 194) 79–80, as quoted in Robert F. Blomquist, '"To Stir Up Public Interest": Edmund S. Muskie and the US Senate Special Subcommittee' Water Pollution,

When he went back to Rumford after completing his studies, he observed the 'pollution problem' of the Androscoggin River, which ran through his hometown, and the intense pollution of the air from nearby paper mill smokestacks.[196] This matter inspired Muskie's 1954 gubernatorial campaign and eventually led to the enactments of Maine's first significant water pollution statute. As governor, he began to understand the complexity of the 'environment issue'—which involved so much more than air and water pollution—at a time when no other politician seemed to be genuinely interested in addressing it.[197] In those years, the protection of certain environmental components was still largely linked to the possibility of their exploitation. Federal regulation of water, for example, which had begun in the late nineteenth century with the adoption of the Rivers and Harbors Acts, had initially been targeted exclusively at "promoting water transportation and commerce."[198] It was only after the first half of the twentieth century that the goal of federal regulation started shifting away from an exclusive focus on protecting navigability, and toward a concern for preventing environmental degradation. The shift, which culminated in the passage of the Clean Water Act in 1972, was largely due to the leadership, foresight, and extreme patience and perseverance of Edmund Muskie.

In 1963, after being "the first Democrat ever to be popularly elected in Maine as a United States Senator,"[199] Muskie was appointed by Pat McNamara, the new Chairman of Public Works, as chairman of the newly formed subcommittee on air and water pollution. Over the course of two decades as chairman of the subcommittee, Senator Muskie had a hand in crafting the majority of the most important American federal environmental statutes,[200] earning the informal

---

Investigations and Legislative Activities. 1963–66—A Case Study in Early Congressional Environmental Policy Development' (1997) 22(1) *Columbia Journal of Environmental Law* 1, 6.

196 Joel K. Goldstein, 'Edmund S. Muskie: The Environmental Leader and Champion' (2015) 67(2) *Maine Law Review* 226.

197 Donald Elliot et al., 'Toward a Theory of Statutory Evolution: The Federalization of Environmental Law' (1985) 1 *The Journal of Law, Economics & Organization* 313, 327.

198 Sam Kalen, 'Commerce to Conservation: The Call for a National Water Policy and the Evolution of Federal Jurisdiction Over Wetlands' (1993) 69 *North Dakota Law Review* 873, 877.

199 Robert F. Blomquist, 'Senator Edmund S. Muskie and the Dawn of Modern American Environmental Law: First Term, 1959–1964' (2002) 26 *William & Mary Environmental Law & Policy Review* 509.

200 The major federal environmental protection statutes adopted during the 1970s include: Clean Air Act, 42 U.S.C. § 7401 et seq. (1970); Clean Water Act, 33 U.S.C. § 1251 et seq. (1972); Federal Insecticide, Fungicide, and Rodenticide Act, 7 U.S.C. § 136 et seq. (1972); Noise Control Act, 42 U.S.C. § 4901 et seq. (1972); Coastal Zone Management Act, 16 U.S.C. § 1451 et seq. (1972); Endangered Species Act, 16 U.S.C. § 1531 et seq. (1973); Safe

nickname of 'Mr. Clean'.[201] In less than ten years, this "great environmental legislator"[202] succeeded in establishing a comprehensive legal framework, that was not anymore limited to water and air pollution but encompassed nearly every aspect of environmental protection and natural resource conservation.

This brief sketch of legislative achievements does not even begin to suggest the difficulties and challenges Muskie and his associates faced during those two decades. One challenge in particular had proven to be especially grueling—namely, the problematic nature of American federalism and the need to work within the constraints provided by the constitutional design for law-making.[203]

3.2 *The Commerce Clause and the Limits to Federal Environmental Law-Making*

The power of the US Congress over interstate commerce is as old as the Constitution itself. It was actually a major motivation for replacing the Articles of the Confederation in the first place.[204] As recalled by James Madison, "it should never be forgotten, that the great object of the Convention was to provide, by a new Constitution, a remedy for the defects of the existing one [and] that among these defects was that of a power to regulate foreign commerce."[205] Indeed, the poor conditions of American commerce and the proliferating trade rivalries among the states were the immediate provocations for the calling of the Constitutional Convention.[206] In response to those concerns,

---

Drinking Water Act, 42 U.S.C. § 300 et seq. (1974); Forest Rangeland Renewable Resources Planning Act, 16 U.S.C. § 1600 et seq. (1974); Toxic Substances Control Act, 15 U.S.C. § 2601–2629 (1976); Resource Conservation and Recovery Act, 42 U.S.C. § 6901 et seq. (1976); Federal Land Policy and Management Act, 43 U.S.C. § 1701 et seq. (1976); Surface Mining Control and Reclamation Act, 30 U.S.C. § 1201 et seq. (1977); Outer Continental Shelf Lands Act, 43 U.S.C. § 1331 et seq. (1978).

201 Blomquist, 'What is Past is Prologue' (n 194) 89.

202 See 'Tribute by Senator Ernest F. Hollings of South Carolina', in United States Senate, *Edmund S. Muskie: Late a Senator from Maine—Memorial Tributes*, S. Doc. No. 104-17 (1996), 3.

203 Lazarus, *The Making of Environmental Law* (n 186) 29.

204 Kathleen M. Sullivan and Noah Feldman, *Constitutional Law* (Foundation Press, 2013), p. 109.

205 Papers of James Madison, 10:29. Indeed, Article 9 of the Articles of Confederation explicitly stated that "no treaty of commerce shall be made whereby the legislative power of the respective States shall be restrained from imposing such imposts and duties on foreigners, as their own people are subjected to, or from prohibiting the exportation or importation of any species of goods or commodities whatsoever," thereby ruling out the possibility to adopt any national trade policy. See Irwin, *Clashing Over Commerce* (n 6) 52.

206 Sullivan and Feldman, *Constitutional Law* (n 204) 109.

the Constitution, Art, 1, §8, cl. 3, granted Congress the power "[t]o Regulate Commerce with foreign Nations, and among the Several States, and with the Indian Tribes."[207] As Alexander Hamilton wrote in *Federalist No. 22*, a central purpose of that grant was to suppress the "interfering and unneighborly regulations of some States"—regulations which, "if not restrained by a national control," would prove to be ever more "serious sources of animosity and discord."[208] It was hoped that the national commerce power "would help end hostile state restrictions, retaliatory trade regulations, and protective tariffs on imports from other states."[209]

It was precisely this power that allowed Cordell Hull to promote the Reciprocal Trade Agreement Act and that served as a constitutional basis for all the treaties of commerce entered into by the United States over the years. This very same power legitimized the presence of the American delegation at Havana in 1947 and during the previous years in the many commercial talks that the US government conducted with Britain.

On the other hand, the Constitution lacked any clear textual foundation for federal environmental protection law: while the power "to regulate commerce among the states" appears among the enumerated powers of the federal government, no reference was ever made to the environment. Furthermore, none of the other enumerated sources provided a ready fit with environmental concerns.[210] The lack of constitutional foundation is generally explained with the mismatch between the values and premises of a legal regime for environmental protection on the one hand, and the "basic cultural norms of liberty, prosperity, and freedom from governmental restraint upon which the United States was founded and that are embedded in the US Constitution and Bill of Rights."[211]

---

207 U.S. Const., art. 1, § 8, cl. 3.

208 The Federalist No. 22 (Alexander Hamilton).

209 Sullivan and Feldman, *Constitutional Law* (n 204) 109.

210 Lazarus, *The Making of Environmental Law* (n 186) 30.

211 Ibid., p. 28. See Bruce Yandle, 'Escaping Environmental Feudalism' (1992) 15 *Harvard Journal of Law & Public Policy* 517; Roger Pilon, 'Property Rights, Takings, and a Free Society' (1983) 6 *Harvard Journal of Law & Public Policy* 165. The Clean Water Act, for example, while affording wetlands previously unavailable protection, was often attacked as authorizing takings of private property without just compensation. See e.g. Flint B. Ogle, 'The Ongoing Struggle Between Private Property Rights and Wetlands Regulation: Recent Developments and Proposed Solutions' (1993) 64 *University of Colorado Law Review* 573.

Yet, because environmental problems often affect more than one state,[212] limiting regulation to the state level was not always enough. A possible solution to this problem was sought in an expansive interpretation of the Commerce Clause, based on the "theory that activities adversely affecting the environment have *substantial effects* on interstate commerce."[213] The so-called 'substantial economic effects' test[214] and the 'stream of commerce' test[215] had been used since the early years of the twentieth century to expand the scope of application of the clause to legitimize national regulatory authority on a "wide range of problems, not commonly regarded as commercial in *character*, which vitally affect the national safety and welfare," including environmental protection.[216] In a 1981 case, the Supreme Court found that the *Surface Mining Control and Reclamation Act* of 1977 did not violate the Commerce Clause because surface coal mining had substantial effects on interstate commerce: "the commerce power extends not only to 'the use of channels of interstate or foreign commerce' and to 'protection of the instrumentalities of interstate commerce ... or persons or things in commerce,' but also to 'activities affecting commerce'."[217] Similarly, the assertion of federal jurisdiction over wetlands under the *Clean Water Act* was based on the sweeping powers of Congress under the Commerce Clause. The Act recognizes federal jurisdiction only over 'navigable waters' and, traditionally, the test of navigability had been whether "a stream or body of water in its natural state [was] susceptible to use as a highway of commerce."[218] On the basis of the 'substantial economic effects' test, the United States Army Corps of Engineers—responsible for the protection of American wetlands—have progressively expanded the definition of 'navigable waters' to include not only those waters that are susceptible for use in interstate commerce, but "[a]ll

212 "... community or state jurisdictions bear little or no relationship to the geographic spread of air pollution." Edmund S. Muskie, 'Role of the Federal Government in Air Pollution Control' (1968) 10 *Arizona Law Review* 17, 18.

213 Lazarus, *The Making of Environmental Law* (n 186) 37 (emphasis added).

214 See *Houston E. & W. T. Ry. Co. v. United States* [The Shreveport Rate Case], 234 U.S. 342 (1914).

215 See *Swift & Co. v. United States*, 196 U.S. 375 (1905).

216 Cushman, 'The National Police Power under the Commerce Clause of the Constitution' (1919) 3 *Minnesota Law Review* 289, 319. In particular, Congress had used this approach to deal with problems of morality and criminality. See *Champion v. Ames* [The Lottery Case], 188 U.S. 321 (1903); *Hipolite Egg Co. v. United States*, 220 U.S. 45 (1911); and *Hoke v. United States*, 227 U.S. 308 (1913).

217 *Hodel v. Virginia Surface Mining Ass'n*, 452 U.S. 264 (1981), quoting *Perez v. United States*.

218 Ogle, 'The Ongoing Struggle' (n 211) 575.

other waters … the use, degradation or destruction of which *could affect* interstate or foreign commerce," which include wetlands.[219]

If, on the one hand, the Commerce Clause has proven essential in legitimizing Congress' environmental law-making power, on the other, this approach makes congressional control dependent on a commercial nexus and, although commerce can be relevant to environmental protection, it is not ultimately this area of law's central concern. Moreover, the Court has not been consistent in its attitude towards congressional action under the commerce power[220] and has struck down a number of laws precisely on Commerce Clause grounds.[221] The result has been that, although federal regulation of the environment is generally preferred, it can only be exercised within the strict and uncertain boundaries set by the Commerce Clause. Moreover, the Commerce Clause set yet another limit to environmental regulation, this time at the state level: as Chapter 3 will explain, the US Supreme Court has interpreted the Commerce Clause's conferral of authority to Congress over interstate commerce to create, by negative implication, a limit on state laws that unduly burden interstate commerce, by, for example, protecting the environment (see later the *Dormant* Commerce Clause).

219 The Corps began expanding the definition of 'navigable waters' after conservation groups brought a suit against them challenging their use of traditional tests of navigability (*Natural Resources Defense Council Inc. v. Callaway*). On July 25, 1975, the Corps published interim regulations to expand the definition of 'navigable waters' and then published an expanded definition in 1977.

220 For example, in the early decades of the XX century, the Court frequently struck down national regulatory laws as exceeding the proper scope of the commerce power (See *Railroad Retirement Board v. Alton Railroad Co.*, 295 U.S. 330 (1935); *Schechter Poultry Corp. v. United States*, 295 U.S. 495 (1935); and *Carter v. Carter Coal Co.*, 298 U.S. 238 (1936)). Beginning in 1937, the Court started showing great deference to congressional action under the commerce power and for nearly six decades no law was struck down on Commerce Clause grounds. See Sullivan and Feldman, *Constitutional Law* (n 204) 131. In *NLRB v. Jones & Laughlin Steel Corp*, 301 U.S. 1 (1937), Chief Justice HUGHES stated that "[the] Congressional authority to protect interstate commerce from burdens and obstructions is not limited to transactions which can be deemed to be an essential part of a 'flow' of interstate or foreign commerce [but also] if they have such a close and substantial relation to interstate commerce that their control is essential or appropriate to protect that commerce from burdens and obstructions, Congress cannot be denied the power to exercise that control." See also *United States v. Darby*, 312 U.S. 100 (1941); *Wickard v. Filburn*, 317 U.S. 111 (1942); *Heart of Atlanta Motel, Inc. v. United States*, 379 U.S. 241 (1964); *Katzenbach v. McClung*, 379 U.S. 294 (1964); *Perez v. United States*, 402 U.S. 146 (1971).

221 In *Solid Waste Agency of Northern Cook County v. Army Corps. of Eng'rs*, 531 U.S. 159 (2001), the Court preferred to avoid the challenge and narrowly construed the jurisdictional scope of the Clean water Act to avoid constitutional issues regarding the applicability of the Commerce Clause.

3.3 *The Economic Purpose of Early European Environmental Efforts*

This account of US federal environmental law-making as dependent on Congress' power to regulate interstate commerce may remind the reader of another similar story, that was unfolding on the other side of the Atlantic. On May 9, 1950, then French Foreign Minister Robert Schuman delivered a famous Declaration marking the creation of the European Community of Steel and Coal—the first step towards European integration. The reasons that pushed six European countries to gather in Paris and create the Community were the same underlying the Constitutional Convention in Philadelphia in May 1787 and the post-war Anglo-American talks in 1943–1948: removing unnatural obstructions to trade with a view to preserving and strengthening peace and stability. In fact, in the 1950 Declaration, Robert Schuman proclaimed that "by pooling basic production and by instituting a new high authority, whose decisions will bind France, Germany and other member countries, this proposal will lead to the realization of the first concrete foundation of a European federation indispensable to the preservation of peace."[222]

This first step was followed a few years later by the creation of the European Economic Community. The Treaty of Rome, which entered into force in 1958, provided for the creation of a single common market in Europe, based on a customs union, the prohibition of restrictions to the free movement of goods, workers, services and capital among the Member States, a competition policy and a common commercial policy, as well as common policies on agriculture and transport.[223] In less than ten years, Italy, Germany, France, Belgium, Holland, and Luxembourg had succeeded in creating a single, unrestricted Western European market in nearly all goods. And for nearly 20 years that was all that mattered.

Just like the US Constitution, the Treaty of Rome did not contain any reference to the environment, and the framers showed no intention to give the Community powers in this area.[224] It was only after Stockholm that the heads of State of the EEC Member States convened a Summit where they declared that "economic expansion was not an end in itself" and 'non-material' values,

222 'Documents relatifs au projet français de mise en commun des productions de charbon et d'acier et à l'institution d'une Haute Autorité', La documentation française. Notes et études documentaires, No. 1339 (June 13, 1950).

223 Damian Chalmers et al., *European Union Law* (Cambridge University Press, 2010), p. 12.

224 Maria Lee, *EU Environmental Law: Challenges, Change and Decision-making* (Hart, 2005), p. 1; Wolfgang E. Burhenne and Thomas J. Shoenbaum, 'The European Community and Management of the Environment: A Dilemma' (1973) 13 *Natural Resources Journal* 494, 496.

such as environmental protection, were crucial for the achievement of the objectives of the Community. As a result of the Summit, the following year, the First Program of Action of the European Communities on the Environment was adopted.[225]

However, as the EEC could only act within the limits of the powers conferred upon it by the Treaties and towards its specific objectives,[226] the adoption of environmental legislation could only be based on an expansive interpretation of the provisions of the Rome Treaty—which contained no reference to the environment—and was therefore constrained by the need to ensure and promote the functioning of the common market.[227] Three provisions were initially used as a basis for environmental legislation: Article 2, which sets out the objectives of the Community, Article 100, which deals with 'approximation' or 'harmonization' of laws, and Article 235.

Article 235, in particular, provides law-making power where action by the Community appears necessary to achieve one of the treaty objectives, and the treaty itself has not provided for the necessary powers of action.[228] However, environmental protection was not included among the objectives in the Rome Treaty:

> The Community shall have as its task, by establishing a common market and progressively approximating the economic policies of Member States, to promote throughout the Community a harmonious development of economic activities, a continuous and balanced expansion, an

---

225 Declaration of the Council of the European Communities and of the representatives of the Governments of the member States meeting in the Council of 22 November 1973 on the programme of action for the European Communities on the environment [1973] O.J. C112/1. See Elisa Morgera, 'European Environmental Law', in Alam et al (eds.), *Routledge Handbook of International Environmental Law* (Routledge, 2012).

226 Principle of conferral or of attributed properties, as set out in Article 5.2 of the EEC Treaty: "Under the principle of conferral, the Union shall act only within the limits of the competences conferred upon it by the Member States in the Treaties to attain the objectives set out therein. Competences not conferred upon the Union in the Treaties remain with the Member States." Treaty Establishing the European Economic Community, Art. 5.2 March 25, 1957, 298 U.N.T.S. 11. [hereinafter EEC Treaty].

227 Morgera, 'European Environmental Law' (n 225).

228 EEC Treaty, article 235 reads: "If action by the Community should prove necessary to attain, in the course of the operation of the common market, one of the objectives of the Community and this Treaty has not provided the necessary powers, the Council shall, acting unanimously on a proposal from the Commission and after consulting the European Parliament, take the appropriate measures." See Burhenne and Shoenbaum, 'The European Community' (n 224) 498.

> increase in stability, an accelerated raising of the standard of living and closer relations between the States belonging to it.[229]

Although some have tried to read into the objective of "an accelerated raising of the standard of living" an implicit reference to the protection of the environment, Community action aimed at the latter would be admissible only to the extent that it contributed to achieving non-environmental goals. Article 100, on the other hand, was often used to justify directives which, although cloaked in environmental terms, were actually part of a program to harmonize national laws to remove distortions of competition, being adopted pursuant to the so-called 'General Program for the elimination of technical barriers to trade within the Community'.[230]

It was only with the adoption of the Single European Act in 1986 that the environment was featured among the Community's objectives, and environmental action at the Community level gained a clear and unequivocal legal basis in the text of the treaty. Until then, the Rome Treaty contained no reference to the environment as an objective of the Community and, in this regard, it was not a rare bird. No commercial treaties or trade agreements negotiated and signed before Stockholm—and for a few years after Stockholm as well—showed any sign of the environment. And neither did the GATT.

3.4 *The Environment Overlooked at Havana*

On January 1, 1948, when the GATT entered into force, international cooperation on trade matters had finally been made official. Twenty-three countries had succeeded in agreeing on a small but powerful set of rules embodied by the agreement: open markets, non-discrimination, institutional stability, transparency, and the use of tariffs, to be gradually reduced, as the sole instrument of protection.[231]

The need to cooperate on trade matters, however, was not the only issue concerning the delegations gathered at Havana. The United States, despite its role as leader, agreed to accommodate demands coming from both the United Kingdom and developing countries. Throughout the long Anglo-American post-war talks, the British had always been very vocal about the difficulties that would face the country after the end of the war.[232] As a result, a temporary

---

229 EEC Treaty, Art. 2.

230 Council Resolution of May 28, 1969, 12 O.J. C 76/1 (1969). See Burhenne and Shoenbaum, 'The European Community' (n 224) 499.

231 Culbert, 'War-time Anglo-American Talks' (n 55) 381–2.

232 In his *Proposal*, Meade advocated the need "to retain the right to impose more general restrictions on purchases of inessential goods or on unnecessary payments abroad so

exception for balance-of-payment difficulties and related to the liquidation of government surpluses was introduced in the text of the Agreement.[233] At the same time, a number of less-developed countries, such as Australia, India, China, Brazil, and Chile, wanted to ensure that any agreement reached during the GATT negotiations would not prevent them from using trade restrictions to promote employment and development goals. In London, they presented proposals for the introduction of a "developing country exception" that would allow them to use quantitative restrictions to foster industrialization,[234] and provisions to this end were introduced in the final text.[235]

The protection of the environment, on the other hand, was not a concern for any of the delegations involved in the drafting of the GATT. It was never discussed during the negotiations, and the word itself was not included in the final draft of the Agreement. Even one of the provisions of the Agreement that are today considered 'environmental'—Article XX(b)—was not originally drafted with the environment in mind (*see* Chapter 3). The provision, which in its original formulation covered restrictions "for the protection of public health or for the protection of animals or plants against disease, insects and harmful parasites," had been part of bilateral treaties of commerce since their inception, together with those covering measures adopted for national defense or to organize the parties' internal trade.[236] The 1904 Treaty of Commerce between Italy and Switzerland, for instance, allowed the parties to introduce export, import, or transit prohibitions in the following circumstances:

> i) Dans des circonstances exceptionnelles, par rapport aux provisions de guerre ; ii) Pour les raisons de sûreté publique; iii) Par égard à la police sanitaire et en vue de la protection des animaux, ainsi que des plantes utiles contre les maladies, les insectes et parasites nuisibles ; and iv) Par égard aux monopoles d'État.[237]

long as we are faced with an acute problem of restoring equilibrium to our international balance of payments." Meade, *Proposal* (n 86) para. 5. See Culbert, 'War-time Anglo-American Talks' (n 55) 384; Irwin, Mavroidis, and Sykes, *The Genesis of the GATT* (n 1) 32.

233 Chapter III, Section C.2 of the *Proposals* reads: "Members confronted with an adverse balance of payments should be entitled to impose quantitative import restrictions as an aid to the restoration of equilibrium in the balance of payments."

234 Irwin, Mavroidis, and Sykes, *Genesis of the GATT* (n 1) 79.

235 See GATT, Article XVIII.

236 Nolde, 'Droit et technique' (n 87) 384.

237 Treaty of Commerce between Italy and Switzerland, 1904. Ibid., 378.

It had become such an inherent component of trade treaties that Clair Wilcox defined what later became Article XX of the GATT as "routine exceptions copied from previous commercial treaties and trade agreements,"[238] and even as "almost boilerplate."[239] The purpose of such "routine" exception clause was to build safety valves into the system and allow the Parties to pursue certain legitimate domestic policy goals, perfectly in line with the embedded liberalism's vision of the market as 'embedded' in a broader social fabric and of multilateralism as predicated upon domestic interventionism.

Despite the importance of this exception clause, which was regarded as fundamental to strike a balance between the demands of the international economy and those of domestic social groups, it had nothing to do with the environment, at least not in its original formulation. Even the Draft ITO Charter, which was intended to cover many more topics in addition to trade in goods—such as labor, investment, and competition—was never intended to address environmental protection. It was only after Stockholm, and after the first disputes with an environmental dimension were brought to the GATT adjudicative body, that the exception was given an environmental touch. And even then, as the next chapter will show, it is debatable whether it could provide countries with any real space to protect the environment. In fact, when the environment started being introduced in these exception clauses, embedded liberalism, which recognized their importance and value, had given way to the neoliberal thought which quickly became the prevailing ideology in international trade.

3.5 *UNEP and the Organizational Challenge*

The challenge of being a late-comer was not limited to having to shape new environmental norms within the constraints of the existing legal framework, whether at the domestic, regional, or international level. Issues also arose with regard to the choice of the institutional structure to be developed to deal with the 'environment issue'.

Towards the end of May 1971, 40 key decision-makers from governments, international agencies, and the scientific community met for three days in Rensselaerville, New York, under the auspices of the former US Judge on the International Court of Justice, Phillip C. Jessup. This meeting had been organized by the Institute on Man and Science and the Aspen Institute of

238 Wilcox, *A Charter for World Trade* (n 54) 179.

239 International Trade Organization, *Hearings Before the Committee on Finance*, Part I, U.S. Senate, 80th Congress, 1st Session, at 412, as quoted in Steve Charnovitz, 'Exploring the Environmental Exceptions in GATT Article XX' (1991) 25 *Journal of World Trade* 44.

Humanistic Studies at the former's idyllic headquarters.[240] For those three days, all the discussions revolved around a fundamental question which, curiously enough, nobody had really given much thought to until then. The question was—what kind of international organizational arrangements will be needed after Stockholm? And it was indeed a crucial and pressing one.

When the 'environment issue' emerged in the late 1960s, international organizations already played a vital role in the political structure of international relations and constituted a fundamental vehicle for international cooperation. During the quarter-century since the end of World War II, despite the persistence of vigorous nationalism, the number of intergovernmental organizations had more than doubled and the United Nations had clearly established itself as the principal focal point in this network.[241] Despite some opposition,[242] there was hardly any doubt that the UN was the best forum to deal with the newly emerged 'environment issue', and this feeling was shared by the 40 decision-makers gathered in Rensselaerville.

The real question was how to square this new issue within the existing UN machinery. After 25 years since the creation of the UN and many of its specialized agencies, any proposal had to necessarily come to terms with the existence of quite a large number of international organizations, some of which had already been working for many years on separate aspects of subjects now subsumed under the environmental label. The World Meteorological Organization (WMO), for instance, had been dealing with atmospheric pollution, the World Health Organization (WHO) with environmental health, and the Food and Agricultural Organization (FAO) with the conservation of soil, forest, and animal resources.[243] To further complicate things, unlike most subjects dealt by the UN, the environment was not just another separate sectoral issue, but rather a system of interacting relationships that extends through all

240 Institute on Man and Science, *International Organization and the Human Environment: Proceedings of an International Conference*, Rensselaerville, N.Y., May 1971.

241 Maurice F. Strong, Lecture delivered at Carlton University, Ottawa: Development, Environment and the New Global Imperative—The New Technological Order (1970–1) (on file with the Environmental Science and Public Policy Archives at Harvard University, Maurice F. Strong Papers, Box 29[292]).

242 See e.g. the view advanced by George Kennan that the United Nations was not the proper forum for dealing with environmental problems while a better solution would be the creation of an environmental agency run by developed countries, given that these problems were mainly caused by ten of the world's most industrialized countries. George F. Kennan, 'To Prevent a World Wasteland: A Proposal', 48(3) *Foreign Affairs*, Apr. 1970, 401–413.

243 Richard N. Gardner, 'The Role of the UN in Environmental Problems' (1972) 26(2) *International Organization* 237, 245.

sectors of activity.[244] As a result, the view was largely shared that, in order to avoid wasteful duplications, it would have been more efficient to rely on the already existing machinery than to create a whole new specialized agency or operating body: all functions which could best be performed by existing organizations should be assigned to those organizations. To be able to give the necessary weight to the environmental context as a whole, what was necessary was the creation, next to the existing machinery, of a body or a system able to coordinate the environmental activities of the different UN agencies.

After those three days of intense discussions, an international workshop was organized in Aspen during the following summer, which produced a set of general institutional recommendations.[245] On this basis, a secretariat paper was completed at the end of the year and sent to Governments, before being considered at the final meeting of the Preparatory Committee in March 1972.[246] The result was the creation of UNEP, which would influence the activities of other organizations, promote international cooperation on environmental matters, provide general policy guidance, and constantly keep under review the world environmental situation.[247]

The same approach was adopted when discussing whether to establish an international environmental court.[248] Once again, in the end, efficiency prevailed: to avoid wasteful duplications, it was deemed sufficient to be able to bring environmental disputes to any of the already existing courts, depending on the parties and the subject matter involved. None of these fora, however, had a truly environmental mandate or expertise and, when the chips were down, while they would take environmental factors into account, there could on occasion be a real conflict between their primary responsibilities and their consideration of the environment.

3.6 *The Environment as an 'Add-On': The Origin of the Nexus*

The chronological unfolding of the events that led to the creation of the trade and environmental regimes contributed greatly to the way in which their

244 The UN organizations have been created on the traditional sectoral pattern which had been developed, and still prevails, in most national governments. United Conference on the Human Environment, The UN System and the Human Environment, A/CONF.48/12 (Dec. 17, 1971).

245 International Institute for Environmental Affairs, 'The Human Environment: Science and International Decision-Making' (1971).

246 Gardner, 'The Role of the UN' (n 243) 243.

247 UNEP was created with G.A. Res. 2997 (XXVII) of December 15, 1972. See Article II.2 for the list of tasks and responsibilities of the Governing Council of UNEP.

248 Jessup, 'Do New Problems Need New Courts?' (n 170).

relationship was perceived. The norms and institutions of international trade are rooted in a legal order established decades before environmental protection began to be considered and valued at the global level. When James Meade traveled to Washington to discuss future trade cooperation with Harry Hawkins and all the other members of the State Department, no one even thought of discussing the environment. Their mandate was itself limited to trade and economic objectives.[249] Similarly, the drafters of the GATT could not have envisioned the types of environmental problems that would be addressed 25 years later in Stockholm, or the role that trade measures would have played in that context. Their one and only goal, instead, was to address international economic problems and, most important of all, to avoid protectionist revivals by diminishing trade barriers and encouraging the expansion of commerce.[250]

As a matter of fact, the international legal framework established in the 1940s by the actors described in the first part of this chapter had been designed to guarantee peace and economic cooperation. The environment came later and was 'added' to this framework, thanks to the work and vision of equally brilliant individuals.

The world of international law and relations that had developed during the twentieth century soon appeared to work on a 'first come, first served' basis: economic matters ruled the roost and the environment could be regulated *only* to the extent permitted by economic considerations and *only* as long as it did not produce any detrimental effects on inter-state trade flows. The result was that the need to protect commerce from undue burdens overrode any environmental protection concerns: *la libertè du commerce* had become the overarching rule, and environmental protection merely the exception.

---

249 See i.e. the list of "overall and principal trade negotiating objectives of the United States", 19 U.S.C. § 2901(b), 2397 note.

250 GATT, *GATT Activities in 1960–61* (Geneva, June 1962).

CHAPTER 3

The *Exception-Based* Model

The timing of the emergence of the 'environment issue', vis-à-vis international cooperation on economic matters, contributed greatly to shaping the relationship between the international environmental and trade regimes. However, the chronological unfolding of these events does not, in itself, explain the environment being forced in a corner of the international trade regime and being treated merely as an 'exception'. It is not simply a matter of *when* these regimes emerged, but also of *how* they were perceived by their respective founders. By the time environmental protection emerged as an international concern in the 1970s, trade policy had become the province of a technocracy, a *trade policy elite*, embodied by the Secretariat of the General Agreement on Tariffs and Trade (GATT)—although including a much larger community of trade experts—which was insulated from all other areas of international cooperation.[1] After the GATT founders, moved largely by political interests, had made sure that the Agreement would contain exception clauses—such as Article XX—to provide countries with the necessary space to pursue domestic policy goals, the *trade policy elite* recast 'embedded liberalism' as 'economics', and "economics became ideology, the ideology of free trade."[2] From this perspective, government intervention, even when it pursued legitimate policy goals, was regarded with suspicion as potential protectionism in disguise.

Soon, the trading system came to be seen as being "for free trade and free markets, and against governmental interference,"[3] as opposed to environmental protection, which could not be realized through trade liberalization and market mechanisms alone but required governmental intervention instead. As a result, the relationship between trade and the environment started being framed in terms of *conflicts*.

As the international trade system was considerably more mature than any part of international environmental law, and had continued to develop largely divorced from environmental considerations, it should be no surprise that, as soon as the first conflicts between economic and environmental

1 Robert Howse, 'From Politics to Technocracy—And Back Again: The Fate of the Multilateral Trading Regime' (2002) 96 *American Journal of International Law* 94, 98.

2 Ibid., 99.

3 Andrew Lang, *World Trade Law After Neoliberalism. Re-Imagining the Global Economic Order* (Oxford University Press, 2013), p. 4.

values emerged, the approach adopted to address them was strongly trade-centered: trade rules became the frame of reference and environmental measures the 'object' to be evaluated, rather than the other way around.

1 The Environment Cornered in Exception Clauses

> It is not surprising that the environment/trade debate is focused on how environmental issues can be squared with the one internationally accepted legal framework that does exist—the GATT.[4]
>
> EDITH BROWN WEISS, 1992

During the first years of coexistence of the two regimes, the interface between their respective goals—economic growth and environmental protection—was framed in terms of *conflict*. When these conflicts first emerged, trade norms and institutions had already been in place for several decades and had developed into a full-fledged legal regime. On the contrary, environmental norms and institutions were still highly fragmented, lacking a focal point comparable to the GATT, or a dedicated dispute settlement mechanism similar to the one available under first the GATT, and then under the World Trade Organization (WTO).

It should be no surprise then, borrowing Edith Brown-Weiss' words, that when the tensions between trade and environmental objectives suddenly emerged at the dawn of the 1990s, they were framed from a trade law—rather than an environmental law—perspective. How could one "simply dismiss the obligations of the GATT where they conflict with environmental values [when] over 100 countries are party to the GATT and ... it is one of the most highly-developed international regimes"?[5] Indeed, it seems that one simply could not.

Soon, trade rules became the framework of reference and environmental measure the 'object' to be evaluated, rather than the other way around.[6] Just

---

4 Edith Brown Weiss, 'Environment and Trade as Partners in Sustainable Development: A Commentary' (1992) 86 *American Journal of International Law* 728, 729.

5 Ted L. McDorman, 'The 1991 U.S.—Mexico GATT Panel Report on Tuna and Dolphin: Implications for Trade and Environment Conflicts' (1992) 17 *North Carolina Journal of International Law & Commercial Regulation* 461, 479.

6 More often than not, the conflict occurs between an international trade norm (i.e. of the GATT or a free trade agreement) and a domestic environmental law or policy (legitimacy conflict). It is rare that the conflict materializes between two international norms (a trade and an environmental norm, which would constitute a normative conflict). Most environmental treaties do not require state-parties to adopt measures that are inconsistent with the GATT, but rather they usually set out a goal or a target, leaving the parties free to decide the measures to adopt to fulfill it. The fact that most trade/environment conflicts are legitimacy

like by wearing glasses with red lenses everything around us suddenly becomes red—the pale colors become pink and the dark colors crimson—using trade law as the framework or 'lens' through which environmental measures are evaluated leads to a somehow distorted vision of such measures, which end up being translated in economic jargon and assessed for their economic importance and impact on trade flows, rather than for their inherent environmental or social values: lax environmental laws were immediately labelled as implicit subsidies, and measures that restricted trade in highly polluting—or otherwise environmentally harmful—products were simply referred to as non-tariff barriers.[7] Indeed, while each and every form of governmental action has an impact on trade, identifying certain actions as 'barriers to trade' requires a certain shared understanding of what constitutes an acceptable form of government intervention and what does not.[8] This 'shared understanding', just like the language that prevailed to describe environmental measures and the parameters used to assess their trade restrictiveness, were those spoken and developed by the trade community, and largely reflected the neoliberal economic thought which provided their shared narrative.

And it was precisely this 'shared understanding' that ensured, once the first questions on the relationship between trade and the environment arose, that the latter would be 'cornered' in exception clauses. In fact, as this chapter will show, these clauses had not been drafted with the environment in mind, and if they soon became the only place where environmentalists could find refuge, it was because of the debate being approached from a free-trade perspective and neoliberalism being the dominant shared narrative.

1.1 *The Environment Seen through Free Trade Glasses*

In his preparation for the Stockholm Conference, Maurice Strong had asked the GATT Secretariat to prepare a document on the link between trade and the environment. The outcome was a study entitled *Industrial Pollution Control and*

conflicts can explain, at least in part, why they are addressed using trade law as the framework of reference.

7 Jeffrey L. Dunoff, 'Rethinking International Trade' (1998) 19(2) *University of Pennsylvania Journal of International Economic Law* 347, 355.

8 See John W. Evans, *The Kennedy Round in American Trade Policy: The Twilight of the GATT?* (Harvard University Press, 1971); Daniel K. Tarullo, 'Logic, Myth and the International Economic Order' (1985) 26 *Harvard International Law Journal* 553, and 'Beyond Normalcy in the Regulation of International Trade' (1987) 100 *Harvard Law Review* 546; Judith Goldstein, *Ideas, Interests, and American Trade Policy* (Cornell University Press, 1993); Howse, 'From Politics to Technocracy' (n 1) 94; and Lang, *World Trade Law After Neoliberalism* (n 3) 170.

International Trade,[9] which marked the first step taken by the trade community in the unexplored territory of environmental protection. In this endeavor, the Secretariat surveyed a number of issues that national anti-pollution measures might raise for international trade law, having specific regard to the provisions and objectives of the GATT. The approach adopted in the report was based on a very simple question: *how could environmental issues be accommodated within the existing body of international trade law without disrupting it*?

Since then, the early explorations of the trade/environment nexus clearly reflected this main analytical perspective: a perspective adopted for many years by trade theorists, and often referred to as "single-minded free trade perspective" or "pro-trade bias."[10] And the trade community, imbued with neoliberal economic thinking, argued that the environment could be accommodated within the basic paradigm of free trade, which represented the parameter to evaluate the legitimacy of environmental measures. In other words, it "was the trade community viewing environmental measures, rather than the environmental community viewing the trade system."[11] As a result, scholars have long approached the trade/environment nexus by identifying and analyzing environmental issues that have raised questions of consistency with the GATT, and then applying GATT rules to such issues.[12] The GATT itself has contributed to

9 GATT, *Industrial Pollution Control and International Trade, Note by the GATT Secretariat*, L/ 3538, June 9, 1971.

10 J. Owen Saunders, 'Trade and Environment: The Fine Line Between Environmental Protection and Environmental Protectionism' (1992) 47(4) *International Journal* 723, 726. Robert Howse and Makau Mutua, 'Protecting Human Rights in a Global Economy: Challenges for the World Trade Organization' (2002) International Center for Human Rights and Democratic Development, Policy Paper. Sungjoon Cho, 'Linkage of Free Trade and Social Regulation: Moving Beyond the Entropic Dilemma' (2005) 5 *Chicago Journal of International Law* 626, 640. This approach has also been criticized for leading to a kind of 'myopic view' of the trading system. See Philip Nichols, 'Trade Without Values' (1996) 90 *Northwestern University Law Review* 658, 701.

11 Charles S. Pearson, 'The Trade and Environment Nexus: What is New Since '72?' in Durwood Zaelke et al. (eds.), *Trade and the Environment. Law, Economics, and Policy* (Island Press, 1993) pp. 23–4.

12 See e.g. Frederic L. Jr. Kirgis, 'Effective Pollution Control in Industrialized Countries: International Economic Disincentives, Policy Responses, and the GATT' (1972) 70 *Michigan Law Review* 859; James Cameron and Jonathan Robinson, 'The Use of Trade Provisions in International Environmental Agreements and their Compatibility with the GATT' (1991) *Yearbook of International Environmental Law* 3; Thomas J. Shoenbaum, 'Free International Trade and Protection of the Environment: Irreconcilable Conflict?' (1992) 86 *American Journal of International Law* 700; Robert Housman and Durwood Zaelke, 'Trade, Environment, and Sustainable Development: A Primer' (1992) 15 *Hastings International & Comparative Law Review* 535; McDorman, 'The 1991 U.S.—Mexico GATT Panel Report' (n 5); Thomas E. Skilton, 'GATT and the Environment in Conflict: The Tuna-Dolphin Dispute

the debate, starting from the assumption that environmental laws and regulations are subject to the trade regime's control,[13] as perfectly illustrated by the 1992 *Trade and Environment* Report: "… *under* GATT *rules*, governments can employ many different measures to protect and improve the local environment … There is also *nothing in the* GATT *that prevents* contracting parties from taxing or regulating domestic producers who engage in polluting activities."[14]

Similarly, the EMIT group, established in 1972, despite the quite broad title 'Group on Environmental Measures and International Trade', had been conceived with the very same mindset. The EMIT group was created with the specific purpose of trying to "ensure that the efforts of governments to combat pollution did not result in the introduction of new barriers to trade or impede the removal of existing barriers."[15] Once again, the ultimate goal remained economic in nature.[16]

The very fact that the relationship between trade and environmental objectives has been framed as "trade and …" already presupposes a certain perspective on the issue: constructing certain values as 'trade values' and others as 'non-trade values' at some level favors the former over the latter when it comes to defining their relationship.[17] And representatives of the environmental community have themselves been framing the relationship in these terms. The Stockholm Conference, in the part of its Action Plan that dealt with the relationship between trade and the environment, adopted principles similar to those suggested in the 1971 GATT study. Recommendation 104, for instance, entrusted the United Nations (UN) with the task to identify "the major threats

---

and the Quest for an International Conservation Strategy' (1993) 26 *Cornell International Law Journal* 455; Steve Charnovitz, 'A Taxonomy of Environmental Trade Measures' (1993) 6(1) *Georgetown International Law Review* 1; John H. Jackson, 'World Trade Rules and Environmental Policies: Congruence or Conflict?' (1992) 49 *Washington and Lee Law Review* 1227; Ernst-Ulrich Petersmann, 'International Trade Law and International Environmental Law. Prevention and Settlement of International Environmental Disputes in GATT' (1993) *Journal of World Trade* 43.

13 Patti Goldman, 'Resolving the Trade and Environment Debate: In Search of a Neutral Forum and Neutral Principles' (1992) 49 *Washington & Lee Law Review* 1279.

14 GATT, *Trade and the Environment* (1992), 12 (emphasis added).

15 GATT, 'GATT, The Uruguay Round and the Environment' (1991) 85 *GATT Focus* 3.

16 It should not come as a surprise, then, that environmentalists feared that the Group would end up "subjugating environmental protections to trade's regimes as opposed to finding some way of reconciling the concerns of both trade and environmental interests." Housman and Zaelke, 'Trade, Environment, and Sustainable Development' (n 12) 572.

17 Dunoff, 'Rethinking International Trade' (n 7) 383.

to exports … that arise from environmental concerns."[18] Twenty years later, the text of Agenda 21 was drafted in accordance with the line adopted by the GATT Secretariat in its 1992 Report on *Trade and the Environment*, calling for the compatibility of environmental trade measures with 'international obligations'—namely the GATT—rather than requiring the compatibility of these 'international obligations' with environmental necessities.[19] And even during the negotiations of specific multilateral environmental agreements, this trade-centered approach continued to characterize the discussions. During the negotiation of the *Montreal Protocol for the Protection of the Ozone Layer*, for instance, the participants invited a legal expert from the GATT Secretariat to advise them on the compatibility of the trade restrictions envisaged in the Protocol with multilateral trade rules.[20]

Everyone was looking to the GATT to define what environmental measures should be allowed. It was the trade community who set the rules of the game and who, guided by the prevailing neoliberal narrative, defined what constituted a 'trade issue' and what did not, what constituted the 'rule' and what was an 'exception'. For its part, the environmental community, young and lacking a united front, found itself forced in a corner, incapable of effectively challenging the *elite*'s supremacy.[21] As a result, environmental measures were depicted

18 United Nations Conference on the Human Environment, An Action Plan for the Human Environment, A/CONF.48/5 (Feb. 9, 1972) [hereinafter Stockholm Action Plan], Recommendation 104(a).

19 United Nations Conference on Environment and Development, Rio de Janeiro, Brazil, June 3–14, 1992, *Agenda 21: Programme of Action for Sustainable Development*, U.N. Doc. A/CONF.151/26 (1992) [hereinafter Agenda 21], para. 2.22(c). See Charles Arden-Clarke, 'An Action Agenda for Trade Policy Reform to Support Sustainable Development: A United Nations Conference on Environment and Development Follow-Up', in Zaelke et al. (eds.), *Trade and the Environment* (n 11) 73, 4.

20 Housman and Zaelke, 'Trade, Environment, and Sustainable Development' (n 12) 580.

21 Furthermore, this same approach has characterized the way in which the GATT system has been dealing with measures designed to serve a much broader array of non-trade or non-economic values. As a matter of fact, free traders were seeing environmental regulation as just one of the many challenges faced by the world trading system, such as antitrust policy, labor, or health standards. GATT, *Trade and the Environment* (n 14). The 1971 GATT study, for instance, recognized that environmental "standards or their enforcement may well cause distortions of, or discrimination in foreign trade but the problems will not be different in kind from those created by standards used to promote health or safety in general." GATT, *Industrial Pollution Control and International Trade* (n 9) 2. See e.g. John H. Jackson, 'International Economic Problems and their Management in the 21st Century' (1979) 9 *Georgia Journal of International & Comparative Law* 497; 'Dolphins and Hormones: GATT and the Legal Environment for International Trade after the Uruguay Round' (1992) 14(3) *University of Arkansas at Little Rock Law Journal* 429, 438; 'GATT and the Future of International Trade Institutions' (1992) XVIII(1)

as a threat to the smoothness and speed of international trade flows and to the integrity of the international trade regime as a whole. A threat that had to be removed and, to the extent that total elimination was not possible, limited and kept at bay.

1.2 *Who's Afraid of Environmental Measures?—Part 1. Environmental Measures as Non-Tariff Barriers*

The main consequence of looking at environmental measures through the lenses provided by the international trade law framework has been a partial, and somehow misleading reading of such measures. Translating environmental principles and norms in economic terms means that environmental laws and regulations are only seen as non-tariff barriers, capable of disrupting the whole trading system, while the values they embody are not fully—if at all—captured.[22]

The environment made its first appearance on the stage of GATT talks precisely when the issue of non-tariff barriers (NTBs) first emerged. Tariff negotiations had been the main item of business in the first six GATT negotiation rounds, up until the Kennedy Round, which was concluded in 1967.[23] Once tariffs were reduced, other types of (non-tariff) barriers began to surface and, starting from the Tokyo Round, GATT parties have been focusing most of their efforts on addressing these newly emerged, and potentially much more dangerous, types of trade barriers.[24] They can be more dangerous because

---

Brooklyn Journal of International Law 11; 'International Economic Law: Reflections on the "Boilerroom" for International Relations' (1995) 10(2) *American University Journal of International Law & Policy* 595; 'Reflections on International Economic Law' (1996) 17(1) *University of Pennsylvania Journal of International Economic Law* 17, 25; and 'Reflections on Constitutional Changes to the Global Trading System' (1996) 72 *Chicago-Kent Law Review* 511.

22 Dunoff, 'Rethinking International Trade' (n 7) 355. According to DiMatteo et al, the situation did not change with the advent of the WTO, which seemed to still largely ignore non-trade concerns, as its "monolithic mandate of liberalising international trade generally does not allow the consideration of legal or ethical factors involving the environment, animal rights, consumer rights, labor rights, or sovereignty." Larry A. DiMatteo et al., 'The Doha Declaration and Beyond: Giving Voice to Non-Trade Concerns Within the WTO Trade Regime' (2003) 36 *Vanderbilt Journal of Transnational Law* 95, 133. See also Nichols, 'Trade Without Values' (n 10) 660.

23 As noted in the 1960 Annual Review of the Work of the GATT, the Agreement "was negotiated primarily as a tariff agreement and its trade rules are essentially designed to prevent the nullification, by other kinds of restrictive measures, of the tariff concessions negotiated between contracting parties." GATT, *The Activities of GATT 1959/60* (Geneva, 1960), 8.

24 The Tokyo Declaration specifies that "the negotiations are to cover tariffs, non-tariff barriers and other measures which impede or distort international trade in both industrial and agricultural products, including tropical products and raw materials, whether in primary

non-tariff barriers are much more diversified, changeable, and hence more difficult to grasp than tariffs.[25] Often, they are adopted for perfectly legitimate reasons, such as national security, public safety, or environmental protection. Nevertheless, they might create obstacles to trade and, to the extent that they do, they should be removed.[26]

At first, their removal was motivated by the fear that they might bring back the specter of protectionism, the very evil that the GATT drafters worked so hard to defeat and eradicate. Although free traders acknowledged that environmental measures could sometimes be adopted for legitimate purposes, they always emphasized the benefits of free trade and the "dangers of 'old-fashioned' protectionism masquerading as environmental concern."[27] Over time, however, the meaning of 'free trade', around which the GATT system had been built, began to change and, rather than referring simply to a trade free from discrimination against foreign countries, as it had been envisioned by the GATT founders, it started to gain a broader meaning, as a trade free from burdens and government intervention. The latter, according to neoliberal economic theory, should have been kept to a minimum, regardless of its more or less legitimate purpose, stemming from the belief that "naturally functioning markets are better than those structured by government intervention."[28] Liberalized trade was therefore portrayed as even conducive to the fulfilment of environmental goals, as it resulted in economic growth which, in turn, enabled governments to raise resources for a variety of purposes, including environmental protection, enabled technologies aimed at environmental protection to be imported where they had not been developed yet, and might even lead to a shift in production patterns with beneficial environmental effects.[29]

---

form or at any stage of processing." GATT, *GATT Activities in 1973* (Geneva, 1974), 18. See Gilbert R. Winham, *International Trade and the Tokyo Round Negotiations* (Princeton University Press, 1985), p. 17.

25 GATT, *GATT Activities in 1973* (n 24) 26.

26 Steven Shrybman, 'International Trade and the Environment: An Environmental Assessment of the General Agreement on Tariffs and Trade' (1990) 20(1) *The Ecologist* 30.

27 Mark Williams, 'International Trade and the Environment: Issues, Perspectives and Challenges' (1993) 2(4) *Environmental Politics* 80, 89; Shoenbaum, 'Free International Trade' (n 12) 715–6.

28 Williams, 'International Trade and the Environment' (n 27) 89.

29 This theory posits that the demand for environmental quality rises with the income, as reflected in the Environmental Kuznets Curve model. See Jagdish Bhagwati, 'The Case for Free Trade' (1993) *Scientific American*. James K.R. Watson, *The WTO and the Environment* (Routledge, 2013). Peter Newell, *Globalization and the Environment: Capitalism, Ecology and Power* (John Wiley & Sons, 2013).

The use of trade measures to address environmental problems, on the other hand, was simultaneously described as inefficient and often ineffective, as well as dangerous for international trade and unjustifiable on economic grounds.[30] And it did not take long before business interests in several countries began enlisting the aid of trade rules in the GATT or in Free Trade Agreements (FTA s) to attack environmental regulations as non-tariff barriers, blinded by the fear of the potential harm they might suffer and oblivious to the inherent environmental and societal value of such regulations.[31] The first dispute ever decided under the 1988 United States-Canada Free Trade Agreement (USCFTA), for instance, dealt with certain provisions of the *Canadian Fisheries Act*,[32] which required that all fish caught for commercial purposes in Canadian waters must be landed first in Canada for biological sampling, which was challenged by the United States (US) as violating Canada's obligations under the FTA.[33] The same agreement was then invoked on many other occasions by both governments to attack environmental and resource-conservation initiatives on both sides of the border, such as Canadian acid-rain-reduction programs or fish conservation policies, and US asbestos regulations and paper-recycling laws.[34] As a result of the pressures caused by such threats, many environmental measures were modified or removed one after the other. So, a reforestation program introduced in British Columbia was scrapped immediately after being attacked by the US timber industry as an illegitimate subsidy, and a US bill banning the importation on American soil of wild-caught birds was first delayed and ultimately watered down in Congress because of its alleged incompatibility with the GATT.[35] Similarly, the European Communities (EC) and Canada have relied on the text of the GATT, and in particular on Article III:2, to challenge a tax on petroleum imposed by the United States on the basis of the so-called *Superfund Act* of 1986.[36]

---

30 See e.g. World Bank, *World Development Report 1992* (Oxford University Press, 1992), p. 67; and Ingo Walter, 'Pollution and Protection: US Environmental Controls as Competitive Distortions' (1974) 110 *Weltwirtschaftliches Archiv*, 104, 112.

31 Steven Shrybman, 'Trading Away the Environment' (1991/92) 9(1) *World Policy Journal* 93, 104. Housman and Zaelke, 'Trade, Environment, and Sustainable Development' (n 12) 575.

32 Fisheries Act, R.S.C., 1985, c. F-14.

33 *In re* Canada's Landing Requirement for Pacific Coast Salmon and Herring, Canada-US Trade Commission Panel, Oct. 16, 1989, 2 TCT 7162. See Housman and Zaelke, 'Trade, Environment, and Sustainable Development' (n 12) 575.

34 Shrybman, 'Trading Away the Environment' (n 31) 93.

35 Lori Wallach, 'Hidden Dangers of GATT and NAFTA', in Ralph Nader et al. (eds.), *The Case Against Free Trade* 23–64 (North Atlantic Books, 1993), p. 26.

36 Superfund Amendments and Reauthorization Act, 42 U.S.C. § 9601 et seq. (1986). This Act, passed on October 17, 1986, amended the Comprehensive Environmental Response,

1.3 *Who's Afraid of Environmental Measures?—Part II. The Harmonization Agenda*

The story does not end here. Even when a measure was found to be a *lawful* trade restriction rather than disguised protectionism, the very fact that different countries had different environmental standards, policies, and regulations, was seen as a trade barrier in itself. Faced with the impossible task of removing these standards or regulations as they were all 'legitimate', the solution designed by the trade community has been to harmonize them. Again, USCFTA perfectly illustrates this agenda. Chapters six and seven of the Agreement required the parties to harmonize technical and agricultural standards, and Canada, as part of the bargain, "agreed to 'work toward equivalence' with a risk-benefit regulatory model for pesticide registration."[37] This bargain, however, required Canada to abandon a more stringent system and ultimately settle for lower levels of environmental protection, forcing the country to "accept US food imports that contain 30 per cent more pesticide residues than were allowed under their national laws before [the agreement]"[38]

The early activities of the European Community in the context of environmental management were equally aimed at harmonization. Being motivated primarily by economic concerns, the goal of the Community was to unify the common market and eliminate obstacles that would prevent free movement of products between the Member States.[39] In fact, according to Article 2 of the Treaty of Rome (EEC Treaty),

> It shall be the aim of the Community, by establishing a Common Market and progressively approximating the economic policies of Member States, to promote throughout the Community a harmonious development of economic activities, a continuous and balanced expansion, an

---

Compensation, and Liability Act (CERCLA) of 1980. The *Superfund Act*, among other things, re-imposed an excise tax on petroleum at higher rates, re-imposed a tax on certain chemicals, and imposed a new tax on certain imported substances produced or manufactured from taxable feedstock chemicals. The dispute brought by the EC and Canada was addressed by a GATT panel in June 1987. See Report of the GATT Panel, *United States—Taxes on Petroleum and Certain Imported Substances*, L/6175, 34S/136 (June 17, 1987).

37 Shrybman, 'International Trade and the Environment' (n 26) 33.

38 Wallach, 'Hidden Dangers of GATT and NAFTA' (n 35) 26.

39 See Christina Ruth Meltzer, 'The Environmental Policy of the European Economic Community to Control Transnational Pollution—Time to Make Critical Choices' (1990) 12 *Loyola of Los Angeles International & Comparative Law Review* 579, 586–7; Owen Lomas, 'Environmental Protection, Economic Conflict and the European Community' (1988) 33 *McGill Law Journal* 506.

> increased stability, an accelerated raising of the standard of living and closer relations between its Member States.[40]

Because the Council of the Community lacked an environmental mandate and could only issue directives "for the establishment or functioning of the common market," environmental initiatives were justified on the basis that they removed obstacles to the creation and functioning of the common market.[41] Such initiatives mostly relied on two provisions of the Treaty of Rome, Articles 100 and 235.[42] Article 100, in the relevant part, reads:

> The Council shall, acting unanimously on a proposal from the Commission, issue directives for the approximation of such provisions laid down by law, regulation or administrative action in Member States as directly affect the establishment or functioning of the common market.[43]

Differences in national standards—including environmental differences—were seen as creating technical barriers to trade, as even the GATT Secretariat had stated in its 1971 study: "very substantial trade barriers can and do arise from differences in national standards ... even when no protection is intended."[44] Article 100 was therefore often used to justify directives that, although cloaked in environmental terms, were actually part of a program to harmonize national laws to remove distortions of competition, being adopted pursuant to the 'General Program for the elimination of technical barriers to trade within the Community'.[45] On this basis, in 1970, the Community adopted a Directive regarding petrol-engine vehicles that, among other things, set limit

---

40 Treaty Establishing the European Economic Community, Mar, 25, 1957, 298 U.N.T.S. 11 [hereinafter Rome Treaty], Art. 2.

41 Lomas, 'Environmental Protection' (n 39) 506.

42 Article 235 of the Rome Treaty reads: "If action by the Community should prove necessary to attain, in the course of the operation of the common market, one of the objectives of the Community and this Treaty has not provided the necessary powers, the Council shall, acting unanimously on a proposal from the Commission and after consulting the European Parliament, take the appropriate measures."

43 Rome Treaty, Art. 100.

44 GATT, *Industrial Pollution Control and International Trade* (n 9) 12. See Auke Haagsma, 'The European Community's Environmental Policy: A Case-Study in Federalism' (1988) 12(2) *Fordham International Law Journal* 312, 316.

45 Council Resolution of May 28, 1969, 12 O.J. C 76/1 (1969). See Wolfgang E. Burhenne and Thomas J. Shoenbaum, 'The European Community and Management of the Environment: A Dilemma' (1973) 13 *Natural Resources Journal* 494, 499.

values for emissions of carbon monoxide and hydrocarbons.[46] This Directive, just as those that followed over the next few years,[47] was not motivated by environmental concerns: the Community had recognized that the fact that some Members States were introducing more stringent measures than others to control these emissions risked creating barriers to intra-Community trade and thus prejudicing the creation of a common market.[48] As a result, the only obligation placed on Member States was to *not* introduce values *more stringent* than those set out in the Directive and, by doing so, it preempted planned legislation in several European countries, such as Germany, that would have required stricter standards.[49]

The risk of pursuing such 'harmonization agenda', as depicted by the two examples provided above, is that environmental rules and standards might be compromised on the lowest level. As long as concern for the environment is not a factor and environmental policy is controlled by an economic agenda—whether that of the European Community or of the international community at large—the picture does not seem promising for the environment.

1.4 *The Exception to the Rule*

This trade-centered approach has led to a system where free trade is the rule and environmental protection is the exception; where trade law is the framework of reference, while environmental measures are simply the object to be evaluated on the basis of that framework. The word 'environment' does not even appear throughout the pages of the GATT, the Rome Treaty, or most trade agreements negotiated over the twentieth century up to the early 1990s.[50]

46 Council Directive of 6 February 1970 on the approximation of the laws of the Member States relating to the type-approval of motor vehicles and their trailers, 70/156/EEC O.J. (L 42).

47 Council Directive 70/157/EEC of 6 February 1970 on the approximation of the laws of the Member States relating to the permissible sound level and the exhaust system of motor vehicles, as amended by Directives Council Directives 73/350/EEC, 1973 O.J. (L 321), 77/212/EEC, 1977 O.J. (L 66), 84/372/EEC, 1984 O.J. (L 196), 84/424/EEC, 1984 O.J. (L 238), 87/354/EEC, 1987 O.J. (L 192), 89/491/ EEC, 1989 O.J. (L 238), 92/97/EEC, 1992 O.J. (L 371), 96/20/EC, 1996 O.J. (L 92), 1999/101/EC, 1999 O.J. (L 334), 2007/34/EC, 2007 O.J. (L 155).

48 Lomas, 'Environmental Protection' (n 39) 525.

49 Burhenne and Shoenbaum, 'The European Community' (n 45) 501.

50 Free Trade Agreement, EU-Switzerland-Liechtenstein, July 22, 1972; Free Trade Agreement, EU-Iceland, Dec. 19, 1972; Free Trade Agreement, EU-Norway, May 14, 1973; Asia-Pacific Trade Agreement, July 31, 1975; Free Trade Agreement, Australia-Papua New Guinea, Nov. 6, 1976; South Pacific Regional Trade and Economic Cooperation Agreement, Jan. 1, 1981; Latin American Integration Association, Aug. 12, 1980; Free Trade Agreement, United States-Israel, Apr. 22, 1985; Global System of Trade Preferences among Developing

When these treaties were drafted, the environment was not thought of as a subject requiring international cooperation and its potential relationship with trade was still largely ignored, leading to their substantive provisions being crafted "with little if any regard for the environmental consequences that may flow from them."[51]

Because of the late emergence of the environment issue vis-à-vis international cooperation on trade matters, there is no mention of the environment in any trade agreement signed before the 1970s and the first attempts to regulate the environment—both at the domestic and international level—necessarily had to depend on states' economic powers. Once the question of the relationship between the two bodies of law was first tabled and the first disputes arose, Article XX of the GATT—an *exception clause*—was immediately presented as the natural and sole possible entry point for environmental considerations, while there seemed to be no room for the environment in any of the agreement's substantive provisions. In fact, none of the 'rules' of the GATT or any other trade agreement allowed for environmental differentiation or for the pursuit, in any other way, of environmental objectives. It was impossible, for instance, to defend an environmental internal regulation on the basis that it did not discriminate between two products—for instance a bag of shrimps that came from a country that requires turtle excluder devices and one that did not[52]—arguing that the two products were not 'like' under Article III:4 of the GATT.[53] In other words, states were not allowed "to use the process characteristic as the basis for trade restrictive measures" as the "result would be to open a

---

Countries, Apr. 13, 1988. There are of course some exceptions, such as the 1986 Single European Act (SEA) and NAFTA.

51 Shrybman, 'Trading Away the Environment' (n 31) 94.

52 This example in inspired by the facts of the well-known WTO dispute *US-Shrimps*.

53 According to Article III:4 of the GATT, "The products of the territory of any contracting party imported into the territory of any other contracting party shall be accorded treatment no less favorable than that accorded to *like products* of national origin in respect of all laws, regulations and requirements affecting their internal sale, offering for sale, purchase, transportation, distribution or use. The provisions of this paragraph shall not prevent the application of differential internal transportation charges which are based exclusively on the economic operation of the means of transport and not on the nationality of the product." (emphasis added). It is important to stress that the prohibition in Article III:4 of the GATT only applies to 'like' products. For an analysis of the notion of likeness in international trade law, see e.g. Robert E. Hudec, '"Like Products": The Differences in Meaning in Articles I and III', in Thomas Cottier and Petros Mavroidis (eds.), *Regulatory Barriers and the Principle of Non-Discrimination in World Trade Law* (University of Michigan Press, 2000), pp. 101–123; Won-Mog Choi, *'Like Products' in International Trade Law* (Oxford University Press, 2003).

Pandora's box of problems that could open large loopholes in the GATT."[54] The only available option would have been to rely on Article XX.

Rather than being able to enter trade agreements through the main door, the environment was allowed access through a small crack in a window, the window in question being an *exception clause*. Most trade law instruments, in fact, contain a clause labelled 'general exceptions', recognizing that countries might want to pursue perfectly legitimate non-economic goals, even when in order to do so they adopt a trade restrictive measure, provided that certain conditions are met. And, despite not mentioning the term 'environment', it is precisely in these exceptions that environmentalists were expected to find some comfort.

GATT Article XX—replicated in almost all other trade agreements signed in the years that followed the signing of the GATT—allows GATT parties to adopt measures *inter alia* "(b) necessary for the protection of human, animal, and plant life or health; or (g) relating to the conservation of exhaustible natural resources if such measures are made effective in conjunction with restrictions on domestic production or consumption," as long as the requirements of the *chapeau* are fulfilled.[55] Similarly, Article 36 of the Treaty of Rome "allows member states to adopt measures which are *prima facie* incompatible with Articles 30 to 34 for the purpose of protecting a series of non-economic values such as … the protection of human health or life, animals or plants," assuming once again that certain conditions are met.[56]

Exceptions of this kind were not new. Rather, they had been part of bilateral treaties of commerce since their inception, together with those covering measures adopted for national defense reasons or to organize the parties' internal trade. As demonstrated by their drafting history, these provisions

---

54 Jackson, 'World Trade Rules and Environmental Policies' (n 12) 1243. The GATT's reluctance to take into account process and production methods (PPMs) reflects one of the underlying differences between the trade and environmental communities: the former concerned only with products and the latter with processes. For a recent analysis of this issue, see David Sifonios and Andreas Ziegler, '"*Tuna—Dolphin* Forever"? The Development of the PPM Debate Related to Trade and Environment in the WTO' (2020) 12 *Indian Journal of International Economic Law* 106.

55 According to the *chapeau* of Article XX, "nothing in this Agreement shall be construed to prevent the adoption or enforcement by any contracting party of measures" falling under one of the subsequent subparagraphs "subject to the requirement that such measures are not applied in a manner which would constitute a means of arbitrary or unjustifiable discrimination between countries where the same conditions prevail, or a disguised restriction on international trade."

56 Damien Geradin, *Trade and the Environment. A Comparative Study of EC and US Law* (Cambridge University Press, 1997), p. 13.

were originally designed to cover a wide variety of legitimate public policy objectives—environmental protection, however, not being one of them. And in this regard, GATT Article XX was not different from all its predecessors.

1.5 *The Real Story of 'Environmental' Exceptions or 'On How They Became Environmental'*

> Mr. fH.M. Catudal (United States): "What is the corresponding safeguard? ... If you are trying to protect yourself, say, from the bubonic plague, it is to exclude any article that might give rise to bubonic plague."[57]

On July 16, 1947, one of the Commissions of the Preparatory Committee of the UN Conference on Trade and Employment—Commission A—met in the Palais de Nations in Geneva to discuss, *inter alia*, the exact formulation of Article 37(b) of the draft, which later became XX(b) of the GATT. Debating whether there was a need to add an explanatory note to the phrase "necessary for the protection of human, animal, and plant life or health," the US delegate, Mr. Catudal, mentioned the bubonic plague as an example of a type of risk that the clause in question could be used to address. Without entering the merits of the debate, it suffices to say that all the other delegates followed the American example and referred to the regulations that Article 37(b) was designed to protect as 'sanitary regulations', adopted to prevent the spreading of diseases.[58]

In a later meeting, in February 1948, the Committee clarified once again that the measures to be published under Article 37(b) were "quarantine and other sanitary regulations."[59] This reading of the clause is not surprising given the legislative history of similar provisions in treaties of commerce up until the 1990s. The Treaty of Commerce between Italy and Switzerland, signed in 1904, for instance, allowed the parties to introduce export, import, or transit prohibitions "par égard à la police sanitaire et en vue de la protection des animaux, ainsi que des plantes utiles contre les maladies, les insectes et parasites nuisibles."[60]

57 E/PC/T/A/PV/30 (July 16, 1947), 11.

58 See e.g. the statements of Mr. Roux (France), or Mr. Cherry (South Africa): "We have been considerably puzzled as to how exactly a country will provide proof that it would take steps, if say someone should say a particular disease did exist in a country when, in fact, that particular disease does not exist in the country." E/PC/T/A/PV/30, 9, 13.

59 E/CONF.2/C.3/SR.35 (Feb. 14, 1948).

60 Treaty of Commerce, Italy-Switzerland.

The Italy-Switzerland Treaty, just as any other trade agreement negotiated until the 1990s, did not mention the environment and did not in any way suggest that the clause could be used to justify measures designed to protect the environment broadly speaking.[61] Similarly, the 1927 *Preliminary Draft for the International Agreement for the Abolition of Import and Export Prohibitions and Restrictions*, which was used as a blueprint for the GATT, featured an exception covering restrictions solely "for the protection of public health or for the protection of animals or plants against disease, insects, and harmful parasites."[62]

In those years, and up until the 1970s, environmental protection was simply not a public issue, as it was not during the negotiations of the GATT, when these debates were taking place. Nor was it a public issue in 1950, when the Treaty of Rome was being drafted. In fact, environmental protection does not in itself figure in Article 36 of the Treaty:[63] we will have to wait until 1979 for Article 36 to be considered, among other things, as an environmental exception. It had already been argued that environmental measures may be designed to protect some of the values listed therein,[64] but it was only with the establishment of the *rule of reason* in *Cassis de Dijon* that the environment could truly penetrate Article 36. In its famous decision, the European Court of Justice (ECJ), recognized that Member States may, when adopting measures which applied equally to domestic and imported products, restrict intra-Community trade for reasons other than those specifically recognized by Article 36:[65]

> Obstacles to movement within the Community resulting in disparities between the national laws relating to the marketing of the products in question must be accepted in so far as those provisions may be recognized as being necessary in order to satisfy mandatory requirements relating in particular to the effectiveness of fiscal supervision, the protection of

61 The fact that some treaties did not use the word 'sanitary' is not here considered meaningful in terms of what the objective and scope of the clause was. But see Steve Charnovitz, 'Exploring the Environmental Exceptions in GATT Article XX' (1991) 25 *Journal of World Trade* 37.

62 Preliminary Draft for the International Agreement for the Abolition of Import and Export Prohibitions and Restrictions (1927 World Economic Conference).

63 Like GATT Article XX, Article 36 of the EEC Treaty simply refers to "the protection of human health or life, animals or plants."

64 See B. Jadot, 'Observations—Mesures Nationales de Police de l'Environnement, Libre Circulation des Marchandises et Proportionalité' (1990) *Cahiers de Droit Européen* 408, 411.

65 See Derrick Wyatt and Alan Dashwood, *European Community Law* (Sweet & Maxwell, 3rd ed., 1993) p. 230; Stephen Weatherill and Paul Beaumont, *EU Law* (Penguin, 1993), p. 439.

> health, the fairness of commercial transactions and the defense of the consumer.[66]

And the few doubts whether environmental protection did indeed fall within the *Cassis de Dijon* requirements were definitively removed in 1980, when the EC Commission underlined the importance of environmental protection as a potential limitation on the prohibition contained in Article 30.[67] And a few years later, in the *Danish Bottles* case, the Advocate General "accepted that environmental protection was an imperative requirement justifying measures prima facie contrary to Article 30."[68]

For many years, after the drafting of the GATT, no mention was made of the environment being somehow associated to the exceptions of Article XX. When the issue of non-tariff barriers emerged, in the early 1970s, it was acknowledged that some might have perfectly legitimate reasons—such as national security, or public health safety—but the focus was, once again, on health and safety, rather than on the environment *per se*.[69] Twenty years later, in the *Tuna/Dolphin* case, the panel itself defined the measures covered by Article XX(b) as 'sanitary measures', when assessing the applicability of the clause to the US import prohibition.[70]

Along very similar lines, paragraph (g) of Article XX, was initially thought of as a much more limited exception, being the environment once again far from the drafters' minds. The reasons for the amendment proposed by the Australian delegation to the text of then Article 37(g) are quite self-explanatory in this regard:

> Pre-war experience in Australia showed that it was necessary to prohibit the exportation of *iron ore*, partly on the grounds that it seemed likely to be used for military purposes by the purchasing country. It is therefore the view of the Australian Delegation that there should be in the Charter, a provision enabling a Member to prohibit exports of such essential materials *in the long term interests of its security*.[71]

66 Case C-120/78, Rewe-Zentral AG v. Bundesmonopolverwaltung fiir Branntwei, 1979, E.C.R. 649, 662.

67 Geradin, *Trade and the Environment* (n 56) p.14.

68 Cameron and Robinson, 'The Use of Trade Provisions' (n 12) 25.

69 GATT, *GATT Activities in 1972*, 26.

70 Report of the GATT Panel, *United States—Restrictions on Imports of Tuna*, DS21/R-39S/155 (Sept. 3, 1991) (not adopted) [hereinafter *US—Tuna I*], para. 5.26. This is the first dispute where the Respondent relied on Article XX(b) to justify an allegedly environmental measure. In the previous disputes, only paragraph (g) had been raised.

71 E/PC/T/W/264 (Aug. 6, 1947) (emphasis added).

The mention of minerals, such as iron ore or manganese,[72] and the reference to national security in the context of arguments made by several delegates that export restrictions should be permitted for the preservation of scarce natural resources, has led many to argue that the phrase "exhaustible natural resources," as written in 1947, only referred to finite resources, such as minerals, and not to biological resources, such as plants or animal species. If it is true that the drafting history of GATT Article XX(g) "does not demonstrate an intent on the part of the framers *to exclude* "living" natural resources from the scope of application"[73] of the provision, it is also true that in no circumstance they expressed their intention to *include* such resources. And as a result, up until the Appellate Body report in US-*Shrimps* in 1998, the parties to the WTO were still debating as to the precise scope and content of the clause.[74]

1.6 *The Indeterminacy of Trade Law and The Neoliberal Turn*

The late emergence of the environment issue vis-à-vis international cooperation on trade matters explains why there is no mention of the environment in any trade agreement signed before the 1970s. However, it does not explain why, once the first disputes arose, the obvious conclusion seemed to be to relegate the environment to an exception clause, whether GATT Article XX, Article 36 of the Treaty of Rome, or similarly worded clauses in regional and bilateral trade agreements. This was not necessarily the idea of the GATT founders, precisely because that very provision had been drafted with several legitimate domestic concerns in mind, none of which even remotely related to the environment. None of the GATT provisions had been drafted to address environmental concerns, yet Article XX immediately became the sole solution. It was not, however, the only option. In a different, parallel scenario, one could imagine the environment entering the GATT through Article III rather than Article XX. In other words, when the first disputes broke out, a possible solution could have been to allow several kinds of trade-related environmental measures without finding a violation of national treatment, simply by defining the notion of 'like products' or of 'less favorable treatment' differently. Article XX would then only be used to justify quantitative restrictions and, more broadly, violations of Article XI of the GATT, as it was originally set up.

---

72 The example of manganese was used by the Brazilian delegate, Mr. Kafka, during a meeting held on November 18, 1946 (E/PC/T/C.II/QR/PV/5), 79.

73 Appellate Body Report, *United States—Import Prohibition of Certain Shrimp and Shrimp Products*, WT/DS58/AB/R (Oct. 12, 1998) [hereinafter *US—Shrimps*], fn. 114.

74 Ibid., paras 127–8.

The truth is that international trade law is, and always has been, largely indeterminate. It contains a series of "ambiguous and generally-worded principles," leaving the entire regime potentially compatible with a broad and diverse array of political choices and programs.[75] Hudec describes the ambiguity of the GATT text as necessary to ensure sufficient flexibility in the law so to reflect whatever consensus prevailed at a particular point in time.[76] The notion of 'non-discrimination', for instance, is susceptible to a number of different interpretations, and it has indeed been interpreted differently since the adoption of the GATT. For the architects of the post-war international trading order, the non-discrimination norm contained in GATT Article III was read as an 'anti-protectionism' norm, applicable against those internal measures that were motivated by protectionist intents.[77] A few decades later, and in particular in the 1980s and 1990s, the concept of 'discrimination' came to be treated as more or less synonymous with the economic concept of market distortion. As a result, all measures which had a negative impact on international trade—even when not protectionist in their purpose—began to fall under the scope of the norm and were therefore at risk of violating the GATT.

This change in understanding over the years was possible because nothing necessarily links the trade regime to a particular understanding of 'non-discrimination' and it has been explained with reference to a change in the ideational basis of the nature and purpose of the trade regime itself, from embedded liberalism to a resurgence of liberal economic thinking (neoliberalism).

Among post-war planners, the prevailing ideological orientation was embedded liberalism, which "combined limited and qualified support for free trade with a commitment to large-scale state interventionism."[78] Free trade was read as 'trade free from discrimination', and the principle of non-discrimination

75 Lang, *World Trade Law After Neoliberalism* (n 3) 5.

76 According to Hudec, "the ability to express ideas in this vague and cloudy manner allows the community to bring to bear whatever degree of consensus does exist. A suggestive statement, however ambiguous, provides something formal and official on which the community can focus its attitudes. The statement itself will point to the preferred result, and support expressed for that statement can create some pressure of consensus toward that end. Part of that pressure lies in the possibility that, faced with a specific case, the community may find itself willing to take a more positive stand than it has taken before. The ambiguous gesture invites such a development and furnishes a vehicle through which it may come about." Robert E. Hudec, 'The GATT Legal System: A Diplomat's Jurisprudence' (1970) 4 *Journal of World Trade Law* 615, 630, as quoted in Lang, *World Trade Law After Neoliberalism* (n 3) 204.

77 Lang, *World Trade Law After Neoliberalism* (n 3) 254.

78 Ibid., p. 4.

represented the pillar on which the GATT was founded. As aptly put by Viner, "[t]he case for equality of treatment as the general rule is a strong one. It is the only general rule in this field which is of general applicability."[79] As the previous chapter has described, the GATT was created to avoid the trade wars of the 1930s, soon associated in the public eye not only with the Great Depression but with the horrors of the war. Discriminatory trade, on the other hand, was regarded as a dangerous threat to international peace. In the words, once again, from Viner, "tariff discriminations are invariably resented by the countries which are discriminated against, and three centuries of experience demonstrate that under all circumstances they operate to poison international relations and to make more difficult the task of maintaining international harmony."[80]

As a result, the immediate priority of the GATT negotiators was to remove the more restrictive trade practices introduced over the course of the interwar period, as they risked subverting the core objectives of the regime they were attempting to create.[81] The focus was in particular on border measures, such as quotas, foreign exchange restrictions, and licensing requirements, ultimately prohibited with the insertion of Article XI in the text of the GATT. As to internal measures, on the contrary, "only a few very specific categories were made visible as barriers to trade" while all the others "were implicitly understood to be normal or background regulation, never intended to be subject to GATT oversight."[82]

The Tokyo Round of trade negotiations, which was concluded in 1979, witnessed a significant economic turmoil of global proportions, which "helped to erode political support for the normative priorities of embedded liberalism" and instead provided "the conditions for the re-emergence and re-strengthening of a purer form of economic liberalism—neoliberalism," which

79 Jacob Viner, 'Conflicts of Principle in Drafting a Trade Charter' (1947) 25 *Foreign Affairs* 612, 616.

80 Ibid.

81 As explained by Srinivasan, "it is clear that the signatories viewed discriminatory treatment in international commerce, not as being unfair in some relevant sense ... but as subverting the broad objectives that signatories sought to promote through GATT." T.N. Srinivasan, 'Nondiscrimination in GATT/WTO: Was there Anything to Begin with and is there Anything Left? (2005) 4 *World Trade Review* 69, 74–5. See also Robert E. Hudec, *Essays on the Nature of International Trade Law* (Cameron May, 1999), pp. 227–250.

82 Lang, *World Trade Law After Neoliberalism* (n 3) 209. This reading of Article III of the GATT was possible because it was based on a shared understanding of the purpose and objectives of the trade regime, which was primarily 'shared' among the key negotiators.

would quickly become the prevailing ideology in international trade governance for the coming decades.[83]

This transformation, which can be attributed to both the economic turmoil of the 1970s and the expansion in the number and diversity of GATT participants, and which could no longer guarantee the survival of the 'shared' consensus that had characterized the embedded-liberalism years, had a strong ideational basis. On the one hand, the notion of 'trade barrier' came to be regarded as synonymous to the idea of 'trade distortion'. According to neoliberal thinking, the goal of the trade regime was to remove all governmental interventions because distortive of international trade flows.[84] As a result, the scope of application of the overall regime expanded, and virtually all aspects of countries' domestic policies became potentially subject to the GATT/WTO discipline as "potentially" trade-distortive. On the other hand, the regime came to be 're-imagined' as a marketplace, thus justifying the series of game theory explanations of the GATT which, became influential through the 1980s.

The GATT/WTO regime had significantly changed its character, becoming more formalized and 'technicalized', as well as motivated by economic and ideological concerns rather than the political ones that had inspired the founders of the regime. This transformation had significant influence on the interpretation and application of the principle of non-discrimination enshrined in Article III of the GATT, whose potentially "significant substantive bite"[85] was becoming apparent only in the context of the disputes that immediately followed the conclusion of the Tokyo Round. Indirectly, it had an equally significant influence on the way in which the relationship between trade and the environment was approached for several decades, contributing to the solidification of an approach that left no other space to the environment than exception clauses. The treatment of all forms of government intervention in the economy as trade-distortive and the focus on economic effects in the context of the likeness analysis under Article III—rather than on the distinction between legitimate domestic regulation and regulation with protectionist motives—resulted in a significant expansion of the prohibitive effect of the

83 Ibid., p. 222.

84 As David Kennedy put it, within neoliberal thought, "[l]aw emerged as a *limit* on the state—on the discretion of administrators and the mandate of legislators. Private rights, constitutional procedures, judicial review, and international obligations—all constrained the neoliberal state." David Kennedy, 'The "Rule of Law," Political Choices, and Development Common Sense', in David M. Trubek and Alvaro Santos (eds.), *The New Law and Economic Development: A Critical Appraisal* (Cambridge University Press, 2006), p. 138.

85 Lang, *World Trade Law After Neoliberalism* (n 3) 208.

norm, leaving no space for environmental regulations other than that provided by Article XX, an exception clause.

This approach was further exacerbated by the complete isolation in which the two communities continued working for years, unaware of each other's values and goals, and rarely perceiving their respective realms as even remotely interconnected. And the deep cultural differences between the two communities—the different languages, assumptions, and philosophical underpinnings—did nothing but deepen the divide, undermining any attempt of communication or interaction.

2 Rivalry

In the Spring of 1992, posters mysteriously appeared in Washington D.C., depicting GATTzilla, a gigantic monster, evocative of Japanese monster Godzilla, "chewing the globe, trampling the Capitol, and spewing DDT, while clutching a squealing dolphin."[86] The headline blared '*GATT is Coming. What You Don't Know Will Hurt You*'. The posters had been plastered on the construction walls surrounding the building that housed the offices of the United States Trade Representative (USTR) and were soon followed by condemnatory advertisements in the *New York Times* and the *Washington Post* under the headline 'sabotage', announcing an approaching GATTastrophe, and displaying the slogan 'GATT—Guaranteeing A Toxic Tomorrow.'[87]

These fervent protests had been triggered by the GATT panel decision in the *Tuna/Dolphin* case, loudly criticized by environmentalists all over the Western hemisphere, who raged with fury and denounced free trade for blindly fostering the exploitation of natural resources, and for ultimately contributing to environmental destruction.[88] The GATT was depicted as a sinister character

86 Jan C. McAlpine and Pat LeDonne, 'The United States Government, Public Participation, and Trade and Environment', in Zaelke et al. (eds.), *Trade and the Environment* (n 11) 203.

87 See Daniel C. Esty, *Greening the GATT. Trade, Environment, and the Future* (Institute for International Economics), p. 35. Jagdish Bhagwati, 'Trade and the Environment: The False Conflict?' in Zaelke et al. (eds.), *Trade and the Environment* (n 11) 161; and Sylvia Ostry, 'Energy Security and Sustainable Development: The WTO and the Energy Charter Treaty', in Marina Larionova (ed.), *Making Global Economic Governance Effective: Hard and Soft Law Institutions in a Crowded World* (Routledge, 2016), p. 131.

88 Report of the GATT Panel, *US—Tuna I*. In addition to threatening US environmental and conservation laws and policies, the decision was perceived as putting other domestic laws, as well as newly adopted multilateral environmental treaties, at risk of being GATT-inconsistent. The European Parliament, for instance, had recently presented a proposal to introduce a ban on imports of tuna caught with driftnets or purse-seine nets, along very

allowing 'big business' "a free hand to plunder the bounty of the natural world" to the point that free trade itself, in the view of certain environmentalists, could destroy the environment.[89] Just like that, the (in)famous decision had raised the "specter" of an obscure international trade tribunal, with no environmental sensitivity or expertise, challenging and overriding environmental laws and regulations.[90] On the other side of the barricade, free-trade proponents welcomed the GATT panel decision with praise and excitement, as it was perceived as an important victory against the environmental lobby. They regarded the challenged US measure as an example of eco-colonialism, and as a dangerous attempt to influence the environmental standards of its trading partners, and began to fear that the GATT could be "in danger of becoming the latest sacrifice" of this out-of-control 'green gang'.[91]

The *Tuna/Dolphin* case was the first dispute that witnessed a direct collision of the two communities. As they first came in contact, environmentalists saw "free traders living in a world of economic theory that distracts them from environmental realities" and worried that, by liberalizing trade without taking the environment into account, countries would "lose the right to determine their own environmental standards" leading to ever-increasing environmental degradation.[92] Free traders, on the other hand, looked on nervously as environmental agreements began incorporating trade measures,[93] regarding

similar lines as the US ban. In light of the Tuna/Dolphin Decision, however, as warned by the EC Commissioner for Cultural Affairs and Information, John Dondelinger, such legislation would not be compatible with the Community's obligations under the GATT. 'European Parliament Calls for EC Ban on Imports of Tuna Caught by Purse-Seines', BNA Int'l Envt. Daily, Nov. 27. See Skilton, 'GATT and the Environment in Conflict' (n 12) 456; and Matthew H. Hurlock, 'Note. The GATT, US Law and the Environment: A Proposal to Amend the GATT in Light of the Tuna/Dolphin Decision' (1992) 92 *Columbia Law Journal* 2098, fn. 171.

89 Martin Kohr, 'The GATT and Environmental Protection' (1990) *Greenpeace* 14, 15; Virginia I. Postrel, 'The Big Green Trade-Killing Machine', *Wall Street Journal*, Sep. 21, 1990, A18; and Patricia Dodwell, 'Trade Row Looms over US Dolphin-Friendly Tuna Policy', *Financial Times*, Jan. 30, 1992, 22, as quoted in Shoenbaum, 'Free International Trade' (n 12) 700.

90 See Esty, *Greening the GATT* (n 87) 29.

91 William H. Lash III, 'Green Gang's GATT Holdup', *Journal of Commerce*, Dec. 10, 1993.

92 Esty, *Greening the GATT* (n 87) 39; David Runnalls and Aaron Cosbey, 'Trade and Sustainable Development. A Survey of the Issues and A New Research Agenda', (1002) IISD Report, 12.

93 Using trade tools to achieve environmental goals was not a new idea. Examples can be found, e.g., in the following conventions: North Pacific Fur Seals Convention, July 7, 1911, 37 Stat. 1542–1543; Convention for the Protection of Migratory Birds, Aug. 16, 1916, 39 Stat. 1702–1704; Plant Protection Convention, Dec. 6, 1951, 150 U.N.T.S 67; London Convention for the Preservation of Fauna and Flora in Their Natural State, Nov. 8, 1933, 172 L.N.T.S. 254, 256. For an overview of these conventions, see Charnovitz, 'Exploring the Environmental

the application of such measures as a potential "threat to the trading system and to international harmony more generally,"[94] reviving the specter of protectionism—the very reason behind international economic cooperation.

However, this was not the first time the collision between industrialized and less developed countries came to the forefront with regards to the adoption of trade restrictions to protect the environment. Their differences vis-à-vis the introduction of the environment issue at the top of the international agenda had already emerged during the Stockholm Conference and in the days spent by several delegations in Founex a few weeks before the Conference commenced. It was precisely in the developing world that the *trade elite*, moved by the neoliberal ideas that by the early 1990s had become the prevailing force behind the trade regime, found a precious ally.

2.1 *Dialogue of the Deaf*

> It was comforting to have one place (one might almost say a club) where likeminded people could get together and do their work in peace.[95]
>
> ROBERT E. HUDEC, 1975

A few years into the creation of the GATT, "the administration and incremental development of the trade system was increasingly entrusted to a specialized policy elite insulated from, and not particularly interested in, the larger political and social conflicts of the age."[96] What had developed in those years has been defined as a *trade policy elite*, which did not just include some of

Exceptions' (n 61) 42. More recent examples (post-Stockholm) include the following treaties: Convention on International Trade in Endangered Species of Wild Fauna and Flora, Mar. 3, 1973, 993 U.N.T.S.; Montreal Protocol on Substances that Deplete the Ozone Layer, Sept. 16, 1987, 1522 U.N.T.S. 3.; Basel Convention on the Control of Transboundary Movements of Hazardous Wastes and their Disposal, Mar. 22, 1989, 1673 U.N.T.S. 57, 28 I.L.M. 657. Rotterdam Convention on the Prior Informed Consent Procedure for Certain Hazardous Chemicals and Pesticides in International Trade, Sept. 10, 1998, 2244 U.N.T.S. 337; Stockholm Convention on Persistent Organic Pollutants, May 22, 2001, 2256 U.N.T.S. 119; United Nations Framework Convention on Climate Change, May 9, 1992, 1771 U.N.T.S. 107, 31 I.L.M. 849; Convention on Biological Diversity, June 5, 1992, 1760 U.N.T.S. 79; International Tropic Timber Agreement, Jan. 27, 2006, 2797 U.N.T.S. 75.

94 Esty, *Greening the GATT* (n 87) 39.

95 Robert E. Hudec, *The GATT Legal System and World Trade Diplomacy* (Praeger, 1975), p. 57.

96 Howse, 'From Politics to Technocracy' (n 1) 98. Howse argues that this lack of interest for the broader political agenda was concurrent with the fact that, with the Cold War, "the high politics of international relations increasingly focused ... on matters of international security and the East-West conflict" and moved away from questions of trade and economic cooperation.

the officials employed in the GATT Secretariat but, more importantly, a larger group of 'experts' which, although formally *outside* of the GATT system, in the sense that they never held official positions at the GATT, were, for all purposes, *insiders*.[97] Despite their differences in terms of national or personal interests, these *insiders* formed a network that tended to understand the system in terms of "the policy science of economics [rather than] a grand normative political vision,"[98] as it had been the case in the 1940s.

A network that can be defined, in constructivist terms, as an *epistemic community*. As aptly explained by Joseph Weiler,

> The GATT successfully managed a relative insulation from the 'outside' world of international relations and established among its practitioners a closely-knit environment revolving round a certain set of shared normative values (of free trade) and shared institutional ambitions. GATT operatives became a classical 'network' of first-name contacts and friendly personal relationships.[99]

The environmental community, on the other hand, was considerably more fragmented, often incapable of speaking with just one voice. In Stockholm, for instance, despite the slogan *Only One Earth*, the press that was covering the Conference used the headline *Only 113 Earths* to reflect the fragmentation within the community and the vast array of diverging views, in particular between developed and developing countries. As a matter of fact, the Stockholm Conference had revealed that the environment was perceived and valued differently between countries, depending on their different level of environmental sensitivity and awareness as well as their particular stage of economic and social development.[100] As a result, there were significant differences between the environmental agenda of the North and that of the South.

---

97 They included, among others, "former or current governmental trade officials, GATT-friendly academics who often sat on GATT/WTO dispute settlement panels and were invited to various conferences and meetings of the GATT/WTO, international civil servants in other organizations preoccupied with trade matters, and a few private attorneys, consultants, and former politicians." Howse, 'From Politics to Technocracy' (n 1) 98.

98 Ibid.

99 Joseph Weiler, 'The Rule of Lawyers and the Ethos of Diplomats: Reflections on the Internal and External Legitimacy of Dispute Settlement', in Roger B. Porter et al. (eds.), *Efficiency, Equity, and Legitimacy: The Multilateral Trading System at the Millennium* (Brookings Institution Press, 2001), pp. 336–37.

100 Winfried Lang, 'Is the Protection of the Environment a Challenge to the International Trading System?' (1995) 7 *Georgetown International Environmental Law Review* 463, 473.

The latter, for instance, was inextricably intertwined with the struggle for social and economic justice and regarded with suspicion the Northern technocratic approach to environmental protection.[101] Ultimately, the heterogeneity of the members of the environmental community was also reflected in their approach to the trade/environment nexus and, while some environmentalists supported the idea of 'greening the GATT', others did not trust the trade regime to administer any linkage between trade and the environment.[102]

What is more, the trade and environmental communities spoke different languages, relying on entirely different vocabularies, and ended up often 'talking past' one another.[103] The use of the term 'protection', as pointed out by Daniel Esty, offers a particularly fitting example of the way in which the language used by the two communities could become a source of confusion: "the word 'protection' warm[ed] the heart of environmentalists but sen[t] chills down the spine of free traders."[104] Another notable example is the word 'dumping', which could reflect two very different concepts, depending on whether one looked at it from a trade or environmental viewpoint: in the trade jargon, it is commonly used to mean the sale of exports below domestic market prices, while in the environmental world it refers to waste being unloaded into rivers, oceans, or soil.[105]

Such differences in the meaning and value attached to certain words had potentially far-reaching effects beyond mere semantics. In fact, the two communities have generally been inclined to approach similar problems in very different ways.[106] One could think, for instance, of the risks that might derive from permitting regulatory diversity. From a free trade perspective, regulatory diversity exposes the world to the danger that countries will set their environmental regulations and standards 'too high', thereby creating obstacles to the free flow of commerce. Environmentalists, on the other hand, would fear that

---

101 Carmen G. Gonzalez, 'Beyond Eco-Imperialism: An Environmental Justice Critique of Free Trade' (2001) 78(4) *Denver University Law Review* 981, 985–6.

102 David W. Leebron, 'Linkages' (2002) 96(1) *American Journal of International Law* 5, 16.

103 Daniel C. Esty, 'Integrating Trade and Environment Policy Making: First Steps in the North American Free Trade Agreement', in Zaelke et al (eds.), *Trade and the Environment* (n 11) 47; Peter L. Lallas, Daniel C. Esty, and David J. van Hoogstraten, 'Environmental protection and International Trade: toward Mutually Supportive Rules and Policies' (1992) 16 *Harvard Environmental Law Review* 271, 274.

104 Esty, 'Integrating Trade and Environment Policy Making' (n 103) 36.

105 Esty, *Greening the GATT* (n 87) 36.

106 Daniel Magraw, 'Environment and Trade: Talking Across Cultures', *Environment*, Mar. 19, 1994.

countries will be tempted to set their regulations and standards 'too low', externalizing harms onto others and ultimately harming the environment.[107]

During the first years of their 'coexistence', the strong divide between the two communities was not limited to differences in language and vocabulary. Rather, it could be better defined as what some scholars have called an actual *clash of cultures*, encompassing differences in traditions, procedures, and philosophical underpinnings.[108]

The level of openness of the policy-making process is particularly illustrative of these tensions. Public participation and transparency are the keywords characterizing the environmental regulatory system both at the domestic and international level. In the United States, for instance, public participation has always been an essential component of the process through which environmental statutes become law and are later implemented and enforced.[109] Similarly, in the context of international environmental negotiations, drafts of the agreements are always made accessible to the public and discussed openly.[110] On the other hand, trade negotiations have traditionally been conducted behind closed doors, in what environmentalists call a 'black box'.[111] When a draft of the North American Free Trade Agreement (NAFTA) text,[112]

107 Esty, *Greening the GATT* (n 87) 44.

108 Ibid., pp. 36–41; Esty, 'Integrating Trade and Environment Policy Making' (n 103) 45, 47; John H. Jackson, 'Greening the GATT: Trade Rules and Environmental Policy', in James Cameron et al. (eds.), *Trade and the Environment: the Search for Balance* (Cameron May, 1994), p. 39.

109 The National Environmental Policy Act requires federal agencies to prepare an Environmental Impact Statement for any proposed "legislation [or] major Federal actions significantly affecting the quality of the human environment." The Statement should include, among others, "i) the environmental impact of the proposed action; ii) any adverse environmental effects which cannot be avoided should the proposal be implemented, and iii) alternatives to the proposed action." 42 U.S.C. § 4332 (1988). See McAlpine and LeDonne, 'The United States Government'(n 86) 207.

110 The Brundtland Report of 1987 advised that "At the national level, governments, foundations, and industry should also greatly extend their cooperation with NGOs in planning, monitoring, and evaluating as well as in carrying out projects when they can provide the necessary capabilities on a cost-effective basis. To this end, governments should establish or strengthen procedures for official consultation and more meaningful participation by NGOs in all relevant intergovernmental organizations." World Commission on Environment and Development, *Our Common Future* (Oxford University Press, 1987) [hereinafter Brundtland Report].

111 See Brian Shoenborn, 'Public Participation in Trade Negotiations: Open Agreements, Openly Arrived At?' (1995) 4 *Minnesota Journal of Global Trade* 103.

112 North American Free Trade Agreement, US-Can.-Mex, Dec. 17, 1992, 32 I.L.M. 289 (1993) [hereinafter NAFTA].

which was being negotiated in complete secrecy, was leaked to the public, the official reaction of the three governments was to deny its accuracy and, even after the agreement was signed, the Bush Administration only agreed to make public a short summary. The complete document was not available until the President left office in 1993, and was sold to the public for the 'reasonable' price of 41 USD.[113]

The openness and transparency of the environmental regulatory system can be explained with the very nature of the object it aims to regulate: the environment. Environmental regulation is often triggered by public demand, and because it imposes positive obligations on governments, it is often essential to mobilize public support for environmental solutions.[114] On the other hand, according to trade specialists, the secrecy of trade negotiations is required by the competitive nature of world trade, which calls for high levels of confidentiality.[115] Moreover, the trade system continued to be a 'black box' even after negotiations were successfully completed: the settlement of disputes, for instance, was once again conducted behind closed doors, and non-governmental organizations (NGOs), which are among the main actors inhabiting the environmental world, were not 'welcome' in the proceedings.[116]

At a deeper level, the trade community that had formed during the 1970s and 1980s was largely driven by economic principles, such as efficiency and comparative advantage, while environmentalists share a law-based worldview. As a matter of fact, economists tend to approach any trade-environment issue as a matter of weighing the relative costs and benefits of trade and environmental policies in maximizing social welfare, starting from the premise that "trade increases income and therefore the capacity to be environmentally conscientious."[117] Moreover, free traders rely on a narrow definition of economics, including only those factors that are readily quantifiable, while environmental problems are generally not,[118] leading them to ignore environmental variables

---

113 Goldman, 'Resolving the Trade and Environment Debate'(n 13) 1283. Ralph Nader and Lori Wallach, 'GATT, NAFTA, and the Subversion of the Democratic Process', in Jerry Mander and Edward Goldsmith (eds.), *The Case Against the Global Economy: and for a Turn Toward the Local* 92–107 (Sierra Club Books, 1996).

114 Goldman, 'Resolving the Trade and Environment Debate'(n 13) 1282–3.

115 See McAlpine and LeDonne, 'The United States Government'(n 86) 210–11.

116 The reluctance to involve NGOs can be due to the fact that the GATT's structure reflects the international order as it was right after the World War II, when nation-states were the only actors involved. See Esty, *Greening the GATT* (n 87) 27.

117 Runnals and Cosbey, 'Trade and Sustainable Development' (n 92) 18.

118 As very clearly explained by Esty, "ecological problems are characterized by threshold effects; time lags between emissions and detection; biological, chemical, and physical interactions that are not well understood; and sometimes substantial scientific

in their analyses: "if you can't put a number on it, leave it out of the equation." Finally, trade specialists have the habit of thinking in terms of products, while environmentalists have always been more concerned with processes, how a good is made, as that is the most relevant stage from an environmental standpoint.[119]

2.2 *Everyone for Themselves*

By behaving like a 'black box', the trade community reflected the 'club model' of multilateral cooperation, where each club is responsible for a specific 'issue-area' and is able to keep outsiders out. The result was the almost absolute lack of opportunities for the two communities to interact and resolve their differences. Rather, this reciprocal isolation did nothing but exacerbate the aforementioned *clash of cultures,* contributing to the stratification of trade norms oblivious to their environmental repercussions. As the US-Canadian experience of the late 1980s is particularly illustrative of this clinical isolation, let us consider two events that took place only a few months apart in Toronto and Washington D.C.

On June 27, 1988, over 300 academics, policymakers, scientists, corporate and environmental leaders from 48 countries gathered in Toronto. They had all been invited to participate in the World Conference on the Changing Atmosphere, chaired by Stephen Lewis, Canada's Ambassador to the United Nations, and co-sponsored by the United Nations Environment Programme (UNEP). The Conference coincided with the worldwide occurrence of sudden extreme weather events—from heat waves in Central Europe, to floods in Africa, and droughts in the Midwestern corn belt of the United States[120]—and was driven by the resulting increased attention devoted to the scientific and social implications of climate change.[121]

Despite the sensitive topic and the difficulties in reaching a consensus on almost every issue that was put on the table, the final plenary session was able to agree on a Conference statement that was "strong, direct, explicit, and

---

uncertainties over the source, scope, and magnitude of public health or habitat damage." Esty, *Greening the GATT* (n 87) 40.

119 Robert W. Jerome, 'Traders and Environmentalists', *Journal of Commerce,* Dec. 27, 1991, 4A.

120 Peter Usher, 'World Conference on the Changing Atmosphere: Implications for Global Security' (1989) *Environment, Science and Policy for Sustainable Development,* 25.

121 The topics covered during the Conference were, however, not limited to climate change but also included the protection of the ozone layer, long-range transport of atmospheric pollutants, and acid deposition. 1988 was also the year that saw the creation of the Intergovernmental Panel on Climate Change (IPCC) as a joint effort of the United Nations Environment Programme and the World Meteorological Organization.

readable."[122] One of the more startling recommendations contained in the statement called for a 20 per cent cutback on global carbon dioxide (CO_2) emissions from current levels by 2005, a reduction which could be achieved through increased energy efficiency, reduced energy consumption, and a shift towards low CO_2-emmiting fuels. These actions were considered to be necessary given that, as solemnly declared by Norway's Prime Minister Gro Harlem Brundtland in her opening statement, "the impact of climate change may be greater and more drastic than any challenges mankind has faced with the exception of nuclear war."[123]

Only a few months later, on September 9, then US President Ronald Reagan ratified the United States-Canada Free Trade Agreement, describing it as "an economic constitution for North America."[124] Unfortunately, this new constitution contained several provisions that were fundamentally at odds with the recommendations penned at the Toronto Conference in June. An entire chapter of the agreement was devoted to the relaxation of regulatory controls to encourage greater energy development and trade,[125] while at the same time shielding subsidies in the oil and gas sector from attacks under the trade protection laws of either country, by providing them with a special status which was by no means extended to subsidies intended to encourage energy efficiency and conservation.[126]

These contradictions were the result of economic and environmental policy objectives having been pursued, for about 20 years, on entirely separate tracks. Trade and environmental policy-makers had been working in clinical isolation, unaware of the potential synergies between economic and environmental policy objectives. When confronted with the obvious contradictions between the new provisions of USCFTA and the need to actively protect the environment, the Canadian government objected that the former was "a commercial accord

122 F. Kenneth Hare, 'World Conference on the Changing Atmosphere: Implications for Security, held at the Toronto Convention Centre, Toronto, Ontario, Canada, during 27–30 June 1988' (1988) 15(3) *Environmental Conservation*, 282.

123 Excerpt from Prime Minster Brundtland's opening statement, quoted in 'Toronto Climate Conference Calls for Sharp Cuts in Carbon Dioxide Emissions' (1988) 1(3) *Climate Alert* 9.

124 United States—Canada Free Trade Agreement, 27 I.L.M. 281 (1988) [hereinafter USCFTA].

125 Article 904 of USCFTA explicitly prevented either government from restricting the export of energy resources for any other than "national security" reasons, unless supplies are rationed to the same extent domestically.

126 Article 906 provides: "Both parties have agreed to allow existing or future incentives for oil and gas exploration, development and related activities in order to maintain the reserve bases for future energy resources." The only other category of government subsidy that is accorded this special status is defense spending. See Shrybman, 'International Trade and the Environment' (n 26) 95, 97.

between the world's two largest trading partners. It [was] not an environmental agreement ... [and] the environment was not, therefore, a subject for negotiations."[127] The very same spirit animated the first years of the NAFTA negotiations, with the Bush administration refusing to acknowledge the link between trade and the environment.[128] US Trade Representative Carla Hills—who only a few years later would proudly define NAFTA the "greenest trade agreement ever negotiated"[129]—vocally argued that environmental issues had absolutely no place in trade agreements.[130]

Along the same lines, despite representatives of several countries declared the importance of tackling the 'environment issue' as part of the ongoing multilateral trade talks,[131] their requests remained largely unanswered and the environment ended up being completely left out of the 1986–1993 GATT negotiations. Once talks had begun, the doors of the Uruguay Round were closed shut, leaving the environmental community out in the cold, as environmental organizations were neither being consulted nor given the opportunity to participate or comment.[132] As a result, it was the sole prerogative of a few thousand "gold-card-carrying members" of the free trade elite to set the agenda for

127 As quoted in Frank Tester, 'Free-Trading the Environment', in Duncan Cameron (ed.), *The Free Trade Deal* (Lorimer and Company, 1988); and Shrybman, 'Trading Away the Environment' (n 31) 95.

128 The goal of the NAFTA negotiations was "to achieve economic growth through the gradual elimination of trade barriers over a fifteen-year period and to create a financial environment which encourages investment while fully protecting industrial and intellectual property rights." James E. Bailey, 'Free Trade and the Environment–Can NAFTA Reconcile the Irreconcilable' (1992) 8 *American University Journal of International Law and Policy* 839, 843–4. See e.g. 'Oil Exploration, Environment, Immigration Should Not Be in FTA, Mexican Official Says', *International Trade Reporter*, Oct. 31, 1990, 1637; 'USTR Reluctance to Debate Social Aspects of Mexico Pact Worries FTA Backers', *Inside U.S. Trade*, Jan. 4, 1991, 8.

129 Carla A. Hills, 'The Trade Pact is Our Best Deal', *N.Y. Times*, Aug. 17, 1993.

130 See John Audley, 'Why Environmentalists Are Angry about the North American Free Trade Agreement', in Zaelke et al (eds.), *Trade and the Environment* (n 11) 193.

131 The *Brundtland Report* had urged the Uruguay Round to address "the impacts of trading patterns on the environment" and stressed "the need for more effective instruments to integrate environment and development concerns into international trading arrangements."

132 Shrybman, 'International Trade and the Environment' (n 26) 30. For the objectives of the Round, as spelled out in the Punta dl Este Declaration, see GATT, *GATT Activities in 1986* (Geneva, 1987), 16. See James Cameron and Halina Ward, 'The Multilateral Trade Organization: A Revised Perspective', in Cameron et al. (eds.), *Trade and the Environment* (n 108) 99.

the multilateral efforts to expand global commerce in such diverse areas as service, agriculture, and intellectual property rights.[133]

2.3 *Between Two Fires*

The insisting requests to integrate the 'environment issue' in the Uruguay Round negotiations agenda came almost solely from a handful of developed countries, led by the United States. The US had been the motivating force behind the drafting of the NAFTA's environmental side agreement, enacted a few years prior to the conclusion of the Uruguay Round,[134] and continued exercising its economic and political leverage to ensure the treatment of environmental matters by GATT negotiators. Two congressional proposals had been advanced to this end in the House of Representative. One of them even led to the passing of a resolution which called "upon the President to initiate and complete negotiations, as part of the current Uruguay Round GATT talk" to make the GATT compatible with a number of US health and environmental laws.[135]

Halfway through the Uruguay Round, similar requests were made by the representatives of several other developed countries. Switzerland, speaking on behalf of the members of the European Free Trade Association (EFTA), declared that there was an urgent need to gain a better understanding on the subject of environmental policies and GATT rules. Similar calls came from Sweden, Austria, the EU, as well as Association of South-East Asian Nations (ASEAN) countries.[136] The EU, for its part, had already extensively incorporated environmental protection into its trade policies, to the point of becoming "a model for the rest of the international community"[137] and brought this disposition to the multilateral trade negotiations in Punta del Este as well.

These requests, however, were opposed by a coalition of developing countries, who expressed vehement opposition to measures designed to link trade

---

133 Lenora Todaro, 'Attack of the Killer Kapitalists', *The Village Voice*, Nov. 30, 1999.

134 Daniel P. Blank, 'Target-Based Environmental Trade Measures: A Proposal for the New WTO Committee on Trade and Environment' (1996) 15 *Stanford Environmental Law Journal* 61, 78. For a detailed account of the role played by the US in this context, see Richard H. Steinberg, 'Trade-Environment Negotiations in the EU, NAFTA, and WTO: Regional Trajectories of Rule Development' (1997) 91 *American Journal of International Law* 231, 245–9.

135 See H. R. Con. Res. 246, 102d Cong. (1st Sess. 1991), Sec. 1, and Pub. L. 102–582, 106 Stat. 4900, Sec. 203 (1992).

136 See GATT, *GATT Activities in 1990* (Geneva, 1991), 16.

137 Philippe Sands, 'European Community Environmental Law' (1991) 100 *Yale Law Journal* 2511.

and environmental protection, fearing that such measures would be used by developed countries to block imports of their products.[138] Along the same lines, during the final sessions of the Uruguay Round, when the role and mandate of the 'Group on Environmental Measures and International Trade' (EMIT Group) was being discussed, delegations from developing countries fought against transforming the Group into a more permanent mechanism to avoid giving the environment a permanent place within the new Organization, arguing that it was a 'trade' organization after all, and fearing that mainstreaming environmental discussions in the newly-established WTO might be used to limit their development options.[139] These countries were able to keep this position during the first years of life of the WTO as well, up until the latest—and largely unsuccessful—Doha Round.

Developing countries, who for years had been following the debate with some suspicion from the sideline, had a major interest in defending the integrity of the multilateral trading system, free from environmental or other non-economic considerations, and they finally had the chance to voice their concerns and defend their position.[140] While in the past richer, larger economies had been able to effectively steer the direction of multilateral trade deals, when the Uruguay Round agreements were being negotiated, nearly all of the Group of 77 developing countries were participating as a single negotiating bloc and were finally capable of asserting their interests. As a result, the picture that emerged from the negotiations was starkly different from the traditional model of power politics, with the "greatest commitment to the multilateral trading system coming from the developing world rather than industrialized states," as sharply noted by Peter Sutherland.[141]

---

138 See William Drozdiak, 'Poor Nations Resist Tougher Trade Rules', *Washington Post*, Apr. 14, 1994, A20; see also Jessica Matthews, The Great Greenless GATT, *Washington Post*, Apr. 11, 1994, A19. See also Gonzalez, 'Beyond Eco-Imperialism' (n 101) 982, fn. 7.

139 Rodrigo J. Prudencio and Stewart J. Hudson, 'Suggestions on an Environmental Reform Agenda at the World Trade Organization', Papers presented at the GATT Symposium on Trade, Environment and Sustainable Development, July 28, 1994, 9–14, 10; Gregory C. Shaffer, 'The World Trade Organization under Challenge: Democracy and the Law and Politics of the WTO's Treatment of Trade and Environment Matters' (2001) 25 *Harvard Environmental Law Review* 1, 23; and Esty, *Greening the GATT*, (n 87) 37.

140 See Piritta Sorsa, 'GATT and the Environment: Basic Issues and Some Developing Country Concerns', in Patrick Low (ed.), *World Bank Discussion Papers: International Trade And The Environment* 325 (1992), p. 326.

141 Quoted in Bartram Brown, 'Developing Countries in the International Trade Order' (1994) 14 *Northern Illinois University Law Review* 347, fn. 223.

Both free traders and representatives from developing countries saw the GATT as the "guardian of the international trading system,"[142] which risked being challenged by environmental considerations, and the environmental community found itself between the proverbial two fires. Even after the Uruguay Round was completed, a large part of the trade community, with the support of less developed countries, kept arguing that environmental issues were best kept out of the trade policy-making process.[143] In 1999, Jagdish Bhagwati drafted a statement, signed by 99 intellectuals and NGOs from the Third World, asking the WTO, and trade negotiators more broadly, to 'bury' the "linkage of labor and environmental standards to WTO and to trade treaties."[144] In their view, the 'moral face' of the countries supporting this linkage was nothing more than "a mask which [hid] the true face of protectionism."[145] They argued that by allowing such linkage, the real goal of the WTO—trade liberalization—would be harmed, as linking non-trade issues "undermines both the freeing of trade and the advancing of our social agendas"[146] because one instrument (WTO rules) cannot be used to achieve two targets:

> The underlying reason for such an unsatisfactory outcome is that you are trying to kill two birds with one stone. Generally, you cannot. So, trying to implement two objectives, the freeing of trade and advancing social and moral agendas, through one policy instrument such as WTO, you will undermine both. You will miss both birds.[147]

The very same view had been expressed, a few years prior, by Indian Prime Minister Pranab Mukherjee who, voicing the concerns of many developing countries and vowing to fight the inclusion of any social or environmental clause in multilateral trade rules, stated that he saw "no merit whatsoever in the attempt to force linkages where they do not exist; trade policy cannot be made the arbiter of all concerns."[148]

---

142 Sorsa, 'GATT and the Environment' (n 140) 339.

143 Daniel C. Esty, 'Bridging the Trade-Environment Divide' (2001) 15(3) *Journal of Economic Perspectives* 113.

144 Jagdish Bhagwati, 'Third World Intellectuals and NGOs Statement Against Linkage (TWINS-SAL)', 1999.

145 Ibid.

146 Jagdish Bhagwati, 'On Thinking Clearly About the Linkage Between Trade and the Environment' (2000) 5 *Environment & Development Economics* 483, 494.

147 Bhagwati, 'Third World Intellectuals' (n 144).

148 Quoted in Drozdiak, 'Poor Nations Resist Tougher Trade Rules' (n 138).

2.4 *Development First*

Seemingly overnight, the environment issue—and the question of its role and place vis-à-vis international trade norms and policies—saw the development and the free-trade agendas standing next to each other on the same side of the barricade, adding a North-South dimension to the already clear free trade v. environment dichotomy. Indeed, "environmental diplomacy is often said to run along the lines of the North-South divide, with opposite positions being advocated by the developed world versus the developing countries."[149] This divide had already emerged loud and clear in 1972 in Stockholm, as evidenced by Maurice Strong's strenuous efforts to ensure developing countries' participation in the Conference.

In truth, the international development movement has much older roots when compared to the environmental one. Grown out of the decolonization process following World War II and anchored in the recognition that newly-independent developing nations were justified to aspire to the same level of economic and social development of their industrialized counterparts, by the 1960s, the development movement had become one of the most prominent forces in global relations.[150] In September 1961, almost a year before Nixon declared that the 1970s would be 'the environmental decade', John F. Kennedy had launched a proposal for making the 1960s the 'UN *Development* Decade.' This proposal was followed by an increasing engagement of the international community with the issue of development, through a variety of actions both within and outside of the UN. Within the UN, in particular, different institutions were created to deal with different facets of the issue, such as the United Nations Conference on Trade and Development (UNCTAD), established in 1964 and, the following year, the United Nations Development Program (UNDP).

When the Stockholm Conference was convened, all the efforts and energy of the developing world were devoted to the goal of development, while terms like 'environmental degradation' and 'environmental quality' seemed like luxurious preoccupations and had an abstract ring about them to societies whose immediate concerns were food, housing, employment, medical care, and education.[151] Unlike industrialized nations, where a growing number of

149 Gaetan Verhoosel, 'Beyond the Unsustainable Rhetoric of Sustainable Development: Transferring Environmentally Sound Technologies' (1998) 11 *Georgetown International Environmental Law Review* 49.

150 Claire Brighton, 'Unlikely Bedfellows: The Evolution of the Relationship between Environmental Protection and Development' (2017) 66 *International and Comparative Law Quarterly* 209, 213.

151 J. Lee, 'Environmental Considerations in Project Appraisal, United Nations Conference on the Human Environment', Panel of Experts on Development and Environment, Working

environmental, health, conservation, and consumer advocates were being vocal about emerging environment problems, large segments of the public opinion in developing countries regarded the consideration and discussion of these problems with suspicion and even hostility.[152] Thy feared that such 'obsessive' concern with problems of the environment might "divert national and international attention from the urgent problems of the economic and social development of the underdeveloped world" or even undermine their industrialization process.[153]

Developing countries' claim to a 'right' to industrialize stood in stark contrast with the kind of environmental problems developed nations denounced in Stockholm: many of these problems were occurring precisely as a result of the same industrialization processes that had produced "such unparalleled levels of wealth and prosperity" in the industrialized world.[154] Just like developed nations did a few centuries ago, developing countries should now be free to build their industries as they wish, pollution or not.

There is no denying that environmental protection was felt as an important issue in the developing world as well. However, the environmental agenda of the North and that of the South differed greatly. The latter, in particular, was inextricably intertwined with the struggle for social and economic justice, which was instead completely neglected by Northern environmentalists.[155] The meeting organized in Founex, Switzerland, a few weeks before the Stockholm Conference, was designed precisely to mediate these diverging, and seemingly irreconcilable views. One of the views that emerged from Founex was the causative link between underdevelopment and environmental degradation: although it was indeed true that developing countries were not unconcerned with environmental problems, it was also true that the major problems they were facing were different from those characterizing industrialized nations, as they mostly reflected poverty and lack of development and, rather

Paper No. 7 (4 June 1971) (on file with the Environmental Science and Public Policy Archives at Harvard University, Maurice F. Strong Papers, Box 40[396]), 3.

152 Lori Wallach, 'Hidden Dangers of GATT and NAFTA' (n 35) 26–7. Enrique Iglesias, 'Development and the Human Environment', United Nations Conference on the Human Environment, Panel of Experts on Development and Environment, Working Paper No. 1 (June 4, 1971), para. 20.

153 Iglesias, Development and the Human Environment (n 152) para. 19.

154 Maurice F. Strong, 'ECO'92: Critical Challenges and Global Solutions' (1991) 44 *Journal of International Affairs* 287.

155 Gonzalez, 'Beyond Eco-Imperialism' (n 101) 985–6.

than being the result of the development process, could be overcome by the process of development itself.[156]

Brazil's Ambassador Miguel Ozorio De Almeida, one of the driving forces behind developing countries' positions in Stockholm, called for the Conference to become an "economic development conference,"[157] to be able to tackle effectively the South's environmental concerns. On the other side, some delegates, including Maurice Strong himself, stressed the need to ensure that the Conference not "become another UNCTAD,"[158] emphasizing that development objectives should not be allowed to "flood out any serious consideration of the questions of pollution and other uses of natural resources which were ... the original purpose of the Conference."[159] Despite the seeming 'victory' of the North, with the Conference being centered around the 'human environment' (rather than development, at it would be the case 20 years later in Rio), Founex ended up introducing a claim to prioritization: environmental policies that reinforced economic growth in the global South would be more readily accepted and supported compared to those conflicting with economic growth, for example by hampering trade.[160]

As a result, those environmental considerations that resulted in new, tighter regulation and control in industrialized countries were seen as operating to developing countries' disadvantage.[161] Let us take the example of tuna, which led environmentalists to take to the streets and wave banners in Washington D.C. in the Spring of 1992. More often than not, tuna harvested in developing and least-developed countries was found to have higher levels of contamination than those established in the US as maximum levels, and was fished with techniques that were often far from being environmentally safe.[162] Limiting trade to tuna fished respecting US levels would have meant the cutting off of

---

156 *Founex Report on Development and Environment* (1971).

157 Miguel A. Ozorio de Almeida, 'The Confrontation Between Problems of Development and Environment' (1970–1) 39 *International Conciliation* 37, 53.

158 Note of Conversation with Mr. Maurice Strong on 11 February 1971, Geneva, attached to Letter from R. Arculus, 9 Feb 1971 to Mr. Ure, 'Preparatory Committee for the UN Conference of the Human Environment: Second Session: Geneva—8 to 19 February 1971', United Kingdom National Archives, Folder FCO 55/670.

159 Letter DM Kitching to Mr. Williams and Mr. Mathieson (first initials not given), UK Foreign and Commonwealth Office, 24 September 1971, United Kingdom National Archives, folder FCO55/672.

160 Brighton, 'Unlikely Bedfellows (n 150) 214.

161 Maurice Strong's interview for the Canadian Broadcasting Corporation on 'Limits to Growth' (Mar. 1975) (on file with the Environmental Science and Public Policy Archives at Harvard University, Maurice F. Strong Papers, Box 27[268]), 26.

162 Ibid.

a major market for some Asian countries.[163] It then should be no surprise that the first generation of trade/environment disputes often opposed developed and less developed countries, the former defending a certain environmental measure and the latter challenging it because it was trade-restrictive and ultimately affecting their economies and industries.[164]

2.5 *To Each His Own Fear*

The *Tuna/Dolphin* case marked the beginning of an intense international debate on the legitimacy and legality of unilateral trade measures to protect the environment. Some countries, however, had been using trade sanctions to compel other nations to implement environmental measures for nearly two decades.[165] The most well-known example of a national statute authorizing the adoption of such 'environmental' trade sanctions is probably the 1971 *Pelly Amendment* to the US *Fishermen' Protective Act* of 1967.[166] The famous amendment, named after Thomas M. Pelly, the Congressman who proposed it at the very end of his long career in the US House of Representatives, was introduced in response to Denmark, Norway, and West Germany's refusal to ban high salmon fishing. The ban, which had been established in 1969 by the International Commission for the Northwest Atlantic Fisheries (ICNAF) to conserve fishing resources in the area, was presented in a manner that allowed countries to ignore it without technically violating the terms of the ICNAF.[167] This represents a clear example of a situation where, despite being preferable, multilateral consensus is often difficult to achieve and unilateral action might present itself as the better option from an environmental standpoint. As a matter of fact, the three countries' refusal to comply with the ban "effectively nullified any benefits that would come"[168] from it, thus motivating the US Congress to vote for Pelly's proposal. As ultimately drafted, the Amendment authorized the President to prohibit the importation of any product from a foreign country whose nationals conducted fishing operations that diminished

---

163 Ibid.

164 See *US—Tuna I* (complainant: Mexico); *US—Gasoline* (complainant: Venezuela and Brazil); *US—Shrimps* (Complainant: India, Malaysia, Pakistan, and Thailand). This of course was not always the case and several disputes have been registered during the same years where developed countries acted both as complainants and respondents.

165 Gonzalez, 'Beyond Eco-Imperialism' (n 101) 1004.

166 22 U.S.C. §§ 1971 et seq.

167 Gene S. Martin and James W. Brennan, 'Enforcing the International Convention for the Regulation of Whaling: The Pelly and Packwood-Magnuson Amendments' (1989) 17 *Denver Journal of International Law & Policy* 293, 294.

168 Ibid., 295.

"the effectiveness of an international fishery conservation program" or engaged in trade that diminished "the effectiveness of any international program for endangered or threatened species."[169]

In 1992, the *Pelly Amendment* was revised to expand the range of products against which a US President could invoke countermeasures and, two years later, President Bill Clinton relied on it to impose a ban on all wildlife products from Taiwan to stop the sale of rhinoceros horns and tiger bones which were undermining the 1973 Convention on International Trade in Endangered Species of Wild Fauna and Flora (CITES).[170] Environmentalists in developed countries immediately applauded the sanctions against Taiwan "as one of the top five environmental successes of 1994," recognizing them as an extremely effective tool "in helping curb the deadly commerce in endangered species.'[171] Others, on the other hand, harshly criticized the sanctions as entirely oblivious to the specific interests of developing countries and as a means of simply imposing American values on Taiwan's culture.[172] For the exact same reasons, several Southeast Asian governments and their allies in the developing world had challenged, in a session of the GATT Council, the legality of an Austrian law which prescribed 'ecolabelling' for imported tropical timber and timber products.[173]

These events, which ultimately culminated in the *Tuna-Dolphin* controversy, reflected a conflict with respect to the use of unilateral 'environmental' trade sanctions between free trade and environmental protection, and between Northern environmentalists and developing countries. This conflict has often been described as one between 'high-level' and 'low-level' countries to stress that the opposing views pit countries with high environmental standards against those with lower ones.[174]

---

169 22 U.S.C. § 1978(a)(1)-(2) (1988 & Supp. IV 1992), as quoted in Howard F. Chang, 'An Economic Analysis of Trade Measures to Protect the Global Environment' (1995) 83 *Georgetown Law Journal* 2131, 2137.

170 The ban was lifted less than year after it was imposed, after Taiwan adopted critical measures to halt commercial trade in rhinocero horns and tiger bones. See Blank, 'Target-Based Environmental Trade Measures' (n 134) 62–3.

171 'The Best Environment of 1994', *Time*, Dec. 26, 1994, 144; Press Release from the World Wildlife Fund, World Wildlife Fund Statement on US Government Decision to Lift Pelly Amendment Sanctions Against Taiwan (June 30, 1995) (on file with the *Stanford Environmental Law Journal*).

172 James Sheehan, 'Most Favored Fauna Treatment', *Washington Times*, May 31, 1994, at A12.

173 GATT Doc. C/M/260, 40–56 (Nov. 26, 1992). See Lang, 'Is the Protection of the Environment'(n 100) 465–6.

174 See e.g. Ileana M. Porras, 'The Puzzling Relationship Between Trade and the Environment: NAFTA, Competitiveness and the Pursuit of Environmental Welfare Objectives' (1995) 3 *Global Legal Studies Journal* 65; Jagdish Bhagwati and T.N. Srinivasan,

Representatives of the former category justified the legitimacy and legality of their unilateral measures on both economic and environmental grounds. First, differential (and in this case 'lower') environmental practices were seen as conferring 'unfair' trade advantages to low-level countries' producers. Maintaining low environmental standards allowed domestic producers to incur lesser costs and was therefore compared to a subsidy or dumping practice. This position was explained with extreme clarity by US Senator Boren in the context of the adoption of the *International Pollution Deterrence Act*:

> We can no longer stand idly by while some US manufacturers, such as the US carbon and steel alloy industry, spend as much as 250 percent more on environmental controls as a percentage of gross domestic product than do other countries ... I see the unfair advantage enjoyed by other nations exploiting the environment and public health for economic gain when I look at many industries important to my own state of Oklahoma ... [175]

As a consequence, environmentalists in the industrialized world further feared that their own countries would then be forced by political pressure to lower their own environmental protection standards in order to remain competitive. Otherwise, their industries would relocate to low-level countries leading to a snowballing race to the bottom.

Developing countries, for their part, regarded these arguments as mere excuses and continued labelling unilateral sanctions as clear examples of 'green protectionism' and 'eco-imperialism' or, in other words, as developed countries' newly found way to impose their own "pollution control and resource conservation strategies on the South, notwithstanding the South's conflicting environmental preferences, economic preferences, and priorities."[176] Ultimately, developing countries saw restricting trade on grounds of differences in environmental standards as the pure and simple imposition of values by importers upon exporters, as an expression of disapproval of a country's environmental behavior by forcing compliance with more acceptable standards. The underlying question is: "acceptable according to whom?" Or, in other words, what can

---

'Trade and the Environment: Does Environmental Diversity Detract from the Case for Free Trade?' Discussion paper Series No. 718 (January 1995).

175 International Pollution Deterrence Act of 1991. Statement of Senator David L. Boren, Senate Finance Committee, October 25, 1991.

176 Esty, *Greening the GATT* (n 87) 181–192. See e.g. Bill L. Long, 'Identifying Environmental Options in Development' (January 1972). *Development Digest* Vol. IX No. 1.

be considered an 'acceptable' level of pollution or environmental degradation and who gets to decide?

What developed countries saw as an unfair trade advantage, developing countries guarded as a fundamental expression of their own sovereignty over resource management and pollution control decisions. And while developed countries saw the adoption of sanctions as an effective way to 'level the playing field', the developing world regarded them as the unjustified imposition of Northern ethical preferences to countries characterized by a different level of environmental awareness, a different stage of economic and social development, as well as different endowments in financial and technological resources.

2.6 *Like Riding Bicycles*

This perspective on trade and environment was shared by both developing countries and free traders, albeit with different emphases.[177] Developing countries based their arguments on their sovereign right to formulate their own environmental goals, while free trade economists and advocates praised differential standards across nations as they determine a nation's comparative advantages, on which trade rules are based to increase welfare.[178]

The many challenges the 'environment issue' had to face once introduced on the international agenda, and in its relationship with trade in particular, were somehow exacerbated and crystallized by the predominance of the neoliberal economic thought. The latter framed the trading system as being "for free trade and free markets, and against governmental interference,"[179] while all forms of government intervention, even when they pursued legitimate policy goals, were regarded with suspicion as potential protectionism in disguise.

In line with neoliberal economic thinking, in the 1999 statement signed by *Third World Intellectuals*, Bhagwati identified trade liberalization as the "true objective" of the multilateral trading system.[180] By reading the Preamble to the GATT, however, one can gather that trade liberalization, rather than being the goal of the agreement, is just a means serving broader goals, namely "raising standards of living, ensuring full employment and a large and steadily growing volume of real income and effective demand, developing the full use of the resources of the world and expanding the production and exchange of

177 Saunders, 'Trade and Environment'(n 10) 726.

178 Robert E. Hudec, 'Differences in National Environmental Standards: The Level-Playing-Field Dimension' (1996) 50 *Minnesota Journal of Global Trade* 1, 22.

179 Lang, *World Trade Law After Neoliberalism* (n 3) 4.

180 Bhagwati, 'Third World Intellectuals' (n 144).

goods."[181] To achieve these objectives, the drafters identified two—necessary but not sufficient—means, namely the substantial reduction of tariffs and other barriers to trade, and the elimination of discriminatory treatment in international commerce.[182]

As the 1999 statement shows, however, members of the trade community, and economists in particular, can sometimes "lose sight of these goals by narrowing the operational goal of trade agreements to that of trade liberalization."[183] This narrow understanding of the goal of the trade regime can be explained with the strong influence of the 'bicycle theory' of trade liberalization on the trade community, according to which an open trading system will be maintained only if forward momentum for trade liberalization continues to avoid that the bicycle might fall over.[184]

After the 'environment issue' emerged in the early 1970s, the major constant goal of the GATT, and any other bilateral or regional trade agreement, remained the "establishment and preservation of an open world trading system,"[185] and whenever trade specialists were required to address subjects that today would be subsumed under the environmental label, they would do so keeping both eyes on their ultimate—economic—goal. When, for instance, the issue of natural resources and natural resource-derived products was raised during the Uruguay Round, the discussion, far from addressing the need to protect natural resources, revolved around a proposal to remove trade barriers to their free flow, which, if successful, would have led to higher demand and unsustainable resource management,[186] rather than conservation—as advocated by environmentalists.

Along the very same lines, when the US adopted a measure based on the *Marine Mammal Protection Act* (MMPA) of 1972[187] prohibiting the import of foreign tuna caught with commercial fishing technology which resulted in the

181 GATT, Preamble. The language of the GATT preamble was inspired by Point 5 of the Atlantic Charter, which read: "Fifth, they desire to bring about the fullest collaboration between all nations in the economic field with the object of securing, for all, improved labor standards, economic advancement and social security."

182 See Victoria Curzon, 'The Management of Trade Relations in the GATT', in Andrew Shonfield (ed.), *International Economic Relations of the Western World 1959–1971*, Vol. I 143–283 (Oxford University Press, 1976), p. 147.

183 Gregory Shaffer, 'Retooling Trade Agreements for Social Inclusion' (2019) 1 *University of Illinois Law Review* 1, 5.

184 Fred Bergsten, *Toward a New International Economic Order* (Lexington Books, 1975).

185 GATT, *GATT Activities 1980* (Geneva, 1981). The reports of GATT Activities until 1990 do not touch upon the environment issue either.

186 See Housman and Zaelke, 'Trade, Environment, and Sustainable Development'(n 12) 562.

187 Marine Mammal Protection Act, 16 U.S.C. § 1361-1423h (1972) [hereinafter MMPA].

incidental killing or serious injury of dolphins, a GATT panel declared the measure inconsistent with trade rules. Just like the GATT negotiators who faced the 'natural resources issue', the panel, composed of members of the very same trade community, concluded that trade restrictions in response to other countries' lower environmental practices were *per se* inconsistent with the GATT.[188] As argued by Howse, this ruling was "without textual basis in GATT law" but was rather based "on some intuitive notion that allowing trade measures to address global environmental externalities was somehow countenancing a slippery slope towards unconstrained green protectionism" and therefore risked undermining the trade liberalization goal of the GATT itself.[189] While the trade community welcomed the decision with praise, environmentalists strongly criticized it—and the GATT in general—for its environmental insensitivity: "the panel's rulings may be legally sound" read the *Washington Post* only a few days after the decision was made public "but they are environmental nonsense."[190]

The environment had found itself at a great disadvantage: not only had it emerged on the international political agenda later than other—economic and developmental—concerns, but it also found itself at the mercy of the prevailing neoliberal doctrine, which inspired the trade community, and of the suspicions and hostilities of the developing world. Not only had the environment been cornered into exception clauses, but, as addressed in the following paragraphs, the neoliberal turn taken by the trade regime contributed to a strict and narrow interpretation of such exception clauses vis-à-vis the protection of the environment. This strictness, once again, was not part of the GATT founders' original grand vision.

3 How Exceptions Work: The Environment Upstaged

According to the GATT Report on *Industrial Pollution Control and International Trade* of 1971, national standards to address pollution concerns "are *already*

188 Report of the GATT Panel, *US—Tuna I*, paras 5.27, 5.32, and 6.2.

189 Robert Howse, 'The World Trade Organization 20 Years On: Global Governance by Judiciary' (2016) 27(1) *European Journal of International Law* 9, 36–7.

190 The article continues: "No country can protect its own smidgen of air or ocean or living part of the global commons. Trade measures are often the only means short of a multilateral treaty to influence the behavior of other countries." See Jessica Matthews, 'Dolphins, Tuna and Free Trade', *Washington Post*, Oct. 18, 1991, A21, as quoted in Hurlock, 'Note' (n 88) 2131.

covered in a general way in GATT, especially through exceptions in Article XX, permitting imposition of restrictions on goods harmful to public health and safety."[191] In other words, in the view of trade officials, trade law already addressed the concerns of environmentalists by providing, through the exceptions in Article XX, the necessary leeway for countries to adopt domestic environmental regulations.

Exception clauses were introduced in the text of the GATT by its founders, right next to the principles of non-discrimination and tariff reduction, to combine trade liberalization with the assurance that countries would be able to pursue a variety of social policies. As the trade community came to be characterized, after the 1970s, by a "crude economist ideology and strong deregulatory orientation,"[192] not only was Article III given a more expansive interpretation, but Article XX—the only refuge left to environmental protection—was deprived of its original meaning and it became nearly impossible to justify domestic policies under this clause. As a matter of fact, this approach has done nothing but amplify certain features typical of exception clauses in general—widely used in international law—which already make them hard to rely on: they are generally narrowly defined, strictly interpreted and applied, and whoever invokes them bears the burden of persuasion.

3.1 *A Clause to Prevent All Abuses*

On November 13, 1946, the Preparatory Committee of the International Conference on Trade and Employment (Preparatory Committee) was getting close to completing its first session at Church House, in London.[193] Committee II, one of the working committees that had been established to divide and speed up the work, was in charge of 'General Commercial Policy', and it was under its aegis that the very first draft GATT articles were prepared.[194] When the discussion turned to Article 32 of the draft—which later became Article 37 and finally Article XX—Mr. Cherry, the delegate from South Africa,[195] called

191 GATT, *Industrial Pollution Control and International Trade* (n 9) 12 (emphasis added).

192 Howse, 'The World Trade Organization 20 Years On' (n 189) 48.

193 The first session of the *Preparatory Committee* ran from October 15, 1946 to November 20, 1946.

194 The other working committees were: Committee I: *Employment and Economic Activity*; Committee III: *Restrictive Business Practices*; Committee IV: *Intergovernmental Commodity Arrangements*; and Committee V: *Administration and Organization*. See Douglas A. Irwin, Petros C. Mavroidis, and Alan O. Sykes, *The Genesis of the GATT* (Cambridge University Press, 2008), p. 107.

195 During this session of Committee II, Delegates of six different nationalities acted as rapporteurs (Belgium, Czechoslovakia, New Zealand, South Africa, UK, and US).

everyone's attention to a delicate issue that had been raised a few weeks prior by the Belgian and Dutch delegates: the issue that, often, the stipulations "to protect animal or plant life or health" are misused for indirect protection.[196]

The risk that these exceptions might lead to abuse had already been observed many years before as "under the guise of biological protection, it is very easy to introduce economic protection."[197] To avoid such abuses, by the mid-1920s, many treaties started imposing conditions on their exceptions. The Treaty between Japan and Mexico of 1924, for instance, required animal and plant laws and regulations to be "applicable to all countries or to countries in similar circumstances."[198] However, these conditions, which were then reproduced in several commercial agreements, did not seem adequate or sufficiently clear to the Church House negotiators.[199] Something else was needed. Something that would shield the provision from any possible future abuse.

After long discussions, Mr. Cherry recommended the insertion of a preambular clause that would prohibit abuse of these exceptions and, in general, the attainment of results that were incompatible with the aim of the Agreement.[200] To this end, the UK delegate, Mr. Rhydderch, proposed to add the following clause as an introduction to Article 32:

> The undertakings in Chapter IV of this Charter relating to import and export restrictions shall not be construed to prevent the adoption or enforcement by any Member of the following measures, provided that they are not applied in such a manner as to constitute a means of arbitrary discrimination between countries where the same conditions prevail, or a disguised restriction on international trade.[201]

196 E/PC/T/C.II/32 (Oct. 30, 1946), 11. See also E/PC/T/C.II/W.20 (June 11, 1946).

197 Percy W. Bidwell, *The Invisible Tariff. A Study of the Control of Imports into the United States* (Council on Foreign Relations, 1939), p. 17.

198 Treaty between Japan and Mexico, 36 L.N.T.S. 278 (no longer in force). Another example is provided by the *Treaty between Czechoslovakia and Sweden* of 1925, which required measures adopted to protect animal or plant life or health to be "in conformity with the universally recognized international regulations"—whatever they might be. See Charnovitz, 'A Taxonomy' (n 12) 41.

199 The phrase "provided that corresponding safeguards are applied in the importing countries if similar conditions exist in that country," which was added to text of Article XX(b)—then 37(b)—was later removed because considered unclear and inadequate (E/PC/T/A/PV/30, at 11–13). The phrase was first introduced by the Drafting Committee of the Preparatory Committee of the United Nations Conference on Trade and Employment on February 11, 1947 (E/PC/T/C.6/55/Rev.1).

200 E/PC/T/C.II/50 (Nov. 13, 1946), 6.

201 Ibid., 7.

The UK proposal was welcomed by all the other delegates and, with a few changes, found its way in the New York draft and later in the final version of GATT Article XX.[202] The insertion of the *chapeau* reveals the fears that surrounded this exception clause. It is true that it had been part of trade agreements for more than a century, but its scope had become broader—it originally used to only apply to import prohibitions and restrictions while it now started covering a much wider field[203]—and it had now become part of a multilateral agreement, with potentially much more far-reaching consequences.

The decision of the GATT drafters to introduce the *chapeau* was motivated by the intention of framing it as an 'anti-protectionism' norm, applicable against those internal measures that were motivated by protectionist intents. Over time, however, all forms of government intervention in the economy began to be regarded as potentially trade distortive and the importance of distinguishing between legitimate domestic regulation and regulation with protectionist motives was somehow lost. As a result, the *chapeau* became a shield against all internal measures that had a negative impact on international trade, regardless of the intent behind their adoption. By doing so, it ultimately reiterated the primacy of GATT's main objective vis-à-vis countries' intentions to protect the environment: "[w]hile the exceptions of Article XX may be invoked as a matter of legal right, they should not be so applied as to frustrate or defeat the legal obligations of the holder of the right under the substantive rules of the General Agreement."[204] In other words, states can adopt policies, regulations, and standards to protect the environment only as long as they do not constitute (unnecessary) barriers to trade:[205] this way, the need to protect commerce from undue burdens seemed to effectively override any environmental protection concerns.

---

202 See E/PC/T/C.6/55 (Feb. 5, 1947); E/PC/T/C.6/55/Rev.1; E/PC/T/142 (Aug. 1, 1947); and E/PC/T/154 (Aug. 6, 1947). Interestingly, a clause similar to the current *chapeau* of Article XX could already be found in the forefather of this provision, Article 4 of the 1927 *Preliminary Draft for the International Agreement for the Abolition of Import and Export Prohibitions and Restrictions* ("The following classes of prohibitions and restrictions are not prohibited by the present Convention, on condition, however, that they are not applied in such a manner as to constitute a means of arbitrary discrimination between foreign countries where the same conditions prevail, or a disguised restriction on international trade.")

203 E/PC/T/C.II/50, 7 (Remarks of the UK delegate, Mr. Rhydderch).

204 Panel Report, *United States—Standards for Reformulated and Conventional Gasoline*, WT/DS2/R (May 20, 1996) [hereinafter *US—Gasoline*], 22.

205 This approach was already clear in both the 1971 and 1992 studies of the GATT Secretariat on the relationship between trade and the environment.

A very similar approach characterized domestic experiences as well. In the United States, for instance, the existing division of authority between federal and state created very similar obstacles to states enacting laws that are more protective of the environment. The US Supreme Court has interpreted the Commerce Clause's conferral of authority to Congress over interstate commerce to create, by negative implication, a limit on state laws that unduly burden interstate commerce (*Dormant* Commerce Clause).[206] States are free to protect the environment—together with other legitimate public interests—within the restraints imposed by the Commerce Clause itself.[207] These restraints do not appear in the words of the Clause, but have been developed and clarified by the Supreme Court in a long series of decisions, which have reflected "an alertness to the evils of 'economic isolation' and protectionism."[208]

According to the interpretation of the Court, while discriminatory restrictions on commerce—regardless of the purpose—are virtually *per se* invalid,[209] when a statute "regulates even-handedly to effectuate a legitimate level public interest, and its effects on interstate commerce are only incidental, it will be upheld *unless the burden imposed on such commerce is clearly excessive* in relation to the putative local benefits."[210] In other words, "no state action can survive a commerce clause analysis if its effect on interstate commerce is heavily burdensome or if it discriminates against interstate commerce."[211] While more lenient than the test applied through GATT Article XX, nevertheless regulation of interstate commerce maintains a privileged position in the constitutional scheme.[212] Once again, the benchmark to decide whether a measure

---

206 This prohibition was first recognized in *Gibbons v. Ogden*, 22 U.S. 1 (1824), 1, 209–11 (1824). On the dormant commerce clause, see generally Martin H. Redish and Shane Nugent, 'The Dormant Commerce Clause and the Constitutional Balance of Federalism' (1987) *Duke Law Journal* 569.

207 *Philadelphia* v. *New Jersey*, 437 U.S. 617, 623 (1978).

208 Ibid., 623–4.

209 The Court set forth the controlling principle in case of discriminatory measures in *Dean Milk v. Madison*, 340 U.S. 349 (1951). Here the Court held: "Madison plainly discriminates against interstate commerce. This it cannot do, even in the exercise of the unquestioned power to protect the health and safety of its people, if reasonable non-discriminatory alternatives, adequate to conserve legitimate local interests, are available." 354.

210 *Pike v. Bruce Church, Inc.*, 397 U.S. 137, 142 (1970) (emphasis added). See also *Oregon Waste Sys. v. Environmental Dep't*, 511 U.S. 93 (1994).

211 Ira Steven Lefton, 'Constitutional Law—Commerce Clause: Local Discrimination in Environmental Protection Regulation' (1977) 55(2) *North Carolina Law Review* 461, 465.

212 See *C&A Carbone Inc. v. Town of Clarkstown*, 511 U.S. 383 (1994); *Oregon Waste Sys. v. Environmental Dep't; Chemical Waste Management, Inc. v. Hunt*, 504 U.S. 334 (1992); *Fort Gratiot Landfill v. Michigan Dep't of Natural Resources*, 504 U.S. 353 (1992); *Philadelphia v. New Jersey*.

can survive a commerce clause analysis is its trade restrictiveness, rather than the potentially protectionist motivations behind its adoption.

Very similar language to the one used by the Supreme Court in the majority opinion delivered in its 1970 landmark decision in *Pike v. Bruce Church* can be found in the *Guiding Principles Concerning the Economic Aspects of Environmental Policy* adopted by the Council of the Organization for Economic Cooperation and Development (OECD) on May 26, 1972:

> Measures taken to protect the environment should be framed as far as possible in such a manner as to avoid the creation of non-tariff barriers to trade ... In conformity with the provisions of the GATT, measures taken within an environmental policy should be applied in accordance with the principle of national treatment and with the principle of non-discrimination.[213]

Similarly, the Action Plan adopted in Stockholm in the very same year clarified that environmental concerns should not be used as a pretext or as an excuse to violate the trade rules agreed on in Havana: according to Recommendation 103, for instance, "it is recommended that Governments take the necessary steps to ensure: (a) That all States participating in the Conference agree not to invoke environmental concerns as a pretext for discriminatory trade policies or for reduced access to markets ..."[214]

Along the same lines, both 1990s *Tuna/Dolphin* panels gave significant weight in their decisions to the fact that permitting the challenged US measure would in their view radically jeopardize the Parties' rights under the GATT, which would "no longer constitute a multilateral framework for trade among all contracting parties but would provide legal security only in respect of

---

213 The extract continues: "[environmental policies] should not be accompanied by subsidies that would create significant distortions in international trade and investment ... Governments should seek harmonization of environmental policies ... to avoid the unjustified disruption of international trade patterns and of the international allocation of resources which may arise from diversity of national environmental standards ..." Taken from Maurice F. Strong, Address as the Southwestern Economic Association Meetings, Dallas: Economic Development and International Response to Environmental Decay (Mar. 23, 1973) (on file with the Environmental Science and Public Policy Archives at Harvard University, Maurice F. Strong Papers, Box 28[287]).

214 Stockholm Action Plan, Recommendation 103(a). See also the remaining text of Recommendation 103 and 104.

trade between a limited number of contracting parties with identical internal regulation."[215]

3.2 *A 'Narrowly Defined' Exception*[216]

Considering that the goal of the GATT was equated with trade liberalization which, in the neoliberal thought, required by its nature the removal of government interventions, and mindful of the risk that broadening GATT exceptions might undermine this goal, GATT panels have consistently ruled that exceptions should be narrowly construed.[217]

This narrow approach can be explained by looking at who sat on these ad-hoc panels and whom they answered to. The *Understanding on Dispute Settlement* specifies that "in order to facilitate the constitution of panels, the Director-General should maintain an informal indicative list of governmental and non-governmental persons *qualified in the fields of trade relations, economic development, and other matters covered by the General Agreement.*"[218] As a result, panels ended up being composed of individuals with an expertise in trade and economic matters, and with at least some knowledge of the GATT and, because use of governmental panelists was generally preferred,[219] panels tended to "inevitably consist of government officials in the trade area."[220] In other words, panels were "made up of various members of the insider network ... closely associated with the GATT 'community',"[221] had the support of the GATT bureaucracy and were, to a certain extent, controlled by it.

In *Tuna/Dolphin,* the panel observed that "Article XX provides for an exception to obligations under the General Agreement [and that] the long-standing practice of panels has accordingly been to interpret this provision narrowly, in a manner that preserves the basic objectives and principles of the General Agreement."[222] This approach reaffirmed an interpretation that was already

---

215 Report of the GATT Panel, *US—Tuna I,* para. 5.27. See also Report of the GATT Panel, *United States—Restrictions on Imports of Tuna,* DS29/R (June 16, 1994) [hereinafter *US—Tuna II*], para. 5.26.

216 This is how the GATT Secretariat described Article XX in its 1992 Report on *Trade and the Environment,* 8.

217 See Jackson, 'Greening the GATT'(n 108) 46.

218 Understanding Regarding Notification, Consultation, Dispute Settlement and Surveillance, GATT B.I.S.D. 200 (26th Supp.) para. 13 (1980) (emphasis added).

219 Decision on Dispute Settlement Procedures, GATT B.I.S.D. (31st Supp.) at 9–10 (1984).

220 William J. Davey, 'Dispute Settlement in GATT' (1987) 11(1) *Fordham International Law Journal* 52, 88–9.

221 Howse, 'The World Trade Organization 20 Years On'(n 189) 15.

222 Report of the GATT Panel, *US—Tuna I,* at 5.22. For later statements of this same principle, see Panel Report, *US—Shrimps,* WT/DS58/R (May 15, 1998), paras 7.36 and 7.37; and

strict by virtue of the very nature of these clauses—after all, they had been framed as exceptions *stricto sensu*. In fact, the Panel's decision to interpret Article XX narrowly in this landmark case was consistent not only with prior GATT decisions[223] and with the legislative history of the Agreement, but also with the pronouncements of other international courts, all following the Latin maxim *exceptio est strictissimae applicationis*.[224] In its dissenting opinion in the *North Sea* case in relation to Article 6 of the 1958 Continental Shelf Convention, for instance, Judge Tanaka suggested that the "special circumstances" clause, because of its exceptional nature, should have been subject to a strict interpretation.[225] Likewise, in *Qatar v. Bahrain*, the International Court of Justice observed that "the method of straight baselines, which is an exception to the normal rules for the determination of baselines ... must be applied restrictively."[226] Similar pronouncements have been made by arbitral tribunals as well as by the European Court of Justice (ECJ).[227] The latter, in particular

Appellate Body Report, *United States—Measure Affecting Imports of Woven Wool Shirts and Blouses from India*, WT/DS33/AB/R (April 25, 1997) [hereinafter *US—Shirts and Blouses*], 16 ("Articles XX and XI:1(2)(c)(i) are limited exceptions from obligations under certain other provisions of the GATT 1994, not positive rules establishing obligations in themselves").

223 See Report of the GATT Panel, *United States—Section 337 of the Tariff Act of 1930*, B.I.S.D. 36S/345, 385 (Nov. 7, 1989) [hereinafter *US—Section 337*], para. 5.9. ("Article XX(d) thus provides for a limited and conditional exception from obligations under other provisions"). See Hurlock, 'Note' (n 88) 2127.

224 The authoritative source governing treaties' interpretation, the Vienna Convention on the Law of Treaties (VCLT), does not contain any explicit rules regarding the interpretation of exceptions. The principle that exceptions should be interpreted restrictively has been drawn from the domestic practice of interpreting exceptions in statutes, as well as from the Latin maxim *exceptio est strictissimae applicationis* which is part of general international law and is consistently referred to by international tribunals. Vienna Convention on the Law of Treaties, May 23, 1969, 1155 U.N.T.S. 331 [hereinafter VCLT]. See Jorge E. Viñuales, 'Seven Ways of Escaping a Rule: Of Exceptions and Their Avatars in International Law', in Lorand Bartels and Federica Paddeu (eds.), *Exceptions and Defences in International Law* (Oxford University Press, 2020).

225 North Sea Continental Shelf (Ger. v. Den.), 1969 I.C.J. 3 (Feb. 1969) (dissenting opinion of Judge Tanaka, at 186).

226 Maritime Delimitation and Territorial Questions Between Qatar and Bahrain (Qatar v. Bahr.) Merits 2001 I.C.J. 40 (Mar. 2001).

227 NAFTA Arbitral Panel Established Pursuant to Chapter Twenty: In the Matter of Cross-Border Trucking Services (Secretariat File no. USA-MEX-98–2008–01) [in this case, however, the reference to the principle *exceptio est strictissimae applicationis* was made with respect to a reservation, and not an exception]. See Asif H. Qureshi, *Interpreting WTO Agreements. Problems and Perspectives* (Cambridge University Press, 2006), p. 105. Case C-169/00, Commission of the European Communities v. Republic of Finland, 2002 E.C.R. I-02433.

has made clear, in a consistent line of case law, that Article 36 must be strictly interpreted.[228]

The individual requirements of paragraphs (b) and (g) have equally been narrowly construed by the panels, who justified the restrictive interpretation of paragraph (b) by relying on its drafting history. The delegates had all agreed that the stipulation "to protect animal or plant life or health" could be misused for indirect protection,[229] and it is clear from the record of the discussions that the "Commission [was] against any possibility of this provision being used as a measure of protection in disguise."[230]

Just like it happened for the *chapeau*, the restrictive and narrow interpretation given to Article XX(b) and (g) as soon as the first disputes arose, did not reflect the original intent of the Drafting Commission and were not motivated by fear of protectionism but rather by the hostility towards all forms of government intervention which might have affected international trade. Once again, the importance of the distinction between legitimate domestic regulation and regulation with protectionist motives disappeared and the only relevant standard to evaluate such measures was the extent of their impact on trade flows. As a result, the word 'necessary' was initially interpreted as the 'least restrictive alternative':[231] in the words of John Jackson, "if there are two or more alternatives that a government could use to protect human life or health, it is not 'necessary' to choose the one that places more restrictions on trade, when an alternative that is equally efficient in protecting human life or health exists."[232]

228 See e.g., Case C-229/83, Leclerq, 1985, E.C.R. 1, 35; Case C-95/81, Commission v. Italy, 1982, E.C.R. 2,187, 2,204; Case C-113/80, Commission v. Ireland, 1981, E.C.R. 1,625,1,638; Case C-13/68, Salgoil, 1968, E.C.R. 453, 463; Case C-7/68, Commission v. Italy, 1968, E.C.R. 423, 431.

229 E/PC/T/C.II/32 and E/PC/T/C.II/50.

230 GATT, *Analytical Index: Notes on the drafting, interpretation and application of the Articles of the General Agreement*, (3rd edition, 1970), 116. E/PC/T/A/PV/30.

231 Throughout the years, the interpretation of the 'necessity test' under Article XX(b) has become less stringent, see later Chapter 4.

232 Jackson, 'World Trade Rules and Environmental Policies' (n 12) 1240. Report of the GATT Panel, *Thailand—Restrictions on Importation of and Internal Taxes on Cigarettes*, DS10/R-37S/91 (Nov. 7, 1990) [hereinafter *Thailand—Cigarettes*], para. 75 ("The panel concluded that the import restrictions imposed by Thailand could be considered 'necessary' ... only if there were no alternative measure consistent with the General Agreement, or less inconsistent with it, which Thailand could reasonably be expected to employ to achieve its health policy objectives"). The panel refers to the report in *US—Section 337*, which referred "to XX(d), but they are considered to have the same objective: to allow contracting parties to impose trade restrictive measures inconsistent with the General Agreement to pursue overriding public policy goals to the extent that such inconsistencies are unavoidable." See Report of the GATT Panel, *US—Section 337*, para. 5.26. For a later decision, see Panel Report, *US—Gasoline*, para. 6.24.

The underlying idea, stressed by several panels, was that "this paragraph of Article XX was intended to allow contracting parties to impose trade restrictive measures inconsistent with the General Agreement to pursue overriding public policy goals *to the extent that such inconsistencies were unavoidable.*"[233] The same interpretation was given to the exception clause contained in Article 36 of the EEC Treaty. The ECJ in the *Danish Bottles* case clarified that "if a member-State has a choice between various measures to achieve the same objective, it should choose the means which least restrict the free movement of goods."[234]

Moreover, the panel in the *Tuna/Dolphin* decision repeated the GATT Secretariat's dislike for unilateralism[235]—a dislike for which, once again, no trace can be found in the discussions and intentions of the GATT founders:

> The Panel considered that if the broad interpretation of Article XX(b) suggested by the United States were accepted, each contracting party could *unilaterally* determine the life or health protection policies from which other contracting parties could not deviate without jeopardizing their rights under the General Agreement. The General Agreement would then no longer constitute a multilateral framework for trade among all contracting parties but would provide legal security only in respect of trade between a limited number of contracting parties with identical internal regulations.[236]

This approach does not take into account, however, that, from an environmental standpoint, unilateralism can sometimes be good. Although multilateral action is preferable, consensus is often difficult to achieve, and faced with the choice between waiting for multilateral action and doing nothing or

---

233 Report of the GATT Panel, *US—Tuna I*, para. 5.27 (emphasis added). See also Report of the GATT Panel, *Thailand—Cigarettes*, paras 73–4.

234 Case C-302/86, Commission v. Denmark, 1988 E.C.R. 4607. See Philippe Sands, 'Danish Bottles and Mexican Tuna' (1992) 1(1) *RECIEL* 28, 29.

235 See the 1992 GATT Secretariat's report on *Trade and the Environment* which, as pointed out by Charnovitz, mentions the word 'unilateral' 25 times in a 35-page document, never in a favorable light. Steve Charnovitz, 'GATT and the Environment. Examining the Issues' (1992) 4(3) *International Environmental Affairs* 203 (1992). See also a Resolution adopted by the United Nations Conference in Trade and Development (UNCTAD) in 1992 and the Rio Declaration, Principle 12. UNCTAD, *A New Partnership for Development: The Cartagena Commitment*, February 1992, para. 152; United Nations Conference on Environment and Development, Rio de Janeiro, Brazil, June 3–14, 1992, *Rio Declaration on Environment and Development*, U.N. Doc. A/CONF.151/26/Rev.1 (Vol. I), Annex I (Aug. 12, 1992) [hereinafter Rio Declaration], Principle 12.

236 Report of the GATT Panel, *US—Tuna I*, para. 5.27 (emphasis added).

acting unilaterally, from an environmental perspective, the latter is a much better option. Not only has there been, for more than a hundred years, a fruitful interplay between unilateral environmental actions and the negotiation of multilateral environmental treaties,[237] but unilateralism is also good for the environment because it allows individual countries to set their own ecological goals and standards.[238]

Finally, the panel clarified that the application of the exception was limited to domestic restrictions and could not be used to justify measures of extraterritorial nature, and reached this conclusion by analyzing the legislative history of the provisions which, according to the panel, indicated that "the concerns of the drafters ... focused on the use of sanitary measures ... *within the jurisdiction of the importing country*."[239] However, as pointed out by Charnovitz, this reading presented by the panel is incomplete, as it does not take into account "either the historical context of the 'life and health' exception in trade treaties, or the laws that might have motivated such an exception."[240] The reluctance to accept an extrajurisdictional application of Article XX(b) was, at least in part, motivated by the fear that environmental trade measures would be used to influence other countries. But, because virtually each and every environmental regulation or standard can influence foreign exporters, this reading of the provisions leaves very little room for environmental policy-making and standard-setting. Even more if one considers that the distinction between a nation's environment and the rest of the world's—as the one made by the panel in *Tuna/Dolphin*—is unhelpful when dealing with global environmental resources or migratory species: "if no country is permitted to take extrajurisdictional action, then much of our biosphere would be unreachable by environmental trade measures."[241]

The rejection of extrajurisdictionality is not limited to paragraph (b) of Article XX but extends, for the very same reasons, to paragraph (g) as well.[242]

237 For example, the US ban of 1897 on fur seal imports led to the adoption of the *North Pacific Fur Seals Convention* of 1911, while the US ban of 1969 on the importation of endangered species spurred the negotiation of the *Convention on International Trade in Endangered Species of Wild Fauna and Flora* of 1973. See Charnovitz, 'GATT and the Environment' (n 235).

238 Setting their own standards for internal and external commerce had been criticized, in particular by developing and least developed countries, as 'eco-imperialism', 'gunboat environmentalism' or 'green vigilantism.' See e.g. Gijs M. d Vries, 'How to Banish Eco-Imperialism' (Apr. 30, 1992) *Journal of Commerce* 8A.

239 Report of the GATT Panel, *US—Tuna I*, para. 5.26 (emphasis added).

240 Charnovitz, 'GATT and the Environment' (n 235).

241 Ibid.

242 Report of the GATT Panel, *US—Tuna I*, para. 5.32.

What is different between the two paragraphs is the strength of the link required between the measure at stake and the policy purpose set out in the provision. Unlike paragraph (b), the letter (g) does not require the measure at stake to be 'necessary' to the conservation of exhaustible natural resources. Rather, it suffices that the measure be 'relating to' the achievement of such an objective. As noted by the panel in *Canada—Salmon and Herring*, "this suggests that Article XX(g) does not only cover measures that are necessary or essential for the conservation of exhaustible natural resources but a wider range of measures."[243] Nevertheless, a significant link between the measure and the policy objective was initially required, and the term 'relating to' has accordingly been interpreted as the measure being 'primarily aimed at' the conservation of exhaustible natural resources.[244] Although broader than (b), the panel has been very clear in stating that Article XX(g) should not be interpreted so expansively as to subvert the object of the Agreement, but merely to make sure that countries do have the possibility to adopt measures to protect natural resources.[245]

The result is that Article XX, a provision that on paper could have represented a safe harbor for many important environmental initiatives, turned out to be anything but safe. While Article XX was the result of a 'compromise' reached by the GATT negotiators between multilateralism and domestic interventionism, and was designed precisely to allow countries to pursue domestic policy objectives, as long as they were legitimate and not protectionism in disguise, the advent of neoliberalism swept away this distinction, transforming the clause into a shield against any trade restrictive or distortive measure. In fact, limiting the application of the exception by placing strict requirements on the term 'necessary' and 'relating to'—in addition to the requirements of the *chapeau*—have significantly diminished the ability of the provision to reconcile environmental and economic goals.[246] What is more, because these increasingly stringent tests have been established by panels on an *ad hoc* basis, they have created an environment of unpredictability, where national

243 Report of the GATT Panel, *Canada—Measures Affecting Exports of Unprocessed Herring and Salmon*, L/6268-35S/98 (Mar. 22, 1988) [hereinafter *Canada—Herring and Salmon*], para. 4.6.

244 Ibid.

245 Panel Report, *US—Gasoline*, paras 6.38-6.41. The Appellate Body, instead, also stated that "Nor may Article III:4 be given so broad a reach as effectively to emasculate Article XX(g) and the policies and interests it embodies." Appellate Body Report, *US—Gasoline*, WT/DS2/AB/R (Apr. 29, 1996), 18.

246 Housman and Zaelke, 'Trade, Environment, and Sustainable Development' (n 12) 535.

authorities may not know whether, at any given time, their environmental policies conform with the GATT or not.[247]

3.3 *Who Bears the Risk of Non-Persuasion?*

> The United States had not demonstrated to the Panel—as required of the party invoking an Article XX exception—that it had exhausted all options reasonably available to it to pursue its dolphin protection objectives through measures consistent with the General Agreement.[248]
>
> Report of the Panel, US –Tuna, 1991

In ruling against the United States, the *Tuna/Dolphin* panel found that the respondent had not successfully discharged its burden of proof under Article XX. With these words, the panel emphasized a rule that had been applied consistently by international courts and tribunals with respect to the allocation of the burden of proof: "the burden of proof rests upon the party, whether complaining or defending, who asserts the affirmative of a particular claim or defense."[249]

In the allocation of the burden of proof, the general rule is the rule *actori incumbit probatio*, according to which "the party who asserts a fact ... is responsible for providing proof thereof."[250] Accordingly, the party claiming the breach of a GATT substantive provision bears the burden of proving that such breach took place.[251] On the other hand, the respondent who invokes an exception to the general rule carries the burden of demonstrating the compliance with

247 Charnovitz, 'GATT and the Environment' (n 235).

248 Report of the GATT Panel, *US—Tuna I*, para. 5.28.

249 Appellate Body Report, *US—Shirts and Blouses*, at 14. See Henrik Horn and Petros C. Mavroidis, 'Burden of Proof in Environmental Disputes in the WTO: Legal Aspects' (2009) Research Institute for Industrial Economics, IFN Working Paper No. 793, 11. See also Report of the GATT Panel, *Canada—Administration of the Foreign Investment Review Act*, BISD 30S/140 (Feb. 7, 1984) [hereinafter *Canada—FIRA*], para. 5.20; ("Since Article XX(d) is an exception to the General Agreement it is up to Canada, as the party invoking the exception, to demonstrate that the purchase undertakings are necessary to secure compliance with the Foreign Investment Review Act."); and Report of the GATT Panel, *US—Section 337*, para. 5.27. ("it is up to the contracting party seeking to justify measures under Article XX(d) to demonstrate that those measures are 'necessary' within the meaning of that provision").

250 Mojtaba Kazazi, *Burden of Proof and Related Issues: A Study of Evidence Before International Tribunals* (Martinus Nijhoff Publishers, 1996), p. 117.

251 Panel Report, *Japan—Taxes on Alcoholic Beverages*, WT/DS8/R (July 11, 1996) [Addressing the claim under Article II:2, first and second sentence, the panel found that "complainants have the burden of proof to show ... that products are like and ... that foreign products are taxed in excess of domestic ones" with reference to the former, and that "the products concerned are directly competitive or substitutable and that foreign products

the conditions reflected in the exception (*quicumque exceptio invocat eiudem probare debet*).[252]

It should be clarified that the term 'burden of proof' is here used to refer to the 'burden of persuasion'. The burden of proof, broadly speaking, can be broken down in different duties or burdens: the 'burden of raising', which refers to the duty to raise a specific claim, the 'burden of production', meaning the duty to produce evidence, and the 'burden of persuasion', which is the burden of proving or disproving a claim and ultimately convince the trier. While the burden of production rests on both parties, as they share the duty to cooperate in the fact-finding process, the burden of persuasion follows the two rules mentioned above.[253]

The allocation of the burden of proof is particularly important and controversial in trade disputes for a number of reasons.[254] First, the content of many WTO obligations is not entirely clear, and the parties may not know what degree of proof is required for the burden of proof to be successfully discharged (and the same applies to free trade agreements, which often borrow the language of their multilateral counterparts). Second, if defining the allocation of the burden of proof and, in particular, of persuasion, does not necessarily affect the

---

are taxed in such a way so as to afford protection to domestic production." Paras 6.14 and 6.28]. Appellate Body Report, *US—Shirts and Blouses*, 14–16.

252 The GATT panels have stressed this rule in several cases with specific reference to GATT Article XX and the Appellate Body has later extended this interpretation to other provisions deemed to constitute "affirmative defences," besides Article XX. See Report of the GATT Panel, *Canada—FIRA*, para. 5.20. See also Report of the GATT Panel, *US—Section 337*, para. 5.27 and *United States—Measures Affecting Alcoholic and Malt Beverages*, BISD 39S/206 (June 19, 1992), paras 5.41 and 5.52. Later, the Appellate Body continued on this track: see Appellate Body Report, *Thailand—Customs and Fiscal Measures on Cigarettes from the Philippines*, WT/DS371/AB/R (June 17, 2011), para. 176; Appellate Body Report, *Korea—Measures Affecting Imports of Fresh, Chilled and Frozen Beef*, WT/DS161/AB/R (Dec. 11, 2000), para. 157. Appellate Body Report, *US—Shirts and Blouses*, at 14–16; Appellate Body Report, *US –Gasoline*, at 22–3. See also Appellate Body Report, *United States—Measures Affecting the Cross-Border Supply of Gambling and Betting Services*, WT/DS285/AB/R (Apr. 7, 2005), para. 309 [with regard to GATS Article XIV(a)]. Appellate Body Report, *United States—Tax Treatment for 'Foreign Sales Corporations'—Recourse to Article 21.5 of the DSU by the European Communities*, WT/DS108/SB/RW (Jan. 14, 2002), para. 133 [with regard to footnote 59 of the ASCM].

253 See e.g. Joost Pauwelyn, 'Defenses and the Burden of Proof in International Law', in Bartles and Paddeu (eds.), *Exceptions and Defences in International Law* (n 224).

254 The subject of the burden of proof in WTO disputes has been taken up and addressed in a comprehensive manner in Michelle T. Grando, *Evidence, Proof, and Fact-Finding in WTO Dispute Settlement* (Oxford University Press, 2009). See also Joost Pauwelyn, 'Evidence, proof and Persuasion in WTO Dispute Settlement. Who Bears the Burden?' (1998) 1 *Journal of International Economic Law* 227 and, more generally, Kazazi, *Burden of Proof* (n 250).

outcome of a dispute whenever there are strong grounds to rule in favor of one party or the other, the allocation of the burden of proof becomes a crucial question when the evidence is not sufficient or the arguments are in equipoise.

In those cases, the panel will have to find against the party bearing the burden of proof. Because exception clauses represent the only 'window' that countries can use to introduce environmental values, the burden will constantly fall on the party defending the adoption of trade-restrictive environmental measures and the actual chances of successfully justifying them under Article XX become quite scarce. And as a matter of fact, in several GATT environmental cases (although this issue is of course not limited to the use of Article XX for environmental purposes), the inability of the respondent to successfully discharge its burden of persuasion contributed to the ultimate outcome of the decision. In one of the first cases brought by Canada against the United States, for instance, it was precisely because "the United States representative had provided no evidence that consumption of tuna and tuna products had been restricted in the United States," which constituted one of the requirements of GATT Article XX(g)—that the measure at stake be made effective in conjunction with restrictions on domestic production or consumption—that the US prohibition of Canadian tuna could not be justified under the exception clause.[255]

If we combine this procedural requirement with the narrow interpretation reserved to exceptions, the respondent's chances to successfully justify an environmental measure under Article XX become quite scarce. And even scarcer if one pauses to look at the individuals who sat on these panels and what their mandate was.

3.4 *Judges with Limited Mandate and Expertise*

When, among the protests and uprising following the *Tuna/Dolphin* decision, environmentalists decried the obscure international trade tribunal with no environmental sensitivity or expertise that was challenging and overriding environmental laws and regulations, they were not too far from the truth.

Under the GATT, when the parties were unable to settle their differences through consultation or mediation, the resolution of disputes was governed by Article XXIII of the Agreement which, rather than establishing any formal procedures for handling such disputes, simply offered a broad outline of the overall process. Since the early 1950s, the use of panels had become the standard

---

255 Report of the GATT Panel, *United States—Prohibition of Imports of Tuna and Tuna Products from Canada*, L/5198—29S/91 (Feb. 22, 1982) [hereinafter *US—Canadian Tuna*], paras 4.11 and 4.12. See also Report of the GATT Panel, *US—Tuna I*, para. 5.28.

practice:[256] "following the inability of two contracting parties to resolve a dispute through consultations and negotiations, the aggrieved party may request the appointment of a panel to adjudicate the dispute."[257] The panel, generally composed of three or five members, was appointed by the Director General, received the written submissions of the parties and, following the parties' comments to an interim draft, submitted its final report to the GATT council.

Trade disputes that presented an environmental component would require the members of the panel to weigh the merits of competing trade and environmental claims. Such weighing would involve understanding the scientific evidence presented, as well as the societal dimension that tends to characterize environmental disputes.[258] However, such a balancing act of environmental, economic, and other concerns encountered several obstacles along the way.

First, when interpreting and applying GATT rules, the members of the panels established under the GATT lacked the mandate to rely on environmental provisions or principles. To the contrary, the measures at stake in each dispute could be examined *solely* "in the light of the relevant GATT provisions,"[259] as clarified in the *Understanding on Dispute Settlement* adopted at the end of the Tokyo Round, intended to summarize the dispute settlement procedures that had traditionally been used in GATT and which would continue to be used in the future.[260] Accordingly, in *Canada—Salmon and Herring*, the panel refused to take into account certain provisions of the United Nations Convention on

---

256 During the first few years of the GATT, up until 1952, disputes were generally considered by working parties, consisting of the contending nations and several other GATT members.

257 Davey, 'Dispute Settlement in GATT' (n 220) 58.

258 US Congress, Office of Technology Assessment, *Trade and Environment: Conflicts and Opportunities* (US Government Printing Office, May 1992), 77. In 1993, Jeffrey Dunoff argued that "trade-environment conflicts should be heard before an institution that recognizes the interdependent nature of global economic and environmental issues and that has a mandate to advance *both* economic development and environmental protection. This body should have ready access to the scientific and technical expertise that would enable it to resolve trade-environment disputes knowledgeably." Jeffrey L. Dunoff, 'Institutional Misfits: The GATT, the ICJ & Trade-Environment Disputes' (1993) 15 *Michigan Journal of International Law* 1043, 1046.

259 GATT, *Understanding Regarding Notification, Consultation, Dispute Settlement and Surveillance*, 207–8. See Report of the GATT Panel, *US—Canadian Tuna*, para. 4.1; Report of the GATT Panel, *United States—Imports of Sugar from Nicaragua*, L/5607-31S/67 (Mar. 13, 1984) [hereinafter *US—Sugar Quota*], para. 4.1; Report of the Panel, *United States—Trade Measures Affecting Nicaragua*, L/6053 (Oct. 13, 1986), para. 5.15; Report of the Panel, *Canada—Herring and Salmon*, para. 5.3; Report of the Panel, *Thailand—Cigarettes*, para. 2.

260 Davey, 'Dispute Settlement in GATT' (n 220) 58.

the Law of the Sea (UNCLOS) and certain fisheries agreements in its examination of Canada's prohibition of export of unprocessed herring and pink and sockeye salmon.[261] In an earlier decision—US—*Trade Measures Affecting Nicaragua*—the panel, while agreeing with Nicaragua that the GATT could not operate in a vacuum and that GATT provisions had to be interpreted within the context of the general principles of international law, nevertheless considered it to be outside its mandate to address certain non-trade questions because its task was to examine the case before it "in the light of the relevant GATT provisions," although they might be inadequate and incomplete for the purpose.[262] Because trade agreements, as mentioned above, did not feature any environmental rules, it follows that, whenever a dispute arose, it was decided almost solely based on standards developed and applied by trade experts, on the basis of free trade principles.

Moreover, as demonstrated earlier by describing the background of these judges, they generally lacked the required environmental expertise. There was, at least in theory, a way to compensate for this lack of expertise: the *Understanding on Dispute Settlement* explains that "each panel should have the right to seek information and technical advice from any individual or body which it deems appropriate."[263] This provision, although it does recognize the panel's right to consult external experts, does not contain any obligation to do so: it is ultimately a prerogative of the panelists to decide whether such external input is necessary for the resolution of the dispute at hand, and in none of the environmental disputes raised before the establishment of the WTO in 1995, did the panel deem fit to make use of this possibility.[264]

261 Report of the GATT Panel, *Canada—Herring and Salmon,* para. 3.

262 Report of the GATT Panel, *US—Sugar Quota,* para. 5.15.

263 GATT, *Understanding Regarding Notification, Consultation, Dispute Settlement and Surveillance* (n 259) para. 15.

264 The only exception being the *Thailand—Cigarettes* dispute which, however, dealt with a health rather than an environmental measure. In this case, the Panel requested the expert opinion of the World Health Organization (WHO) and relied on its factual determinations throughout the whole report. Here it had been inserted in the Memorandum of Understanding of the Parties that if one of them did ask to consult a competent international organization, the Panel should have proceeded accordingly, and Thailand did ask. Report of the GATT Panel, *Thailand—Cigarettes,* at 73: "In agreement with the parties to the dispute and the expert from the WHO, the Panel accepted that smoking constituted a serious risk to human health and that consequently measures designed to reduce the consumption of cigarettes fell within the scope of Article XX(b)." See Joost Pauwelyn, 'The Use of Experts in WTO Dispute Settlement' (2002) 51(2) *International & Comparative Law Quarterly* 325.

One last limit of the system lay in it being a 'black box', where only the parties to the GATT could participate in the proceedings—those involved in the dispute and any other contracting party having a substantial interest in the matter after having notified the Council.[265] Nongovernmental organizations or other private entities, on the other hand, were not allowed to participate in the GATT dispute resolution process as amici curiae, witnesses, or even observers.[266] However, given the significant involvement of scientific data in environmental disputes, allowing access to environmental NGOs would have increased the information available to the panel, allowing its members to adopt better informed—and more balanced—decisions, and it would have enhanced the legitimacy of the final judgment.[267] In neglecting the role of these organizations, the GATT seems to not only part from the practice shared by the vast majority of international organizations, which largely draw on the expertise of NGOs in their work, but to even forget the original intentions of the Havana negotiators: the Havana Charter itself, which was supposed to establish the International Trade Organization (ITO), provided that the Organization "may make suitable arrangements for consultation and co-operation with nongovernmental organizations concerned with matters within the scope of this Charter."[268]

3.5 *Trade Liberalization First*

What this chapter has described are the concurring circumstances that have led to the adoption of a trade-centered approach to the trade/environment nexus: an approach where economic growth through trade liberalization represents the primary goal of trade agreements, and trade rules simply proscribe government actions that could disrupt the free flow of commerce. Environmental protection is mostly seen as a potential obstacle to smooth

---

265 GATT, *Understanding Regarding Notification, Consultation, Dispute Settlement and Surveillance* (n 259) para 15, and Annex at iv.

266 See Steve Charnovitz, 'Participation of Nongovernmental Organizations in the World Trade Organization' (1996) 17(1) *University of Pennsylvania Journal of International Economic Law* 331, 348–356; David Wirth, 'Reexamining Decision-Making Processes in International Environmental Law' (1994) 79 *Iowa Law Review* 769, 786–7.

267 Charnovitz, 'Participation of Nongovernmental Organizations' (n 266) 351. Without forgetting that it would also increase the legitimacy of the GATT. See Kevin Stairs and Peter Taylor, 'Non-Governmental Organizations and the Legal Protection of the Oceans: A Case Study', in Andrew Hurrell and Benedict Kingsbury (eds.), *The International Politics of the Environment* (1992), p. 134; Pauwelyn, 'The Use of Experts' (n 264) 330.

268 Havana Charter for an International Trade Organization, 1948, U.N. Doc. E/CONF.2/78, Art. 87(2).

trade flows and, as a result, enters trade agreements through narrow exceptions, interpreted and applied by panels who lack any environmental expertise and whose rules and procedures are criticized for being biased towards trade values. Following this approach, environmental standards are addressed only to the extent that they are 'too high' while no mechanism exists to address standards that would qualify as 'too low'. Where the legitimacy of environmental regulations depends solely on what is produced, rather than how it is produced, the environmental footprint of processes and production methods is not taken into account in the substantive provisions of the agreements.

As time went by, environmental and trade values came to clash against each other increasingly frequently, as evidenced by the GATT dispute settlement system being used "more frequently for the settlement of 'environmental disputes' between states than any other international dispute settlement mechanism,"[269] although it was never intended to play this role. Soon, the two communities could not live in isolation any longer, and initiating a constructive dialogue between them became imperative. It was time to address the elephant in the room: countries were increasingly adopting trade measures to protect the environment and more and more environmental agreements started featuring provisions that legitimized them. It was time to find ways for free trade and environmental protection to peacefully coexist, rather than being an 'irreconcilable conflict.'

269 Petersmann, 'International Trade Law and International Environmental Law' (n 12) 53.

CHAPTER 4

The Evolution of the Nexus

The Quest for Balance

On March 15, 1999, Sir Leon Brittan, then Vice President of the European Commission, addressed his audience at the World Trade Organization (WTO) High Level Symposium on Trade and Environment by emphasizing the "need to reconcile the competing demands of economic growth, environmental protection and social development." He then added that "[p]ursuing any one of these three at the expense of the other two [would] inevitably lead to an unbalanced approach."[1] Indeed, Sir Brittan had been one of the most vocal advocates of the importance of pushing the trade and environment debate forward and, just one year prior, had come up with the idea for the symposium as a perfect way to bring together top-level policymakers in both fields. The ideas exposed in his speech—the acknowledgment that both trade and environmental law pursue valuable goals and the need to pursue such goals in a mutually supportive manner—were not new. If anything, his words reflected a sentiment that had been floating around for more than a decade and that found its roots in the report prepared in 1987 by the Brundtland Commission, *Our Common Future*.[2] The *Brundtland Report*, as it is commonly known, introduced the world to the notion of 'sustainable development', which was intended to serve as a frame of reference to avoid or minimize frictions between the two regimes, and as a common language, able of being understood by both free traders and environmentalists.[3]

The 'dialogue of the deaf' that had characterized the previous decades suddenly seemed to be over, as both communities acknowledged the need to balance free trade and environmental protection as two sometimes conflicting, yet complementary, values. Accordingly, the trade regime began increasing the space provided to allow countries to protect the environment, while the international environmental regime came to terms with the idea of balancing the

---

1 Sir Leon Brittan QC, Address at the WTO High Level Symposium on Trade and the Environment, Geneva, Mar. 15, 1999.

2 World Commission on Environment and Development, *Our Common Future* (Oxford University Press, 1987) [hereinafter Brundtland Report], Ch. 3, para. 2.4.

3 David Runnalls and Aaron Cosbey, 'Trade and Sustainable Development. A Survey of the Issues and A New Research Agenda' (1002) IISD Report, 12, 13.

environmental component of sustainable development with economic growth and social inclusion.

One scholar has described this as a "new era in the trade-environment debate," beginning in the mid-1990s, and fostered not only by the increasing attention given to the environment by trade negotiators, but also by an "enlightened" Appellate Body jurisprudence.[4] This "new era" was characterized by countless efforts to avoid or reduce potential and existing conflicts between trade and environmental rules, the core question being how to ensure that trade rules are not used to override environmental regulations, without, at the same time, allowing protectionist measures disguised as environmental policies. The "new era", while embodying a certain evolution of the nexus, has not however proceeded at the same pace at all levels. Within the newly established WTO, the larger and more diverse membership, as well as the increasing power of less developed countries within the Organization, allowed this evolution to proceed at a slower pace, largely limited to the 'enlightened' jurisprudence of the Appellate Body, which has been giving increasing weight to the environmental side of the equation when interpreting WTO provisions. On the other hand, the efforts of many industrialized countries, such as the United States (US) or the countries of the European Union (EU), were not similarly constrained, and it is in bilateral and regional contexts that negotiators have worked towards reducing potential conflicts by introducing environmental language directly in the text of trade agreements.

This is an evolution *à la carte*, as one could define it, and, more importantly, an evolution which, despite all the steps forward, keeps unfolding against the same backdrop we saw in the previous chapter: international trade law continues to provide the framework of reference and to represent the 'official language' of the debate, which ultimately boils down to whether the existing trade norms are adequate to strike a balance between trade liberalization and environmental protection. It should be no surprise then that even when more space is given to environmental values, "that space is always designed as exceptional. And the [neoliberal] narrative guarantees that such exceptions are seen with a skeptical eye."[5]

4 Steve Charnovitz, 'The WTO's Environmental Progress' (2007) 10(3) *Journal of International Economic Law* 685, 686.

5 Harlan Grant Cohen, 'What is International Trade Law For?' (2019) 113(2) *American Journal of International Law* 326, 331.

1 The Need for Balance

> [A] bad [trade] agreement is likely to be defined in Congress and the media as any agreement that doesn't have labor and environment in it.[6]
>
> US Ambassador ROBERT ZOELLICK, 1999

On October 4, 1992, Clinton gave a major speech on the North American Free Trade Agreement (NAFTA) at North Carolina State University where, while expressing his general support for the agreement, he also recognized its deficiencies.[7] In particular, he expressed concerns regarding environmental protection, labor relations, and safeguarding against import surges. Clinton's position was straightforward: he would not sign legislation implementing NAFTA until new "supplemental agreements" had been negotiated with Mexico and Canada regarding these issues.[8]

Candidate Clinton's speech reflected a change of perspective compared to the previous decades. In 1971, the Group on Environmental Measures and International Trade (EMIT Group) had prepared a document describing the negative impacts of pollution control measures on international trade flows, translating the dominant narrative of the time. Clinton's request for the supplemental environmental agreement conveyed two complementary new ideas: first, that the rapid expansion of trade could pose serious problems for the environment,[9] and second, that this undesirable outcome should be

---

6 Ambassador Robert Zoellick, US Trade Representative, quoted in Morton K. Kondracke, *Battles in Seattle Make Free Trade an Election Issue*, Roll. Call. (Dec. 9, 1999), 1999 WL 14666783.

7 Bill Clinton, 'Expanding Trade and Creating American Jobs', at North Carolina State University (Oct. 4, 1992) in (1993) 23 *Environmental Law* 683. See Candidate Bill Clinton's Proposal for Supplemental Agreements on NAFTA, in Rodney Dabell and Michael Henfeld (eds.), *Beyond NAFTA, The Western Hemisphere* 192 (Oolichan Books,1993).

8 See Steve Charnovitz, 'The NAFTA Environmental Side Agreement: Implications for Environmental Cooperation, Trade Policy, and American Treatymaking' (1994) 8 *Temple International & Comparative Law Journal* 257; Robert Housman, 'The North American Free Trade Agreement's Lessons for Reconciling Trade and the Environment' (1994) 30 *Stanford Journal of International Law* 379, 382.

9 David Runnalls, 'Trade Liberalization and Sustainable Development', Papers presented at the GATT Symposium on Trade, Environment and Sustainable Development, July 28, 1994, 19. Many of the papers presented at the GATT Symposium on Trade, Environment and Sustainable Development were prepared by environmental experts and they showed an environmental perspective of the trade/environment nexus. Jeffrey McNeely, of the International Union for the Conservation of Nature (IUCN), for example, argued that "the GATT Agreement ... has significant negative implications for biodiversity and could itself undermine the work initiated by the Earth Summit," stressing that IUCN shares the Rio Conference's concern for the lack of attention given to the environmental implication of international trade. Jeffrey A. McNeely, 'Trade and Biological Diversity: The

avoided at all costs. In other words, it conveyed the message that economic growth had to be sustainable.

The notion that growth and development ought to be sustainable, made 'popular' by the *Brundtland Report*, had its origin more than a decade prior, and more precisely in the thought and work of one of the greatest internationalists of the twentieth century, whose role behind the scenes at the Stockholm Conference is just one of her many contributions to modern society: Barbara "Lady Jackson" Ward.[10]

1.1 *Lady Jackson*

Barbara Ward, also known as "Lady Jackson" after her marriage to Sir Robert Jackson, was born on May 23, 1914 in York, England. Since her early school years, she proved to be a very serious student, and certainly a gifted one, showing great promise, which took her all the way to Oxford. There, she chose to enroll in the newly started School of Philosophy, Politics, and Economics, the very same School that James Meade had attended only a few years before.

It was at Oxford that she began her social activism, which she would carry on for her whole life.[11] In this, she was surely influenced by her father, who "was a man of very liberal opinions and brought [her] up as a Social Democrat" from a very early age.[12] During her college years, she was deeply affected by the massive unemployment of the 1930s, and since her very first book, which she published when she was only 24 years old, she became one of the most articulate and persuasive champions of the poor, making a compelling case for the rich to be more responsive to their needs.[13]

Her interest for the environment came later, during the 1960s, and found its first and most powerful expression in the Pegram Lectures she delivered at Columbia University, which were later published as *Spaceship Earth* in 1966.

Internalization of Environmental Costs', Papers presented at the GATT Symposium on Trade, Environment and Sustainable Development, July 28, 1994, 49, 51–2.

10 For a survey of different opinions regarding the origin of the term 'sustainable development', see Claire Brighton, 'Unlikely Bedfellows: The Evolution of the Relationship Between Environmental Protection and Development' (2017) 66 *International & Comparative Law Quarterly* 209, 222.

11 Jean Gartlan, *Barbara Ward: Her Life and Letters* (A&C Black, 2010), p. 3.

12 Interview with Mary Evelyn Jegen, SND, Rome, Sept. 17, 1973, as quoted in Gartlan, *Barbara Ward* (n 11) 3.

13 The book in question is *The International Share-Out*, published in 1938 and addressing the international tensions created among colonialist nations. Maurice Strong, 'Transcending Divisions: Work for the Stockholm Conference', in David Satterthwaite, *Barbara Ward and the Origins of Sustainable Development* (International Institute for Environment and Development, 2006), p. 14.

In this seminal book, she vocally argued that "our planet is not much more than the capsule within which we have to live as human beings ... We depend upon a little envelope of soil and a rather larger envelope of atmosphere for life itself. And both can be contaminated and destroyed."[14] Ten years later, she demanded from governments and international agencies a higher priority on meeting basic needs for water, sanitation, health and education in both rural and urban areas, and even set out the costs of doing so, thus anticipating the Millennium Development Goals (MDG s) by roughly 30 years.[15]

It was precisely because of her ability to think in terms of both environment and development, that Maurice Strong asked her to co-author with Renè Dubos *Only One Earth*, the volume that served as the scientific basis and conceptual framework for the Stockholm Conference: Strong knew from the very start that Barbara Ward would bring her concern for 'our fragile planet' and, at the same time, would never write a book that did not have poverty reduction and social justice at its core.[16] Her efforts and her vision were necessary to mediate between the diverging approaches and interests of Northern and Southern environmentalists, where the former "have typically adopted a technocratic approach to environmental protection, emphasizing global management of the environment based on scientific principles," neglecting the struggle for social and economic justice which characterized Southern environmentalism.[17]

As a result, *Only One Earth* can be seen as the first book on sustainable development, making it the task of the Stockholm Conference to "define what should be done to maintain the Earth as a place suitable for human life not only now, but also for future generations."[18] The term 'sustainable development' was then used in a report published by the International Institute for Environment and Development, titled *Banking on the Biosphere*, in 1979, when Barbara Ward was Director of the Institute. One year later, in the *1980 World Conservation Strategy*, the notion of sustainable development replaced that of ecodevelopment as the guiding principle.[19]

---

14 Barbara Ward, *Spaceship Earth* (Columbia University Press, 1966), p. 15.

15 Satterthwaite, *Barbara Ward* (n 13) 8.

16 Ibid., p. 11.

17 Carmen G. Gonzalez, 'Beyond Eco-Imperialism: An Environmental Justice Critique of Free Trade' (2001) 78(4) *Denver University Law Review* 981, 985–6.

18 Barbara Ward and René Dubos, *Only One Earth* (W.W. Norton & Company, 1972), p. 25.

19 Satterthwaite, *Barbara Ward* (n 13) 10. See Robert E. Stein and Brian D. G. Johnson, *Banking on the Biosphere* (Aero Publishing Ltd, 1979) and IUCN, UNEP, WWF, FAO, UNESCO *World Conservation Strategy: Living Resource Conservation for Sustainable Development* (1980).

1.2 *Same Game, New Rules*

The notion of sustainable development represented the cornerstone of the discussions that allowed an ad-hoc commission to prepare a second international environmental conference to be held in Rio de Janeiro in 1992. To head the commission, the United Nations (UN) Secretary General deliberately chose a political leader who had become Norway's Prime Minister after serving as the country's Minister of the Environment for several years (1974–79). The political leader in question was yet another woman who, just like Barbara Ward, understood the widespread feeling of frustration around the treatment of developing countries' concerns in Stockholm, while making sure that, at the same time, the environment would remain a central issue in both national and international decision-making.[20] The political leader in question was the woman who has traditionally been associated with the notion of sustainable development, Norway's Prime Minister at the time, Gro Harlem Brundtland.

Drawing on the past intellectual concepts of 'Spaceship Earth' and 'sustainable development', the report produced by the Brundtland Commission managed, for the very first time, to integrate economics with environmental protection, by showing "what conservation might mean for economic policy, [and] how misguided economic policy could degrade the environment."[21] By doing so, the introduction of this new overarching principle changed the rules of the game for both the trade and environmental regimes.

As to the former, this principle shifted the focus away from economic growth plain and simple. The term *development* reflects "some set of desirable goals or objectives for society"[22] which undoubtedly include *but are not limited to* economic growth—intended as a rising level of income per capita. It refers to a process of transformation which combines economic growth with broader social and cultural changes, to enable individuals to achieve a certain 'quality of life' and realize their full potential.[23] At the same time, "the dimension of *sustainability* brings the recognition that [growth and] development must ... adhere to the physical constraints imposed by ecosystems, so that environmental considerations have to be embedded in all sectors and policy areas."[24]

As a result, while the preamble to the General Agreement on Tariffs and Trade (GATT) identified as the core objective of the Agreement—and of the

20 Brundtland Report, pp. xi–x.

21 David Pearce et al., *Blueprint For A Green Economy* (Earthscan, 1990), p. xii.

22 Ibid., p. 1.

23 Neil Carter, *The Politics of the Environment: Ideas, Activism, Policy* (Cambridge University Press, 2018), p. 211.

24 Ibid., p. 212.

multilateral trading system at the time—raising standards of living, ensuring full employment and a large and steadily growing volume of real income and effective demand, the WTO, influenced by the *Report* and the emergence of this new paradigm, was asked to pursue the much broader objective of sustainable development, seeking both to protect and preserve the environment while doing so. Thus, the growth and development promoted by the trade regime would have to be sustainable, and trade rules themselves should not undermine domestic and international efforts towards securing the environmental pillar of sustainable development.

But the rules have not changed just for free traders. Environmentalists too found themselves facing a new reality. In Stockholm, the environment was the undeniable and unrivaled star. The emergence of sustainable development "shifted the debate from traditional environmentalism with its primary focus on environmental protection, to the notion of sustainability, which requires a much more complex process of trading off social, economic, and environmental priorities."[25] Many developing countries had expressed their concern, during the Stockholm Conference—and in particular in the meeting in Founex a few weeks before—that there was a risk that environmental protection measures could be used by industrialized powers to impose environmental conditionality on their development. Twenty years later, these concerns were finally addressed and the Brundtland definition of sustainable development was "as much concerned with economic and social development as it [was] with environmental protection."[26]

1.3 *Which Takes Precedence, Environment or Development?*

On April 2, 1992, Tommy Koh heaved a sigh of relief as he left a small boardroom on the 29th floor of the UN building in New York. Just a few days prior, acting as Chairman of the Preparatory Committee of the Rio Conference, Koh had gathered a small group of representative countries—seven industrialized and seven developing countries—to finalize the draft of what eventually became the *Rio Declaration on Environment and Development*.[27] The Preparatory Committee had met four times over the two years leading up to Rio, but it was not until the fourth meeting that the drafting of the Declaration had actually begun. Over those two years, various proposed drafts had been

25 Ibid., p. 215.

26 Ibid., p. 211.

27 See Howard Mann, 'The Rio Declaration' (1992) 86 *Proceedings of the American Society of International Law* 405, 408, and Jeffrey D. Kovar, 'A Short Guide to the Rio Declaration' (1993) 4 *Colorado Journal of International Environmental Law & Policy* 119, 122.

tabled, revealing the predictable North-South divide.[28] It was only during the very last days that Koh was able to mediate between the two different positions and to negotiate the final compromise.

Although often defined as a balanced compromise between developmental and environmental goals, the final text of the Declaration largely reflected the negotiating text presented by the Group of 77 developing countries (G77). Twenty years earlier, in Founex, the differences between industrialized and developing countries over a number of issues—who was the cause of environmental damage and who would have to pay for it—had emerged as clear as day. In Founex, developing countries did not find themselves sufficiently prepared, and they wanted to avoid committing the same mistake in Rio at all costs. To this end, despite there being differences between the African, Latin American, and Asian segments of the G77, the Group was able to develop a common negotiating strategy, largely as a result of the efforts of the South Center.[29]

The main point of contention between the North and the South, both in Stockholm and in Rio, was whether the emphasis should be on the environment or development. According to industrialized countries, the environment should be the focus of the Conference, while developing countries argued the Conference should be aimed at establishing their right to development.[30] The title of the *Rio Declaration* itself reflects, at least to a certain extent, the South's position: the original title—"Earth Charter"—had been forcefully contested by the G77 and China, as it seemed to suggest an 'undue' emphasis on the environment at the expense of development, and the final title—"On Environment and Development"—while clearly linking the two, did not emphasize the former over the latter, shattering industrialized nations' dream to produce a document focused solely on solving global environmental problems.[31]

---

28 Proposed drafts include those presented by Argentina, Australia, Canada, the European Community, Japan, the United States, a group of Nordic countries, the Group of 77 developing countries and China, the United Kingdom and Denmark (on behalf of several non-governmental organizations), and Russia.

29 See Report of the South Center on Environment and Development, *Towards a Common Strategy for the South in the UNCED Negotiations and Beyond* (South Center, 1991).

30 See e.g. M.P.A. Kindall, 'Talking Past Each Other at The Summit' (1993) 4 *Colorado Journal of International Environmental Law & Policy* 69, 71–2; Mann, 'The Rio Declaration' (n 27) 409; Ved P. Nanda, 'Sustainable Development, International Trade and the Doha Agenda for Development' (2005) 8 *Chapman Law Review* 53, 56; and Chris K. Mensah, 'The Role of Developing Countries', in Luigi Campiglio et al. (eds.), *The Environment After Rio: International Law and Economics* (Springer, 1994), p. 36.

31 Kovar, 'A Short Guide to the Rio Declaration' (n 27) 123, and Nanda, 'Sustainable Development' (n 30) 56–7.

While the title of the Declaration can be seen as ruling out the superiority of environmental concerns over developmental ones without offering, however, a conclusive answer to the old question—"which takes precedence, environment or development?"—, the final text of Principle 3 seems to clear up any confusion on the matter. The Principle, opposed by most industrialized countries, especially the US, and insisted upon by developing ones, explicitly acknowledges the existence of a 'right to development' which "must be fulfilled so as to equitably meet developmental and environmental needs of present and future generations."[32] On the other hand, the Declaration failed to recognize a 'right to a healthy environment', as proposed by the North, and opted instead for the reference to a mere 'entitlement' to a "healthy and productive life in harmony with nature."[33]

The developing countries' insistence on the recognition of a right to development, as well as their broader approach to the Rio negotiations, were fueled by their deep-seated fear that an excessive focus on the environment could be used as a tool to hold back their development opportunities. After all, 20 years had passed but these countries still regarded many environmental measures, in particular when related to trade, as possibly disguising protectionist intents. It was therefore necessary, in their view, to ensure that trade and environment issues would not move forward in isolation from wider development commitments.[34] To this end, a group of Latin American countries, led by Mexico, insisted upon the inclusion of a Principle that would clarify the relationship between trade and the environment, while safeguarding them against trade

---

32 United Nations Conference on Environment and Development, Rio de Janeiro, Brazil, June 3–14, 1992, *Rio Declaration on Environment and Development*, U.N. Doc. A/CONF.151/26/Rev.1 (Vol. I), Annex I (Aug. 12, 1992) [hereinafter Rio Declaration], Principle 3.

33 Ibid., Principle 1. The need for a recognition of a human right to a healthy environment among existing human rights is still debated today. See e.g. John H. Knox and Ramin Pejan (eds.), *The Human Right to a Healthy Environment* (Cambridge University Press, 2018); Philippe Cullet, 'Definition of an Environmental Right in a Human Rights Context' (1995) 13 *Netherlands Quarterly of Human Rights* 25; James T. McClymonds, 'Human Right to a Healthy Environment: An International Legal Perspective' (1992) 37 *New York Law School Law Review* 583; John Lee, 'The Underlying Legal Theory to Support a Well-Defined Human Right to a Healthy Environment as a Principle of Customary International Law' (2000) 25 *Columbia Journal of Environmental Law* 283 (2000); Marc Paellemarts, 'The Human Right to a Healthy Environment as a Substantive Right', in Maguelonne Dejeant-Pons and Marc Paellemarts (eds.), *Human Rights and the Environment* (Council of Europe, 2002); Rebecca Bratspies, 'Do We Need a Human Right to a Healthy Environment?' (2015) 13(1) *Santa Clara Journal of International Law* 31.

34 Scott Vaughan, 'Trade and Environment: Some North-South Considerations' (1994) 27 *Cornell International Law Journal* 591, 591–2.

measures adopted to influence their environmental practices.[35] Principle 12 was added to the Declaration as a result:

> States should cooperate to promote a supportive and open international economic system that would lead to economic growth and sustainable development in all countries, to better address the problems of environmental degradation. Trade policy measures for environmental purposes should not constitute a means of arbitrary or unjustifiable discrimination or a disguised restriction on international trade. Unilateral actions to deal with environmental challenges outside the jurisdiction of the importing country should be avoided. Environmental measures addressing transboundary or global environmental problems should, as far as possible, be based on an international consensus.[36]

The goal of this principle was to prevent industrialized countries from unilaterally imposing trade sanctions against developing countries under the guise of enforcing environmental norms. This language, which has no analogue in the Stockholm documents, recalls the *chapeau* of GATT Article XX to the letter, where it requires trade measures adopted for environmental purposes to "not constitute a means of arbitrary or unjustifiable discrimination or a disguised restriction on international trade", while the third and fourth sentences clearly codify the well-known holding of the GATT panel in the *Tuna/Dolphin* case.[37]

1.4 *Trade Too Can Harm the Environment*

With the development agenda gaining considerable ground both in environmental and trade fora, and with the principle of sustainable development as the overarching principle guiding future negotiations,[38] the rules of the

35 Mensah, 'The Role of Developing Countries' (n 30) 46; and Kovar, 'A Short Guide to the Rio Declaration' (n 27) 132.

36 Rio Declaration, Principle 12.

37 Report of the GATT Panel, *United States—Restrictions on Imports of Tuna,* DS21/R-39S/155 (Sept. 3, 1991) (not adopted) [hereinafter *US—Tuna I*], para. 5.27. See David A. Wirth, 'The Rio Declaration on Environment and Development: Two Steps Forward and One Back, or Vice Versa?' (1995) 29 *Georgia Law Review* 599, 641.

38 Many MEAs contain a caveat such as the one we can find in the chapeau of GATT Article XX. See e.g. Article 3.5 of the United Nations Framework Convention on Climate Change (UNFCCC), Article 3.5. Climate change negotiations represent a particularly fitting example, as trade measures are nearly never discussed as a tool to contribute to climate change mitigation, but rather as a threat to economic development in developing and least-developed countries. The creation of the Forum on the Impact of Implementation of Response Measures in 2011, was aimed precisely as addressing the negative impact that

game for environmentalists had decisively changed, making development an essential component of the evolution of the trade/environment nexus going forward. At the same time, the situation had drastically changed for free traders. In particular, the dimension of *sustainability* brought the recognition that economic growth could no longer be pursued decoupled from environmental considerations, which instead needed to be effectively embedded in all sectors and policy areas.[39]

The consequences of this paradigm shift for the interplay between the two regimes should not be underestimated. For nearly 20 years, the relationship between trade and the environment had been framed in a very one-sided fashion, which may be summed up in the following question: "to what extent may environmental measures act as deterrents to freer trade and how should such deterrents be dealt with?"[40] In other words, the trade community regarded measures adopted for environmental purposes as a potential obstacle to trade liberalization, while the other side of the question—whether liberalized trade could harm the environment—was not even taken into consideration. As convincingly explained by Bhagwati in a piece aptly titled *The Case for Free Trade*, economic growth "enables governments to tax and to raise resources for a variety of objectives, including environmental protection ... freer trade enables pollution-fighting technologies available elsewhere to be imported ... [and] can also lead to better environmental outcomes from a shift in the composition of production."[41] The very same arguments were advanced by global economic institutions, such as the World Bank, who published a report contending that "[l]iberalized trade fosters greater efficiency and higher productivity and may actually reduce pollution by encouraging the growth of less polluting industries and the adoption and diffusion of cleaner technologies."[42]

Overall, these arguments reflected the neoliberal view of "environmental protection through economic means,"[43] which was backed up by a model known as the Environmental Kuznets Curve (EKC), and which supported the hypothesis that during the very first stages of social and economic advancement, there will necessarily be environmental degradation and harm, while

---

mitigation measures adopted by industrialized countries risk having on the economies of less developed ones.

39 Carter, *The Politics of the Environment* (n 23) 212.

40 J. Owen Saunders, 'Trade and Environment: The Fine Line Between Environmental Protection and Environmental Protectionism' (1992) 47(4) *International Journal* 723, 726.

41 Jagdish Bhagwati, 'The Case for Free Trade' (1993) *Scientific American* 43.

42 World Bank, *World Development Report* (Oxford University Press, 1992), p. 67.

43 James K.R. Watson, *The WTO and the Environment* (Routledge, 2013), p. 101.

once a country has reached a higher level, "there will be money and assets free to invest in environmental goods such as pollution control and waste management."[44] As a result, the alarming fears of environmentalists that free trade increases economic growth, which in turn harms the environment, were considered misplaced and rapidly dismissed.[45]

The paradigm shift introduced with the notion of sustainable development, on the other hand, began to quietly shake the confidence of free trade supporters over the entirely beneficial impact of trade liberalization on the environment. Suddenly, the focus was no longer solely on the potential negative impact that environmental measures could have on international trade flows, but equally on the harm that liberalized trade could cause to the environment. Slowly, the trade community itself began to realize that trade could harm the environment in various ways—and not just in low-income countries—and it was therefore necessary to eliminate or reduce this harm to a minimum. And this is precisely when environmental safeguards made their first appearance within the text of trade agreements.

1.5 *Assessing Environmental Impacts*

On November 16, 1999, just a few weeks before the opening of the WTO Ministerial Conference in Seattle, President Clinton issued Executive Order 13,141, committing the US government to conduct environmental reviews of trade agreements for the very first time.[46] It is no coincidence that the Order was issued the same day as the administration's *Declaration on Environmental Trade Policy*, which pledged to "[take] fully into account environmental implications throughout the course of the negotiations, including by performing a written environmental review."[47] Accordingly, the Order committed the US government to "factor environmental considerations into the development of its trade negotiating objectives [through] a process of ongoing assessment and evaluation, and, in certain instances, written environmental reviews."[48]

The Order concluded almost a decade of judicial battles, which found their fountainhead in a provision of the National Environmental Protection

44 Ibid., quoting World Bank, *World Development Report* (n 42).

45 Bhagwati, 'The Case for Free Trade' (n 41) 43; Gene M. Grossman and Alan B. Krueger, 'Economic Growth and the Environment', NBER Working Paper Series, Working Paper No. 4634 (Feb. 1994).

46 Exec. Order No. 13,141, 64 Fed. Reg. 63,169 (Nov. 16, 1999).

47 White House Policy Declaration on Environment and Trade (Nov. 16, 1999). See James Salzman, 'Seattle's Legal Legacy and Environmental Review of Trade Agreements' (2001) 31(3) *Environmental Law* 501, 503.

48 Exec. Order No. 13,141, §1.

Act (NEPA), requiring US federal agencies to prepare Environmental Impact Assessments (EIAs) for proposed major federal actions that may significantly affect the quality of the human environment.[49] Since NEPA's adoption, environmental reviews have become a cornerstone of environmental law, being introduced in the domestic legislation of many other states,[50] as well as in international legal instruments.[51]

When NAFTA was being negotiated, the real question became whether NEPA applied to trade agreements. Convinced that it did and wanting the Office of the United States Trade Representative (USTR) to conduct an assessment of NAFTA, Public Citizen, Sierra Club, and Friends of the Earth filed a suit in US district court to decide on this matter.[52] The suit led to the dispositive case *Public Citizen v. Office of the U.S. Trade Representative*,[53] which ruled against the necessity of EIAs for trade agreements,[54] only to be voided a few years later by Clinton's Executive Order, which made such reviews mandatory.

---

49 NEPA uses the expression 'Environmental Impact Statements' or EIS. According to paragraph 4332, "all agencies of the Federal Government shall include in every recommendation or report on proposals for legislation and other major Federal actions significantly affecting the quality of the human environment, a detailed statement by the responsible official on (i) the environmental impact of the proposed action, (ii) any adverse environmental effects which cannot be avoided should the proposal be implemented, (iii) alternatives to the proposed action, (iv) the relationship between local short-term uses of man's environment and the maintenance and enhancement of long-term productivity, and (v) any irreversible and irretrievable commitments of resources which would be involved in the proposed action should it be implemented." 42 U.S.C. § 4332 (1988).

50 Kevin Gray, 'International Environmental Impact Assessment' (2000) 11 *Colorado Journal of International Environmental Law & Policy* 83, 89.

51 Principle 17 of the Rio Declaration, for instance, provides that "Environmental impact assessment, as a national instrument, shall be undertaken for proposed activities that are likely to have a significant adverse impact on the environment and are subject to a decision of a competent national authority." Rio Declaration, Principle 17. Other international legal instruments providing for EIAs include the Espoo Convention, the Convention on Biological Diversity (CBD), the United Nations Convention on the Law of the Sea (UNCLOS), and the World Charter for Nature. See Convention on Environmental Impact Assessment in a Transboundary Context, Feb. 25, 1991, 1989 U.N.T.S. 309, Convention on Biological Diversity, June 5, 1992, 1760 U.N.T.S. 79, United Nations Convention on the Law of the Sea, Dec. 10, 1982, 1833 U.N.T.S. 397, and United Nations General Assembly Resolution, *World Charter for Nature*, A/RES/37/7 (Oct. 28, 1982).

52 See Steve Charnovitz, 'No Time for NEPA: Trade Agreements on a Fast Track' (1994) 3 *Minnesota Journal of Global Trade* 195, 208; and Salzman, 'Seattle's Legal Legacy' (n 47) 508.

53 *Public Citizen v. Office of the US Trade Representative*, 782 F. Supp. 139, 141 (D.D.C. 1992).

54 While initially dismissed for lack of standing and lack of final agency, the case was refiled and the district court granted a summary judgment and ordered the USTR to prepare an environmental impact assessment of NAFTA. However, the D.C. Circuit reversed the

Even before Clinton's Order, the idea that trade expansion—just as the norms that facilitate it—could be harmful for the environment had started to gain traction. As a result, while the case was still pending in court, although not required to do so by law, the USTR *did* convene an interagency task force with the specific job of examining the environmental issues most likely to arise during the negotiation and drafting of NAFTA, and this 'informal' review, as USTR officials were calling it,[55] ultimately had a quite significant impact on the final text of the agreement. One of the main findings of the review was the potential race-to-the-bottom consequences of the agreement, and NAFTA Article 1114,[56] as well as several provisions of its environmental side agreement (North American Agreement on Environmental Cooperation or NAAEC),[57] were drafted precisely to address these concerns, ensuring that the parties maintained their environmental, health, and safety standards. The review similarly called for assurances that NAFTA would not undermine the parties' obligations under certain environmental agreements, hence Article 104 of NAFTA, which clarifies the relationship between these treaties and NAFTA itself.[58]

Following the NAFTA review and Clinton's Executive Order, the Office of the USTR issued an environmental review of the Uruguay Round, right after the EU had launched its *Sustainability Impact Assessment of the Proposed New Round of Multilateral Trade Liberalization*.[59] These initiatives were perfectly in line with the position taken by many international organizations during the very same years. The Commission on Sustainable Development (CSD), created during the Rio Conference, for instance, encouraged "Governments to develop or strengthen processes to assess the environmental effects of trade policies … and promote transparency and openness to the public in these processes."[60]

---

lower court decision on purely administrative law grounds. See Charnovitz, 'No Time for NEPA' (n 52) and Salzman, 'Seattle's Legal Legacy' (n 47).

55 Salzman, 'Seattle's Legal Legacy' (n 47) 508.

56 See later in the text.

57 North American Agreement on Environmental Cooperation, US-Can.-Mex. 32 I.L.M. 1482 (1993) [hereinafter NAAEC].

58 Another important finding of the review was the environmental degradation caused by maquiladoras along the US-Mexico Border, which led to the adoption of the Integrated Border Environmental Plan.

59 This initiative built on the 1992 EIA of the Common Market. See Salzman, 'Seattle's Legal Legacy (n 47) 512.

60 U.N. ESCOR, Comm'n on Sustainable Dev., 3rd Sess., Supp. No. 12 §69, U.N. Doc. E/CN/.17/1995/36 (1995). A more recent report in April 2000, similarly called for assessments that can "anticipate potentially adverse scale effects of trade liberalization and, where possible, to avoid or mitigate such effects through appropriate environmental policies." See Salzman, 'Seattle's Legal Legacy' (n 47) 511.

Along the very same lines, the Organization for Economic Cooperation and Development (OECD), the United Nations Environment Program (UNEP), and the United Nations Conference on Trade and Development (UNCTAD) began sponsoring projects and developing guidelines for conducting environmental reviews.[61] The importance of conducting EIAs of trade negotiations was also raised at the WTO. During several meetings of the Committee on Trade and Environment (CTE), the representative of the United States emphasized the importance of environmental reviews to develop the necessary information to ensure "the goal of trade liberalization in conjunction with an overall commitment to sustainable development."[62] Along the same lines, the Canadian representative listed the benefits of identifying and discussing the environmental consequences of trade liberalization in relation to specific WTO negotiations: it would help, among other things, "to identify potential problem areas and the positive effects of trade liberalization early in the process … identify ways to mitigate environmental effects and inform decision-makers."[63] These persistent suggestions, however, have gone nowhere and the WTO managed to remain immune to the spreading 'environmental reviews' enthusiasm.[64]

As a result, a number of countries, including the US, the EU, and Canada, have been introducing provisions requiring parties to conduct environmental impact assessments of trade agreements in their bilateral and regional trade negotiations,[65] starting with the NAFTA environmental side agreement, which includes EIAs in the list of the parties' *General Commitments*,[66] up until one of the more recent agreements signed by the EU with Japan, where the parties have committed to monitor, assess, and review the environmental impact of the implementation of the agreement.[67]

Conducting such reviews can indeed prove beneficial for the parties' environments, as they help negotiators identify those aspects of the agreements that are more likely to have a negative environmental impact. This might in turn lead to the introduction of environmental safeguards within the text, just

61 See e.g. OECD, *Methodologies for Environmental and Trade Reviews* 5, OECD Doc. OECD/GD(94)103 (1994); and OECD, *Assessing the Environmental Effects of Trade Liberalization Agreements: Methodologies* (2000).

62 WT/CTE/M/22 (Oct. 29, 1999), para. 8.

63 Ibid., para. 10.

64 Ibid., para. 9. See Salzman, 'Seattle's Legal Legacy' (n 47) 543.

65 See e.g. Free Trade Agreement & Economic Integration Agreement, EU-Republic of Korea, Oct. 6, 2010 [hereinafter EU-S. Kor. FTA], Art. 13.10.

66 NAAEC, Art. 2(e).

67 Free Trade Agreement & Economic Integration Agreement, EU-Japan, July 17, 2018 [hereinafter EU-Japan FTA], Art. 16.11.

like Article 1114 of NAFTA, which was, at least in part, a reaction to the alarming 'maquiladoras' problem, denounced by environmentalists for years, and finally put down in black and white as a result of the USTR's 'informal' review.

1.6 *Maquiladoras, Hazardous Waste, and the Pollution Haven Package*

During the 1960s, the region along Mexico's northern border was facing problematic levels of unemployment and underdevelopment. To address these issues and attract greater foreign investment in the region, in 1965 the federal government established the maquiladora industry.[68] The maquiladora program essentially established a free-trade zone regime, which allowed for raw materials to be imported in Mexico duty-free as long as their output was exported.[69] By 1991, there were more than 1871 maquiladora plants along the northern Mexican border, mostly owned or controlled by American corporations.[70]

The maquiladora program played a key role in the country's economic recovery, attracting foreign investment and currency, promoting local employment, and contributing to the overall development of the region.[71] While beneficial for the Mexican economy, the maquiladora industry was also causing a series of environmental problems, related in particular to the creation of hazardous waste which, when stored improperly and accidentally spilled, risked seeping through the soil and contaminating local groundwater supplies.[72] These concerns were at the heart of environmentalists' uneasiness about the effect that NAFTA would have on the border region: while it would increase trade between the two countries and expand the maquiladora industry, thus benefitting Mexico's economy, it risked further contributing to the region's environmental degradation[73] by driving US and Canadian companies to relocate their

---

68 See Cheryl Schechter and David Frill Jr., 'Maquiladoras: Will the Program Continue' (1992) 23 *Saint Mary's Law Journal* 697, 701.

69 Programs of this kind are generally known as 'duty drawback' programs. Ibid., 698. James E. Bailey, 'Free Trade and the Environment–Can NAFTA Reconcile the Irreconcilable' (1992) 8 *American University Journal of International Law & Policy* 839, 867.

70 See Schechter and Frill Jr., 'Maquiladoras' (n 68) 699; Roberto A. Sanchez, 'Health and Environmental Risks of the Maquiladora in Mexicali' (1990) 30(1) *Natural Resources Journal* 163, 164; and Stephen Lerner, 'The Maquiladoras and Hazardous Waste: The Effects under NAFTA' (1993) 6 *Transnational Law* 255, 258.

71 As of 1993, "the over 1871 maquiladora plants employ over 400,000 workers and comprise over fifteen percent of Mexico's total manufacturing labor force." Bailey, 'Free Trade and the Environment' (n 69) 868.

72 Lerner, 'The Maquiladoras and Hazardous Waste' (n 70) 258. US/Mexico Hazardous Waste Work Group, *Hazardous Waste Management and Maquiladora Industry Manual* (1992), p. 49.

73 Bailey, 'Free Trade and the Environment' (n 69) 868.

operations in Mexico. The creation of this 'pollution haven' along the Mexican side of the border, in turn, could have encouraged both the United States and Canada to lower their own environmental standards to keep companies at home, leading to a snowballing race to the bottom.[74]

These concerns found an answer in a series of provisions of both NAFTA and NAAEC generally referred to as the 'Pollution Haven Package'.[75] To avoid a situation where Mexico would become a 'pollution haven', NAFTA Article 1114 provides that:

> 1. Nothing in this Chapter shall be construed to prevent a Party from adopting, maintaining or enforcing any measure otherwise consistent with this Chapter that it considers appropriate to ensure that investment activity in its territory is undertaken in a manner sensitive to environmental concerns.
> 2. The Parties recognize that it is inappropriate to encourage investment by relaxing domestic health, safety or environmental measures. Accordingly, a Party should not waive or otherwise derogate from, or offer to waive or otherwise derogate from, such measures as an encouragement for the establishment, acquisition, expansion or retention in its territory of an investment of an investor.[76]

The provision, which has often been criticized for being phrased in merely hortatory terms and for lacking an efficient enforcement mechanism,[77] did

---

74 See e.g. Robert Housman and Paul M. Orbuch, 'Integrating Environmental and Labor Concerns in the North American Free Trade Agreement: A Look Back and a Look Ahead' (1993) 8(4) *American University International Law Review* 719, 732.

75 Gary Clyde Hufbauer et al., *NAFTA and the Environment: Seven Years Later* (Peterson Institute for International Economics, 2000), p. 9.

76 North American Free Trade Agreement, US-Can.-Mex, Dec. 17, 1992, 32 I.L.M. 289 (1993) [hereinafter NAFTA], Art. 1114.

77 The only remedy provided to the aggrieved party is consultation and publicity. See e.g. Steve Charnovitz, 'NAFTA's Social Dimension: Lessons from the Past and Framework for the Future' (1994) VIII(1) *International Trade Journal* 39, 52; Housman, 'The North American Free Trade Agreement's Lessons' (n 8) 396; and Daniel C. Esty, 'Integrating Trade and Environment Policy Making: First Steps in the North American Free Trade Agreement', in Durwood Zaelke et al (eds.), *Trade and the Environment. Law, Economics, and Policy* (Island Press, 1993), p. 53. NAAEC seeks to remedy some of these 'shortcomings'. For example, Article 5.1 recasts the hortatory language of NAFTA Article 1114 in legally binding terms by requiring each of the three parties to "effectively enforce its environmental laws." Over time, the term "should" in the original NAFTA evolved into "shall strive to" and finally to "shall" in the recent United States-Mexico-Canada Agreement (USMCA). NAAEC also established two mechanisms to ensure compliance which, however, have proven quite ineffective. See John H. Knox, 'The Neglected Lessons of the NAFTA Environmental Regime' (2010) 45(2) *Wake Forest Law Review* 391, 396–7.

establish an important new principle: for the very first time, a group of nations had deemed the lack of environmental protection an unacceptable means of encouraging investment and had addressed this "objectional behavior" in a trade agreement.[78]

In the first report prepared by the WTO Committee on Trade and Environment, WTO Members recognized the importance of this principle in the context of *trade*, rather than investment, noting that "it would be inappropriate for them to relax their existing national environmental standards or their enforcement in order to promote their *trade*."[79] Throughout the years, the 'pollution haven package' has become a constant and essential component of regional trade agreements, often with reference to both trade and investment: the EU and Singapore, for instance, agreed that "it is inappropriate to encourage *trade or investment* by weakening or reducing the protections afforded in domestic labor and environment laws."[80] Of course if the parties, on the one hand, wanted to make sure that trade rules were not used to override environmental regulations, on the other, not all environmental laws and standards were allowed—more precisely, those that are "used for protectionist trade purposes"[81] were not—perfectly reflecting the tension underlying any attempt to balance economic and environmental goals.

78 Housman, 'The North American Free Trade Agreement's Lessons' (n 8) 397.

79 World Trade Organization, Committee on Trade and Environment (CTE), *Report (1996) of the Committee on Trade and Environment,* WT/CTE/W40 (Nov. 7, 1996) [hereinafter CTE 1996 Report], para. 169 (emphasis added).

80 Free Trade Agreement, EU-Singapore [hereinafter EU-Sing. FTA], Art, 13.1, first sentence (emphasis added). Other examples include, e.g., Free Trade Agreement & Economic Integration Agreement, EU-Colombia-Peru, June 26, 2012 [hereinafter EU-Colom.-Peru FTA], Art. 277; Free Trade Agreement & Economic Integration Agreement, United States-Singapore, May 6, 2003 [hereinafter US-Sing. FTA], Art. 18.2(2); Free Trade Agreement & Economic Integration Agreement, United States-Chile, June 6, 2003 [hereinafter US-Chile FTA], Art. 19.2; Free Trade Agreement & Economic Integration Agreement, United States-Australia, May 18, 2004 [hereinafter US-Austl. FTA], Art. 19.2(2); Free Trade Agreement & Economic Integration Agreement, United States-Republic of Korea, June 30, 2007, Art. 20.3(2); Free Trade Agreement, Turkey-Chile, July 14, 2009, Art. 37(8); Free Trade Agreement & Economic Integration Agreement, India-Japan, Feb. 16, 2011, Art. 99; Free Trade Agreement & Economic Integration Agreement, Canada-Colombia, Nov. 21, 2008 [hereinafter Can.-Colom. FTA], Arts. 815 and 1702; Free Trade Agreement, Chile-Malaysia, Nov. 13, 2010, Art. 9.5(2); Free Trade Agreement & Economic Integration Agreement, Switzerland-China, July 6, 2013, Art. 12.2(2); Free Trade Agreement & Economic Integration Agreement, Republic of Korea-New Zealand, Mar. 23, 2015 [hereinafter S. Kor.-N.Z. FTA], Art. 16.2(2); Free Trade Agreement, EU-SADC, June 10, 2016 [hereinafter EU-SADC FTA], Art. 9(3); Free Trade Agreement, Canada-Ukraine, July 11, 2016 [hereinafter Can.-Ukr. FTA], Art. 12.5; and EU-Japan FTA, Art. 16.2(2).

81 EU-Sing. FTA, Art, 13.1, second sentence.

1.7 *This Is Not Solely an International Story*

The "new era" in the trade/environment debate, which began in the mid-1990s and was largely inspired by the appearance of the overarching principle of sustainable development, was indeed characterized by the quest for balance between the two regimes. It was no longer possible to pursue the environmental and trade agendas on separate tracks and it became compelling to initiate a fruitful dialogue to reconcile what just a few decades earlier was regarded as entirely irreconcilable. This "new era" has often been described as characterized by a 'greening' of trade law. In particular, the incorporation of environmental sensitivities in the text of NAFTA has been deemed to have "permanently changed the dialogue about trade and the environment,"[82] making the agreement the first one of its kind, in directly addressing environmental concerns.[83]

Why was this change of course possible? What had made the North American negotiations 'greener' than all its predecessors? What, even beyond the North American experience, had created the breeding ground for the development of the relationship between trade and the environment towards a more balanced outcome? As argued in the next section—and throughout the whole book—normative changes, while the result of many different and concurring factors, have an indispensable ideational basis, and individuals and communities play a crucial role in creating environments that are more or less conducive to such ideational and normative change.

Before reaching the international plane, most ideas first blossom, spread, and thrive in domestic systems. This is true, for instance, of the ideas conveyed by the *Brundtland Report*, which reflected and built upon notions initially developed in the United States.[84] Some domestic systems, for a variety of reasons, the analysis of which are beyond the scope of this inquiry, have provided the trade/environment nexus with an environment more conducive to change than others. And the relative power that these countries were able to exercise

---

82 Charnovitz, 'NAFTA's Social Dimension' (n 77) 40.

83 Weekly Compilation of Presidential Documents, 1992, at 1425, as quoted in Charnovitz, 'NAFTA's Social Dimension' (n 77) 44. When it was concluded in 1992, William Reilly defined NAFTA as "the greenest trade agreement ever." Carol Browner, then EPA Administrator, claimed without faltering that the Agreement made it "harder to pollute in all three countries," while Congressman Fred Grandy called it "the strongest environmental treaty ever signed ..." See Browner, Former EPA Chief Reilly Push for Support for NAFTA on Capitol Hill, 10 *International Trade Reporter* 1685 (Oct. 6, 1993). Advertisement, *Washington Post,* Oct. 26, 1993, at B5.

84 Robert F. Blomquist, '"Clean New World": Toward an Intellectual History of American Environmental Law, 1961–1990' (1990) 25(1) *Valparaiso University Law Review* 1.

in international fora, vis-à-vis countries with an environment comparatively less conducive to change, is precisely what explains a more or less pronounced evolution of the nexus in different contexts.

It should not come as a surprise that NAFTA negotiations could lead to a 'greener' result compared to those that characterized the seven and half years of the Uruguay Round: unlike NAFTA, the GATT of the 1990s, and later the WTO, had to accommodate a plethora of divergent voices. According to realist thinking, the actual development of an 'environmental agenda' within trade negotiations largely depends on the relative power and interests of those states that advocate for it—for the most part industrialized nations with large economies. Given the increasing number of developing, and especially least-developed, countries actively participating in the Uruguay Round, the power of 'greener' states, like the US and Northern European countries, proved far less effective than in smaller fora or organizations.[85]

This explains, for instance, why, while the US, the EU, and other industrialized countries introduced the practice of conducting environmental impact assessment of trade agreements, the WTO had instead succeeded in remaining immune to the spreading 'environmental reviews' enthusiasm. This lack of enthusiasm becomes obvious if one looks inside the Committee on Trade and the Environment, where representatives of developing countries did not seem to get on board with the US and European proposals. The representative from India, for instance, clarified more than once that, in his view, conducting environmental reviews "was purely a national prerogative."[86] As the next section will demonstrate, the different pace of the development of the 'environmental agenda' within multilateral and regional negotiations has led to an asymmetrical evolution of the nexus which can be defined as *à la carte*.

2 Finding Balance

In 1996, the WTO Committee on Trade and Environment issued its first report, drawn up on the basis of more than 50 proposals and non-papers submitted by the interested Members. In one of its non-papers, dealing with Item 1 of the agenda—the relationship between the provisions of the multilateral trading system and trade measures for environmental purposes—the EU advanced

85 Richard H. Steinberg, 'Trade-Environment Negotiations in the EU, NAFTA, and WTO: Regional Trajectories of Rule Development' (1997) 91 *American Journal of International Law* 231, 232–3.

86 WT/CTE/M/22 (Oct. 29, 1999), para. 9. See Salzman, 'Seattle's Legal Legacy' (n 47) 543.

two different proposals. First, the European document suggested to "improve the consistency of the rules of the multilateral trading system taking into account both the commitment expressed in the first preambular paragraph of the Agreement establishing the WTO and the fact that the environment is already mentioned in several WTO Agreements."[87] The second proposal focused instead on the amendment of GATT Article XX, either by including a reference to "measures taken pursuant to specific [Multilateral Environmental Agreements] MEAs" or "in more general terms, to measures necessary to protect the environment."[88]

These proposals, as well as others advanced by other Members, represent a compromise between the long lists of amendments to the GATT demanded by the environmental community over the previous 20 years,[89] and the firm conviction of the trade community of the complete adequacy of the existing provisions. The underlying assumption of all proposals requesting amendments to GATT Article XX was the "belief that by clarifying trade rules and building greater attentiveness to environmental considerations into the GATT, the breadth and depth of trade-environment clashes [could] be reduced."[90]

To a certain extent, both proposals would be addressed over the years that followed. On the one hand, the newly-created Appellate Body distanced itself from the traditional orientation and ideology that characterized GATT/WTO panels, relying on sources of general international law—including environmental law—even when they were not perfectly in line with the trade agenda. On the other, a new generation of free trade agreements started being negotiated, featuring several references to the environment, including in the text of their GATT-like exception clauses.

87 CTE, *Non-Paper by the European Communities on Item 1*, Feb. 19, 1996.
88 Ibid.
89 Daniel Esty summarizes the standard menu of concerns as generally including "GATT Article XX reform, import prohibitions, export restraints, product standards, restrictions on production processes and methods, taxes and subsidies, unilateral and extraterritorial actions, and the use of trade penalties to enforce environmental agreements." Daniel C. Esty, *Greening the GATT. Trade, Environment, and the Future* (Institute for International Economics), p. 99. See e.g. Eliza Patterson, 'GATT and the Environment—Rule Changes to Minimize Adverse Trade and Environmental Effects' (1992) 26(3) *Journal of World Trade* 99. Peter L. Lallas, Daniel C. Esty, and David J. van Hoogstraten, 'Environmental protection and International Trade: toward Mutually Supportive Rules and Policies' (1992) 16 *Harvard Environmental Law Review* 271; Rodrigo J. Prudencio and Stewart J. Hudson, 'The Road to Marrakech: An Interim Report on Environmental Reform of the GATT and the International Trade System' (1994) National Wildlife Foundation.
90 Esty, *Greening the GATT* (n 89) 100.

2.1 *Free Traders and Environmentalists: Together at Last*

To fully understand these developments, one has to consider the way in which the interactions between the trade and environmental community had evolved over the years. On August 12, 1992, while briefing the press immediately after the signature of NAFTA, US Trade Representative Carla Hills noted that if "never has an agreement offered such a balance of economic growth, opportunity, workers' benefits, and environmental sensitivity," this is in large part due to the "efforts and dedication" of the vast US interagency team, composed of negotiators from ten different agencies. For the very first time, environmental officials were included in the trade negotiations. Russell Train, then Chairman of the World Wildlife Fund and former administrator of the US Environmental Protection Agency (EPA) was appointed to the presidential advisory committee, while Carla Hills had appointed similarly prominent environmental leaders to her policy advisory committees.[91]

To really appreciate the importance of these appointments, it suffices to think that only a few years earlier, Carla Hills herself had vocally argued that environmental issues had absolutely no place in trade agreements,[92] and environmental officials and experts kept watching as the doors of multilateral and regional trade talks closed right in front of them.

However, over the previous few years, many things had changed. The organizations that had been created after the 1970s and that developed and carried the identity of the US environmental movement—such as the Environmental Policy Center, the National Resources Defense Council, and Sierra Club—had established themselves as major actors in the country's political scene, becoming increasingly influential in legislative and administrative politics.[93] Their

91 They include John Sawhill, President and CEO of the Nature Conservancy and former Secretary of Energy (Industry); Peter Berle, President of the National Audubon Society (Agriculture); John Adams, Executive Director of the Natural Resources Defense Council (Services); Jay Hair, President of the National Wildlife Federation (Investment); and James Strock, Secretary for Environmental Protection of the State of California (Intergovernmental). See Daniel C. Esty, 'Economic Integration and the Environment', in Regina S. Axelrod & Stacy D. VanDeveer (eds.), *The Global Environment. Institutions, Law, and Policy* (Sage, 1999), p. 197; Sanford E. Gaines and Albert E. Utton, 'Environmental Laws and Regulations After NAFTA' (1993) 1 *US-Mexico Law Journal* 199, 200.

92 See John Audley, 'Why Environmentalists Are Angry about the North American Free Trade Agreement', in Zaelke et al (eds.), *Trade and the Environment* (n 77) 193.

93 Robert J. Brulle, 'Environmental Discourse and Social Movement Organizations: A Historical and Rhetorical Perspective on the Development of US Environmental Organizations' (1996) 66(1) *Sociological Inquiry* 58; and Samuel P. Hays, *Beauty, Health, and Performance. Environmental Politics in the United States, 1955–1985* (Cambridge University Press, 1989), p. 60.

influence, which resulted from a combination of formal participation in the legislative process and informal contacts with the legislators to whom they provided technical advice, was felt in the context of trade negotiations as well. At a January 1991 meeting on Capitol Hill, only four months before Congress would meet to vote on whether to grant the President 'fast-track' authority to negotiate NAFTA, the hall was packed with environmental groups, labor unions, and human rights supporters.[94] Obtaining 'fast-track' authority, which until then had been a pro forma exercise, was all of a sudden complicated by the presence of these groups, and ultimately became dependent on the government addressing at least some of their concerns. Together, representatives of both governmental and non-governmental environmental groups ended up playing a substantive role in balancing NAFTA's economic goals with environmental concerns.[95]

To better integrate trade and environmental expertise in the development of rules on cross-cutting issues, more permanent fora were created where members of the two communities could exchange ideas, coordinate efforts, and cooperate. In 1994, for instance, the US Trade and Environmental Policy Advisory Committee (TEPAC), co-chaired by the US Trade Representative and the EPA Administrator, was created, to provide policy advice on the intersection of trade and environmental policies.[96] Within the OECD, environmental issues had been a prerogative of the Environmental Policy Committee, added to the Organization's structure in 1970. After a fruitful dialogue began within the Organization on the intersection between trade and the environment, in 1998, the Joint Working Party on Trade and Environment was established within the Environmental Policy Committee.[97] And it was the Joint Working Party that published a study in 2001 titled *Environmental Goods and Services: The Benefits of Further Global Trade Liberalization*,[98] whose Annex contained a list of environmental goods accompanied by the corresponding Harmonized System nomenclature,[99] which, together with the list prepared by the Asia-Pacific

94 Carolyn L. Deere and Daniel C. Esty (eds.), *Greening the Americas. NAFTA's Lessons for Hemispheric Trade* (MIT Press, 2002), p. 99.

95 Labor Unions had a similar role during the finals stages of the negotiations, resulting in the introduction of a 'labor' package within the text of NAFTA.

96 Deere and Esty (eds.), *Greening the Americas* (n 94) 517.

97 OECD, *International Environmental Issues and the OECD 1950–2000. An Historical Perspective, by Bill L. Long* (OECD Publishing, 2000), p. 144.

98 OECD, *Environmental Goods and Services: The Benefits of Further Global Trade Liberalization: The Benefits of Further Global Trade Liberalization* (OECD Publishing, 2001).

99 International Convention on the Harmonized Commodity Description and Coding System, June 14, 1983, 1503 U.N.T.S. 3. The Convention contains more than 5,000 six-digit

Economic Cooperation (APEC) countries, constituted the point of departure for negotiations on liberalizing trade in environmental goods and services.

Furthermore, the conditions that had allowed the trade community to remain an exclusive club, such as the homogeneity of its membership, the supposedly technical nature of the subject, and the consequent media indifference, had begun to vanish. Trade disputes, especially those that dealt with non-trade issues, started making the front pages of the New York Times, the Guardian, and many other papers.[100] Maintaining the previous *clubiness* had become more and more difficult. The result was the beginning of a dialogue between the trade and environmental community: rather than talking past each other, they started talking to one another and, once they started learning each other's language and values, a fruitful conversation could finally begin. As a result, the environmental community played a key role in 'greening' the final months of the Uruguay Round when, as described by a USTR official, environmental non-governmental organizations (NGOs) "were briefed every night and became heavily involved in proposing alternate formulations."[101]

However, at the same time, the WTO membership had become larger and developing countries, which had been given little vote in the past, had become increasingly important players, at least collectively.[102] It should then be no surprise if the level of institutional integration between the trade and environmental communities, and the resulting influence on the evolution of the nexus, are 'softer' within the WTO than in certain domestic and regional experiences.

2.2 *The Committee on Trade and Environment: WTO's 'Softer' Version of Institutional Integration*

During one Uruguay Round negotiating meeting in December 1990, Members of the European Free Trade Association (EFTA) requested the GATT Secretariat to re-activate the long-dormant EMIT Group to ensure the effective participation of the GATT in the fast-approaching UN Conference on Environment

---

subheadings, which may be subdivided further to reflect national administrative and statistical requirements.

100 Joseph Weiler, 'The Rule of Lawyers and the Ethos of Diplomats: Reflections on the Internal and External Legitimacy of Dispute Settlement', in Roger B. Porter et al. (eds.), *Efficiency, Equity, and Legitimacy: The Multilateral Trading System at the Millennium* (Brookings Institution Press, 2001), p. 337. See also Robert O. Keohane and Joseph S. Nye Jr., 'The Club Model of Multilateral Cooperation and Problems of Democratic Legitimacy', in Porter et al. (eds.), *Efficiency, Equity, and Legitimacy*, pp. 269–272.

101 Salzman, 'Seattle's Legal Legacy' (n 47) at fn. 74.

102 Jeffrey A. Frankel,' Assessing the Efficiency Gains for Further Liberalization', in Porter et al. (eds.), *Efficiency, Equity, and Legitimacy* (n 100) 94.

and Development.[103] During the final sessions of the Uruguay Round, the role and mandate of the Group spurred heated discussions among the negotiators. While some delegations saw the need to transform the Group into a more permanent mechanism to effectively address the issues that would arise from the interface between trade and the environment,[104] others—in particular developing countries—wanted to avoid giving the environment a permanent place within the new Organization, arguing that it was a 'trade' organization after all, and fearing that mainstreaming environmental discussions in the WTO might be used to limit their development options.[105] Eventually, developing countries agreed to the creation of the Committee, provided that its agenda reflected their concerns as well. On April 15, 1994, along with the Final Act of the Uruguay Round, the parties adopted the *Decision on Trade and Environment*, which established the Committee on Trade and Environment or CTE.[106]

---

103 Proposal to convene the EMIT Working Group, submitted by member countries of the European Free Trade Association, in Statement on Trade and the Environment. See MTN.TNC/W/47 (Dec. 3, 1990). What these northern European countries had at heart when they requested to reinvigorate the Group, however, was not the environment as such. Rather, despite their 'green' reputation, they simply wanted the GATT to confront "the rising tide of environmental measures and international environmental agreements" because many used trade measures to realize their objectives. Trade interests, hence, rather than environmental concerns, led to the convening of the Group, as evidently demonstrated by its mandate: although certain parties—in particular the EU and the US—had been criticizing the original mandate of the Group because too narrow, the Group had been careful to "ensure that the scope of its discussions remained well within its mandate and GATT's competence, namely the trade-related aspects of environment policies which may result in significant trade effects for GATT contracting parties." C/M/247 (Mar. 5, 1991), p. 22, as quoted in Gregory C. Shaffer, 'The World Trade Organization under Challenge: Democracy and the Law and Politics of the WTO's Treatment of Trade and Environment Matters' (2001) 25 *Harvard Environmental Law Review* 1, 17, fn. 51. See also *Report by the Chairman of the Group on Environmental Measures and International Trade presented to the Contracting Parties at their Forty-ninth Session*, GATT B.I.S.D. (40th Supp.), p. 75, para. 9 (1995) (reporting to the January 25 and 26 1994 meeting of GATT members, the work of the EMIT Working Group in 1993, L/7402).

104 Manisha Sinha, 'An Evaluation of the WTO Committee on Trade and Environment' (2013) 47(6) *Journal of World Trade* 1285, 1290.

105 Prudencio and Hudson, 'Suggestions on an Environmental Reform Agenda' (n 89) 10; Shaffer, 'The World Trade Organization under Challenge' (n 103) 23; and Esty, *Greening the GATT* (n 89) 37.

106 Decision on Trade and Environment, April 14, 1994, Marrakesh Agreement Establishing the World Trade Organization Annex 1C, 33 I.L.M. 1267 [hereinafter Decision on Trade and Environment]. See Gregory Shaffer, 'The Nexus of Law and Politics: The WTO's Committee on Trade and Environment', in Richard Steinberg (ed.), *The Greening of Trade Law* 81 (Rowman & Littlefield Publishers, 2002), p. 87.

The creation of the CTE was immediately seen by many environmentalists as a hopeful change in the GATT's approach to the trade/environment nexus. The *Decision on Trade and Environment* clarified the terms of reference of the Committee, which differed greatly from the ones drafted for the EMIT Group: the aim of the CTE was not anymore to simply assess the potentially negative impacts of environmental measures on trade, but rather to contribute to making international trade and environmental measures mutually supportive. To this end, the CTE was asked to

> (a) identify the relationship between trade measures and environmental measures, in order to promote sustainable development; and
> (b) make appropriate recommendations on whether any modifications of the provisions of the multilateral trading system are required, compatible with the open, equitable and non-discriminatory nature of the system ...[107]

Unfortunately, despite the initial high hopes for the work of the Committee—some even predicted it would solve "all outstanding trade and environment matters within two years of the entry into force of the WTO [Agreement]"[108]—the

107 Ibid. Within those terms of reference, the Committee was initially expected to address the following matters: "i) the relationship between the provisions of the multilateral trading system and trade measures for environmental purposes, including those pursuant to multilateral environmental agreements; ii) the relationship between environmental policies relevant to trade and environmental measures with significant trade effects and the provisions of the multilateral trading system; iii) the relationship between the provisions of the multilateral trading system and charges and taxes for environmental purposes and requirements for environmental purposes relating to products; iv) the provisions of the multilateral trading system with respect to the transparency of trade measures used for environmental purposes and environmental measures and requirements which have significant trade effects; v) the relationship between the dispute settlement mechanisms in the multilateral trading system and those found in multilateral environmental agreements; and vi) the effect of environmental measures on market access, especially in relation to developing countries, in particular to the least developed among them, and environmental benefits of removing trade restrictions and distortions."

108 *Action Agenda: Trade and the Environment, Resolution Adopted Unanimously by the 8th GLOBE International General Assembly* (Mar. 2, 1994), as quoted in Steve Charnovitz, 'A Critical Guide to the WTO's Report on Trade and Environment' (1997) 14(2) *Arizona Journal of International & Comparative Law* 341. Along the same lines, the Clinton Administration promised that the CTE would "assist efforts to reach international agreements on environmental issues that affect the entire world, such as ozone depletion, global climate change and biodiversity." Office of The US Trade Representative, *Uruguay Round-Jobs for the United States, Growth for the World* 19 (1994).

first results were quite disappointing.[109] Two years after its creation, rather than solving all "outstanding matters," the CTE issued its first report and it became instantly clear that the road ahead was still long and rocky:[110] After a "grueling negotiating process, culminating in a 36-hour marathon session where the concluding portion of the report was negotiated line-by-line," the report's conclusions merely called for "further work" on all 11 agenda items.[111]

Despite this criticism, the Committee did play a key role in advancing the trade and environment debate, by serving as a laboratory to open up WTO's internal process to the public, and as a venue where national officials from trade and environment ministries could get together and where representatives from MEAs Secretariats and other international environmental organizations could regularly meet with trade officials.[112] The value of such socialization should by no means be underestimated, as it has allowed for constant communication between the two communities, acting as a breeding ground for mutual coordination and cooperation.[113] It was precisely because the two communities had been pursuing their work on separate tracks for years that they had not been able to move past their deeply rooted differences in goals, assumptions, procedures, and traditions. As the delegates representing a state

---

109 See e.g. Charnovitz, 'A Critical Guide' (n 108) 342; Thomas J. Shoenbaum, 'International Trade and Protection of the Environment: The Continuing Search for Reconciliation' (1997) 91 *American Journal of International Law* 268, 269–70.

110 CTE 1996 Report. Several scholars have assessed the work of the CTE over the first few years. See e.g. Geert Van Calster, 'The World Trade Organisation Committee on Trade and Environment: Exploring the Challenges of the Greening of Free Trade' (1996) *European Environmental Law Review* 44; Kristin Woody, 'The World Trade Organization's Committee on Trade and Environment' (1996) 8 *Georgetown International Environmental Law Review* 459; Richard G. Tarasofsky, 'The WTO Committee on Trade and Environment: Is It Making a Difference?' (1999) 3 *Max Planck Yearbook of United Nations Law* 471; and Sinha, 'An Evaluation' (n 104).

111 Shaffer, 'The World Trade Organization under Challenge' (n 103) 36.

112 Shaffer, 'The Nexus of Law and Politics' (n 106) 101; Charnovitz, 'The WTO's Environmental Progress' (n 4) 690.

113 Throughout the years, a number of international environmental institutions have been granted observer status in the CTE, as well as in several other WTO bodies. The Secretariats that enjoy observer status in the CTE include those of the CBD, the Convention of International Trade in Endangered Species of Wild Fauna and Flora (CITES), the International Commission for the Conservation of Atlantic Tuna (ICCAT) and the United Nations Framework Convention on Climate Change (UNFCCC). For a complete list, see https://www.wto.org/english/thewto_E/igo_obs_e.htm. Mutual observership represents one of the several forms of cooperation between trade and environmental organizations, listed in a document prepared by the WTO Secretariat entitled *Existing Forms of Cooperation and Information Exchange Between UNEP/MEAs and the WTO*. See TN/TE/S/2/Rev.2 (Jan. 16, 2007).

in the WTO are not usually the same as those acting for the very same state in the context of environmental organizations,[114] lack of communication and coordination risks leading to conflicting provisions.[115] If trade and environmental goals need to be pursued in a mutually supportive manner, however, this course of action is no longer sustainable.

Outside of the CTE, a certain level of 'greening' can be found in the work of the newly created Appellate Body. Here, seven judges external to the *trade policy elite* were given the opportunity to push the nexus ahead towards further integration.

2.3 *Seven 'Faceless Foreign Judges'*

> This was truly extraordinary language, and a constitutional door opener for approaches that require a broader perspective than just the four corners of the very extensive GATT/WTO treaty language.[116]
>
> JOHN JACKSON, 2005

The language John Jackson was referring to in this often-quoted passage belongs to the Appellate Body Report in the landmark *US—Shrimps* decision. On this occasion, the Appellate Body admonished the first level panel for focusing only on trade, without taking in due account other fundamental policy goals, and entertained these other goals in the process of interpreting the *chapeau* of GATT Article XX.[117] By doing so, the Appellate Body not only criticized the panel's approach but, most importantly, repudiated the traditional approach to environmental trade measures in the GATT/WTO system since the first *Tuna/Dolphin* case.[118]

This traditional approach assumed *a priori,* and without any textual basis, that "unilateral measures that conditioned market access on the policies of the

---

114 See Joost Pauwelyn, *Conflict of Norms in Public International Law* (Cambridge University Press, 2003), p. 15.

115 See e.g. the relationship between Articles 27, 29, and 62 of the Agreement on Trade-Related Intellectual Property Rights (TRIPS) Agreement, and Article 15 of the CBD. See Nuno Pires de Carvalho, 'Requiring Disclosure of the Origin of Genetic Resources and Prior Informed Consent in Patent Applications Without Infringing the TRIPS Agreement: The Problem and the Solution' (2000) 2 *Washington University Journal of Law and Policy* 371.

116 John H. Jackson, 'Justice Feliciano and the WTO Environmental Cases: Laying the Foundations of a "Constitutional Jurisprudence" with Implications for Developing Countries', in Charnovitz et al (eds.), *Law in the Science of Human Dignity* 29 (Cambridge University Press, 2005), p. 40.

117 Ibid.

118 See Robert Howse, 'The Appellate Body Rulings in the Shrimp/Turtle Case: A new Legal Baseline for the Trade and Environment Debate' (2002) 27 *Columbia Journal of Environmental Law* 491, 499.

exporting countries were, as a matter of general principle, not justifiable under Article XX."[119] Reversing this finding, the Appellate Body stated that

> It is not necessary to assume that requiring from exporting countries compliance with, or adoption of, certain policies ... prescribed by the importing country, renders a measure *a priori* incapable of justification under Article XX. Such an interpretation renders most, if not all, of the specific exceptions of Article XX inutile, a result abhorrent to the principles of interpretation we are bound to apply.[120]

In its interpretation of the *chapeau*, the Appellate Body relied on the Preamble to the WTO Agreement, which explicitly listed 'sustainable development' as one of the objectives of the Agreement, to be pursued "seeking both to protect and preserve the environment,"[121] and which added "colour, texture, and shading" to the interpretation of trade provisions.[122] Moreover, the Appellate Body relied on certain developments that occurred after the end of the Uruguay Round and which helped elucidate "the objectives of the members with respect to the relationship between trade and the environment" such as, among others, the establishment of the CTE.[123] In contrast with the reasoning of the panel, which concluded that "the provisions of the GATT are essentially turned toward liberalization of access to markets on a non-discriminatory

---

119 See Panel Report, *United States—Import Prohibition of Certain Shrimp and Shrimp Products* WT/DS58/R (May 15, 1998) [hereinafter *US—Shrimps*], para. 7.50. Howse, 'The Appellate Body Rulings' (n 118) 498.

120 Appellate Body Report, *US—Shrimps* WT/DS58/AB/R (Oct. 12, 1998), para. 121.

121 The Uruguay Round negotiators were not the first nor the last to introduce references to sustainable development and the environment in a purely economic treaty. A very similar wording can be found in the preamble of NAFTA and, even before, in 1986, the Single European Act (SEA) had inserted a title on the 'Environment' into the EEC Treaty, which did not contain any provisions on the environment or on the possible role of the Community in its protection. With this new Title, the Act essentially gave a *constitutional* base to the Community's environmental policy, defining its objectives as preserving, protecting, and improving the quality of the environment; contributing towards protecting human health; and ensuring a prudent and rational utilization of natural resources. Single European Act Amending the Treaties Establishing the European Communities, July 1, 1987, 1987 O.J. L 169/1 [hereinafter SEA]. See Title VII in Part Three of the EEC Treaty, in particular Article 130r(1), as amended by the SEA. See Dirk Vandermeersch, 'The Single European Act and the Environmental Policy of the European Economic Community', in Ludwig Kramer (ed.), *European Environmental Law: A Comparative Perspective* (Routledge, 2003).

122 Appellate Body Report, *US—Shrimps*, para. 153.

123 Ibid., para. 154.

basis,"[124] the Appellate Body recognized the delicate nature of the *chapeau* as a means to strike a balance between two equally important rights.[125]

While early GATT panel holdings had rendered environmental exceptions essentially unusable,[126] the Appellate Body explicitly acknowledged that, sustainable development being one of the objectives of the WTO Agreement, Article XX should be read so as to mediate between the right to an open, non-discriminatory, and equitable multilateral trading system on the one hand, and the right to act for the protection of the environment, and the promotion of sustainable development on the other.[127]

With this decision, and others before,[128] the Appellate Body cut a clear break from the traditional approach of GATT and WTO panels. Some scholars have ascribed this departure to the Appellate Body's composition, which was remarkably different from the one that characterized both GATT and WTO panels.[129] The seven original and founding members of the Appellate Body, who first worked together at "a round table in a corner room of a quiet wing of the Italianate Villa that serves as the global headquarters of the WTO in Geneva," were: Julio Lacarté-Muro of Uruguay, Claus-Dieter Ehlermann of Germany, Florentino Feliciano of the Philippines, Said El-Naggar of Egypt, Mitsuo Matsushita of Japan, Christopher Beeby of New Zealand, and James Bacchus of the United States.[130] With the exception of Lacarté-Muro, none of these seven 'faceless foreign judges', as journalists often referred to them, had any particular ties with the *trade policy elite*. Unlike those sitting in GATT ad-hoc panels, these seven judges had been chosen among "distinguished generalist jurists, not eminent experts in GATT/WTO law."[131] It should be no

124 Panel Report, *US—Shrimps*, para. 7.42.

125 The Appellate Body stated that "[t]he task of interpreting and applying the chapeau is, hence, essentially the delicate one of locating and marking out a line of equilibrium between the right of a Member to invoke an exception under Article XX and the rights of other Members under varying substantive provisions (e.g. Art. XI) of the GATT 1994, so that neither of the competing rights will cancel out the other." Appellate Body Report, *US—Shrimps*, para. 159.

126 Charnovitz, 'The WTO's Environmental Progress' (n 4) 695–6.

127 Appellate Body Report, *US—Shrimps*, para. 154.

128 Appellate Body Report, *Japan—Taxes on Alcoholic Beverages*, WT/DS8/AB/R (Nov. 1, 1996) [hereinafter *Japan—Alcoholic Beverages II*]; *European Communities—Customs Classification of Certain Computer Equipment*, WT/DS62/AB/R (June 5, 1998).

129 See e.g. Robert Howse, 'The World Trade Organization 20 Years On: Global Governance by Judiciary' (2016) 27(1) *European Journal of International Law* 9, and Michael Trebilcock et al. (eds.), *The Regulation of International Trade* (Routledge, 2005), pp. 381–425.

130 James Bacchus, 'Table Talk: Around the Table of the Appellate Body of the World Trade Organization' (2002) 35(4) *Vanderbilt Journal of Transnational Law* 1021, 1022–23.

131 Howse, 'The World Trade Organization 20 Years On' (n 129) 27.

surprise then if, rather than following the trade elite dicta, they adopted a rather different approach, "employing normative benchmarks and legal standards and sources from outside the domain of GATT/WTO law, unrelated to and sometimes in tension with GATT 'collective wisdom'," and relying heavily on the rules of interpretation provided by the Vienna Convention on the Law of Treaties (VCLT).[132]

Unlike GATT panels, WTO adjudicators are explicitly *required to* invoke the rules of interpretation of treaties as a source to clarify WTO Agreements.[133] Such 'rules of interpretation' are contained in Articles 31 and 32 of the VCLT and they require adjudicators to interpret every treaty "in good faith in accordance with the ordinary meaning to be given to the terms of the treaty in their context and in the light of its object and purpose."[134] The principle of sustainable development and the objective of preserving and protecting the environment are now part of the "context, object and purpose" of the covered agreements and should inform the interpretation of any other GATT/WTO rule accordingly. And in fact, in *US—Shrimps*, both the panel and the Appellate Body were required to take into account the "context, object and purpose" of the covered agreements when interpreting the *chapeau* of GATT Article XX. However, the different approach of the two bodies can hardly be missed. On the one hand, the panel concluded that "while the WTO preamble confirms that environmental considerations are important for the interpretation of the WTO agreement, the central focus ... remains the promotion of economic development through trade."[135] On the other, the Appellate Body gave equal importance to the rights of the Members under the substantive—trade liberalization—provisions of the GATT and its exceptions, clarifying that "neither of the competing rights [should] cancel out the other."[136]

132 Ibid., at 31.

133 Understanding on Rules and Procedures Governing the Settlement of Disputes, Apr. 15, 1994, Marrakesh Agreement Establishing the World Trade Organization, Annex 2, 1869 U.N.T.S. 401 [hereinafter DSU], Art. 3.2. In *US—Gasoline* and *US—Shrimps*, the Appellate Body criticized the panel for not following all the steps in applying the customary rules of interpretation of public international law and for overlooking "a fundamental rule of treaty interpretation." Appellate Body Report, *United States—Standards for Reformulated and Conventional Gasoline*, WT/DS2/AB/R (Apr. 29, 1996) [hereinafter *US—Gasoline*], 16–17; Appellate Body Report, *US—Shrimps*, para. 115.

134 Vienna Convention on the Law of Treaties, May 23, 1969, 1155 U.N.T.S. 331 [hereinafter VCLT], Article 31.1.

135 Panel Report, *US—Shrimps*, para. 7.42.

136 Appellate Body Report, *US—Shrimps*, para. 154.

Moreover, together with the context, Article 31(3)(c) of the VCLT demands that "any relevant rules of international law applicable in the relations between the parties" be taken into account, and the Appellate Body has in many instances drawn from the body of law which has developed outside the context of the GATT, including environmental principles and norms, in its interpretation of WTO norms.[137]

A comprehensive analysis of the composition of the Appellate Body at different times and its impact on the interpretation of WTO provisions is beyond the scope of this contribution. It is interesting, however, to note a concomitance between, on the one hand, an Appellate Body composed of members *outside* of the trade policy elite, at least in its founding membership, and on the other, decisions in trade/environment cases that seem to depart from the neoliberal approach typical of the *elite* itself. Besides, this is not the first nor the sole example of the influence that the composition of a judicial body

137 See e.g. *US—Shrimps* (CITES and UNCLOS) and *EC—Bananas III* (Lomè Convention). Appellate Body Report, *US—Shrimps*; *European Communities—Regime for the Importation, Sale and Distribution of Bananas*, WT/DS27/AB/R (Sept. 9, 1997). In a paper presented at the GATT Symposium on Trade, Environment and Sustainable Development in July 1994, Philippe Sands had hoped that "the new WTO language [would] allow WTO panels to take into account the body of law which has developed outside the context of the GATT." Philippe Sands, *GATT 1994 and Sustainable Development: Lessons from the International Legal Order*, Papers presented at the GATT Symposium on Trade, Environment and Sustainable Development, July 28, 1994, 27–30, 28. But see the Panel Report in *EC—Biotech*, where the panel refused to take into account as means of interpretation the CBD and the Protocol on Biosafety because, according to VCLT Article 31.3(c), there shall be taken into account "any relevant rules of international law applicable in the relations *between the parties*," and not all the parties to the disputes were parties to these MEAs. Panel Report, *European Communities—Measures Affecting the Approval and Marketing of Biotech Products*, WT/DS291/R (Sept. 29, 2006). Howse and Horn argue that this difference in approach between the Appellate Body and the Panel can "come down to the [Appellate Body's] interest in enfranchising environmental interests and constituencies in WTO dispute settlement, and the Panel's concern (possibly reflecting the insider perspective of the WTO Secretariat, which has a large influence in the drafting of Panel decisions) to enfranchise those interests and constituencies as little as possible." Robert L. Howse and Henrik Horn, 'European Communities—Measures Affecting the Approval and Marketing of Biotech Products' (2009) 8(1) *World Trade Review* 49, 60. See Joost Pauwelyn, 'The Role of Public International Law in the WTO: How Far Can We Go?' (2001) 95(3) *American Journal of International Law* 535. As noted by Joel Trachtman, "the Appellate Body has not yet definitively addressed the question as to whether the other relevant rules of international law used in interpretation ... are limited to those to which all members subscribe, or whether they only need bind the parties to the particular dispute." Joel P. Trachtman, 'WTO Trade and Environment Jurisprudence: Avoiding Environmental Catastrophe' (2017) 58(2) *Harvard Journal of International Law* 273, 303.

can have on a line of decisions. Another example—outside of the environmental realm this time—is offered by the changing composition of the US Supreme Court. For instance, in 1937, after years of frequently striking down national laws as exceeding the proper scope of the commerce power, the US supreme Court started showing great deference to congressional action under the commerce power and for nearly six decades no law was struck down on Commerce Clause grounds.[138] In those years there had been rapid changes in the composition of the Court. From 1937 through 1941, President Roosevelt made several appointments to the Court—Justices Black, Reed, Frankfurter, Douglas, Murphy, Byrnes, and Jackson—cementing the dominance of a deferential judicial stance toward Congress' commerce power. A simple change in the Justices sitting on the bench let several state laws survive the Court's scrutiny. Just like those seven Justices shared a certain deferential judicial stance toward Congress' commerce power, which led to a line of decisions interpreting the Clause broadly, so an Appellate Body composed by international jurists rather that trade technocrats, led to a different—less trade-centered—interpretation of GATT Article XX in cases such as *US—Shrimps, EC—Asbestos,* and *EC—Hormones.*[139]

2.4 *Finding Balance through Interpretation*

The approach adopted by the Appellate Body allowed for an increasingly expansive interpretation of the exception clauses applicable *inter alia* to the environment. As such, the individual subparagraphs of Article XX have been given a progressively more expansive reading. For many years, GATT panels had adopted a restrictive interpretation of the 'necessary' requirement under Article XX(b), applying the so-called 'least trade restrictive' test.[140] The latter was very narrow and did not acknowledge the political reality of environmental policy-making processes.[141] After the establishment of the WTO, however,

---

138 Noah Feldman and Kathleen M. Sullivan, *Constitutional Law* (Foundation Press, 2013), p. 131.

139 See e.g. B.S. Chimni, 'WTO and Environment. Shrimp-Turtle and EC-Hormones Cases' (2000) 35(20) *Economic and Political Weekly* 1752; Robert Howse and Elizabeth Tuerk, 'The WTO Impact on Internal Regulations—A Case Study of the Canada-EC Asbestos Dispute', in George A. Bermann and Petros C. Mavroidis (eds.), *Trade and Human Health and Safety* (Cambridge University Press, 2006); Andrew Green and Tracy Epps, 'The WTO, Science, and the Environment: Moving Towards Consistency' (2007) 10(2) *Journal of International Economic Law* 285; Charnovitz, 'The WTO's Environmental Progress' (n 4).

140 See Chapter 3, Section 3.2.

141 Janine Ferretti, 'The Internalization of Environmental Costs and the Implications for the Trading System', Papers presented at the GATT Symposium on Trade, Environment and Sustainable Development, July 28, 1994, 33, 36.

the Appellate Body in *Korea—Beef* introduced a new test for 'necessity',[142] clarifying that the term 'necessary' is not limited to measures that are 'indispensable'.[143] For measures that are not indispensable to achieve the objective set out in Article XX(b), the 'necessary' standard is to be judged in every case through a process of weighing and balancing a series of factors.[144]

The factors to be weighed and balanced are the importance of the values furthered by the challenged measure, the contribution of the measure to the realization of such values, and the restrictive impact of the measure on international trade flows.[145] In this context, the Appellate Body Report in *Brazil—Tyres* explicitly referred to measures adopted to tackle environmental

142 In *Korea—Beef*, like a few years later in *Brazil—Tyres*, the Appellate Body was required to interpret the word 'necessary' under Article XX(d), but the same reasoning has been considered applicable to XX(b). Appellate Body Report, *Korea—Measures Affecting Imports of Fresh, Chilled and Frozen Beef*, WT/DS161/AB/R (Dec. 11, 2000) [hereinafter *Korea—Beef*]; Appellate Body Report, *Brazil—Measures Affecting Imports of Retreaded Tyres*, WT/DS332/AB/R (Dec. 3, 2007) [hereinafter *Brazil—Tyres*]. This test was applied to Article XX(b) for the first time by the Appellate Body in *EC-Asbestos*. See Appellate Body Report, *European Communities—Measures Affecting Asbestos and Products Containing Asbestos*, WT/DS135/AB/R (Mar. 12, 2001) [hereinafter *EC—Asbestos*], para 172. Nevertheless, the importation of the Article XX(d) test to Article XX(b) has been criticized by some scholars. See e.g. Anupam Goyal, *The WTO and International Environmental Law* (Oxford University Press, 2006), pp. 139–140.

143 In *Korea—Beef*, the Appellate Body continued explaining that "[a]s used in Article XX(d), the term 'necessary' refers, in our view, to a range of degrees of necessity. At one end of this continuum lies 'necessary' understood as 'indispensable'; at the other end, is 'necessary' taken to mean as 'making a contribution to'. We consider that a 'necessary' measure is, in this continuum, located significantly closer to the pole of 'indispensable' than to the opposite pole of simply 'making a contribution to'." Appellate Body Report, *Korea—Beef*, para. 161. See also Appellate Body Report, *Brazil—Tyres*, para. 141.

144 Charnovitz, 'The WTO's Environmental Progress' (n 4) 697–8. This new test has then been confirmed in several other cases, such as: Appellate Body Report, *China—Measures Affecting Trading Rights and Distribution Services for Certain Publications and Audiovisual Entertainment Products*, WT/DS363/AB/R (Dec. 21, 2009) and *China—Measures Related to the Exportation of Various Raw Materials*, WT/DS394/AB/R (Jan. 30, 2012) [hereinafter *China—Raw Materials*].

145 Appellate Body Report, *Korea—Beef*, para. 164; Appellate Body Report, *Brazil—Tyres*, paras. 142–3; and Appellate Body Report, Appellate Body Report, *United States—Measures Affecting the Cross-Border Supply of Gambling and Betting Services*, WT/DS285/AB/R (Apr. 7, 2005) [hereinafter *US—Gambling*], para. 306. Note the departure from the 'traditional' approach adopted up until the panel report in *Korea—Beef*: "To demonstrate that the dual retail system is 'necessary', Korea has to convince the Panel that no alternative measure consistent with the WTO Agreement is reasonably available at present in order to deal with misrepresentation in the retail beef market as to the origin of beef." Panel Report, *Korea—Beef*, WT/DS161/R (July 31, 2000), para. 659.

problems—climate change and global warming in particular. In this regard, the Appellate Body concluded that even if the contribution of a measure—including an import ban—to these objectives is not immediately observable, it can still be justified under Article XX(b) on the basis of a demonstration that it is "apt to produce a material contribution to the achievement of its objective," considering in particular that

> certain complex public health or environmental problems may be tackled only with a comprehensive policy comprising a multiplicity of interacting measures. In the short-term, it may prove difficult to isolate the contribution to public health or environmental objectives of one specific measure from those attributable to the other measures that are part of the same comprehensive policy. Moreover, the results obtained from certain actions … can only be evaluated with the benefit of time.[146]

This test appears to be far less stringent than the 'least trade restrictive' test in terms of the kind of relationship that is required between the measure adopted and the policy objective pursued, thus expanding the policy space provided for environmental protection measures.[147]

Even more so if one looks at how the determination of the second element of the test—the existence of a less trade-restrictive alternative—has evolved over time: to be viable, the alternative needs to not only allow for the same level of protection as that desired by the Member adopting the measure, but it also needs to be technically and financially feasible.[148] Moreover, the allocation of the burden of proof in presenting the panel with a viable alternative provides the member defending the environmental measure with a further advantage: while under the 'least trade restrictive' test, it was understood that

146 Appellate Body Report, *Brazil—Tyres*, para. 151. A few years prior, in *US—Gasoline*, the Appellate Body had reached similar conclusions in the context of GATT Article XX(g): "in the field of conservation of exhaustible natural resources, a substantial period of time, perhaps years, may have to elapse before the effects attributable to implementation of a given measure may be observable." Appellate Body Report, *US—Gasoline*, 21.

147 Gabrielle Marceau and Julian Wyatt, 'The WTO's Efforts to Balance Economic Development and Environmental Protection: A Short Review of Appellate Body Jurisprudence' (2013) 1(1) *Latin American Journal of International Trade Law* 291, 300.

148 In *US—Gambling*, the Appellate Body recognized that an alternative measure may be found not to be 'reasonably available' not only where it does not achieve the responding Member's chosen level of protection but also "where it is merely theoretical in nature, for instance, where the responding Member is not capable of taking it or where the measure imposes an undue burden on that member, such as prohibitive costs or substantial technical difficulties." Appellate Body Report, *US—Gambling*, para. 308.

the country invoking Article XX would have to prove the absence of an alternative,[149] in *Brazil—Tyres*—and even before in *US—Gambling*—the Appellate Body clarified that "while the responding Member must show that a measure is necessary, it does not have to show, in the first instance, that there are *no* reasonably available alternative to achieve its objectives."[150]

Article XX(g) has been characterized by a similar increasingly expansive interpretation. In *US—Shrimps*, the Appellate Body, while interpreting Article XX(g), concluded that the provision could not be "read as referring only to the conservation of exhaustible mineral or other non-living natural resources."[151] Rather than the finding itself, which was not entirely new to the GATT/WTO system,[152] the reasoning of the Appellate Body is of particular interest. As a matter of fact, this conclusion was motivated not solely by the language of the WTO Preamble[153] but equally by the fact that the *Brundtland Report* denounced "growing scientific consensus that species are disappearing at rates never before witnessed on the planet,"[154] and that "all of the seven recognized species of sea turtles are today listed in Appendix 1 of [the Convention on International Trade in Endangered Species of Wild Fauna and Flora] CITES."[155] This line of reasoning is even more impressive if one stops for a moment to think that, only ten years before, the GATT panel in *Canada—Salmon and Herring* had refused to even look at the United Nations Convention on the Law of the Sea (UNCLOS) because its mandate was "limited to the examination of Canada's measures in the light of the relevant provisions of the GATT."[156]

---

149 See e.g. Report of the GATT Panel, *United States—Section 337 of the Tariff Act of 1930*, B.I.S.D. 36S/345, 385 (Nov. 7, 1989), para. 5.27.

150 Appellate Body Report, *US—Gambling*, para. 309; Appellate Body Report, *Brazil—Tyres*, para. 156.

151 Appellate Body Report, *US—Shrimps*, para. 131.

152 In the 1988 GATT Panel Report on *Canada—Salmon and Herring*, the Panel agreed with the parties that salmon and herring stocks were 'exhaustible natural resources'. Report of the Panel, Report of the GATT Panel, *Canada—Measures Affecting Exports of Unprocessed Herring and Salmon*, L/6268-35S/98 (Mar. 22, 1988) [hereinafter *Canada—Herring and Salmon*], para. 4.4.

153 Ibid.

154 Brundtland Report, p. 13, as quoted in fn. 106 of the Appellate Body Report, *US—Shrimps*.

155 Appellate Body Report, *US—Shrimps*, para. 132. Besides CITES, the Appellate Body relied on several other environmental treaties to support this argument, including UNCLOS, the CBD, Agenda 21, and the Resolution of Assistance to Developing Countries adopted in conjunction with the Convention on the Conservation of Migratory Species of Wild Animals. See Appellate Body Report, *US—Shrimps*, para. 130.

156 Report of the GATT Panel, *Canada—Herring and Salmon*, para. 5.3.

Regarding the second prong of this subparagraph—that a measure be "relating to" the conservation of exhaustible natural resources—the Appellate Body seems to have distanced itself from the traditional GATT jurisprudence, which had given the term a strict meaning of "primarily aimed at" for several years. In *US—Shrimps*, the Appellate Body seemed to abandon the interpretation of "relating to" as "primarily aimed at," to embrace a more nuanced approach, examining the relationship between the general structure of the measure and the conservation policy goal it purports to serve, and concluding that the means were "reasonably related" to the ends.[157] Since then, the "relating to" requirement has been defined as a "close and genuine relationship of ends and means."[158]

Finally, in the context of the same dispute, the Appellate Body adopted a new approach with regards to the issue of *amicus curiae* briefs, by holding that both panels and the Appellate Body have the authority to accept and examine *amicus* briefs from non-state actors, including environmental NGOs. While recognizing, in line with the panel's reasoning, that the panel's authority to seek information and technical advice does include "the authority to decide not to seek such information or advice," the Appellate Body concluded that Article 13 of the Dispute Settlement Understanding (DSU) does not contain the prohibition to accept information which has been submitted without having been requested by the panel.[159] The same seems to apply to the Appellate Body, considering that it did accept an unsolicited brief precisely in *US—Shrimps*.[160]

157 Ibid., paras. 136–7, and 141–2. See Charnovitz, 'The WTO's Environmental Progress' (n 4) 701.

158 Appellate Body Report, *US—Shrimps*, para. 136; Appellate Body Report, *China—Raw Materials*, paras. 356, 361. See Trachtman, 'WTO Trade and Environment Jurisprudence' (n 137) 295–6.

159 Appellate Body Report, *US—Shrimps*, paras. 104 and 108.

160 Later in *US—Lead and Bismuth II*, the Appellate Body explicitly ruled that unsolicited *amicus curiae* briefs are admissible in Appellate Body proceedings: "We are of the opinion that we have the legal authority under the DSU to accept and consider amicus curiae briefs in an appeal in which we find it pertinent and useful to do so. In this appeal, we have not found it necessary to take the two amicus curiae briefs filed into account in rendering our decision." Appellate Body Report, *United States—Imposition of Countervailing Duties on Certain Hot-Rolled Lead and Bismuth Carbon Steel Products Originating in the United Kingdom*, WT/DS138/AB/R (May 10, 2000). See Arthur E. Appleton, 'Amicus Curiae Submissions in the Carbon Steel Case: Another Rabbit from the Appellate Body's Hat?' (2000) 3(4) *Journal of International Economic Law* 691; Denise Prévost, 'WTO Subsidies Agreement and Privatised Companies. Appellate Body Amicus Curiae Briefs' (2000) 27 *Legal Issues Economic Integration* 279. See also Jacqueline Peel, 'Giving the Public a Voice in the Protection of the Global Environment: Avenues for Participation by NGOs in Dispute Resolution at the European Court of Justice and the World Trade Organization' (2001) *Colorado Journal of International Environmental Law & Policy* 47.

This position was strongly attacked by trade experts, academic commentators, and Member delegates, in particular from developing countries. Regardless, the Appellate Body had entered into a dialogue with outsider constituencies, which had contributed to its "enlightened" jurisprudence.

This "enlightened" jurisprudence represents, together with the discussions within the CTE, the only concrete attempts to search for a balance between trade and environmental considerations at the WTO. The very same quest was proceeding at a faster pace in certain domestic systems—mostly industrialized countries—and was reflected in the position they brought forward in their bilateral and regional talks. In these contexts, simply giving exception clauses a more expansive interpretation did not seem like a sufficient response to the quest for balance: a gap that could instead be filled by drafting new 'greener' exceptions.

2.5 *FTA s and the Introduction of 'Updated' Exceptions*

> Nothing short of GATT reform is acceptable ... [We urge] Congress to ... seek fundamental reforms which will ensure the rights of GATT Contracting Parties to take trade actions consistent with the protection of the global resources and recognizing the validity of worldwide environmental treaties.[161]
>
> DAVID PHILLIPS, Hearing Before the Subcommittee on Health and the Environment, 1991

David Phillips, of the Earth Island Institute, uttered these words as part of his testimony in the congressional hearings conducted by the US Subcommittee on Health and the Environment of the Committee on Energy and Commerce in 1991. Phillip's voice was not an isolated one. Over the course of the same hearings, Steven Shrybman, of the Canadian Environmental Law Association, suggested an amendment to the GATT to allow national governments to assert their "sovereign prerogative [of doing] what they believe is necessary in the public interest to protect the environment and conserve resources."[162] To this end, he even presented a written proposal containing a model for an amended Article XX, which began with the following words:

---

161 See *GATT: Implications on Environmental Laws: Hearing Before the Subcomm. on Health and the Environment of the House Comm. on Energy and Commerce*, 102d Cong., 1st Sess. 1 (1991), at 62 (Testimony of David Phillips).

162 Ibid., 95 (Testimony of Steven Shrybman), as quoted in Thomas E. Skilton, 'GATT and the Environment in Conflict: The Tuna-Dolphin Dispute and the Quest for an International Conservation Strategy' (1993) 26 *Cornell International Law Journal* 455, 485.

> (1) Nothing in this agreement shall be construed to prevent any party from taking any action which it may deem necessary to protect the environment, including the establishment of import or export restrictions and the use of subsidies to: (i) prevent or remedy adverse environmental effects, and/or; (ii) conserve natural resources.[163]

Along the same lines, and only a few years later, the European Union participated in the first round of discussions at the newly stablished CTE by proposing, among other things, the amendment of GATT Article XX, either by including a reference to "measures taken pursuant to specific MEAs" or "in more general terms, to measures necessary to protect the environment."[164]

However, none of these proposed amendments were introduced in the text of the GATT. The Appellate Body's 'enlightened' jurisprudence on Article XX has proven to be the only means to address some of the concerns underlying these proposals, at least at the multilateral level. It was instead in the context of bilateral and regional trade negotiations that many of these proposals found a much more promising breeding ground.

163 The proposed Article continued: "(2) For greater certainty, "actions necessary to protect the environment" shall include national and international initiatives, including, but not restricted to: (i) the establishment of regulatory regimes including environmental standards, objectives, guidelines and codes of practice; (ii) approval processes relating to environmental impact assessment of projects or programs that may have significant environmental con- sequences, including the determination of whether approval for such projects or programs shall be granted; (iii) measures intended to encourage public participation and standing in the decision-making processes that may affect the environment, and; (iv) access to information on matters relating to the environment. (2) For the purpose of resolving or adjudicating any dispute that may arise under this agreement with respect to any action taken to protect the environment, the onus shall be upon the complainant to prove that: (i) the action or measure was not taken in good faith, and; (ii) is unreasonable."

164 CTE, *Non-Paper by the European Communities on Item 1*. This is just one of many similar proposals. Hurlock, for example, suggests the introduction of an additional subparagraph under GATT Article XX—letter (k)—related to measures adopted pursuant to multilateral environmental agreements. For the complete text of the proposed provision, see Matthew H. Hurlock, 'Note. The GATT, US Law and the Environment: A Proposal to Amend the GATT in Light of the Tuna/Dolphin Decision' (1992) 92 *Columbia Law Journal* 2098, 2148. Other proposals are even more drastic. Over the course of the Uruguay Round, US Senator Max Baucus, for example, had been advocating the negotiations of a GATT side-agreement that would account for environmental issues, an 'Environment Code', along the lines of the Tokyo codes on subsidies or on technical barriers to trade. See Max Baucus, 'NAFTA Needs Environmental Side Agreements' (1993) 10 *Environmental Forum* 30. See also Skilton, 'GATT and the Environment in Conflict' (n 162) 484 and William H. Lash III, 'Green Gang's GATT Holdup', *Journal of Commerce*, Dec. 10, 1993.

At a first glance, the general exceptions contained in most free trade agreements (FTAs) seem to simply reproduce those found in WTO agreements and, in some instances, this is exactly the case.[165] Other agreements, instead, formulate their own exception clauses with the goal of providing for greater policy space for environmental regulations. First, a number of FTAs do explicitly refer to the environment in their exception clauses. The *EU-Colombia-Peru* FTA, for instance, revisits the GATT wording to explicitly include environmental measures.[166] A similar result is achieved by the *US-Jordan* FTA, which, in the context of trade in goods, clarifies that "[t]he Parties understand that the measures referred to in GATT 1994 Article XX(b) include environmental measures necessary to protect human, animal or plant life or health, and that GATT 1994 Article XX(g) applies to measures relating to conservation of living and non-living exhaustible natural resources."[167]

Besides explicitly qualifying their exception clauses as 'environmental', some agreements omit the word "necessary" when reproducing GATT Article XX(b) and simply refer to measures "justified on grounds of ... the protection of health and life of humans, animals or plants,"[168] thus eliminating the necessity test required by the GATT which, despite having become far more flexible than it used to be, still represents an obstacle to be overcome by the party defending a given environmental measure.

A third way in which new FTAs innovate with regards to the drafting of exception clauses is by expanding their scope of application *beyond* the chapter on trade in goods. As a matter of fact, article XX only applies to claims made under the GATT or, at least, under agreements with provisions that refer to GATT Article XX.[169] However, the more recent environmental disputes brought

165 See e.g. Free Trade Agreement, EU-Iceland, Dec. 19, 1972, Art. 21; and Free Trade Agreement, EU-Norway, May 14, 1973, Art. 20.

166 Article 106 refers to measures "(b) necessary to protect human, animal or plant life or health, including those environmental measures necessary to this effect; [...] (g) relating to the conservation of living and non-living exhaustible natural resources, if such measures are made effective in conjunction with restrictions on domestic production or consumption."

167 Free Trade Agreement & Economic Integration Agreement, United States-Jordan, Oct. 24, 2000, Art. 12. See also e.g. Free Trade Agreement & Economic Integration Agreement, China-New Zealand, Apr. 7, 2008 [hereinafter China-N.Z. FTA], Art. 200(2); Free Trade Agreement, EFTA-Canada, Jan. 26, 2008, Art. 22; Free Trade Agreement & Economic Integration Agreement, Japan-Peru, May 31, 2011 [hereinafter Japan-Peru FTA], Art. 10; and Free Trade Agreement & Economic Integration Agreement, Australia-China, June 17, 2015, Art. 9.8(2).

168 Free Trade Agreement, EU-South Africa, Oct. 11, 1999 [hereinafter EU-S. Afr. FTA], Art. 27.

169 See e.g. SPS Agreement, Articles 1 and 2.4. According to Article 1, Members desire "to elaborate rules for the application of the provisions of GATT 1994 which relate to the

to the WTO rarely require the application of GATT provisions, as the challenged measures generally include local-content requirements, conditional subsidies, tax rebates, and artificial limits on inputs, also known as 'green industrial policy' measures.[170] Unlike the GATT, none of the disciplines governing these trade measures—such as the Agreement on Subsidies and Countervailing Measures (ASCM) or the Anti-Dumping Agreement (ADA)—contain an environmental exception that allows for a balancing test.[171] And even those agreements that do include general exceptions, such as Article XIV of the General Agreement on Trade in Service (GATS), do not always mirror the exact terms of GATT Article XX.[172]

Some of the more recent FTAs address these concerns by expanding the scope of application of GATT-like exceptions to numerous chapters of the agreement, or by introducing new exception clauses in chapters that traditionally did not feature one. So, the *EU-Colombia-Peru* FTA, among others, expands the scope of its "trade in services" exception clause by including a subparagraph on measures "relating to the conservation of exhaustible natural resources," a category that corresponds to GATT Article XX(g) but does not instead feature in GATS Article XIV.[173] Article 21.1 of the *US-Singapore* FTA, instead, extends GATT Article XX to its chapters 2 through 6 (National Treatment and Market Access for Goods, Rules of Origin, Customs Procedures, Textiles, Technical Barriers to Trade).[174]

---

use of sanitary or phytosanitary measures, in particular the provisions of Article XX(b)," while Article 2.4 reads as follows: "Sanitary or phytosanitary measures which conform to the relevant provisions of this Agreement shall be presumed to be in accordance with the obligations of the Members under the provisions of GATT 1994 which relate to the use of sanitary or phytosanitary measures, in particular the provisions of Article XX(b)." Agreement on Sanitary and Phytosanitary Measures, Apr. 15, 1994, Marrakesh Agreement Establishing the World Trade Organization, Annex 1A, 1867 U.N.T.S. 3 [hereinafter SPS Agreement].

170 Salzman and Wu define these disputes as "Next Generation" trade and environment conflicts, as opposed to the "Classic" trade and environment disputes that revolved around the imposition of import restrictions for environmental purposes. See Mark Wu and James Salzman, 'The Next Generation of Trade and Environment Conflicts: The Rise of Green Industrial Policy' (2014) 108(2) *Northwestern University Law Review* 401.

171 Ibid., 452, 454.

172 Marceau and Wyatt, 'The WTO's Efforts' (n 147) 305.

173 EU-Colom.-Peru FTA, Art. 167(c).

174 See also e.g. US-Chile FTA, Art. 23; Free Trade Agreement & Economic Integration Agreement, Canada-EU, Oct. 30, 2016 [hereinafter CETA], Art. 28.3; Free Trade Agreement & Economic Integration Agreement, China-Singapore, Oct. 23, 2008, Art. 105; Free Trade Agreement & Economic Integration Agreement, Australia-Chile, July 30, 2008 [hereinafter Austl.-Chile FTA], Art. 22.1; Free Trade Agreement & Economic Integration Agreement, Canada-Peru, May 29, 2008, Art. 2201; Free Trade Agreement & Economic Integration

The applicability of Article XX, in particular, to the ASCM has been the subject of heated debates.[175] The Agreement, introduced at the conclusion of the Uruguay Round, initially contained a temporary escape clause for environmental measures—albeit narrowly drafted—which elapsed in 2000 and was never renewed by the Members.[176] The recent case law regarding renewable energy subsidies[177] has brought to the surface the inherent shortcomings of the existing subsidies discipline: the one-size-fits-all approach adopted by the Agreement, where all subsidies are lumped in the same basket, has been widely criticized for not allowing the distinction between undesirable subsidies and those that are adopted for legitimate reasons.[178]

Agreement, Costa Rica-Singapore, Apr. 6, 2010, Art 18.2; and Free Trade Agreement & Economic Integration Agreement, Mexico-Panama, Apr. 3, 2014 [hereinafter Mex.-Pan. FTA], Art. 19.2. The agreement between Singapore and Turkey, e.g., extends the applicability of Article XX to the Chapter of Investment as well. See Free Trade Agreement & Economic Integration Agreement, Turkey-Singapore, Nov. 14, 2015 [hereinafter Turk.-Sing. FTA], Art. 12.24.

175 The 2006 *World Trade Report* of the WTO Secretariat, in its legal analysis, suggests: "While Article XX in principle would apply to subsidies, the more specific rules of the ASCM in any case are explicitly geared to remedying trade distortions arising from subsidization," 201.

176 Article 8 of the ASCM, now no longer in force, allowed subsidies devoted to the "assistance to promote adaptation of existing facilities to new environmental requirements imposed by law and/or regulations which result in greater constraints and financial burden on firms" provided that some conditions were met. See e.g. Paolo D. Farah and Elena Cima, 'World Trade Organization, Renewable Energy Subsidies and the Case of Feed-in Tariffs: Time for Reform Toward Sustainable Development?' (2015) 27 *Georgetown International Environmental Law Review* 516.

177 Appellate Body Report, *Canada—Certain Measures Affecting the Energy Generation Sector,* WT/DS412AB/R (May 6, 2013) [hereinafter *Canada—Renewable Energy*] and *Canada—Measures Relating to the Feed-In Tariff Program* WT/DS426AB/R (May 6, 2013) [hereinafter *Canada—FIT Program*]. Appellate Body Report, *India—Certain Measures Relating to Solar Cells and Solar Modules,* WT/DS456/AB/R (Sept. 16, 2016).

178 Alan Sykes, 'The Economics of WTO Rules on Subsidies and Countervailing Measures' (2003) University of Chicago Law & Economics, Olin Working Paper No. 186, 1. See also Steve Charnovitz and Carolyn Fischer, 'Canada-Renewable Energy: Implications for WTO Law on Green and Not-So-Green Subsidies' (2015) 14(2) *World Trade Review.* Petros C. Mavroidis and Aaron Cosbey, 'A Turquoise Mess: Green Subsidies, Blue Industrial Policy and Renewable Energy: The Case for Redrafting the Subsidies Agreement of the WTO' (2014) EUI Working Paper RSCAS 2014/17. Moreover, because the GATT covers measures—such as total bans and quotas—which are widely known as more restrictive and trade-distorting than subsidies, the lack of an exception in the ASCM would end up according more distorting measures a more favorable treatment. See Robert Howse, 'Climate Mitigation Subsidies and the WTO Legal Framework' (2010) IISD; Luca Rubini, 'Ain't Wastin' Time No More: Subsidies for Renewable Energy, the SCM Agreement, Policy Space and Law Reform' (2012) 15 *Journal of International Economic Law* 525.

Scholars have been discussing ways to fill this gap and different views have been put on the table, from reinstating the category of non-actionable subsidies—or introducing a new one—to extending the application of GATT Article XX to the ASCM.[179] Once again, FTAs seem to have started addressing these concerns. Article 12.9 of the *EU-Japan* FTA, for instance, extends GATT Article XX to its chapter on subsidies, while other agreements, as the next section will explain in further detail, have introduced a different kind of environmental escape clause in their subsidies chapter, precisely to allow the distinction between undesirable subsidies and subsidies that pursue legitimate (environmental) policy goals.

2.6 *An Exception and Nothing More*

While the Appellate Body's jurisprudence of the last 30 years has provided WTO Members with greater environmental policy freedom through means of interpretation, free trade agreements, beginning with NAFTA, have allowed the environment to have a more significant presence in their text: by means of treaty interpretation and negotiation, the dialogue about trade and the environment appears to have permanently changed.

However, without detracting at all from this discernible evolution, the dominant narrative has hardly changed: the environment continues to be treated as nothing more than an exception, although a much broader one than it used to be, as "GATT Article XX remains the arbiter, balancing environmental protection against trade protectionism when conflicts arise."[180] If it is true that, unlike the pre-*Tuna/Dolphin* and pre-WTO era, it is generally acknowledged that environmental and trade goals can and should be pursued in a mutually supportive manner trying to avoid or minimize all possible conflicts, on the other hand all the efforts towards this end seem to concentrate solely on how

179 For different proposals, see Andrew Green, 'Trade Rules and Climate Change Subsidies' (2006) 5 *World Trade Review* 377, 408–10; Robert Howse, 'Do the World Trade Organization Disciplines on Domestic Subsidies Make Sense? The Case for Legalizing Some Subsidies', in Kyle W. Bagwell et al. (eds.), *Law and Economics in Contingent Protection in International Trade* 85–102 (Cambridge University Press, 2009), p. 94; Howse, 'Climate Mitigation Subsidies' (n 178) 21; Tracey Epps and Andrew Green, *Reconciling Trade and Climate* 256–57 (Edward Elgar, 2010); Rubini, 'Ain't Wastin' Time No More' (n 178) 570–77; Gary Horlick and Peggy Clarke, 'Rethinking Subsidy Disciplines for the Future' (2016) E15 Task Force on Rethinking International Disciplines—Policy Options Paper, ICTSD; Elena Cima, 'Caught between Trade and Climate Change. The Economic Rationale of "Green Subsidies"', in Klaus Mathis and Bruce R. Huber (eds.), *Environmental Law And Economics* 379–404 (Springer, 2017), pp. 400–1; Wu and Salzman, 'The Next Generation of Trade and Environment Conflicts' (n 170) 456.

180 Wu and Salzman, 'The Next Generation of Trade and Environment Conflicts' (n 170) 413.

to best use the space provided by GATT exceptions. And even in the context of the more recent disputes concerning the environment, although not based on the GATT but on other WTO Agreements, the debate continues to be framed in terms of 'exceptions'. The debate on the (lack of) space provided by the ASCM provides a good example of this trend, as most proposals have been revolving around the need to either extend the application of GATT Article XX to the ASCM, or to draft a brand-new exception clause within its text.

Along the same lines, no matter how many times the Appellate Body declares that the *chapeau* of Article XX should be interpreted as a means to strike a balance between two equally important rights, environmental protection is hardly recognized as a *right* in the WTO system, and framing them merely as an exception effectively prevents environmental goals from standing on equal footing with economic ones.

Accordingly, trade law continued to be used as the framework of reference through which to evaluate environmental measures: despite the recognition that countries can pursue environmental objectives, and although they now seem to have more freedom to do so, ultimately the limit is still the respect of trade norms and the preservation of the integrity and smoothness of international trade flows. The importance of this limit has been reiterated even by the Appellate Body which, in *US—Gasoline*, held that, although "WTO Members have a large measure of autonomy to determine their own policies on the environment ... that autonomy is circumscribed ... by the need to respect the requirements of the GATT and other covered agreements."[181]

A similar message can be found in paragraph 6 of the Doha Ministerial Declaration which, despite all the enthusiasm it generated, still subordinates states' ability to enact whatever environmental protection measures they please "to the requirement that they are not applied in a manner which would constitute a means of arbitrary or unjustifiable discrimination between countries where the same conditions prevail, or a disguised restriction on

181 Appellate Body Report, *US—Gasoline*, 30, quoted by the Panel in *US—Shrimps*, at 7.26. This message can be found loud and clear in the text of several WTO Agreements, such as the SPS Agreement, where Article 5.6 provides that "when establishing or maintaining sanitary or phytosanitary measures to achieve the appropriate level of sanitary or phytosanitary protection, Members shall ensure that such measures *are not more trade-restrictive* than required to achieve their appropriate level of sanitary or phytosanitary protection" (emphasis added). Similarly, Article 5.4 provides that "Members should, when determining the appropriate level of sanitary or phytosanitary protection, take into account the objective of minimizing negative trade effects."

international trade, and are otherwise in accordance with the provisions of the WTO Agreements."[182]

After all, although the two communities have managed to overcome the clinical isolation that had characterized the GATT-era, the level of integration has remained relatively weak, especially at the multilateral level. Within the WTO, the rules governing the institutional ties between the CTE and international environmental organizations had been unclear and contested for several years,[183] their discussions dominated by a clear hierarchy between trade and environmental rules, and observers did not participate beyond formal reporting.[184] It should then be no surprise to find that the 1996 CTE report, while acknowledging "certain complementary objectives between the WTO and MEAS ... subordinates MEAS' trade-related environmental measures (TREMS) to trade obligations."[185] Because of the diverging positions of the representatives of developed and developing countries, the weak language of the 1996 Report seemed necessary to provide the foundation around which these divergent interests could converge and a consensus text could be constructed. Moreover, it has been argued that the ten-point work program of the CTE weakened its original mandate, by targeting specific environmental issues while moving away from the promotion of sustainable development and lacking direct opportunities to recommend changes to the multilateral trading system.[186] Overall, the discussions within the CTE and Ministerial negotiations

182 World Trade Organization, Ministerial Declaration of 14 November 2001, WT/MIN(01)/DEC/1, 41 I.L.M. 746 (2002) [hereinafter Doha Declaration], para. 6.

183 Observership in the WTO is regulated by the 1996 *Guidelines on Observer Status for International Intergovernmental Organizations in the WTO*, WT/L/161 (July 25, 1996) [hereinafter *Guidelines*]. Granting observer status is usually related to specific sessions or specific organs of the Organization and each request is assessed on a case-by-case basis, taking into account, among other factors, the nature of the work of the organization concerned, the nature of its membership, the number of WTO Members in the organization, and reciprocity with respect to access to proceedings.

184 As to the rights of the observers, the *Guidelines* specify that representatives of organizations accorded observer status, beside receiving copies of the main WTO documents and of other documents relating to the work of the subsidiary bodies which they attend as observers, have the right to speak after Members have spoken and may be able to circulate papers or make proposals if expressly invited to do so. On the other hand, the *Guidelines* are clear when they specify that these rights do not in any event include the right to participate in any decision-making activity.

185 Melissa Gabler, 'Norms, Institutions and Social Learning: An Explanation for Weak Policy Integration in the WTO's Committee on Trade and Environment' (2010) 10(2) *Global Environmental Politics* 80.

186 Rachel McCormick, 'A Qualitative Analysis of the WTO's Role on Trade and Environment Issues' (2006) 6(1) *Global Environmental Politics* 102, 111. The original mandate, outlined in the 1994 Ministerial Declaration on the Environment, was twofold: (i) "identify the

reflected a style of interaction between the trade and environmental communities based on simple learning about environmental norms to satisfy trade interests.[187] The same can be said for the CTE Special Sessions (CTESS),[188] whose mandate indicated that the possibilities for substantial changes in the prevailing trade-centered stance would be very limited. First, with regards to the first topic to be addressed by the CTESS—the relationship between WTO rules and specific trade obligations set out in MEAs—Ministers clarified that "negotiations shall be limited in scope to the applicability of ... existing WTO rules as among Parties to the MEA in question [and that] the negotiations shall not prejudice the WTO rights of any Member that is not a Party to the MEA."[189] Second, outcomes "shall be compatible with the open and non-discriminatory nature of the multilateral trading system and shall not add to, diminish or alter the balance of the rights and obligations of Members under existing WTO Agreements."[190]

The very same message can be found in bilateral and regional trade agreements as well. Despite being much 'greener' than their multilateral counterparts, they have continued to subordinate the parties' freedom to protect the environment to the condition that by doing so trade is not excessively restricted. Article 104 of NAFTA, for instance, which was considered revolutionary at the time because it defined the relationship between a trade agreement and multilateral environmental treaties for the first time,[191] clarifies that, in case of inconsistency between NAFTA and the specific trade obligations set

relationship between trade measures and environmental measures in order to promote sustainable development;" and (ii) "make appropriate recommendations on whether any modifications of the provisions of the multilateral trading system are required, compatible with the open, equitable and non-discriminatory nature of the system."

187 Gabler, 'Norms, Institutions and Social Learning' (n 185) 105.

188 The Committee on Trade and Environment Special Sessions (CTESS) held its very first meeting on March 22, 2002, back-to-back with the regular meeting of the CTE. See WTO CTESS, *Statement by the Chairperson of the Special Session of the Committee on Trade and Environment to the Trade Negotiations Committee*, TN/TE/1 (Apr. 12, 2002).

189 Doha Declaration, para. 31(i). The other topics to be covered by the CTESS are "(ii) procedures for regular information exchange between MEA Secretariats and the relevant WTO committees, and the criteria for the granting of observer status; [and] (iii) the reduction or, as appropriate, elimination of tariff and non-tariff barriers to environmental goods and services."

190 Ibid., para. 32.

191 To be entirely correct, the Havana Charter did directly address the MEA issue. Article 45 provided an exception for measures "taken in pursuance of any inter-governmental agreement which relates solely to the conservation of fisheries resources, migratory birds or wild animals." See Charnovitz, 'A Critical Guide' (n 108) 346.

out in certain MEAs,[192] the latter shall prevail to the extent of the inconsistency. However, the same provision further clarifies that "where a Party has a choice among equally effective and reasonably available means of complying with" the MEAs obligations, the Party will have to choose the alternative that is "the least inconsistent" with NAFTA.[193] And the same caveat can be easily spotted after every provision that addresses environmental concerns in nearly all free trade agreements signed since then.

3 Beyond Exceptions

The reader, who has followed the story up until this point, will have observed a quite discernible evolution of the relationship between the international trade and environmental regimes towards a greater mutual supportiveness,[194] as suggested in the *Brundtland Report,* in Rio, and in nearly every single international environmental conference or summit since then. This evolution, nevertheless, continues to follow traditional patterns: the assumption is always the possibility of conflicts between the goals of the two regimes and what has emerged is rather the willingness to solve them; the relationship between trade liberalization and environmental protection continues to be approached from a purely free trade perspective and, as a result, even when more space is given to environmental values, this space is always designated as exceptional.

Looking more closely, however, the situation seems to be gradually changing and the evolution itself appears to be taking a rather different turn. This new direction, however, cannot be detected at all levels and in all fora at the same

192 NAFTA Article 104 in particular refers to CITES, the Montreal Protocol on Substances that Deplete the Ozone Layer, and the Basel Convention on the Control of Transboundary Movements of Hazardous Wastes and Their Disposal.

193 NAFTA, Art. 104. Similar language characterizes the SPS and TBT chapters of the agreement. For a more recent example, see also e.g. Article 292(3) of the agreement between the EU and Ukraine: "Nothing in this Agreement shall limit the rights of a Party to adopt or maintain measures to implement the multilateral environmental agreements to which it is a Party. Such measures shall not be applied in a manner which would constitute a means of arbitrary or unjustifiable discrimination between the Parties or a disguised restriction on trade." Free Trade Agreement & Economic Integration Agreement, EU-Ukraine, June 27, 2014 [hereinafter EU-Ukr. FTA], Art. 292(3).

194 For a discussion on the principle of mutual supportiveness in the context of the relationship between international trade and environmental law and, more broadly, in the context of fragmentation of international law, see Laurence Boisson de Chazournes and Makane Moïse Mbengue, 'A "Footnote as a Principle." Mutual Supportiveness in an Era of Fragmentation', in Holger P. Hestermeyer et al. (eds.), *Coexistence, Cooperation and Solidarity—Liber Amicorum Rüdiger Wolfrum—Vol. II* (Martinus Nijoff Publishers, 2011).

time, or even with the same intensity. Once again, it is those countries that are pursuing, both domestically and internationally, a 'greener' agenda that are paving the way for a brand-new chapter in the trade/environment story. A new chapter where the trade community appears more and more willing to open the front door to let the environment in and take its seat at the table, if not within the WTO, at least in the context of bilateral and regional negotiations. The EU and the US are once again on the frontline, together with other developed countries like Canada, architects of a new generation of trade agreements where the idea of 'greening trade law' acquires a whole new meaning. These agreements feature provisions that give the environment a new status within their text, far beyond what we generally define as 'exceptions'. Environmental exemptions, or carve-outs, give states an autonomous right to pursue environmental objectives and so do those provisions that recognize countries' regulatory sovereignty in the environmental realm, integrate general environmental principles, and provide for environmental obligations of a mandatory nature.

3.1 *The (Not So) Thin Line between Exceptions and Exemptions*

> (1) A procuring entity shall not prepare, adopt or apply any technical specification or prescribe any conformity assessment procedure with the purpose or the effect of creating unnecessary obstacles to international trade.
> (6) For greater certainty, a Party, including its procuring entities, may, in accordance with this Article, prepare, adopt or apply technical specifications to promote the conservation of natural resources or protect the environment.
>
> Government Procurement Agreement, Revised Text, 2012, Article X

Article X of the Revised Agreement on Government Procurement (GPA) contains an environmental 'exemption' in its discipline on technical specifications. Although an 'exemption' should *never* be confused with an 'exception', the risk of confusion is fairly common. In fact, the term 'exception' is often used—misleadingly—in a very broad and over-comprehensive fashion, to encompass all clauses which identify situations where trade rules do not apply or prevail in order to accommodate domestic policies. The reason why using the term 'exception' interchangeably may be misleading is that several different techniques exist to achieve such exclusion, and each of them carries different legal implications.[195]

---

195 Viñuales, for example, identifies up to seven techniques that can be employed in treaties to "escape a rule." The seven techniques identified are: i) delimitation of the scope of a

The escape clauses discussed so far—mainly GATT Article XX—can be characterized as exceptions *stricto sensu*. However, over the course of the years, a different type of escape clause—referred to as 'exemption' or 'carve out'—has been gradually introduced to allow countries to pursue, among others, environmental objectives. The agreements on Technical Barriers to Trade (TBT) and on Sanitary and Phytosanitary Measures (SPS), for instance, contain exemptions that are relevant for the environment.[196] Article X of the Revised Agreement on Government Procurement (Revised GPA), quoted at the beginning of this section, similarly contains an environmental exemption.[197] Interestingly, this provision was only added when the Agreement was amended in 2012 while, when the GPA was first drawn up during the Uruguay Round, it did not contain any reference to the environment in its provision on technical specifications.[198] Between 1995 and 2012, a number of bilateral negotiations had led to the adoption of FTAs whose chapters on government procurement began introducing the very same exemption, which ultimately found its way on the table of the Revised GPA negotiators.[199]

Recent FTAs feature a wider variety of environmental exemptions. Many examples can be found in their investment chapters. Annex 8-A of the EU-Canada Comprehensive Economic and Trade Agreement (CETA), for example, explicitly excludes from the definition of 'indirect expropriation' "non-discriminatory regulatory actions by a Party that are designed and applied to protect legitimate public welfare objectives, such as public health, safety and the environment" except in rare circumstances.[200] Similar environmental

---

norm or set of norms; ii) specific carve-outs or exemptions; iii) flexibilities; iv) derogations; v) exceptions *stricto sensu*; vi) excuses; and vii) circumstances precluding wrongfulness. Jorge E. Viñuales, 'Seven Ways of Escaping a Rule: Of Exceptions and Their Avatars in International Law', in Lorand Bartels and Federica Paddeu (eds.), *Exceptions and Defences in International Law* (Oxford University Press, 2020).

196 See SPS Agreement, Art. 3.3 and, Agreement on Technical Barriers to Trade, Apr. 15, 1994, Marrakesh Agreement Establishing the World Trade Organization, Annex 1A, 1868 U.N.T.S. 120 [hereinafter TBT Agreement], Art. 2.4.

197 WTO, Committee on Government Procurement, *Decision on the Outcomes of the Negotiations under Article XXIV:7 of the Agreement on Government Procurement*, GPA/113, Apr. 2, 2012 [hereinafter Revised GPA], Art. X.

198 See Agreement on Government Procurement, April 14, 1994, Marrakesh Agreement Establishing the World Trade Organization, 1869 U.N.T.S. 508 (1994) [hereinafter GPA], Art. VI.

199 See Austl.-Chile FTA, Art. 15.12(6); Can.-Colom. FTA, Art. 1407; Japan-Peru FTA, Art. 149(5). For later examples, see S. Kor.-N. Z. FTA, Art. 13.13(6); Can.-Ukr. FTA, Art. 10.10(6); CETA, Art. 19.9.6; and Free Trade Agreement & Economic Integration Agreement, Japan-Australia, July 8, 2014, Art. 17.7(8).

200 CETA, Art. 8.12 and Annex 8-A. Other examples include US-Chile FTA, Annex 10-D, US-Austl. FTA, Annex 11-B; China-N. Z. FTA, Annex 13; Turk.-Sing. FTA, Annex 12-A; Free Trade

carve-outs can be found in other investment provisions, such as those on the prohibition of performance requirements,[201] as well as in the Chapters dealing with marking and labelling, government procurement, and trade facilitation.[202]

The *EU-Singapore* FTA stands out as it provides for an exemption within its subsidies discipline, marking a stark departure from the multilateral subsidies discipline that does not even feature an exception clause. The agreement allows the two parties to provide for subsidies that *do* have trade effects on the other party—as long as such effects are contained and the subsidy is limited to the minimum needed to achieve the objective—when such subsidies are necessary to achieve an objective of public interest, explicitly including subsidies "for environmental purposes."[203]

Agreement & Economic Integration Agreement, United States-Morocco, June 15, 2004, Annex 10-B; Free Trade Agreement & Economic Integration Agreement, Dominican Republic-Central America-United States, Aug. 5, 2004, Annex 10-C; Free Trade Agreement & Economic Integration Agreement, Canada-Panama, May 14, 2010, Annex 9.11; Free Trade Agreement & Economic Integration Agreement, Republic of Korea-Vietnam, May 5, 2015, Annex 9-B; and Free Trade Agreement & Economic Integration Agreement, Costa Rica-Colombia, May 22, 2013, Annex 12-B. This type of carve-out has been invoked in a number of recent disputes, which clearly show the legal implications of using carve-outs rather than exceptions. See e.g. *Adel A Hamadi Al Tamimi v. Sultanate of Oman*, ICSID Case No. ARB/11/33, Award (Nov. 3, 2015) [hereinafter *Al Tamimi v. Oman*].

201 More precisely, the prohibition to impose or enforce the requirement to achieve a given level or percentage of domestic content, to purchase, use, or accord a preference to goods produced in its territory, or to purchase goods from persons in its territory, or to transfer a particular technology, production process, or other proprietary knowledge to a person in its territory, does not apply to measures "(ii) necessary to protect human, animal, or plant life or health; or (iii) related to the conservation of living or non-living exhaustible natural resources." See NAFTA, Art. 1106, US-Chile FTA, Art. 10.5, Mex.-Pan. FTA, Art. 10.7(7), and US-Sing FTA., Art. 15.8. See also Free Trade Agreement & Economic Integration Agreement, United States-Peru, Apr. 12, 2006, Art. 10.9; Free Trade Agreement & Economic Integration Agreement, Peru-Mexico, Apr. 6, 2011, Art. 11.7(2); Free Trade Agreement & Economic Integration Agreement, Canada-Republic of Korea, Sept. 22, 2014, Art. 8.8(2).

202 According to the EU-Colom.-Peru FTA, Parties that require mandatory marking or labeling or products shall not require the approval, registration, or certification of labels or marking as a precondition for sale in their respective markets "d) unless necessary in view of the risk of the products to human, animal or plant health or life, the environment or national safety." Art. 81. See also EU-S. Kor. FTA, Art. 61(g), Free Trade Agreement & Economic Integration Agreement, EU-Chile, Nov. 18, 2002, Art. 161.

203 EU-Sing. FTA, Art. 12.8, Annex 12-A(e). See also Annex IX of the EU-S. Afr. FTA. Another example is provided by the European Economic Area (EEA). Article 61, which regulates state aid, prohibits "any aid granted by EC Member States, EFTA States or through State resources in any form whatsoever which distorts or threatens to distort competition by favouring certain undertakings or the production of certain goods [...] in so far as it affects trade between Contracting Parties." However, under Article 61.3(c), "aid to facilitate the

Although sometimes articulated in very similar terms, exceptions and exemptions operate in a very different manner. *Exceptions* identify circumstances in which the breach of other provisions of an agreement is justified. On the other hand, *exemptions* do not assume the breach of any provision, as they function as a removal of a given measure from the scope of application of a rule or set of rules, with the effect that said rule (or set of rules) will not apply to the carved-out measure.[204] This distinction is very important as it carries with it different legal implications, in particular with reference to the allocation of the burden of proof and interpretation.[205]

As to the allocation of the burden of proof, the maxim that the respondent bears the burden of proving the exception only applies to *exceptions* and not to *exemptions*. In the presence of an *exemption*, in fact, the burden will not be on the respondent but rather on the complainant to prove that a general rule has been violated by the respondent and that the respondent does not fall under the situation foreseen by the excluding provision.[206] In *EC—Hormones*, the

---

development of certain economic activities or of certain economic areas, where such aid does not adversely affect trading conditions to an extent contrary to the common interest" may be compatible with the functioning of the Agreement. See Cima, 'Caught between Trade and Climate Changeo' (n 179) 400–1.

204 The WTO Appellate Body has grasped and clarified this distinction on several occasions. In *US—Shrimps*, it defined Article XX of the GATT as a "limited and conditional exception from the substantive obligations contained in the other provisions of the GATT 1994" (para. 157), following the approach of earlier GATT panels. By contrast, in *Canada—Periodicals*, referring to GATT Article III:8, it stated that this provision exemplifies "the kinds of programs which are exempted from the obligations of Articles III:2 and III:4." Appellate Body Report, *Canada—Certain Measures Concerning Periodicals*, WT/DS31/AB/R (June 30, 1997), 33–4. In subsequent cases, it was further clarified that the measures falling under Article III:8 "do not violate Article III" and are not subject to the national treatment obligations set out therein. The distinction between the two categories of provisions was made even clearer in cases arisen under the TBT and SPS Agreements. In *EC—Hormones*, discussing the scope of Article 3.3 of the SPS Agreement, the Appellate Body reversed the panel's finding that a "general rule—exception" relationship existed between Article 3.1 and 3.3 of the SPS Agreements, to explain that there is a qualitative difference between this relationship and the one between Articles I and III and Article XX of the GATT, precisely because Article 3.1 "simply excludes from its scope of application the kinds of situations covered by Article 3.3." Appellate Body Report, *European Communities—Measures Concerning Meat and Meat Products*, WT/DS26/AB/R (Jan. 16, 1998) [hereinafter *EC—Hormones*], paras 104 and 172.

205 The distinction between different techniques is not a prerogative of trade agreements but applies to international treaties broadly. See Viñuales, 'Seven Ways of Escaping a Rule' (n 195).

206 Michelle T. Grando, *Evidence, Proof, and Fact-Finding in WTO Dispute Settlement* (Oxford University Press, 2009).

Appellate Body reversed the panel's finding that the burden of proof regarding SPS Article 3.3 had to be assigned to the respondent and clarified that it was for the United States and Canada (the complainants) to prove that the excluding norm did not apply.[207]

Because the panel or Appellate Body have to find against the party bearing the burden of proof when the evidence is not sufficient or the arguments are in equipoise, framing an excluding provision as an *exception* or an *exemption* can produce far-reaching effects. An element that further exacerbates the distance between the two scenarios is the standard of proof required to prove the violation of a primary norm vis-à-vis the applicability of an exception. The burden of persuasion imposed on the complainant to prove the violation of a general obligation (such as those contained in Articles I, III, and XI of the GATT), is generally rather 'light' when compared to that borne by the respondent,[208] leading some scholars to argue that it is precisely the 'light' burden imposed on the complainant to have contributed towards some (type II) errors, where a measure that should have been allowed is found inconsistent instead.[209]

Another element that makes exemptions more advantageous for the respondent in an hypothetical trade/environment dispute is the way in which these provisions are interpreted by the adjudicating bodies. The traditional approach in international practice has been to give primary norms an expansive interpretation, leading to a broad range of measures falling under their scope, and to interpret exception clauses restrictively.

---

207 Appellate Body Report, *EC—Hormones* paras 107–9. This statement formed the basis of Appellate Body decisions in later TBT cases, such as *EC—Sardines*, where the Appellate Body stressed that "it [was] for Peru—as the complaining Member seeking a ruling on the inconsistency with Article 2.4 of the TBT Agreement of the measure applied by the European Communities—to bear the burden of proving its claim," as the second part of TBT Article 2.4 represents an exemption and not an exception. Appellate Body Report, *European Communities—Trade Description of Sardines*, WT/DS231/AB/R (Sept. 26, 2002), paras. 275 and 282.

208 For example, with regard to both Article III and XI of the GATT, no adverse effects need to be shown to establish a violation. If we break down these provisions into their various components, we reach similar conclusions. With regard to Article III, for example, when determining whether a product has been taxed "in excess," even a minimal tax differential is sufficient. See Appellate Body Report, *Japan—Alcoholic Beverages II*, at. 23. See also Henrik Horn and Petros C. Mavroidis, 'Burden of Proof in Environmental Disputes in the WTO: Legal Aspects' (2009) Research Institute for Industrial Economics, IFN Working Paper No. 793, 14.

209 Based on the distinction between *Type I* errors, where a truly guilty defendant escapes liability, and *Type II* errors, where a truly innocent defendant is found liable. Horn and Mavroidis, 'Burden of Proof' (n 208) 41.

It is true that recent Appellate Body reports seem to have re-interpreted the principle of strict interpretation to deny that it constitutes a mandatory principle to be followed by adjudicative bodies. In *EC—Hormones*, the Appellate Body stated that

> ... merely characterizing a treaty provision as an 'exception' does not by itself justify a 'stricter' or 'narrower' interpretation of that provision than would be warranted by examination of the ordinary meaning of the actual treaty words, viewed in context and in the light of the treaty's object and purpose, or, in other words, by applying the normal rules of treaty interpretation.[210]

However, as it has been suggested, with this statement the Appellate Body has simply clarified that qualifying a provision as an exception does not automatically trigger a strict interpretation, *not* that exceptions should not be interpreted restrictively.[211] Moreover, the Appellate Body has often emphasized that exceptions operate in a limited and conditional way. In *US—Shrimps*, for instance, it stressed the "limited ambit of such exceptions because the lack of their determinacy could otherwise endanger the integrity of the primary obligations under the relevant treaty."[212] The *chapeau* of Article XX, in addition, puts further limitations on the operability of the exceptions under GATT Article XX.[213]

Exemptions have not been addressed as thoroughly as exceptions with respect to their interpretation. If one were to follow the principle according to which "the more exceptional the clause the more restrictive the interpretation," as explained by Viñuales, being exemptions less exceptional than

210 Appellate Body Report, *EC—Hormones*, para. 104.

211 Asif H. Qureshi, *Interpreting WTO Agreements. Problems and Perspectives* (Cambridge University Press, 2006), p. 109. Similarly, referring to general rules of treaty interpretation does not change much in practice, as the principle *exceptio est strictissimae applicationis* "is not independent of this treaty material but rather draws from it." Ibid., p. 110.

212 Appellate Body Report, *US—Shrimps*, para. 157.

213 As to the principle of effective interpretation, it refers only to the right to invoke exceptions, which should not be rendered illusory by an overly restrictive interpretation thereof. As the Appellate Body clarified in *US—Gasoline*, if the exceptions in GATT Article XX should not "be read so expansively as seriously subvert the purpose and object of Article III:4, ... Article III:4 [should not] be given so broad a reach as effectively to emasculate Article XX(g) and the policies and interests it embodies." By contrary, this principle should not "enable exception clauses to exceed their profile as exceptions and *encroach* on what is regulated under the 'primary provisions' under the treaty." Appellate Body Report, *US—Gasoline*, 18. See Alexander Orakhelashvili, *The Interpretation of Acts and Rules in Public International Law* (Oxford University Press, 2008), p. 428.

exceptions, it would follow that their interpretation should be less restrictive.[214] The investment dispute *Mesa v. Canada* provides a quite clear example of such an approach.[215] The claimant (Mesa) suggested that NAFTA "Article 1108(7)(a) must be interpreted restrictively because it is an exception,"[216] while the tribunal qualified the provision as a carve-out, whose function is "to exclude all procurement activities from the scope of some of the obligations of Chapter 11,"[217] and sided with the Appellate Body in *Canada—Renewables* in interpreting the term 'procurement' broadly.[218]

The importance of the use of exemptions in the context of the trade/environment debate is not limited to the legal implications studied in this section. The introduction of these clauses marks a departure from the traditional way in which the nexus has been approached, in that they identify a country's autonomous right to pursue environmental objectives, rather than simply an exception from a general treaty obligation, as clearly explained by the Appellate Body in *EC—Hormones*: "The right of a Member to determine its own appropriate level of sanitary protection is an important right ... this right ... is an autonomous right and not an 'exception' from a 'general obligation.'"[219] The same result is achieved with those provisions, increasingly featured in FTAs, which recognize countries' regulatory 'environmental' sovereignty.

3.2 *The Right to Protect the Environment*

> ... relating to the level of protection, we note that it is undisputed that WTO Members have the right to determine the level of protection of health that they consider appropriate in a given situation.
>
> Appellate Body Report, EC—Asbestos, para. 168

In 1997, France introduced a ban on asbestos and on products containing asbestos fibers.[220] Asbestos had been long known to be a deadly carcinogen and France was determined to eradicate this serious health hazard once and for

214 Viñuales, 'Seven Ways of Escaping a Rule' (n 195).

215 *Mesa Power Group, LLC v. Government of Canada*, UNCITRAL, PCA Case No. 2012–17 [hereinafter *Mesa v. Canada*]. See Viñuales, Seven Ways of Escaping a Rule' (n 195).

216 *Mesa v. Canada*, para 405.

217 Ibid., para 427.

218 Ibid., paras 411–413. Appellate Body Report, *Canada—FIT Program*, para 5.59, where the Appellate Body understood "the word 'procurement' to refer to the process pursuant to which a government acquires products." Viñuales, 'Seven Ways of Escaping a Rule' (n 195).

219 Appellate Body Report, *EC—Hormones*, para. 172.

220 Décret no. 96–1133 relatif à l'interdiction de l'amiante, pris en application du code de travail et du code de la consummation (Jan. 1, 1997).

all. Even though the ban applied to both domestically produced and imported asbestos, Canada argued that the kind of asbestos it exported (chrysotile) did not present any health risks when used in a safe manner and should therefore be allowed into the French market.[221]

Both the panel and the Appellate Body, when addressing the applicability of GATT Article XX(b) to the French ban, started from the assumption that countries could set their own level of protection, and concluded that the analysis of the 'necessity' of the ban had to be based on the specific level chosen by France. That the choice of the level of protection deemed appropriate is a prerogative of the member concerned rather than the panel or Appellate Body had already been established in *Australia—Salmon*: "We do not believe that Article 11 of the DSU ... entitles the Panel or Appellate Body ... to substitute its own reasoning about the implied level of protection for that expressed consistently by Australia."[222] It follows that each member can choose the level of risk they are willing to endure and, in both cases, France and Australia chose the risk to be equal to zero—so-called 'zero risk'.[223] France, in particular, was determined to halt the spread of asbestos-related health risks, and that is precisely why such a trade-restrictive measure—a total import ban—was chosen. Despite Canada's attempts to argue, in appeal, that 'controlled use' could represent a reasonably available alternative that would serve the same end,[224] the Appellate Body was firm in ruling that "such an alternative measure would, in effect, prevent France from achieving its chosen level of health protection" and therefore deemed the French ban to be necessary.[225]

Although these disputes deal with public health, WTO Members enjoy the same 'regulatory sovereignty' in the context of environmental protection. Under WTO law, however, the right to define one's own level of protection is not an "absolute or unqualified right."[226] Even though countries are free to choose

221 Appellate Body Report, *EC—Asbestos*, para. 16.

222 Appellate Body Report, *Australia—Measures Affecting Importation of Salmon*, WT/DS18/AB/R (Oct. 20, 1998) [hereinafter *Australia—Salmon*], para. 199. See also Appellate Body Report, *US—Gasoline*, at 30 and Appellate Body Report, *EC—Hormones*, para. 172: "The rights of a Member to determine its own appropriate level of sanitary protection is an important right ... made clear by the sixth preambular paragraph of the *SPS Agreement:* 'Desiring to further the use of harmonized sanitary and phytosanitary standards ... without requiring Members to change their appropriate level of protection of human, animal, or plant life or health'." See also Appellate Body Report, *Brazil—Tyres*, para. 140.

223 Appellate Body Report, *Australia—Salmon*, para. 124–5; Appellate Body Report, *EC—Asbestos*, para. 168.

224 Appellate Body Report, *EC—Asbestos*, para. 173.

225 Ibid., para. 174.

226 Appellate Body Report, *EC—Hormones*, para. 173.

the level of protection they deem appropriate, they are generally required to use international standards.[227] The underlying rationale is to achieve a certain harmonization of domestic environmental standards, as diverging standards are still seen as barriers to smooth trade flows. The SPS and TBT Agreements allow Members to exceed the protection of such international standards *but only* provided that certain conditions are met.[228]

Once again, free trade agreements take it one step further. NAFTA, in its Chapters 7 and 9, removes these conditions simply stating that:

> Nothing in paragraph 1 shall be construed to prevent a Party, in pursuing its legitimate objectives, from adopting, maintaining or applying any standards-related measure that results in a higher level of protection than would be achieved if the measure were based on the relevant international standard.[229]

As a result, the agreement manages to favor harmonization while at the same time preserving the parties' right to choose higher levels of protection and ensuring that such harmonization does not occur in a downward fashion,[230] introducing a provision that has become an essential component of the environmental chapter of many modern FTA s.

Moreover, the new generation of free trade agreements has been taking this trend to the next level. Many explicitly recognize the parties' right to determine the level of environmental protection they deem suitable considering their national priorities, and the sovereignty over the enforcement of environmental measures.[231] They have also started including provisions that are slowly shaping them into instruments that can be actively used to pursue environmental objectives.

---

227 SPS Agreement, Art. 3.1, and TBT Agreement, Art. 2.4.

228 See SPS Agreement, Arts. 3.3 and 5.

229 NAFTA, Art. 905.3. The exact same wording can be found in Article 713.3.

230 See Housman, 'The North American Free Trade Agreement's Lessons' (n 8) 405.

231 See all FTAs signed by the US after NAFTA, as well as the following agreements: EU-S. Kor. FTA, Art. 13.3; EU-Colom.-Peru FTA, Art. 268; EU-Ukr. FTA, Art. 290; EU-Sing. FTA, Art, 13.2; EU-SADC, Art. 9.1; CETA, Art. 24.3; EU-Japan, Art. 16.2; Free Trade Agreement & Economic Integration Agreement, EU-Caribbean Forum, Oct 15, 2008, Art. 184.1; Free Trade Agreement & Economic Integration Agreement, EU-Georgia, June 27, 2014, Art. 228; and Free Trade Agreement & Economic Integration Agreement, EU-Moldova, June 27, 2014, Art. 364. See also e.g. Agreement on Environmental Cooperation, Canada-Chile, Feb. 1997, Art. 3; and Free Trade Agreement & Economic Integration Agreement, EFTA-Philippines, Apr. 28, 2016, Arts. 11.3 and 11.4.

3.3 FTAs' Environmental Framework

In 1994, in his seminal book *Greening the GATT*, Daniel Esty called for the creation of a Global Environmental Organization (GEO) to act as counterbalance to the then soon-to-be-established WTO.[232] The features of the GEO would have included: i) the definition of general environmental principles; ii) the development of a "cohesive set of norms, rules, methodologies and procedures" for countries to follow in their efforts to protect the environment, as well as baseline environmental obligations; iii) the creation of a forum for settling environmental disputes; and iv) of a focal point to facilitate the exchange of information and data, as well as the transfer of clean technologies, to gather data on environmental trends, refine analytical tools, and develop environmental indicators.[233]

All these features were seen as necessary to ensure that "environmental values [were] not overwhelmed by more established interests, such as trade liberalization."[234] After almost 30 years, there is no sign of a Global Environmental Organization. What is there, instead, is a new generation of FTAs, which seem to be slowly moving in this precise direction: unlike in the GATT/WTO system, which only reflects the classical free trade principles (such as nondiscrimination) and only contains obligations related to trade liberalization and the elimination of protectionist behaviors,[235] these new FTAs create a framework that increasingly resembles that of the GEO envisioned by Esty. Figure 1 offers a visual representation of the aforementioned framework.

3.3.1 Environmental Principles

Besides the recognition of the parties' right to pursue environmental objectives, all the main environmental principles have found their way in the intricate jungle of trade rules that dominate these agreements. These are the principles that, after making their first appearance in the Declaration signed in Stockholm in 1972, were further developed 20 years later in Rio and, in many cases, have acquired the status of norms of customary international law.[236]

232 See e.g., Daniel C. Esty, 'The Case for a Global Environmental Organization', in Peter B. Kenen (ed.), *Managing the World Economy: Fifty Years after Bretton Woods* (Institute for International Economics, 1994), p. 287; Steve Charnovitz, 'A World Environmental Organization' (2002) 27 *Columbia Journal of Environmental Law* 323; Frank Bermann, *A World Environmental Organization. Solution or Threat for Effective International Environmental Governance* (Routledge, 2005).

233 Esty, *Greening the GATT* (n 89) 82.

234 Ibid., p. 79.

235 See the language of GATT Articles II and XI, among many others.

236 For an analysis of the Rio principles, see Jorge E. Viñuales (ed.), *The Rio Declaration on Environment and Development: A Commentary* (Oxford University Press, 2015); Kovar,

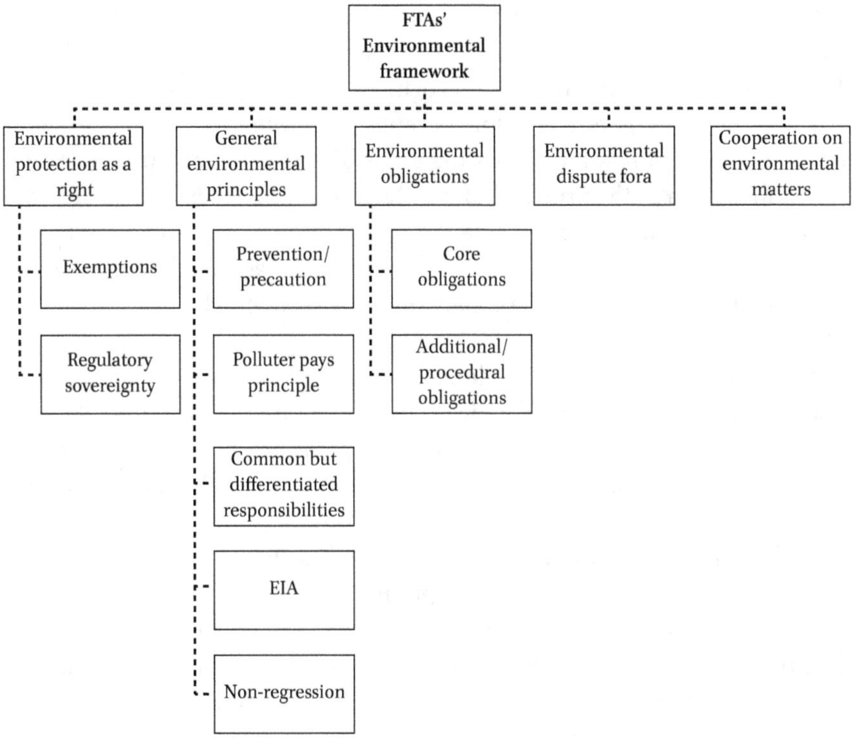

FIGURE 1 Environmental 'Framework' within trade agreements

The EU, Colombia, and Peru, for instance, have agreed to "address global environmental challenges in accordance with the principle of common but differentiated responsibilities,"[237] while the parties to the European Economic Area (EEA) have committed to base any action related to the environment "on the principles that preventive action should be taken, that environmental damage should as a priority be rectified at the source, and that the polluter should pay."[238] Another environmental principle that has found its way in modern

'A Short Guide' (n 27) 119. See e.g. Jonathan Vessey, 'The Principle of Prevention in International Law' (1998) 3 *Austrian Review of International and European law* 181; John H. Knox, 'The Myth and Reality of Transboundary Environmental Impact Assessment' (2002) 96(2) *American Journal of International Law* 291; Philippe Cullet, *Differential Treatment in International Environmental Law* (Ashgate, 2003); Priscilla Schwartz, 'Polluter Pays Principle', in Malgosia Fitzmaurice et al. (eds.), *Research Handbook on International Environmental Law* (Edward Elgar, 2010), p. 243.

237 EU-Colom.-Peru FTA, Art. 267(4).

238 EEA, Art. 73.2.

FTAs is the principle of non-regression. The idea of non-regression is old in international environmental law.[239] It can already be found in Principle 1 of the Stockholm Declaration, which recognizes man's responsibility "to protect and improve the environment for present and future generations," so as to avoid regressing in relation to existing levels of environmental protection.[240] The introduction of the principle of non-regression in the text of recent FTAs, motivated by the desire to mitigate the possibility to fail to enact or enforce environmental laws as a source of competitive advantage, has been translated in actual obligations for the states party to the agreement.[241]

3.3.2 Environmental Obligations

Next to the classical free-trade obligations—prohibition to discriminate or to impose quantitative restrictions—many FTAs feature environmental obligations which, unlike their trade counterparts, are not merely negative obligations but also include affirmative duties. The core obligations, which constitute part of the 'Pollution Haven Package' examined earlier, require the parties to enforce their environmental laws and prohibit them from lowering their level of environmental protection to attract trade or investment, thus translating the principle of non-regression examined above. Around these core commitments, FTAs generally specify additional, and often procedural, obligations. According to CETA, the parties are required to "take into account relevant scientific and technical information … when preparing and implementing measures aimed at environmental protection that may affect trade or investment between the Parties."[242] Moreover, they have committed to ensure public awareness of the respective environmental laws and enforcement compliance procedures, and to promote public participation—by encouraging public debates and submissions—with respect to the development and definition

239 Michel Prieur, 'Le principe de non régression en droit de l' environnement, condition du développement durable' (2013) *Revue Africaine de Droit de l'Environnement* 17.

240 United Nations Conference on the Human Environment, Stockholm, Sweden, June 5–16, 1972, *Stockholm Declaration on the Human Environment*, U.N. Doc. A/CONF.48/14/Rev.1, Principle 1. This principle can also be found in a wide variety of multilateral environmental agreements, such as *inter alia* the Paris Agreement on climate change.

241 Elena Cima and Makane M. Mbengue, 'ESIL Reflection—"Kind of Green". The U.S. Proposal to Advance Sustainability through Trade Rules and the Future of the WTO' (2021) 10(1) *ESIL Reflections*. With reference to investment agreements, see Andrew D. Mitchell and James Munro, 'No Retreat: An Emerging Principle of Non-regression From Environmental Protections In International Investment Law' (2019) 50 *Georgetown Journal of International Law* 626, 649.

242 CETA, Art. 24.8.

TABLE 1 Environmental obligations in FTAs

Core obligations	
Not lowering of levels of environmental protection	
Enforcement of environmental laws	
Additional obligations	
Scientific knowledge	Scientific knowledge when designing environmental measures Scientific knowledge when conducting environmental risk assessment
Public awareness and participation	Publication of environmental laws and regulations Public participation in the development of environmental laws and policies Public participation in environmental impact assessment
Environmental impact	Monitor the state of the environment Conduct and review environmental impact assessments Exchange information on assessment methodologies
Invest in environmental research and science	

of new environmental laws and policies.[243] Similarly, parties often commit to monitor, assess, and review the environmental impact of the implementation of the agreement, as in the FTA between the EU and Singapore.[244] *Table 1* offers an overview of these obligations, as included in the FTAs examined.

3.3.3 Dispute Settlement

Any violation of these environmental obligations by one of the parties to the FTA can be challenged by the other party(ies), just like any other obligation contained in the agreement. Most agreements, such as those signed by the EU—or by the US before 2007—establish a special dispute settlement

243 Ibid., Art. 24.7.
244 EU-Sing. FTA, Art. 13.14.

mechanism under their 'Sustainable Development' or 'Environment' chapters, which is able to settle any claims raised under the provisions contained therein.[245]

Although, in the vast majority of cases, these chapters are not covered by the general dispute settlement mechanism, the mere existence of environmental provisions or chapters within these agreements may have quite far-reaching consequences in the way trade/environment disputes are handled and ultimately decided. While trade provisions as such have not been invoked yet, and no relevant case law exists,[246] an increasing number of disputes brought under the investment chapter of FTAs shows an environmental component[247] and can provide us with an insight into the role that all these environmental norms can play in disputes involving FTAs. A particularly good example is provided by the interpretation of the minimum standard of treatment by the tribunal in *Al Tamimi v. Oman*, an investment dispute raised under the *US-Oman* FTA.[248] The dispute, which arose with respect to the enforcement of environmental laws against a limestone quarry project, required the definition by the arbitral tribunal of the exact content of the minimum standard of treatment, as set out in Article 10.5 of the FTA.[249]

If the preamble to the WTO Agreement has been used by the panels and the Appellate Body to "add color, texture, and shading" to the interpretation of WTO rules, the existence of an entire chapter dedicated to the 'environment'

---

245 Similarly, the "investment" chapter is generally excluded from the operation of the dispute settlement mechanism established by the FTA, as it requires the parties to settle their disputes through the traditional methods of investor-state arbitration.

246 The lack of disputes under the dispute settlement mechanisms established by FTAs can sometimes be explained with the decision of the complainant to bring the dispute at the WTO. This can happen in any case of overlapping jurisdiction, which may occur whenever trade disputes arise between the Parties to an FTA, who are also WTO Members regarding obligations that are the same or similar to those of a covered agreement. See Gabrielle Marceau, 'The Primacy of the WTO Dispute Settlement System' (2015) *Questions of International Law* (2015).

247 See Jorge E. Viñuales, 'Foreign Investment and the Environment in International Law: The Current State of Play', in Kate Miles (ed.), *Research Handbook on Environment and Investment Law* (Edward Elgar, 2019).

248 Ibid. *Al Tamimi v. Oman.*

249 According to Article 10.5: "1. Each Party shall accord to covered investments treatment in accordance with customary international law, including fair and equitable treatment and full protection and security [and] 2. For greater certainty, paragraph 1 prescribes the customary international law minimum standard of treatment of aliens as the minimum standard of treatment to be afforded to covered investments." Free Trade Agreement & Economic Integration Agreement, United States-Oman, Jan. 19, 2016 [hereinafter US-Oman FTA], Art. 10.5.

in the the *US-Oman* FTA, featuring mandatory obligations for the parties to comply with, can have an even greater impact on the way in which any other norm of the agreement is interpreted. In this specific instance, the tribunal referred to both Article 10.10 and Chapter 17 of the agreement in interpreting the minimum standard of treatment.

Article 10.10 is an environmental provision within the investment chapter of the *US-Oman* FTA, which provides for the protection of the right of both parties to adopt, maintain, and enforce any measure to ensure that "investment activity in [their] territory is undertaken in a manner sensitive to environmental concerns."[250] As part of the investment chapter, Article 10.10 falls under the jurisdiction of the tribunal, who relied upon it to construe Article 10.5.[251] Chapter 17, entitled 'Environment,' on the other hand, does not fall directly within the tribunal's jurisdiction. Nevertheless, the tribunal gave substantial weight to this chapter in interpreting the content of the minimum standard of treatment, as it "provides further relevant context in which the provisions of Chapter 10 must be interpreted."[252] In the exact words of the tribunal,

> ... the very existence of Chapter 17 exemplifies the importance attached by the US and Oman to the enforcement of their respective environmental laws ... When it comes to determining any breach of the minimum standard of treatment under Article 10.5, the Tribunal must be guided by the forceful defense of environmental regulation and protection provided in the express language of the Treaty.[253]

This interpretation of the minimum standard of treatment offers a meaningful example of the way in which environmental provisions are applied and used in the context of FTA s. Unlike WTO panels and Appellate Body, panels established under an FTA will not be constrained in their mandate by an underlying purely economic rationale when performing their function. It follows that, in case of disputes administered under an FTA, free trade principles and obligations on

250 US-Oman FTA, Art. 10.10.

251 *Al Tamimi v. Oman*, para. 387.

252 Ibid., para. 388.

253 Ibid., para. 389. This reasoning is perfectly in line with Article 10.21 of the US-Oman FTA, entitled "Governing Law," which states in the relevant part that "the tribunal shall decide the issues in dispute in accordance with this Agreement and applicable rules of international law." Thus, while the tribunal's jurisdiction is limited to the provisions within Chapter 10, it must read them in the context and purpose of the Agreement as a whole.

the one hand, and environmental principles and obligations on the other, will have to be balanced against one another in each individual dispute.

3.4 *The Road Ahead*

The final declaration adopted by the Singapore Ministerial Conference on December 7, 1996 stated that "the full implementation of the WTO Agreements will make an important contribution to achieving the objectives of sustainable development."[254] As indicated in the Preamble to the Marrakesh Agreement, sustainable development does indeed represent one of the objectives of the Organization. The story of the evolution of the trade/environment debate as told so far, however, paints a different picture. The developments described in this chapter, although significant, have not been aimed at protecting the environment through trade norms, but rather at ensuring that trade rules would interfere less than before with countries' domestic environmental policy goals, provided, of course, that these rules are nevertheless respected. In other words, the space devoted to the environment within international trade law has been increasing but has remained 'exceptional'.

The new generation of FTA s described in the final section of this chapter—although limited to a small number of countries—presents certain features that can no longer be explained exclusively with the prevailing narrative. The environment has become more than simply an exception, it has also become a rule. At the same time, however, the underlying rationale of these new provisions is the same as that of the expansive reading of GATT Article XX offered by the Appellate Body in the last two decades: to allow for a fairer balance of economic and environmental goals, in order to facilitate their mutual supportiveness and reduce conflicts to a minimum. Moreover, even when the parties agree to protect the environment—for instance, by liberalizing trade in environmental goods and services—the language used in nearly all agreements is hortatory rather than providing enforceable binding obligations.

The story told so far reflects the dominant narrative generally used to describe it. This narrative is oblivious to the origin and historical evolution of the trade and environmental regimes, painting their relationship in conflictual terms. Over time, we have witnessed, as these chapters have demonstrated, changes in the composition and interactions of the respective communities, which have allowed the inherent synergy between the two regimes to gradually reach the surface. What the next chapter of this book will depict is an even more radical transformation, where trade norms are seen as instrumental to

254 Shoenbaum, 'International Trade and Protection of the Environment' (n 109) 270.

environmental protection, showing this synergy, which had remained buried under layers of reciprocal suspicion, misconception, and, more often than not, simple unawareness for a long time. Just like trade rules were initially drafted in Havana with the ultimate goal of maintaining long-awaited peace, they can now work towards the protection of our common environment and the fulfillment of sustainable development goals.

CHAPTER 5

Can Trade Work for the Environment?

The Promotion-Based *Model*

On September 19, 2000, the Committee on Trade and the Environment (CTE) issued a document entitled *Matrix on Trade-Related Measures Pursuant to Selected Multilateral Environmental Agreements.*[1] The goal of the Matrix was to clarify which multilateral environmental treaties contained trade-related environmental measures, and to assess their relationship with the rules of the World Trade Organization (WTO) Agreements. Clarifying the relationship between trade-related provisions in multilateral environmental agreements (MEAs) and WTO rules was indeed part of the mandate of the Committee, stated first in the 1994 *Decision on Trade and Environment* and later confirmed in Doha.[2] There are several reasons why MEA negotiators might decide to regulate trade or mandate the use of trade restrictions: for instance, to ensure the integrity of the regulatory framework created with the MEA itself, to artificially control the supply of a given product, when satisfying the demand to its fullest would deplete the resources on which it is based, or to prohibit trade in certain substances or products with non-parties to provide incentives both to join the agreement and to comply with its obligations.[3] Indeed, environmental

1 WT/CTE/W/160 (Sept. 19, 2000) [hereinafter Matrix on Trade Measures Pursuant to Selected MEAs]. The document has been revised several times: WT/CTE/W/160/Rev.1 (June 14, 2001), WT/CTE/W/160/Rev.2 (Apr. 25, 2003), WT/CTE/W/160/Rev.3 (Feb. 16, 2005), WT/CTE/W/160/Rev.4 (Mar. 14, 2007), WT/CTE/W/160/Rev.5 (June 15, 2011), WT/CTE/W/160/Rev.6 (Oct. 4, 2013), WT/CTE/W/160/Rev. 7 (Sept. 4, 2015), WT/CTE/W/160/Rev.6 (Oct. 9, 2017).

2 World Trade Organization, Ministerial Declaration of 14 November 2001, WT/MIN(01)/DEC/1, 41 I.L.M. 746 (2002) [hereinafter Doha Declaration], para. 31(i).

3 An example of the third reason is offered by the Montreal Protocol which, developed under the framework of the Vienna Convention for the Protection of the Ozone Layer, creates a regime that limits the release of ozone-depleting substances into the atmosphere. Allowing the import of such substances from non-parties would frustrate the whole system and therefore import and export from or to non-parties are banned. The Convention on International Trade in Endangered Species of Wild Fauna and Flora (CITES), on the other hand, offers an example of a treaty that incorporates trade measures to artificially control the supply of a given product to achieve its objectives. Finally, both the Montreal Protocol and the Basel Convention on the Control of Transboundary Movements of Hazardous Wastes and Other Wastes provide for more trade-restrictive measures to be adopted only against non-parties to incentivize membership.

treaties have been featuring such provisions for decades, and there is absolutely nothing surprising in a multilateral environmental treaty providing for trade restrictions to fulfill specific environmental protection objectives.[4] As *environmental* treaties, these instruments pursue their environmental protection goals in a variety of ways including, when deemed more effective, through the regulation of trade measures. There's nothing shocking about any of that.

What would instead be surprising is finding similar provisions within the text of trade agreements rather than environmental one—and this is precisely what this chapter will show: trade negotiations and agreements that *neither* ignore the environment *nor* expand exception clauses to accommodate environmental concerns within the hard-driving logic of trade. Rather, trade rules that have been designed with environmental protection in mind. The backdrop against which this new chapter of the trade/environment nexus unfolds is provided by the *2030 Agenda for Sustainable Development* (*2030 Agenda*), which has fortified the acknowledgment that environmental degradation, lack of access to clean and affordable water, and spreading hunger and poverty have become the most pressing concerns faced by the international community, and that trade can play an important role in securing their solution.[5] After many decades, the notion that the trade regime is meant for something greater than trade liberalization and the instrumental role of trade instruments and norms had finally resurfaced.

1 Tables Have Turned

> What will trade be like in 2030?
> How can we shape it to fit our priorities?
> How can we make it more sustainable?
>
> ROBERTO AZEVÊDO, WTO Public Forum, October 2, 2018

In his opening speech delivered at the WTO Public Forum on October 2, 2018, Roberto Azevêdo, former Director-General of the WTO, welcomed more than 2000 people by asking his audience these difficult, yet fundamental questions.[6]

4 See e.g. Edith Brown Weiss, 'The Evolution of International Environmental Law' (2011) 54 *Japanese Yearbook of International Law* 1.

5 United Nations General Assembly, *Transforming Our World: The 2030 Agenda for Sustainable Development*, A/RES/70/1 (Sept. 25, 2015) [hereinafter 2030 Agenda].

6 Roberto Azevêdo, WTO Director-General, Opening Remarks at the WTO Public Forum (Oct. 2, 2018). The text of the speech is available at https://www.wto.org/english/news_e/spra_e/spra238_e.htm (last accessed August 3, 2021).

The third question resonated in particular among the hundreds of environmentalists in the room, whether national delegates, leaders of non-governmental organizations (NGOs), businessmen, or students. This very question was given center stage throughout the day, with a series of events following one after another unremittingly, all tied together by the same theme: "Making Trade Work for the Environment, Prosperity, and Resilience."[7]

The idea first came to Azevêdo and Eric Solheim, former Director of United Nations (UN) Environment, about a year before, and was announced to the public in January 2018. Although over the past 20 years, the trade and environmental agendas had been slowly brought closer together, the two leaders agreed that more needed to be done.[8] In his speech, Azevêdo acknowledged that "trade is a powerful tool to make green technologies more affordable and to help sustainable business expand," making it his priority to ensures that trade "delivers benefits for people and the environment everywhere."[9] Over the course of the many events that took place on that October day in Geneva, many proposals were advanced, all pointing to ways in which trade institutions and instruments could be used and trade rules modified to foster environmental—and more broadly sustainable development—goals. Some panelists, for instance, called for trade policies in support of the widespread dissemination of environmentally friendly technologies such as those needed for renewable energy. Others debated approaches to eliminate fossil fuel subsidies, and most of them agreed on the importance of introducing new rules on subsidies in the fisheries sector. Most of these ideas seemed to be widely shared by the representatives of both the trade and environmental communities. Azevêdo himself mentioned the agreement on deep cuts in fish-depleting subsidies and the scaling back of trade barriers on environmental goods and services as examples of ways to ensure the 'sustainability' of trade. What is more, he seemed entirely confident that "the WTO [would be] the place to deliver progress on these issues."[10]

This statement, and the launch, on the very same day, of a joint WTO/UN Environment publication entitled—just like the series of events—*Making*

7 The series of events were co-organized by the WTO and UN Environment. See https://www.unenvironment.org/events/conference/making-trade-work-environment-prosperity-and-resilience (last accessed August 3, 2021).

8 Roberto Azevêdo, WTO Director-General, Address at the High-Level Panel on Making Trade Work for the Environment, Prosperity, and Resilience (Oct. 2, 2018).

9 Ibid.

10 Ibid.

Trade Work for the Environment, Prosperity, and Resilience,[11] broke new ground. Not even 20 years had passed since another WTO Director General, Renato Ruggiero, had penned the following words reflecting on the events that had unfolded in Seattle in November 1999: "This Organization [the WTO] cannot be allowed to gradually drift away from its trade vocation. It would serve neither the WTO nor any other cause if it were to pretend it could offer solutions to every non-trade issue."[12] Now, the Director General in charge looks at the WTO and sees a forum where progress on making trade work for a variety of non-trade concerns is possible, if not even desirable. And so do environmental organizations: in a meeting of the CTE in January 2008, a representative from the United Nations Environment Program (UNEP) had declared with confidence that "the WTO was the most promising international forum for effectively disciplining fisheries subsidies,"[13] one of the thorniest issues at the interface between trade and the environment.

The thick lines that had been drawn by the *trade policy elite* to distinguish what qualified as a 'trade issue' and what did not have become increasingly blurry, to the point of nearly fading. And, while bilateral and regional trade negotiations had been addressing them since NAFTA, this was the first time the WTO itself was depicted as a forum "to deliver progress on these issues."[14]

The 2018 joint publication broke new ground also with regards to the previous record of cooperation between the two organizations. In 2009, Pascal Lamy and Achim Steiner, then Directors of, respectively, the WTO and UNEP, presented the first joint study ever carried out together by the two organizations, a detailed and comprehensive report on climate change and trade.[15] The document, groundbreaking at the time given the decades of isolation between the two communities, still reflected the traditional trade-centered approach to the nexus: it took WTO rules for granted and addressed the question of how to best address climate change within the boundaries of international trade law, as it was based on the assumption that "there is considerable scope and flexibility under WTO rules for addressing climate change at the national level."[16]

11 WTO/UN Environment, *Making Trade Work for the Environment, Prosperity, and Resilience* (2018).

12 Roberto Ruggiero, 'Reflections After Seattle' (2000) 24(9) *Fordham International Law Journal* 9, 11. See also Jagdish Bhagwati, 'On Thinking Clearly About the Linkage Between Trade and the Environment' (2000) 5 *Environment & Development Economics* 483.

13 WT/CTE/M/45 (Jan. 9, 2008), para. 15.

14 Roberto Azevêdo, Address at the High-Level Panel (n 8).

15 WTO/UNEP, *Trade and Climate Change* (2009).

16 Ibid., p. v. The Report focuses on three broad categories of national climate change policies—price and market mechanisms, financial mechanisms, and technical

The question at the core of the new report published on October 2, 2018, on the other hand, was a significantly different one: how to best use trade policies and design trade rules that are conducive to environmental protection.[17] Not only did this report represent the first output of a brand-new joint initiative by the two organizations on trade and the environment, but, most importantly, it signaled a change of course and began a new chapter in the trade/environment story.

1.1 *The Instrumental Role of Trade*

The dimension of *sustainability* was at the center of one of the most recent WTO Public Forums, held in Geneva in October 2018. Even the title of the Forum—'Trade 2030'—was imbued with 'sustainability' language, as it clearly echoed the *2030 Agenda for Sustainable Development*, launched in 2015.[18] The latter set targets to be achieved by 2030 in areas such as poverty reduction, health, education, and the environment, and the Forum, acknowledging the role that trade can play in achieving sustainable development goals (SDGs), focused precisely on the contribution that the WTO could make to the *2030 Agenda*. The launch of the *2030 Agenda*, however, was not the first time that trade was recognized as a powerful tool to achieve a sustainable future.

In 2002, world leaders had gathered in Johannesburg, South Africa, to further build on the achievements made since the Conference on Environment and Development held in Rio ten years before. The Johannesburg Summit, which brought together tens of thousands of participants, from heads of State and national delegates, to leaders from NGOs, business, and many other major groups, focused on poverty eradication, changing unsustainable patterns of production and consumption, and protecting and managing natural resources.[19] In this context, for the very first time, the parties recognized "the major role that trade can play in achieving sustainable development and in eradicating

---

requirements—and on their compatibility with trade rules. As a matter of fact, each section of the report devoted to these categories of measures provides a description of the measures first, followed by the overview of the relevant WTO rules they fall under, assessing their compatibility with them. Trade norms are here clearly used as the relevant legal framework, and climate change policies as the object to be evaluated against such framework.

17 This Report is based on the *2030 Agenda* and on the assumption that trade should be "at the service of a more sustainable, inclusive, and resilient world." WTO/UN Environment, *Making Trade Work for the Environment* (n 11) 2.

18 2030 Agenda.

19 See e.g. Luc Hens and Bhaskar Nath (eds.), *The World Summit on Sustainable Development* (Springer, 2005).

poverty" and encouraged "members of the World Trade Organization to pursue the work program agreed at their Fourth Ministerial Conference."[20]

The *Johannesburg Plan of Implementation*, in particular, encouraged the completion of the Doha Round of negotiations suggesting, among others, the reform of the existing subsidies disciplines, in particular with reference to those subsidies "that have considerable negative effects on the environment and are incompatible with sustainable development."[21] The *Johannesburg Plan of Implementation* therefore, for the first time, emphasized the potential role that trade rules could play in achieving sustainable development. It further added that "States should cooperate to promote a supportive and open international economic system that would lead to economic growth and sustainable development in all countries to better address the problems of environmental degradation."[22]

The instrumental nature of an open and well-functioning economic system was by no means something new. In the first half of the twentieth century, Cordell Hull had been arguing fiercely that "unhampered trade dovetailed with peace,"[23] while fighting for the establishment of an open international economic system precisely to ensure peaceful relations among nations and avoid the horrors of the two wars. When the General Agreement on Tariffs and Trade

---

20 World Summit on Sustainable Development, Johannesburg, South Africa, August 26-September 4, 2002, *Plan of Implementation of the World Summit on Sustainable* Development, U.N. Doc. A/CONF.199/20, Annex (Sept. 4, 2002) [hereinafter Johannesburg Plan of Implementation], para. 90.

21 Ibid., para. 97(b).

22 Ibid., para. 101, first sentence. See also United Nations International Conference on Financing for Development, Monterrey, Mexico, March 18–22, 2002, *Financing for development: Monterrey Consensus of the International Conference on Financing for Development: the final text of agreements and commitments adopted at the International Conference on Financing for Development*, paras. 26–38; and United Nations, Follow-up International Conference on Financing for Development to Review the Implementation of the Monterrey Consensus, Doha, Qatar, Nov. 29—Dec. 2, 2008, *Doha Declaration on Financing for Development: outcome document of the Follow-up International Conference on Financing for Development to Review the Implementation of the Monterrey Consensus*, A/CONF.212/L.1/Rev, paras. 30–39. It should also be noted, however, that the *Johannesburg Plan of Implementation* takes the multilateral trade law framework for granted when it states that Countries should "establish and strengthen existing trade and cooperation agreements, *consistent with the multilateral trading system*, with a view to achieving sustainable development [and] support voluntary *WTO-compatible* market-based initiatives for the creation and expansion of domestic and international markets for environmentally friendly goods and services." Johannesburg Plan of Implementation, para. 99(a) and (b) (emphasis added).

23 Cordell Hull, *The Memoirs of Cordell Hull* (Macmillan, 1948), p. 81.

(GATT) was drafted, its preamble emphasized that trade was useful only insofar as it served broader goals.[24] When the WTO was established 50 years later, the instrumental role of trade was once again reaffirmed but, rather than being merely conducive to economic growth and to ensure peace among nations, it was now supposed to serve much broader social and developmental goals, in other words, sustainable development. As the years went by, the need for the trading system to pursue sustainable development goals has become more and more important, as environmental degradation, lack of access to clean and affordable water, spreading hunger and poverty have become today as pressing as ensuring peaceful inter-state relations was when Hull was arguing for the first steps towards international trade cooperation.

This message was reiterated and made even more explicit in the UN General Assembly Resolution *The Future We Want*, adopted in 2012, where trade appears in the list of means of implementation (together with finance, technology, capacity-building, and registry of commitments).[25] The Resolution stressed the role that international trade cooperation can and should play to achieve sustainable development in all its three dimensions,[26] and singled out two issues that were deemed especially relevant to frame trade as a means of implementation: subsidies and trade in environmental goods and services.[27] The problem of fisheries subsidies, in particular, caught the drafters' attention as they

24 In the GATT Preamble, the Contracting Parties recognized that "entering into reciprocal and mutually advantageous arrangements directed to the substantial reduction of tariffs and other barriers to trade and to the elimination of discriminatory treatment in international commerce" was instrumental to "raising standards of living, ensuring full employment and a large and steadily growing volume of real income and effective demand, developing the full use of the resources of the world and expanding the production and exchange of goods." General Agreement on Tariffs and Trade, Oct. 30, 1947, 61 Stat. A-11, 55 U.N.T.S. 194 [hereinafter GATT], preamble.

25 G.A. Res. 66/288, U.N. Doc. A/RES/66/288 (Sept. 11, 2012) [hereinafter The Future We Want], paras. 281–2. In Rio, instead, trade does not yet feature as having any kind of instrumental role. Agenda 21, for example, does not list it among the means of implementation, as *The Future We Want* did in 2011. The means of implementation in the text of Agenda 21 included: i) Financial resources and mechanisms; ii) Transfer of environmentally sound technology, cooperation and capacity-building; iii) Science for sustainable development; iv) Promoting education, public awareness and training; v) National mechanisms and international cooperation for capacity-building in developing countries; vi) International institutional arrangements; vii) International legal instruments and mechanisms; viii) Information for decision-making. Agenda 21, paras. 33.1–40.30. See also the Programme for the Further Implementation of Agenda 21. G.A. Res. 19/2, U.N. Doc. A/RES/S-19/2 (Sept. 19, 1997) [hereinafter Programme for the Further Implementation of Agenda 21], paras. 76–115.

26 The Future We Want, para. 19.

27 Ibid., para. 281.

decided to build on the commitment taken ten years prior in Johannesburg "to eliminate subsidies that contribute to illegal, unreported and unregulated [IUU] fishing and overcapacity ... and to conclude multilateral disciplines on fisheries subsidies."[28] The Resolution did not stop there and went on to address the thorny issue of fossil fuel subsidies as well:

> Countries reaffirm the commitments they have made to phase out harmful and inefficient fossil fuel subsidies that encourage wasteful consumption and undermine sustainable development. We invite others to consider rationalizing inefficient fossil fuel subsidies by removing market distortions, including restructuring taxation and phasing out harmful subsidies, where they exist, to reflect their environmental impacts ...[29]

Only three years later, world leaders, meeting at the UN Headquarters in New York, as the Organization celebrated its seventieth anniversary, embarked on a new journey agreeing on a "comprehensive, far-reaching and people-centered set of universal and transformative Goals and targets."[30] Seventeen goals, to be precise, and 169 associated targets, which constituted "the result of over two years of intensive public consultations and engagement with civil society and other stakeholders around the world ..."[31]

The role of trade as a means of implementation appears in two manners in the text of the *2030 Agenda for Sustainable Development*: as a specific section under the heading 'means of implementation', and as a target under some of the 17 SDGs. As to the former, the instrumental role of trade is envisioned almost exclusively with regards to the *developmental* component of the goals. This explains the reference being mostly to those norms and mechanisms relevant for assisting developing and least-developed countries in their path

---

28 Ibid., para. 173. IUU fishing was originally defined in 2001 within the context of the *International Plan of Action to Prevent, Deter, and Eliminate Illegal, Unreported and Unregulated Fishing*. *Illegal* fishing refers to fishing and related activities conducted in contravention of national, regional and international laws. *Unreported* fishing covers non-reporting, misreporting, or under-reporting of information on fishing operations and their catches. And *unregulated* fishing includes fishing by stateless vessels fishing in convention areas of Regional Fisheries Management Organizations (RFMOs) by non-party vessels, fishing activities not regulated by states and with monitoring and accounting difficulties, and fishing in areas or stocks for which there were no conservation or management measures. See FAO statement at the CTE. WT/CTE/M/63 (Sept. 27, 2017), para. 1.1.

29 The Future We Want, para. 225.

30 2030 Agenda, para. 2.

31 Ibid., para. 6.

towards sustainable development,[32] and therefore only indirectly linked to the environment issue. After all, environmental protection represents only one of the components of sustainable development and needs constant balance with the social and economic goals of all countries—in particular developing and least-developed ones.

Under specific SDGs, instead, trade is explicitly identified as a tool with high potential when it comes to protecting certain environmental components. Examples include enhancing "international cooperation to facilitate access to clean energy research and technology, including renewable energy, energy efficiency and advanced and cleaner fossil fuel technology,"[33] rationalizing and phasing out fossil fuel subsidies "to reflect their environmental impact,"[34] prohibiting "certain forms of fisheries subsidies which contribute to overcapacity and overfishing" and eliminating those "subsidies that contribute to illegal, unreported and unregulated fishing,"[35] and finally enhancing "global support for efforts to combat poaching and trafficking of protected species."[36] Assessed together, all these targets suggest the importance of 'greening' the economy.

1.2 *A Global Green New Deal*

The origin of the term 'green economy' can be traced back to a 1989 publication by a number of prominent economists titled *Blueprint for the Green Economy*, which presented, for the first time, practical proposals on how to 'green' modern economies and put them on the path to sustainable development.[37] Although it was initially presented as a conceptual challenge, and was later characterized as a sub-category of sustainable development, the concept of 'green economy' differs from that of sustainable development: while the latter is all about internalizing negative environmental externalities and "doing as well in economic terms while respecting the environment", the concept of

32 Ibid., Goal 17 involves strengthening the means of implementation of the other SDGs, one of which is trade. In particular, targets 17.11 and 17.12 refer to "significantly increase[ing] the exports of developing countries, in particular with a view to doubling the least developed countries' share of global exports by 2020" and realizing "timely implementation of duty-free and quota-free market access on a lasting basis for all least developed countries, consistent with World Trade Organization decisions, including by ensuring that preferential rules of origin applicable to imports from least developed countries are transparent and simple, and contribute to facilitating market access." See also Target 10.a.

33 Ibid., Targets 7.a and 7.b.

34 Ibid., Target 12.c.

35 Ibid., Target 14.6.

36 Ibid., Target 15.c.

37 David Pearce et al., *Blueprint For A Green Economy* (Earthscan, 1990).

'green economy' suggests an evolution towards designing a whole new economic paradigm to fit new environmental imperatives, because doing well in economic terms requires focusing on green opportunities.[38]

All of a sudden, protecting the environment is no longer a matter merely of 'responsibility' but rather 'profitability', and states are now urged to build their economic models on environmental considerations in order to do better in economic terms.[39] Through what Esty and Winston call an 'environmental lens', moving from brown to green means moving from green to gold, as going 'green' "is not just a nice strategy tool or a feel-good digression from the real work of a company [but rather] an essential element of business strategy in the modern world."[40]

The idea of a 'green economy' represents the centerpiece of the 'Global Green New Deal', launched by UNEP in 2008, which followed in the footstep of a much earlier 'New Deal'. In July 1932, Franklin D. Roosevelt flew to Chicago to accept the Democratic nomination for President. Dressed in a blue suit with a red rose in his lapel, Roosevelt made his way slowly to the podium and, facing the cheering crowd, promised a 'New Deal' for America.[41] And America was very much in need of a new deal. When, only a few months later, Roosevelt entered the Oval Office as President, the economic crisis was at its most terrifying: about a quarter of the country's labor force was unemployed and more than 50 million people were in desperate poverty.[42] Facing the crisis head on, over the next eight years, the United States (US) government introduced a series of experimental 'New Deal' programs and projects aimed at stabilizing the economy and providing jobs and relief to the many Americans who were suffering.

On December 2, 2008, the United Nations Environment Program convened a meeting of policy experts in its offices in Geneva to discuss a comprehensive global strategy to address a new alarming crisis. By December 2008, it was

38 See Jorge E. Viñuales, 'Foreign Investment and the Environment in International Law: The Current State of Play', in Kate Miles (ed.), *Research Handbook on Environment and Investment Law* (Edward Elgar, 2019). See also Sha Zukang, Secretary-General of the 2012 United Nations Conference on Sustainable Development, statement at the Meeting of the CTE held on July 6, 2011, WT/CTE/M/52 (Sept. 6, 2011), paras. 100–1; UNEP, *Towards a Green Economy: Pathways to Sustainable Development and Poverty Eradication* (2011), pp. 1–2.

39 Viñuales, 'Foreign Investment and the Environment in International Law' (n 38).

40 Daniel C. Esty and Andrew S. Winston, *Green to Gold* (Yale University Press, 2006), p. 4.

41 Anne Schraff, *Franklin Delano Roosevelt* (Saddleback Educational Publishing, 2008), p. 35.

42 Michael J. Heale, *Franklin D. Roosevelt. The New Deal and the War* (Routledge, 1999), pp. 17–18.

already apparent that the world was witnessing its worst financial crisis yet, triggering the start of one of the most severe economic recessions since the Great Depression of the 1930s. What the world needed was the same kind of initiative and government leadership that had been shown by Roosevelt and his 'New Deal', but "at a global scale and embracing a wider vision."[43]

First, this 'New Deal' should be global in scale, given the global scale of the crises the world was confronted with, and all countries would be invited to participate. Second, the financial crisis was just one piece of the puzzle: what the world was facing was in fact multiple crises, including climate change, rising fuel prices, and food and water scarcity.[44] The policy experts gathered in Geneva agreed that these crises shared a common feature, namely the gross misallocation of capital as, over the two previous decades, "much capital [had] been poured into property, fossil fuels, and structured financial assets with embedded derivatives, but relatively little [had] been invested in renewable energy, energy efficiency, public transportation, sustainable agriculture, and land and water conservation."[45] Emerging global threats arising both from ecological crises and inequitable distribution of resources called for a new economic model "capable of delivering enhanced prosperity and growing social equity, within the contours of a finite and fragile planet."[46] Thus, what was necessary in 2008 was to avoid resurrecting an unsustainable 'brown' economy but rather promote structural changes towards an economy that is low carbon, efficient and clean in production, in other words a 'green' economy. The economic recovery promoted by Roosevelt in the 1930s was replaced by a '*global green* recovery', and his 'New Deal' had become a '*Global Green* New Deal', which should lead the world on a pathway towards a sustainable future.

1.3 *Trading Places: A Brief History of Means and Ends*

The objectives of this 'Global Green New Deal' were fourfold: making a major contribution to reviving the world economy, reducing carbon dependency and ecosystem degradation, putting economies on a path to clean and stable development, and furthering sustainable and inclusive growth while ending extreme poverty.[47] Under this agenda, nearly all sectors of the global economy needed

---

43 Edward B. Barbier, *A Global Green New Deal: Rethinking the Economic Recovery* (Cambridge University Press, 2010), p. xvi.

44 UNEP, *Global Green New Deal*, Policy Brief (Mar. 2009), pp. 2–3.

45 Ibid., p. 3.

46 PAGE, *Green Industrial Policy and Trade: A Tool-Box*, UN Environment and UNIDO under the Partnership for Action on Green Economy (2017), p. 7.

47 UNEP, *Global Green New Deal* (n 44) 5.

to be 'greened': domestic policy reforms were recommended to reduce fossil fuels and other perverse subsidies, while creating positive incentives to those sectors that encourage a green economy and appropriate taxes to account for environmental externalities.

Trade policies and other economic instruments, such as investment schemes, play a key role in developing a green, circular economy, which in turn is seen as a core component of the overall strategy to achieve sustainable development and poverty eradication in the near future, as *The Future We Want* clearly emphasizes.[48] The picture that all these new instruments paint is significantly different from the one we were contemplating at the beginning of this book, as much has changed since the beginning of the twentieth century.

The reader certainly remembers the international treaties signed during the end of the nineteenth and the beginning of the twentieth century which, although couched in environmental terms, were aimed at the conservation of certain environmental elements as instrumental to economic growth. Thus, for instance, it was forbidden to kill certain birds—especially insectivores—or destroy their nests, eggs, or hatching, because they proved useful to agriculture,[49] and fur seals were protected from over-exploitation because governments had an interest in their commerce, which could only survive if their exploitation was limited and regulated.[50] In other words, environmental protection was seen as a means to an (economic) end. In his first message to Congress on December 3, 1901, Theodore Roosevelt conveyed this idea loud and clear when he proclaimed that "[f]orest protection is not an end in itself; it is a means to increase and sustain the resources of our country and the industries which depend upon them. The preservation of our forests is an imperative *business* necessity."[51] And the Atlantic Charter itself referred to the importance of access to raw materials purely for economic reasons.[52]

That was still a time when the environment issue had not yet entered any national or international agenda. As the previous chapters have clearly shown, once agreement was found on the importance of environmental protection and international cooperation on environmental matters began, neoliberal

48 The Future We Want, paras. 56–74.

49 Convention for the Protection of Birds Useful to Agriculture, March 19, 1902, 191 C.T.S.

50 Arbitration between the United States and the United Kingdom related to the Rights of Jurisdiction of United States in the Bering's Sea and the Preservation of Fur Seals, August 15, 1983, XXVIII R.I.A.A. 1.002.

51 Theodore Roosevelt, First Annual Message, Dec. 3, 1901 (emphasis added).

52 Point Four of the Charter declared the importance of the "further enjoyment by all States ... of access, on equal terms, to the trade and to the raw materials of the world which are needed for their economic prosperity."

ideas had become the driving force of the trading system, and failed to see that environmental protection and sustainable development represented new goals that the trading system was in the position to pursue. Coherently with this mindset, in a paper prepared for the Founex meeting on June 3, 1971, the Secretariat of the United Nations Conference on Trade and Development (UNCTAD) had identified the major fields in which environmental actions may have an impact on world trade and on international economic relations.[53] Similarly, the GATT Secretariat had, the very same year, published the well-known study entitled *Industrial Pollution Control and International Trade*, which surveyed a number of issues that national anti-pollution measures might raise for international trade.

It took several decades—and this is the story this book has been telling so far—for the synergetic relationship between protection of the environment and trade liberalization, as well as between the respective regimes, to come to the surface, so that environmental protection can finally be portrayed no longer as a means to an (economic) end, but as one of the ultimate goals that economic instruments—trade, financial, and investment policies—are asked to pursue.[54] So, nearly 45 years later, in 2015, UNCTAD issued a policy brief on trade and climate change, which began with the words "trade policies can have an impact on the climate change mitigation efforts of countries,"[55] and looked into how to design trade instruments that did not hamper such efforts, while the WTO Public Forum featured a whole day of discussions on how to make trade work for the environment. The terms of the debate are changing, and trade instruments offer some signs of this change.

---

53 *The Implication of Environment Measures for International Trade and Development*, Background Paper prepared by the UNCTAD Secretariat (June 3, 1971) (on file with the Environmental Science and Public Policy Archives at Harvard University, Maurice F. Strong Papers, Box 40[397]).

54 In the last several years, sustainable development has become the global paradigm guiding the ongoing reform of international investment law. Developments can be seen at the level of both treaty-drafting and investment arbitration. See UNCTAD, *Investment Policy Framework for Sustainable Investment*, 2015. IISD, *International Investment Law and Sustainable Development: Key Cases from 2000–2010* (July 2011), and *International Investment Law and Sustainable Development: Key Cases from the 2010s* (Oct. 2018). See also Jorge E. Viñuales, *Foreign Investment and the Environment in International Law* (Cambridge University Press, 2012), and Pierre M. Dupuy and Jorge E. Viñuales eds., *Harnessing Foreign Investment to Protect the Environment* (Cambridge University Press, 2013). At the level of case law, see e.g. *Chemtura Corporation (formerly Crompton Corporation) v. Government of Canada*, ICJG 464 (PCA 2010) (Aug. 2, 2010); *Parkerings-Compagniet AS v. Republic of Lithuania*, ICSID Case No. ARB/05/8 (Sept. 11, 2007) [hereinafter *Parkerings v. Lithuania*].

55 UNCTAD, 'Trade and Climate Change Policy Beyond 2015', Policy Brief No. 36 (Sept. 2015).

Of course, when stating that economic instruments are starting to be framed as means to an environmental end, it should be clarified that the end is not purely environmental. Protection of the environment is just one of the components of sustainable development, and only some of the SDGs can be defined as 'environmental'. Trade, investment, and finance are therefore a means to implements *all* aspects of sustainable development, including but not limited to environmental ones.[56]

2 Negotiating Trade Rules with the Environment in Mind

In April 1987, delegates from 46 countries met in Geneva. It was one of the many sessions of the negotiation of the *Montreal Protocol for the Protection of the Ozone Layer* where the parties discussed trade restrictions. Because the Protocol created a regime that limited the release of ozone-depleting substances into the atmosphere, allowing the import of such substances from non-parties would have frustrated the whole system. For this reason, trade restrictions were seen by many of the negotiators as necessary to ensure the integrity of the regulatory framework created with the Protocol itself. After many months of discussing different proposals, representatives from the United Kingdom (UK) and the European Commission blocked further discussion until a legal expert from the GATT Secretariat could advise them on the compatibility and permissibility of the trade restrictions that were being proposed with the rules of the General Agreement.[57]

Not even 30 years later, on November 27, 2015, a selected group of trade and environment experts, coming from both practice and academia, met at the Maison International de l'Environnement in Geneva, not too far from the building where the events described above took place, for what turned out to be a very productive day of discussions. The meeting had been organized by UNEP and the International Institute for Sustainable Development (IISD) with a very precise objective in mind: to create a toolkit to guide negotiators of bilateral and regional trade agreements, to help ensure that their final product would contribute to national and international environmental objectives,

56 As a result, one could say that environmental protection is still a 'means' to the extent that it can contribute to the socio-economic development of developing and least-developed countries.

57 Richard E. Benedick, *Ozone Diplomacy: New Directions in Safeguarding the Planet* (Harvard University Press, 2009), p. 91.

and more broadly to sustainable development.[58] In other words, to offer trade negotiators the necessary (environmental) expertise to draft trade agreements that would contribute to environmental protection and preservation.

The antinomy between the two scenarios could not be more evident: in 1987, a group of environmental negotiators asked a trade expert for advice to make sure that the rules they were going to draft would not clash with the goals and rules of the trading system; in 2015, a group of environmental experts were preparing to give advice to trade negotiators to make sure that they would negotiate trade rules that would not undermine, but rather foster, environmental goals.

2.1 *Plenty of Fish in the Sea?*

> Regardless of status, every nation, indeed every person in the world, has a stake in ensuring the resilience of the Ocean. Thus, whether they are fishing nations or not, all WTO members should come together in 2019 and do the right thing for people and planet by prohibiting harmful fisheries subsidies.[59]
>
> PETER THOMSON, UN Secretary General's Special Envoy for the Ocean, January 8, 2019

The *2030 Agenda for Sustainable Development* identifies the removal of certain fisheries subsidies as one of the instruments to achieve Goal 14 of the *Agenda*, namely the conservation and sustainable use of the oceans, seas, and marine resources for sustainable development:

> By 2020, prohibit certain forms of fisheries subsidies which contribute to overcapacity and overfishing, eliminate subsidies that contribute to illegal, unreported and unregulated fishing and refrain from introducing new such subsidies, recognizing that appropriate and effective special and differential treatment for developing and least developed countries should be an integral part of the World Trade Organization fisheries subsidies negotiation.[60]

58 UN Environment/IISD, *A Sustainability Toolkit for Trade Negotiators: Trade and Investment as Vehicles for Achieving the 2030 Sustainable Development Agenda*, available at https://www.iisd.org/toolkits/sustainability-toolkit-for-trade-negotiators/ (last accessed August 3, 2021).

59 Peter Thomson, '2019: The Year to End Harmful Fisheries Subsidies', IISD SDG Knowledge Hub (Jan. 8, 2019), available at https://sdg.iisd.org/commentary/guest-articles/2019-the-year-to-end-harmful-fisheries-subsidies/ (last accessed August 3, 2021).

60 2030 Agenda, Target 14.6.

The first time any action was taken on this issue at the UN level dates back to a Special Session of the UN General Assembly in 1997, which recognized the urgent need to prevent and eliminate overfishing and overcapacity and called on governments to consider the impact of subsidies on the conservation and management of fisheries and start planning appropriate action.[61] In the same year, the United States asked that the issue could be addressed as a matter of WTO negotiations,[62] relying on a study prepared by the Food and Agriculture Organization (FAO), which showed that "the depletion of various fish stocks has occurred in virtually all coastal states throughout the world. Indeed ... this is an inevitable outcome unless appropriate controls are adopted."[63]

After the United States, several other Members, which gradually began to be known with the fitting moniker 'Friends of Fish',[64] proposed to work on fisheries subsidies regulations within the WTO framework.[65] During this period of time, however, there was no consensus on whether an actual need for *new* fisheries subsidies regulations at the WTO existed.[66] In July 1999, during a

---

61 Programme for the Further Implementation of Agenda 21, paras. 36(e) and (f).

62 *Submission by the United States to the Committee on Trade and Environment, Environmental and Trade Benefits of Removing Subsidies in the Fisheries Sector*, WT/CTE/W/51 (May 19, 1997). See also *Environmental Benefits of Removing Trade Restrictions and Distortions.* Note by the Secretariat, WT/CTE/W/67 (Nov. 7, 1997), para. 91. During the Uruguay Round, fisheries issues were discussed in the Negotiating Group on Natural Resources Based Products (NRBPs). Later, they were moved to the Market Access Group along with other subjects and, at the end of the Round, the issue of fisheries subsidies was included under the scope of the Agreement on Subsidies and Countervailing Measures. Because of the environmental aspects it involves, it immediately became a topic of discussion at the CTE. See Chen-Ju Chen, *Fisheries Subsidies under International Law* (Hamburg Studies on Maritime Affairs, Springer, 2010), pp. 45–6.

63 FAO, *Marine Fisheries and the Law of the Sea: A Decade of Change* (FAO Fisheries Department, 1993).

64 The informal term 'Friends of Fish' has been used to refer to a group of WTO Members who have spoken for special WTO regulations on fisheries subsidies. At various times, active members of the 'Friends of Fish' coalition have included Argentina, Australia, Chile, Ecuador, Iceland, New Zealand, Norway, the Philippines, Peru, and the United States.

65 See e.g. *Submission by Australia to the Committee on Trade and Environment, Trade Liberalization and the Environment: A positive Agenda for Trade Reform*, WT/CTE/W/105 (Feb. 2, 1999); *Submission by Iceland to the Committee on Trade and Environment, On the Environmental Impact of Fisheries Subsidies*, WT/CTE/W/111 (Mar. 11, 1999); *Communication from Australia, Iceland, New Zealand, Norway, Peru, Philippines and United States to the General Council, Preparations for the 1999 Ministerial Conference: Fisheries Subsidies*, WT/GC/W/303 (Aug. 6, 1999); *Submission by Japan to the Committee on Trade and Environment, Japan's Basic Position on the Fishery Subsidy Issue, Item 6*, WT/CTE/W/173 (Oct. 23, 2000).

66 See Chen, *Fisheries Subsidies* (n 62) 51.

Special Session of the General Council of the WTO, Iceland made a particularly compelling case that the Members should agree to "eliminate subsidies that contribute to fisheries overcapacity, in view of the fact that they distort trade, seriously undermine sustainable utilization of fish stocks and hamper sustainable development,"[67] and nearly 20 countries expressed support for the proposal, including a relatively large number of developing countries.[68] Less than two years later, UNEP held a technical workshop where it was suggested to place the fisheries subsidies issue on the Agenda of the WTO Ministerial Conference.[69] To facilitate the CTE Members' understanding of the issues, the Committee itself held information sessions with several environmental organizations, including UNEP and the Secretariat of the Convention on Biological Diversity (CBD).[70]

In 2001, the Doha Ministerial Conference responded to these proposals by calling on the Members to "clarify and improve WTO disciplines on fisheries subsidies, taking into account the importance of this sector to developing countries,"[71] and specifying that the issue would form part of the negotiations on trade and the environment.[72] This statement represented a considerable milestone for the WTO: "since Doha, it has been considered that the WTO has an

---

67 *Communication from Iceland to the General Council, Preparations for the 1999 Ministerial Conference: Fisheries Subsidies,* WT/GC/W/229 (July 6, 1999). See also General Council Special Session 7 July 1999, WT/GC/M/44 (July 28, 1999).

68 Gareth Porter, 'Fisheries Subsidies and Overfishing', UNEP—Economics and Trade Unit (Feb. 12, 2001).

69 Ibid. UNEP, UNEP Fisheries Subsidies Workshop Geneva. Chairman's Summary (Feb. 12, 2001).

70 WT/CTE/W/187 (Mar. 15, 2001) and WT/CTE/W/149 (June 28, 2000). In preparation to these sessions, the Secretariat of the CTE had reviewed the work done by other international organizations, such as UNEP and FAO, on the topic. WT/CTE/W/167 (Oct. 16, 2000) and WT/CTE/W/167/Add.1 (June 19, 2001).

71 Doha Declaration, para. 28. The draft Seattle Ministerial Declaration already mentioned the issue, though in passing: "In the context of these negotiations, the areas to be considered shall include, inter alia, certain subsidies that may contribute to over-capacity in fisheries and over-fishing or cause other adverse effects to the interests of Members. The work on fisheries subsidies shall be carried out in cooperation with the FAO and drawing also on relevant work under way within other intergovernmental bodies, including regional fisheries management organizations. It shall consist of (i) the identification and examination of subsidies which contribute to over-capacity in fisheries and over-fishing, or have trade-distorting effects, and (ii) the clarification and strengthening, as appropriate of disciplines under the ASCM with respect to such subsidies." Draft Ministerial Declaration as discussed in Green Room, 3 December 1999.

72 Doha Declaration, para. 31.

unprecedented opportunity to help improve the environmental and economic health of the world's oceans by disciplining harmful fisheries subsidies."[73]

After Doha, the CTE, which had served as an important forum to understand and discuss the issue of fisheries subsidies, passed the baton to the Negotiating Group on Rules (NGR), where discussions would continue from that point on. By the time everything was ready for the Hong Kong Ministerial Conference, the focus of the negotiations had finally shifted once and for all from the question of *whether* there was a need for specific regulations in the fisheries sector to that of the *nature and extent* of such regulations.[74] The Hong Kong Ministerial declaration, issued in December 2005, noted that there was broad agreement among Members to "strengthen disciplines on subsidies in the fisheries sector, including through the prohibition of certain forms of fisheries subsidies that contribute to overcapacity and over-fishing,"[75] and which also indicated that such disciplines should take the form of amendments to the Agreement on Subsidies and Countervailing Measures (ASCM).[76]

The 2007 Chair Text[77] and subsequent proposals by Members have generated several substantive options for amending the WTO subsidies disciplines to account for the specificities of the fisheries sector, assuming the inadequacy of the ASCM in addressing concerns regarding the fish stock depletion and possible trade-distorting effects.[78] As pointed out by several Members, existing

73 Chen, *Fisheries Subsidies* (n 62) 58.

74 See TN/RL/9 (June 25, 2004), para. 8. In particular there was a heated discussion between the proponents of the so-called 'top-down' approach, which would have involved a blanket prohibition followed by a list of exceptions, and those advocating for a 'bottom-up' approach, consisting of a positive list of prohibited subsidies. The countries that supported a top-down approach included Argentina, Chile, Ecuador, New Zealand Peru, the Philippines and the United States, while the coalition arguing for a bottom-up approach featured Members such as Japan, Korea, Taiwan, the European Communities, and some developing country members. For a detailed analysis of these proposals, see Chen, *Fisheries Subsidies* (n 62) 70–76.

75 World Trade Organization, Hong Kong Ministerial Declaration, Dec. 22, 2005, Annex D: Rules I. Anti-Dumping and Subsidies and Countervailing Measures including Fisheries Subsidies, WT/MIN(05)/DEC, para. 9.

76 Lorand Bartels and Tibisay Morgandi, 'Options for the Legal Form of a WTO Agreement on Fisheries Subsidies' (2017) International Centre for Trade and Sustainable Development, 2. Radika Kumar et al, 'The Effectiveness of Fisheries Subsidies as a Trade Policy Tool to Achieving Sustainable Development Goals at the WTO' (2019) 100 *Marine Policy* 132.

77 TN/RL/W/213 (Nov. 30, 2007). The Chair Text provides for an amendment of Article 3 of the ASCM, adding subparagraph (c) to the list of 'prohibited subsidies', namely "subsidies referred to in Article I of Annex VIII", which lists eight different categories of fisheries subsidies.

78 Seung Wha Chang, 'WTO Disciplines on Fisheries Subsidies: A Historic Step Towards Sustainability? (2003) 6(4) *Journal of International Economic Law* 879, 880. Seven

ASCM rules "do not adequately address other negative trade, environment and development impacts of fisheries subsidies, particularly the distinctive production distortions subsidies can cause in the fisheries sector ... [while] the heterogeneous nature of fisheries products, and the diffuse nature of support to the sector, make it harder to demonstrate the existence of market distortions of the kind envisaged by existing ASCM discipline."[79] In particular, the characteristics of fish products are a source of specific technical obstacles to the use of the 'serious prejudice' and 'determination of injury' provisions.[80]

Recently, negotiations have been reinvigorated by the *2030 Agenda*, and in particular by SDG 14.6. In 2017, the Ministers at the 11th WTO Ministerial Conference in Buenos Aires agreed

> to continue to engage constructively in the fisheries subsidies negotiations, with a view to adopting, by the Ministerial Conference in 2019, an agreement on comprehensive and effective disciplines that prohibit certain forms of fisheries subsidies that contribute to overcapacity and

---

proposals have officially been filed up until July 2017: TN/RL/GEN/186 (New Zealand, Iceland, Pakistan); TN/RL/GEN/181/Rev.1 (EU); TN/RL/GEN/189/Rev.1 (Indonesia); TN/RL/GEN/192 (ACP Group); TN/RL/GEN/187/Rev.2 (Argentina, Colombia, Costa Rica, Panama, Peru, Uruguay); TN/RL/GEN/193 (LDC Group); and TN/RL/GEN/191 (Norway). All the proposals can be easily compared in a document prepared by the Chair of the Negotiating Group on Rules, TN/RL/W/273 (July 28, 2017), which served as a basis for discussions at the 11th Ministerial Conference in December of the same year.

79 TN/RL/W/3 (Apr. 24, 2002), 1.

80 According to Article 6.3 of the ASCM, *serious prejudice* may arise when "the effect of the subsidy is to displace or impede the imports of a like product of another Member into the market of the subsidizing Member; (b) the effect of the subsidy is to displace or impede the exports of a like product of another Member from a third country market; (c) the effect of the subsidy is a significant price undercutting by the subsidized product as compared with the price of a like product of another Member in the same market or significant price suppression, price depression or lost sales in the same market; (d) the effect of the subsidy is an increase in the world market share of the subsidizing Member in a particular subsidized primary product or commodity as compared to the average share it had during the previous period of three years and this increase follows a consistent trend over a period when subsidies have been granted." All these instances require the determination of the *likeness* of two products. However, because of the heterogeneity of fish products, products from different species can sometimes be in direct competition while similar products from the same family can require different prices. As a result, it is often difficult to determine *likeness* with certainty. At the same time, the heterogeneity of fish products creates difficulties in establishing the unsubsidized reference prices necessary to demonstrate injury to the domestic industry of another Member or serious prejudice to the interests of another Member (ASCM Arts. 5, 6, and 15). See TN/RL/W/3 and TN/RL/W/12 (July 4, 2002).

> overfishing, and eliminate subsidies that contribute to IUU-fishing recognizing that appropriate and effective special and differential treatment for developing country Members and least developed country Members should be an integral part of these negotiations.[81]

The progress since talks began in the CTE in 1997 has been considerable. While at first, arguments were on whether the existing ASCM disciplines were sufficient, soon the question became how to modify them, and recently they have turned into more and more concrete legal texts, where environmental protection plays a central role. In fact, not only is the prohibition of certain fisheries subsidies motivated by environmental reasons, but the 2018 draft of the new proposed discipline excludes from the definition of subsidy, and therefore from the scope of the future agreement,

> subsidies ... promoting sustainable fisheries ... the adoption of techniques or technology aimed at reducing the environmental impact of wild marine capture (such as by catch reduction or turtle excluder devices) or for improving compliance with fisheries management regimes aimed at sustainable use and conservation ... and for increasing resilience or reducing vulnerability to climate change [as well as] subsidies for the installation of equipment for safety or for control and enforcement purposes, and equipment fitted for the purpose of reducing environmentally harmful emissions.[82]

In other words, according to this formulation, fisheries subsidies that do produce a positive environmental impact would be excluded from the overall discipline. Interestingly, all the proposals submitted to the NGR envisioned such 'environmental subsidies' as carved out of the agreement, rather than listed in a GATT-style exception clause. At the same time, all proposals and discussions reflect the need to provide for special and differential (S&D) treatment and to introduce exceptions to address the concerns raised by

81 World Trade Organization, Fisheries Subsidies. Ministerial Declaration of 13 December 2017, WT/MIN(17)/64, WT/L/1031 (Dec. 18, 2017).

82 TN/RL/W/274/Rev.6 (Nov. 14, 2018), proposed Art. 2(f) and (g). See also Proposal from Indonesia. Revision, TN/RL/GEN/189/Rev.1 (July 12, 2017); Submission of Cambodia on behalf of the LDC Group, TN/RL/GEN/193 (July 17, 2017); Submission from Guyana on behalf of the ACP Group, TN/RL/GEN/192 (July 14, 2017).

some developing countries[83] and, in particular, by small vulnerable coastal states.[84]

Although no agreement has yet been reached and negotiations seem easier said than done, the discussion of these proposals by WTO Members reflects an unprecedented attempt to impose specific obligations on the Members to protect the environment beyond the WTO's traditional focus on trade distortions.[85] In creating trade rules that also protect natural resources, the WTO would fulfill the pledges made more than two decades ago in the Earth Summit's Agenda 21 to "remove or reduce those subsidies that do not conform with sustainable development objectives."[86]

2.2 *The Untapped Green Potential of the Subsides Agreement*

The proposal presented by the US in December 2020, entitled *Advancing Sustainability Goals through Trade Rules to Level the Playing Field* and aimed at amending Article 5 of the ASCM to add the enactment and enforcement of environmental standards below a certain level of environmental protection to

83 See e.g. *Comments from the People's Republic of China on the United States Proposal on Fisheries Subsidies to the Negotiating Group on Rules*, TN/RL/W/88 (May 1, 2003); *Contribution to the Discussion on the Framework for Disciplines on Fisheries Subsidies*. Paper from Brazil to the Negotiating Group on Rules, TN/RL/W/176 (Mar. 31, 2005). *Contribution to the Discussion on the Framework for Disciplines on Fisheries Subsidies*. Paper from Brazil to the Negotiating Group on Rules, TN/RL/GEN/56 (July 4, 2005).

84 See e.g. *Fisheries Subsidies*. Submitted by Antigua and Barbuda, Belize, Fuji Islands, Guyana, the Maldives, Papua New Guinea, Solomon Islands, St. Kitts and Nevis to the Negotiating Group on Rules, TN/RL/W/136 (July 14, 2003); *WTO Fisheries Subsidies Disciplines Architecture on Fisheries Subsidies Disciplines*. Paper from Fiji, Papua New Guinea and the Solomon Islands to the Negotiating Group on Rules, TN/RL/GEN/57 (July 7, 2005); *WTO Fisheries Subsidies Disciplines Architecture on Fisheries Subsidies Disciplines*. Paper from Fiji, Jamaica, Papua New Guinea, and the Solomon Islands to the Negotiating Group on Rules, TN/RL/GEN/57/Rev.1 (Aug. 4, 2005); *WTO Fisheries Subsidies Disciplines Architecture on Fisheries Subsidies Disciplines*. Paper from Antigua and Barbuda, Barbados, Dominican Republic, Fiji, Grenada, Guyana, Jamaica, Papua New Guinea, St, Kitts and Nevis, St. Lucia, Solomon Islands, and Trinidad and Tobago to the Negotiating Group on Rules, TN/RL/GEN/57/Rev.2 (Sept. 13, 2005).

85 Chang, 'WTO Disciplines on Fisheries Subsidies' (n 78) 882. In particular, while members have agreed on the need to prohibit subsidies contributing to IUU fishing, significant differences of view still persist as to subsidies that may contribute to overcapacity and overfishing. To bridge these different views, in March 2019, Australia and the United States proposed a cap-based approach to address these types of subsidies. See TN/RL/GEN/197 (Mar. 25, 2019).

86 United Nations Conference on Environment and Development, Rio de Janeiro, Brazil, June 3–14, 1992, *Agenda 21: Programme of Action for Sustainable Development,* U.N. Doc. A/CONF.151/26 (1992) [hereinafter Agenda 21], Section I, Chapter 2, paragraph 2.21(a) and Chapter 8, paragraph 8.32(b). See UNEP, 'Incorporating Resource Impact into Fisheries Subsidies Disciplines: Issues and Options, a Discussion Paper' (2004).

the list of 'actionable subsidies' can be read under the same light as the negotiations on fisheries.[87] As a matter of fact, the US proposal addresses the role that the subsidies agreement could play in making trade and trade law more sustainable from an unprecedented perspective.

As the previous chapter has described, the important role of the ASCM in this regard has been at the center of heated debates for the past few decades. Most of the arguments, however, have concentrated on the need and opportunities to include exception clauses in the text of the agreement to allow Members to introduce measures in support of their 'green' industries. These arguments, in addition to missing the heart of the problem according to the most recent literature,[88] continue to be grounded in the *exception-based* approach to the trade/environment nexus: whenever the environment is introduced in the debate, its space and role is envisioned as exceptional, with all the ensuing consequences. The US proposal, on the other hand, moves away from this approach. It is no longer about resurrecting the long-dormant 'green box' in Article 8 of the ASCM, which contained a carve-out for certain kinds of measures including certain environmental ones. Nor is it about introducing a brand new exception or extending existing exceptions to the text of the agreement. The focus of the proposal is instead on the role that can be played by trade remedies to advance sustainability goals through trade rules: rather than helping countries' 'green' measures by providing for a way to escape ASCM rules, what the US is suggesting is to 'punish' those countries that do not uphold certain fundamental levels of environmental protection, adding their practices to the list of actionable subsidies, under Article 5 of the Agreement.

Actionable subsidies are permissible under WTO law so long as they do not negatively harm the trade interests of other countries.[89] When this happens,

87 Draft Ministerial Decision, *Advancing Sustainability Goals through Trade Rules to Level the Playing Field*, WT/GC/W/814, 17 December 2020. For an earlier analysis of this proposal, see Elena Cima and Makane M. Mbengue, 'ESIL Reflection—"Kind of Green". The U.S. Proposal to Advance Sustainability through Trade Rules and the Future of the WTO' (2021) 10 (1) *ESIL Reflections*.

88 See e.g. Ilaria Espa, 'New Features of Green Industrial Policy and the Limits of WTO Rules: What Options for the Twenty-First Century?' (2019) 53(6) *Journal of World Trade* 979, and 'Dissecting the Green Component of 21st Century Industrial Policy in the Energy Sector: Implications for the WTO System' in Elena Cima and Makane M. Mbengue (eds.), *A Multifaceted Approach to Trade Liberalization and Investment Protection in the Energy Sector* 16–40 (Brill, 2021).

89 According to Article 5 of the ASCM, "[n]o Member should cause, through the use of any subsidy ... adverse effects to the interests of other Members, i.e.: (a) injury to the domestic industry of another Member11; (b) nullification or impairment of benefits accruing directly or indirectly to other Members under GATT 1994 in particular the benefits of concessions bound under Article II of GATT 199412; (c) serious prejudice to the interests of another Member."

other countries have the choice between a multilateral route (adjudication) or taking unilateral actions under the review of domestic authorities against the other government's subsidy through the imposition of countervailing duties. Countervailing duties are known, together with antidumping duties and safeguards, as 'trade remedies'.[90] These measures consist, essentially, of increasing the price of goods imported from abroad by imposing duties on them, to eliminate the unfair advantage arising from a subsidy given by a state to its exporters. The underlying idea of the US proposal is that "industries located in certain countries benefit from weak or unenforced environmental laws and regulations by not being required to incur, and properly internalize, the costs of preventing or remediating environmental damage resulting from their production processes"[91] and thus gain an unfair competitive advantage, comparable to that obtained by subsidized industries.

This is not the first time the US has adopted a similar position vis-à-vis differential—and in particular low—environmental standards. As previously described in Chapter 3, already in the early 1990s, lower environmental practices were seen as conferring 'unfair' trade advantages to low-level countries' producers and it was argued that maintaining low environmental standards allowed domestic producers to incur lesser costs and was therefore compared to a subsidy or dumping practice.[92] While the attempt to qualify lower environmental standards as subsidies was not successful in the context of the Uruguay Round of negotiations that established the WTO in 1995, the United States, as well as many other—mostly industrialized—countries have turned to the bilateral and regional track to address the issue of differential environmental practices. This model was pioneered by the negotiators of the North American Free Trade Agreement (NAFTA) with the so-called 'Pollution-Haven Package', and has found its way in the vast majority of recent free trade agreements.[93]

Should the US proposal be accepted with the adoption of a ministerial decision, such a decision could serve as a vehicle not only to integrate the principle of non-regression in the corpus of WTO law, but also to introduce the observance of an 'acceptable' standard of environmental protection as a condition for compliance with WTO rules. The implications of such integration could be wide-ranging for the relationship between trade liberalization and environmental protection. To start, it would indicate a drastic change in the traditional

---

90 Generally on trade remedies, see Rüdiger Wolfrum et al. (eds.), *WTO: Trade Remedies* (Brill, 2008); Roberto Soprano, *WTO Trade Remedies in International Law* (Routledge, 2018).

91 Draft Ministerial Decision, *Advancing Sustainability Goals.*

92 See supra Chapter 3, Section 2.6.

93 See supra Chapter 4, Section 1.6.

free-trade approach towards regulatory diversity: rather than focusing on the 'danger' that countries would set their environmental regulations and standards 'too high', thereby creating obstacles to the free flow of commerce, the US proposal stems from the fear—traditionally shared by environmentalists—that countries would instead be tempted to set their regulations and standards 'too low', externalizing harms onto others and ultimately harming the environment. More broadly, it would represent a significant development of the traditional approach to the relationship between international trade and the environment, as it abandons the view that the environment should enter trade agreements only through narrow exceptions, but rather through the clear formulation of environmental principles. As a result, such environmental principles—such as the principle of non-regression—could influence and shape the interpretation and application of trade provisions, as well as other 'environmental' provisions already present in the text of WTO agreements. More importantly, it could suggest that the WTO and the legal framework it administers represent the right forum to address the long-lasting trade and environment debate—or at least a promising candidate.

2.3 *Three Ways to Protect the Environment*

The United States has been at the forefront of the efforts to push the debate forward inside, and mainly, outside of the WTO. In the context of the efforts towards constraining environmentally harmful fisheries subsidies, for instance, a significant step forward has been made by a recent agreement signed by the US with Canada and Mexico. The newly signed agreement is the *United States-Mexico-Canada Agreement*, known with the acronym USMCA, but which many still refer to as 'the new NAFTA'.[94] An in-depth assessment of the environmental chapter of the agreement is beyond the immediate scope of this work, and so is taking part in the discussions on who's greener—NAFTA or USMCA.[95] It is instead of interest to highlight a few specific provisions of the new text, one of which deals precisely with the issue of fisheries subsidies. Not only is this the first free trade agreement (FTA) addressing this thorny question; it has also done so before a final decisive agreement could be reached at the multilateral level, despite the on-going discussions.[96]

94 United States-Mexico-Canada Free Trade Agreement, Nov. 30, 2018 [hereinafter USMCA]. The full text of the Agreement can be found on the website of the USTR at https://ustr.gov/trade-agreements/free-trade-agreements/united-states-mexico-canada-agreement (last accessed August 3, 2021).

95 See e.g., Scott Vaughan, 'USMCA Versus NAFTA on the Environment', IISD, available at https://www.iisd.org/library/usmca-nafta-environment (last accessed August 3, 2021).

96 USMCA, Art. 24.20.

It would not be the first time that countries manage to include in the text of a free trade agreement provisions that proved much harder to agree on in a multilateral context. From an environmental standpoint, in particular, some of the most recent agreements seem to really be making great strides.[97] It suffices to compare the agreement signed by the European Union (EU) with Switzerland in 1972, which did not contain any reference to the environment,[98] with the one signed with Japan which entered into force in February 2019, and which mentions the word environment, in all its variations, 44 times, excluding the annexes. Of course, not all that glitters is gold—or, in our case, green. In many of these new agreements, the parties do acknowledge the importance of protecting and preserving the environment and agree that trade and investment in goods and services beneficial to the environment and sustainable development should be promoted, but are these provisions actually capable of protecting the environment? Do they actually require changes in trade policies and investment schemes to foster environmental goals? Let us have a look at the recent agreement between the European Free Trade Association (EFTA) and the Philippines, which features a provision that has become relatively 'standard' in recent years:

> The Parties *shall strive to facilitate and promote* investment, trade in and dissemination of goods and services that contribute to sustainable

---

97 See e.g. Gehring et al, 'Climate Change and Sustainable Energy Measures in Regional Trade Agreements (RTAs). An Overview' (2013) ICTSD Issue Paper No. 3; Rafael Leal-Arcas, 'Climate Change Mitigation from the Bottom Up: Preferential Trade Agreements to Promote Climate Change Mitigation' (2013) 7 *Carbon & Climate Law Review*; Karolina Milewicz et al. 'Beyond Trade: The Expanding Scope of the Nontrade Agenda in Trade Agreements' (2016) 62(4) *Journal of Conflict Resolution* 743; Elena Cima, 'Promoting Renewable Energy through FTAs? The Legal Implications of a New Generation of Trade Agreements' (2018) 52(4) *Journal of World Trade* 663–695; and Jean-Frédéric Morin, Andreas Dür, and Lisa Lechner, 'Mapping the Trade and Environment Nexus: Insights from a New Data Set' (2018) 18(1) *Global Environmental Politics* 122. The most recent meetings of the CTE have also been devoting a certain 'space' for briefings on the environmental provisions in FTAs. See e.g. WT/CTE/M/58 (MAR. 23, 2015), paras. 2.50–2.60; WT/CTE/M/61 (Oct. 14, 2016), paras. 3.1–3.24; WT/CTE/M/62 (Mar. 20, 2017), paras. 3.1–3.13.

98 Article 20 contains the classical exception: "The Agreement shall not preclude prohibitions or restrictions on imports, exports or goods in transit justified on grounds of public morality, law and order or public security, *the protection of life and health of humans, animals or plants*, the protection of national treasures of artistic, historic or archaeological value, the protection of industrial and commercial property, or rules relating to gold or silver. Such prohibitions or restrictions must not, however, constitute a means of arbitrary discrimination or a disguised restriction on trade between the Contracting Parties" (emphasis added).

> development, such as environmental technologies, sustainable renewable energy, as well as goods and services that are energy efficient, eco-labelled or subject to schemes such as fair and ethical trade. Related non-tariff barriers will be addressed as part of these efforts.[99]

As it is evident from the wording of this provision, while it clearly depicts the intentions of the parties, it is phrased in hortatory rather than mandatory terms and therefore is not concretely capable of contributing to environmental protection or preservation.[100] These types of norms are of course important, similar to preambles, in making explicit the intentions of the parties and in guiding the interpreter in case a dispute arises. They might even lead to a 'greener' interpretation of other provisions of the same agreement, as the previous chapter has shown. However, they do not bind the parties in any way, they do not commit them to actually "*facilitate and promote* investment, trade in and dissemination of goods and services that contribute to sustainable development."

At a closer look, however, there are a handful of agreements that have begun including provisions that do have this concrete capability. Despite their small number and the difficulties in tracking the actual impact on environmental protection policies (since they have been concluded so recently), these efforts do point to possible avenues to be further explored by negotiators in the future. Three avenues, in particular, are worth examining.

First, provisions that *require the parties to eliminate certain trade measures for environmental reasons*. A notable example is Article 24.20 of the newly signed USMCA, which prohibits subsidies that contribute to overfishing. More

99 Free Trade Agreement & Economic Integration Agreement, EFTA-Philippines, Apr. 28, 2016, Art. 11.7 (emphasis added). Other examples include e.g. Free Trade Agreement & Economic Integration Agreement, EFTA-Georgia, June 27, 2016, Art. 10.8; Free Trade Agreement, EU-SADC, June 10, 2016, Art. 10; Free Trade Agreement & Economic Integration Agreement, Republic of Korea-New Zealand, Mar. 23, 2015, Art. 16.4; Free Trade Agreement & Economic Integration Agreement, Canada-Republic of Korea, Sept. 22, 2014, Art. 17.4; Free Trade Agreement, EFTA-Bosnia Herzegovina, June 24, 2013, Art. 39; Free Trade Agreement, Switzerland-China, July 6, 2013, Art. 12.3.

100 Similar hortatory language can be found in those provisions where the parties, rather than simply committing to uphold existing levels of environmental protection, decide to go even further and commit to achieve high levels of environmental protection, further clarifying the they "shall strive to continue to improve those laws" over time. See e.g. Free Trade Agreement & Economic Integration Agreement, EU-Republic of Korea, Oct. 6, 2010 [hereinafter EU-S. Kor. FTA], Art. 13.3; Free Trade Agreement, United States—Jordan, Oct. 24, 2000, Art. 5; and Free Trade Agreement & Economic Integration Agreement, United States-Singapore, May 6, 2003, Art. 18.1.

precisely, two categories of subsidies are prohibited: those "provided to a fishing vessel or operator while listed for IUU fishing" and those "for fishing that negatively affect fish stocks that are in an overfished condition."[101] A second example is the commitment to gradually phase out fossil fuel subsidies, which can be found in the agreement between the EU and Singapore.[102]

Second, provisions that *recognize the parties' right to adopt certain trade measures for environmental reasons*. This category of provisions can be seen as including the exemptions or carve-outs surveyed in the previous chapter. These provisions recognize the countries' autonomous right to pursue environmental objectives and, being drafted as *exemptions* rather than *exceptions,* as already explained, can potentially facilitate the adoption of domestic trade-related environmental measures. In this context, the *EU-Singapore* FTA stands out once again, as it allows the two parties to provide for subsidies that *do* have trade effects on the other party—as long as such effects are contained and the subsidy is limited to the minimum needed to achieve the objective—when such subsidies are necessary to achieve an objective of public interest, explicitly including subsidies "for environmental purposes."[103] The allowance of 'environmental' subsidies can also be found in the agreement between the EU and South Africa, as well as in the one with the European Economic Area (EEA). A different example is provided by article 24.17(3) of the USMCA, which allows the three parties to the agreement to adopt measures that would restrict import of fish or fish products in order to protect or conserve fish or other marine species, as long as the measures are:

101 USMCA, Art. 24.20(1). The explanatory notes to the article further clarify that "the negative effect of such subsidies shall be determined based on the best scientific evidence available" and that "a fish stock is overfished if the stock is at such a low level that mortality from fishing needs to be restricted to allow the stock to rebuild to a level that produces maximum sustainable yield or alternative reference points based on the best scientific evidence available."

102 EU-Sing. FTA, Art. 13.11(3). The commitment is followed by a caveat clarifying that such a reduction should "be accompanied by measures to alleviate the social consequences associated with the transition to low carbon fuels."

103 EU-Sing. FTA, Art. 12.8, Annex 12-A(e). See also Free Trade Agreement, EU-South Africa, Oct. 11, 1999, Annex IX. Another example is provided by the EEA. Article 61, which regulates state aid, prohibits "any aid granted by EC Member States, EFTA States or through State resources in any form whatsoever which distorts or threatens to distort competition by favouring certain undertakings or the production of certain goods ... in so far as it affects trade between Contracting Parties." However, under Article 61.3(c), "aid to facilitate the development of certain economic activities or of certain economic areas, where such aid does not adversely affect trading conditions to an extent contrary to the common interest" may be compatible with the functioning of the Agreement.

(a) based on the best scientific evidence available, as applicable, that establish a connection between the products affected by the measure and the species being protected or conserved;
(b) tailored to the conservation objective; and
(c) implemented after the importing Party has:
  (i) consulted with the exporting Party, in an effort to resolve the issue cooperatively; and
  (ii) provided a reasonable opportunity for the exporting Party to take appropriate measures to address the issue.[104]

Third, provisions that *allow the parties to streamline environmental criteria in domestic laws and policies*. These include provisions that allow the parties to take environmental considerations into account in their public procurement assessments. Government procurement practices are generally considered non-tariff barriers and all the agreements that choose to regulate them contain a blanket prohibition to prepare, adopt, or apply technical specifications, or to prescribe conformity assessment procedures, as they might create unnecessary obstacles to international trade.[105] Some of the more recent agreements, however, exclude from this general prohibition technical specifications adopted for environmental reasons. Article 19.9 of the *EU-Canada Comprehensive Economic and Trade Agreement* (CETA), for instance, allows the parties to "adopt or apply technical specifications to promote the conservation of natural resources or protect the environment"[106] and, despite the general prohibition to do so, further clarifies that the "evaluation criteria set out in the notice of intended procurement or tender documentation *may* include" among other factors, "environmental characteristics."[107] This 'exemption' is in line with the European long-term vision for sustainable development, set out in a 2011 Communication of the Commission, where one of the *actions* refers precisely to "make better use of public procurement to favor environmentally-friendly products and services."[108] While traditionally 'government procurement' provisions in FTAs were focused on avoiding discrimination and

104 USMCA, Art. 24.17(3).
105 The prohibition generally reads: "A procuring entity may not prepare, adopt, or apply any technical specification or prescribe any conformity assessment procedure with the purpose or the effect of creating unnecessary obstacles to trade between the Parties" (or similar language).
106 Free Trade Agreement & Economic Integration Agreement, Canada-EU, Oct. 30, 2016 [hereinafter CETA], Art. 19.0(6).
107 CETA, Art. 19.0(9) (emphasis added).
108 Commission Communication on a Sustainable Europe for a Better World: A European Union Strategy for Sustainable Development, May 15, 2001, COM(2001)264 Final, 7.

offsets in tenders, these new provisions can allow governments to incorporate environment-related criteria into their traditional cost-benefit analysis.[109]

To these three categories of provisions, we should add those that allow the parties to impose trade sanctions in case a norm in the environmental chapter or annex of the agreement is violated, and which, more broadly, provide for the enforcement of their environmental and trade provisions on the same basis. These provisions have been gradually introduced in recent FTAs signed by the US and have proven particularly effective, as the next section will show, in the context of the protection of forests.

2.4 *Trade Sanctions and Forests Protection*

In the past few decades, the number of 'environmental' provisions contained in free trade agreements has exponentially increased.[110] Besides the recognition of the parties' right to pursue environmental objectives, all the main environmental principles have found their way in the text of many FTAs and, next to the classical free-trade obligation, many FTAs feature environmental obligations as well. The final section of the previous chapter has provided the reader with an overview of these provisions. Despite their undeniable potential in terms of promoting environmental protection, however, they often fall short because of a number of reasons, in particular related to their enforcement—or lack thereof.

First, in case of violation by one of the parties of the FTA's environmental norms, the parties generally have limited or no access to the general dispute settlement mechanism provided for in the agreement. Under the *US-Chile* FTA for instance, the parties have access to the general dispute settlement mechanism provided for in Chapter 22 of the Agreement *only* in the case where one of the parties has failed "to effectively enforce its environmental laws, through a sustained or recurring course of action or inaction, in a manner affecting trade between the Parties" and *only* after having exhausted the consultation procedure described in the environmental chapter.[111] Similarly, FTAs signed by the European Union expressly clarify that the title on sustainable development is not subject to the title on dispute settlement.[112]

---

109 *Climate Change and Trade Agreements: Friends or Foes?* Report by The Economist Intelligence Unit (2019), 25–6.

110 See e.g. Cima, 'Promoting Renewable Energy through FTAs' (n 97) and Morin, Dür, and Lechner, 'Mapping the Trade and Environment Nexus' (n 97).

111 Free Trade Agreement & Economic Integration Agreement, United States-Chile, June 6, 2003, Art. 19.6(8) and (9).

112 See e.g. EU-S. Kor. FTA, Art. 13.6; EU-Sing. FTA, Art. 13.16(1); and CETA, Art. 24.16.

Various environmental—or sustainable development—chapters of FTAs do provide for their own procedure in case a violation of one of their provisions is believed to have occurred. However, these procedures generally involve several rounds of consultations and do not allow for the imposition of sanctions. The result is that the environmental chapter of FTAs, despite all these new provisions and obligations, is hardly enforceable.

A series of recent events that have unfolded under the trade agreement signed between the United States and Peru, on the other hand, seem to tell a rather different story. This story is where a trade agreement was used as a legal basis to impose a trade sanction on one of the parties because of non-compliance with its own environmental norms. The story started in 2015 in Tampico, Mexico, on an October morning. The cargo ship *Yacu Kallpa,* which was scheduled to arrive in Houston with lumber harvested from the Amazon rain forest, was ambushed by Homeland Security investigators, who seized the entire cargo: "never before had so much lumber been denied entry at a US port on evidence that it was harvested illegally," read a newspaper describing the events.[113] Because most of the shipment belonged to the Peruvian company Inversiones La Oroza SRL (Oroza), then-US Trade Representative Michael Forman asked Peru to verify whether specific shipments from that particular company complied with Peru's laws and regulations governing the harvest and trade in timber products.[114] The timber verification process initiated shortly thereafter by Peru's Supervisory Agency for Forest and Wildlife Resources (OSINFOR) found that significant portions of the wood had been harvested illegally. Given the outcome of the verification, on October 19, 2017, then-US Trade Representative Robert Lighthizer directed the US Customs and Border Protection to block all shipments from Oroza for three years or until the Interagency Committee on Trade in Timber Products from Peru determines that Oroza complied with all applicable laws, regulations, and other measures of Peru governing the harvest of and trade in timber products.[115]

The trade sanction imposed by the United States against Oroza's exports represented a step forward in the battle to preserve tropical forests and fight organized criminal logging in Peru. The sanction, just like the US request that Peru verified the company's compliance with Peru's environmental and timber

113 Frank Bajak, 'Investigations Show Peru Backsliding on Illegal Logging', *Houston Chronicle*, Apr. 19, 2017.

114 Letter from Michael B.G. Froman, US Trade Rep., to Magali Silva Velarde-Alvarez, Minister of Trade and Tourism, Republic of Peru (Feb. 26, 2016). Law No. 29763, July 22, 2011 (Peru).

115 Press Release, Office of the US Trade Rep., *USTR Announces Unprecedented Action to Block Illegal Timber Imports from Peru* (Oct. 19, 2017).

laws, were not triggered or motivated by an environmental treaty. Rather, they had been adopted within the framework created by the PTPA, the *United States-Peru Trade Promotion Agreement*. Similarly, it was the PTPA that had led to the establishment of OSINFOR in Peru, "as an independent and separate body responsible for the supervision and oversight of forest and wildlife resources primarily at the point of harvest."[116] A free trade agreement, in other words, had led to the creation of an institutional framework precisely devoted to forest and wildlife protection, had pushed Peru to modify and update its environmental laws, and had formed the legal basis to block the entry in the US market of illegally-harvested timber.

All these provisions can be found in an Annex to the agreement, known as the 'Forest Annex', which was drafted to help the parties "combat trade associated with illegal logging and illegal trade in wildlife,"[117] incorporating and further elaborating on the 1973 Convention on International Trade in Endangered Species of Wild Fauna and Flora (CITES). Paragraph 3 of the Annex requires Peru to take a number of actions within 18 months after the entry into force of the Agreement, some of which have an impact on trade, such as imposing penalties to deter violations of any timber laws and regulations, including "suspending the right to export the product as to which a law, regulation, or other measure has been violated,"[118] and establishing "an annual export quota for bigleaf mahogany, covering logs, sawn wood, veneer sheets and plywood, at a level and in a manner consistent with Article IV of [CITES]."[119]

Paragraph 7 further provides that

> on the written request of the United States, Peru shall verify whether, with respect to a particular shipment of timber products from Peru to the United States, the exporter or producer of those products has complied with applicable laws, regulations, and other measures of Peru governing the harvest of, and trade in, those products.[120]

116 US Interagency Committee on Trade in Timber Products from Peru, *Statement Regarding Implementation of the PTPA Forest Annex and Peru's July 2018 Verification Report* (Sept. 17, 2018).

117 PTPA, Annex 18.3.4 on Forest Sector Governance [hereinafter PTPA Forest Annex], para. 1.

118 Ibid., para. 3(c)(ii).

119 Ibid., para. 3(f).

120 Paragraph 7 further specifies in a footnote that "the United States may detain a shipment which is subject to a verification request pending the result of the verification …".

If such request is made, Peru is then required to provide the United States with a written report on the results of the verification.[121] If the report shows the existence of violations or if Peru fails to provide it, the United States can take a number of actions, including "denying entry to the shipment that was the subject of the verification."[122] And, for the very first time in the history of US free trade agreements, the United States Trade Representative (USTR) indeed denied entry of a shipment on environmental grounds—because the timber had been harvested illegally and unsustainably.

All this was possible thanks to the historic *May 10 Agreement*.[123] On May 10, 2007, after several months of behind-the-scene negotiations between the Democrats and the Republican Administration, a bipartisan deal on US trade policy was finally struck, less than two months before the trade promotion authority was expected to expire, and which would have been difficult to renew without the support of the pro-labor and pro-environment Democrats.[124] The *May 10 Agreement* contains a template to be followed by any future US trade agreement with regards to six topics, including the environment.[125] It further incorporates a specific list of multilateral environmental agreements,[126] adding that any violation of these environmental obligations shall be enforced "on the same basis as the commercial provisions" of FTA s, including through trade sanctions:

> We have agreed that all of our FTA environmental obligations will be enforced on the same basis as the commercial provisions of our agreements—same remedies, procedures, and sanctions. Previously, our environmental dispute settlement procedures focused on the use of fines, as opposed to trade sanctions, and were limited to the obligation to effectively enforce environmental laws.[127]

---

121 PTPA Forest Annex, para. 12.

122 Ibid., para. 13(a)(i).

123 Office of the US Trade Representative, Bipartisan Agreement on Trade Policy (May 2007). See H. Rep. 110–421 (Nov. 5, 2007) (describing the May 10 Agreement).

124 See Sunjoon Cho, 'The Bush Administration and Democrats Reach a Bipartisan Deal on Trade Policy', 11(15) *ASIL Insights* (May 31, 2007); Steven R. Weisman, 'Bush and Democrats in Accord on Trade Deals', *New York Times*, May 11, 2007.

125 The other areas covered are labor, investment, government procurement, intellectual property, and port security.

126 The listed MEAs are: Convention on International Trade in Endangered Species, Montreal Protocol on Ozone Depleting Substances, Convention on Marine Pollution, InterAmerican Tropical Tuna Convention, Ramsar Convention on Wetlands, International Whaling Convention, and Convention on Conservation of Antarctic Marine Living Resources.

127 USTR, Bipartisan Agreement on Trade Policy (May 2007).

Further, it contains specific reference to the PTPA, where it provides that "we have agreed to work with the Government of Peru on comprehensive steps to address illegal logging, including of endangered mahogany, and to *restrict imports of products that are harvested and traded in violation of CITES*."[128] On this basis, the United States and Peru drafted the environment chapter of the PTPA and its 'Forest Annex' clarifying that the Annex was subject to the general dispute settlement procedure, set out in Chapter 21, in contrast with all the agreements signed by the US before 2007, where their environmental provisions were subject to a special procedure in case of non-compliance, generally considered far less effective that the one foreseen in case of violation of one of the trade norms. Similarly, the PTPA and its Annex foresee the possibility to impose trade sanctions and import/export restrictions, a possibility that was used in 2017 for the very first time.

Moreover, in January 2019, the USTR requested its very first consultation under the PTPA, where the United States expressed their concern that Peru's decision to move OSINFOR within Peru's Ministry of Environment would have deprived the Agency of its independence, required by the 'Forest Annex', and resulted in Peru's decision to annul the decree at stake only a few months later.[129]

2.5 *A New Kind of Environmental Bargain*

When Canada began negotiating a trade agreement with the United States in 1986, the country's system for regulating pesticides was significantly more stringent than the one in force in the US. The latter relied on a risk-benefit regulatory model for pesticide registration, which had been opposed by environmental groups both in Canada and in the US.[130] As part of the 'bargain' required to complete the negotiations, however, Canadian negotiators agreed to "work towards equivalence" with the US system, which meant settling for lower levels of environmental protection.[131] In order to be able to strike a deal

---

128 Ibid. (emphasis added).

129 Press Release, Office of the US Trade Representative, USTR Requests First-Ever Environment Consultation Under the US-Peru Trade Promotion Agreement (PTPA) (Jan. 4, 2019); Press Release, Office of the US Trade Representative, USTR Successfully Resolves Concerns Raised in First-Ever Environment Consultation Under the US-Peru Trade Promotion Agreement (PTPA) (Apr. 9, 2019).

130 Steven Shrybman, 'International Trade and the Environment: An Environmental Assessment of the General Agreement on Tariffs and Trade' (1990) 20(1) *The Ecologist* 30, 33.

131 Chapter six and seven of USCFTA required the parties to harmonize technical and agricultural standards.

with the United States, Canada had to lower its own environmental standards. This kind of bargain reflected the traditional neoliberal approach to trade and the environment, an approach where trade liberalization is regarded as the supreme goal and differences in domestic (environmental) standards as dangerous trade barriers.

After all, despite the vocal opposition of environmental groups on both sides of the border, advisory committees had been established to assist with the negotiations, and no environmentalists had participated in their discussions, nor had they been invited to do so.[132] Rather, such advisory committees were predominantly composed of representatives of government and business, while environmental and consumer groups were generally left out. This is a classic example of the 'club model' of negotiation and cooperation, as constructivists would describe it.[133] It is based on a clear-cut distinction between issue-areas and on the premise that each club—trade, environment, labor etc.—is strictly responsible for its own issue-area, hence the tendency to exclude *outsiders* from the negotiations.

In December 2003, when the United States concluded its trade negotiations with Chile, the overall situation was significantly different. The clinical isolation between the trade and environmental communities had come to an end, as the trade community struggled to maintain its previous *clubiness* and was 'forced' to involve several groups of 'outsiders' in its work. In 2002, the US Congress passed the new *Trade Act*, which, in Section 2104(e), required that advisory committees provided the President, the US Trade Representative, and Congress with reports required under Section 135(e)(1) of the Trade Act of 1974, as amended, not later than 30 days after the President notified Congress of his intent to enter into an agreement.[134] One of these advisory committees is the Trade and Environment Policy Advisory Committee or TEPAC, which had been created in 1994 and was co-chaired by the US Trade Representative and the Environmental Protection Agency (EPA) Administrator.[135] In particular,

132 Shrybman, 'International Trade and the Environment' (n 130) 33.

133 See Robert O. Keohane and Joseph S. Nye Jr., 'The Club Model of Multilateral Cooperation and Problems of Democratic Legitimacy', in Roger B. Porter et al. (eds.), *Efficiency, Equity, and Legitimacy: The Multilateral Trading System at the Millennium* (Brookings Institution Press, 2001), pp. 264–291.

134 Trade Act of 2002, H.R. 3009, 116 Stat. 933, 19 U.S.C. §§ 3803–3805 (2002) [hereinafter 2002 Trade Act].

135 The other committees include a broad-based Advisory Committee for Trade Policy and Negotiations, a policy advisory committee on industry and one on agriculture, five technical advisory groups on specific agricultural groups, 17 industry sector advisory committees, four industry functional advisory committees, and an intergovernmental policy advisory committee.

with regards to the report to be submitted by TEPAC, the *Trade Act* of 2002 elucidated the principal trade negotiating objectives related to environmental matters, which included (i) "to ensure that a party to a trade agreement with the United States does not fail to effectively enforce its environmental laws,"(ii) "to strengthen the capacity of United States trading partners to protect the environment through the promotion of sustainable development," and (iii) "to reduce or eliminate government practices or policies that unduly threaten sustainable development."[136]

In addition, Section 2012(c)(4) of the 2002 *Trade Act*, together with Executive Order 13,141, require the USTR to conduct several environmental reviews before a trade agreement can successfully be signed. The scope of the review is quite broad and encompasses not only an analysis of the potential impacts of the trade agreement on the environment of the parties involved but it also involves an assessment of their existing environmental legal framework.

At the time of the negotiations, Chile's environmental laws were not as advanced and as protective of the environment as US laws, or as many MEAs would have required. For instance, the country did not have adequate legislation to implement the basic requirements of CITES.[137] To this end, in addition to Chapter 19 of the *US-Chile* FTA, dedicated to the environment, the parties negotiated an environmental side agreement, which, at Article II, established the Joint Commission for Environmental Cooperation, co-chaired by designated high-level officials of the US Department of State and the Chilean Ministry of Foreign Affairs and which would serve as a forum of cooperation between the two countries to work side by side to promote "sustainable development and management of environmental resources, including wild fauna and flora, protected wild areas, and other ecologically important ecosystems."[138] For several years, the US-Chile cooperation conducted through the Joint Commission focused, among others, on strengthening and improving Chile's environmental legal framework and in 2016, Law 20962, which implements CITES, was approved, introducing various adaptations to national legislation in matters of prevention, control and sanction of behaviors related to trafficking and commercialization of threatened species of wild fauna and flora.[139] In 2017, after a thorough review, the CITES Secretariat concluded that Chile's new wildlife

136 2002 Trade Act.

137 USTR, *2018 Trade Policy Agenda and 2017 Annual Report of the President of the United States on the Trade Agreements Program* (Mar. 2018), 68.

138 US-Chile Joint Commission for Environmental Cooperation, 2012–2014 Work Program, 2012.

139 Law No. 20962, Sept. 30, 2016, Diario Oficial [D.O.] (Chile).

law fully satisfied the country's implementation commitments under CITES. As the two countries had committed in the 2015–2017 Joint Commission Work Program, signed in August 2015, they have succeeded in working together to preserve and protect the environment *through* the FTA Environment Chapter and the Environmental Cooperation Agreement.[140]

The two negotiations depicted could not be more different. In 1986, Canada had to agree to lower its own environmental standards to be able to successfully conclude a trade agreement with the United States. Not even 20 years later, Chile had to commit to improve its environmental legal framework—in particular in the area of protection of threatened species of wild flora—to conclude an agreement with, once again, the United States. While in 1986 harmonization of domestic standards and regulations was feared by environmentalists as it tended to occur *downward,* in 2003 it showed the potential to occur *upward.*

2.6 *The EU's Sustainable Commercial Policy*

A similar approach can be found in the *Resolution on Climate Diplomacy* adopted by the European Parliament on July 3, 2018. The latter called on the Commission "to integrate the climate change dimension into international trade and investment agreements and to make ratification and implementation of the Paris Agreement a condition for future trade agreements", while recommending the "development and systematic inclusion of a mandatory fundamental climate change clause in international agreements, including trade and investment agreements."[141] Certain environmental requirements are set out as conditions to negotiate comprehensive trade agreements with the European Union, while only 12 years before, the Communication *Global Europe: Competing in the World*, had identified purely economic criteria to

140 Joint Communique of the United States-Chile Environment Affairs Council and Joint Commission for Environmental Cooperation (Aug.13, 2015).

141 Climate Diplomacy Resolution. These statements were later repeated by the European Parliament after the 2018 Climate Change Conference in Katowice: European Parliament Resolution on the 2018 UN Climate Change Conference in Katowice, Poland (COP24), Oct. 25, 2018, para. 53. The recent decision of the European Council to begin new trade talks with United States irrespective of Trump's decision to withdraw from the Paris Agreement and despite the unfavorable vote of the European Parliament on this point, has been justified arguing that the condition set out in the Climate Diplomacy Resolution only applies to 'comprehensive trade agreements', while the current trade negotiations between the EU and the US will only cover industrial tariffs and conformity assessments. *Opening of Negotiations between the EU and the US,* 2019/2537(RSP) (Procedure Rejected). Council Decision 6052/19 (Apr. 9, 2019).

guide the EU in the selection of partners in FTAs and in their negotiation and conclusion, namely: "the market potential measured in terms of size and economic growth, the level of protection vis-à-vis exports from the EU (customs tariffs, non-tariff barriers), etc., [as well as] negotiations between the EU's potential partners and its competitors, the impact of these negotiations on the EU and the risk that they pose to the partners' preferential access to the Union's markets."[142]

At the same time, however, the *Communication* had also recognized the role that trade cooperation can have in promoting sustainable development when it stated that "in considering new FTAs, we will need to work to strengthen sustainable development through our bilateral trade relations. This could include incorporating new co-operative provisions in areas relating to labor standards and environmental protection."[143]

In the same year, the Council of the European Union adopted the Sustainable Development Strategy:

> 21. The EU will seek to use the full range of policy instruments in the implementation of its policies. The most appropriate economic instruments should be used to promote market transparency and prices that reflect the real economic, social and environmental costs of products and services (getting prices right). Their potential to reconcile environmental protection and smart economic growth and exploit win-win opportunities should be recognized. Additionally, their suitability should be judged against a set of criteria, including their impact on competitiveness and productivity.
>
> 22. Member States should consider further steps to shift taxation from labor to resource and energy consumption and/or pollution, to contribute to the EU goals of increasing employment and reducing negative environmental impacts in a cost-effective way.[144]

---

142 Commission Communication on Global Europe: Competing in the World, Oct. 4, 2006, COM(2006)567.

143 Ibid.

144 Council Review of the EU Sustainable Development Strategy, June 9, 2006, 10117/06. See Commission Communication on a Sustainable Europe for a Better World: A European Union Strategy for Sustainable Development, May 15, 2001, COM(2001)264 Final. See also the *Treaty of Nice*, Declaration on Article 175 of the Treaty establishing the European Community: "The High Contracting Parties are determined to see the European Union play a leading role in promoting environmental protection in the Union and in international efforts pursuing the same objective at global level. Full use should be made of all possibilities offered by the Treaty with a view to pursuing this objective, including the use of incentives and instruments which are market-oriented and intended to promote

The centrality of environmental protection—and sustainable development more broadly—as inherent component of the EU commercial policy, was finally clearly stated by the European Court of Justice in its May 2017 Opinion 2/15.[145] Asked about the competence of the EU with regards to the *EU-Singapore* FTA, the Court, disagreeing with the Advocate General, stated that sustainable development clauses in FTAs fall under EU exclusive competence and that there is an "obligation on the European Union to integrate those objectives and principles into the conduct of its common commercial policy" stemming from the first paragraph of Article 207 of the Treaty on the Functioning of the European Union (TFEU) itself, Article 21 of the Treaty of the European Union (TEU) and Articles 9, 11 and 205 TFEU.[146] The argument goes on with the Court taking a clear position in favor of the entire sustainable development clause having a direct and immediate effect on trade between the EU and Singapore.[147]

2.7 *From Exception to Promotion*

In 1994, when NAFTA was adopted, it was welcomed as the "greenest trade agreement ever negotiated."[148] And it was, at the time. These few paragraphs, however, show us a very different meaning of 'being green'. It is not simply a matter of allowing countries to protect the environment within the rigid boundaries of trade rules anymore. It is instead a matter of designing trade rules that are themselves conducive to environmental protection. New provisions in trade agreements—and even entire agreements if a WTO agreement on fisheries will one day be completed—are now explicitly prohibiting certain

sustainable development." Treaty of Nice amending the Treaty on the European Union, the Treaties Establishing the European Communities and Certain Related Acts, 2001 O.J. C 80/1.

145 ECJ, Opinion 2/15, May 16, 2017.

146 Ibid., para 143. See also Opinion of Advocate General Sharpston, Dec. 21, 2016. According to Article 207 TFEU, "the common commercial policy shall be conducted in the context of the principles and objectives of the Union's external action." Article 9 and 11 of the TEU read: "in defining and implementing its policies and activities, the Union shall take into account requirements linked to the promotion of a high level of employment, the guarantee of adequate social protection, the fight against social exclusion, and a high level of education, training and protection of human health" (Article 9) and "Environmental protection requirements must be integrated into the definition and implementation of the Union's policies and activities, in particular with a view to promoting sustainable development" (Article 11).

147 Giovanni Gruni, 'Towards a Sustainable World Trade Law? The Commercial Policy of the European Union after Opinion 2/15 CJEU' (2018) 13 *Global Trade & Customs Journal* 5, 6.

148 Carla A. Hills, 'The Trade Pact is Our Best Deal', *New York Times*, Aug. 17, 1993.

trade measures because they harm the environment and recognize the right of the parties to restrict trade in the name of environmental protection. In the past—when NAFTA or the WTO agreements were being negotiated—these kinds of provisions could only be found in multilateral environmental agreements.

To really appreciate the groundbreaking nature of these developments, let us consider the case of the protection of wild flora. Certain plant species, threatened with extinction or otherwise endangered, have been protected since 1975 by the *Convention on International Trade in Endangered Species*.[149] The Convention places certain controls on international trade in specimens of selected species, dividing them in two groups—Appendix I, for "species threatened with extinction which are or may be affected by trade" and Appendix II for species which might become threatened with extinction if their trade remains unregulated.[150] The listing of timber species under CITES, for instance, places an obligation on the exporting state willing to export a CITES-listed timber species to demonstrate the legal acquisition of the listed timber in accordance with national law, and provide a scientific non-detriment finding attesting to the sustainability of the amount of listed timber harvested. In parallel, the importing state has the obligation not to accept any listed timber species without the necessary permits and to seize and confiscate any illegally traded listed timber species.[151]

I

When the GATT was negotiated in 1947, no reference was made in the text of the agreement to the protection of forests, timber, or wild fauna and flora more broadly, not even after the WTO was established in 1994. When the issue of natural resources and natural resource-derived products was raised during the Uruguay Round, the discussion, far from addressing the need to protect natural resources, revolved around a proposal to remove trade barriers to their free flow, which, if successful, would have led to higher demand and unsustainable resource management,[152] rather than conservation—as advocated by environmentalists.

---

149 Since 1975, the number of protected species has been constantly growing, as new species are included at nearly each meeting of the Conference of the Parties (COP).

150 Convention on International Trade in Endangered Species of Fauna and Flora, Mar. 3, 1973, 993 U.N.T.S. 243 [hereinafter CITES], Art. II.

151 WT/CTE/M/58, para. 1.34. CITES, Art. VIII(1)(b).

152 See Robert Housman and Durwood Zaelke, 'Trade, Environment, and Sustainable Development: A Primer' (1992) 15 *Hastings International & Comparative Law Review* 532, 562.

The possibility to adopt trade measures to protect endangered species of any kind was highly controversial, as suggested by the reaction of several Southeast Asian governments and their allies in the developing world towards an Austrian law that prescribed 'ecolabelling' for imported tropical timber and timber products. Another example is provided by the US-Taiwan saga under the Pelly Amendment. In that context, the US sanction, which had led Taiwan to take critical steps towards halting commercial trade in tigers and rhinos before it was lifted, was not allowed by GATT rules, and the only refuge for countries wanting to adopt similar measures would have been engaging in an uphill, and most likely unsuccessful, battle under Article XX. Trade liberalization was the overarching rule and the protection of fauna and flora, or the environment more broadly, clearly just an exception.

II

The NAFTA drafters, mindful of the possibility that the parties might introduce measures in compliance with CITES rules, and that these measures might restrict trade between them and violate one or more of the core rules of the agreement, introduced a reference to the Convention in Article 104, clarifying that "in the event of any inconsistency between [NAFTA] and the specific trade obligations set out [in the Convention] such obligations shall prevail to the extent of the inconsistency, provided that where a Party has a choice among equally effective and reasonably available means of complying with such obligations, the Party chooses the alternative that is the least inconsistent with the other provisions of this Agreement."[153]

Although it did not really address the underlying problems, as inconsistencies were not likely to occur between NAFTA and CITES, but rather between NAFTA and a domestic measure adopted within the framework provided by CITES, this provision does acknowledge that the goals pursued by CITES, among other environmental treaties, are valuable and the willingness to try and mediate between the sometimes-conflicting objectives of trade and environmental instruments. On the other hand, however, it still reflects the distinction between 'trade issues', dealt with in the text of NAFTA, and 'non-trade issues'—such as the protection of the environment—dealt with in other agreements outside of the realm of trade law, and the hierarchy that ensues.[154]

153 North American Free Trade Agreement, US-Can.-Mex, Dec. 17, 1992, 32 I.L.M. 289 (1993) [hereinafter NAFTA], Art. 104.

154 As a matter of fact, NAFTA Article 104 specifies that "where a Party has a choice among equally effective and reasonably available means of complying with such obligations, the Party chooses the alternative that is the least inconsistent with the other provisions of this Agreement."

III

The trade agreement between the United States and Peru, in its Annex 18.3.4 (Forest Annex), instead, requires both parties to suspend the right to export a specific timber-product in case a law, regulation, or other measure regulating its harvest and trade has been violated,[155] and to establish "an annual export quota for bigleaf mahogany, covering logs, sawn wood, veneer sheets and plywood, at a level and in a manner consistent with Article IV of CITES."[156] For the first time, the protection of certain species of plants became the rule in the text of a trade agreement, and not just in that of a multilateral environmental treaty. The Annex to the PTPA actually reproduces and further elaborates on certain rules of a multilateral environmental treaty, placing them on equal footing with trade rules, covered by the same general dispute settlement mechanism, and legitimizing trade sanctions for environmental purposes. As explained by the US representative at the CTE, the agreement was supposed to be a tool precisely to assist Peru to combat illegal logging and associated trade and to promote trade in legal wood products.[157]

The concept of 'greening' trade rules seems to have acquired a whole new meaning. These agreements, and others belonging to this 'new' generation, do not ignore environmental concerns, nor they simply 'accommodate' them. Rather, they actively promote the protection and preservation of the environment.

Another example is provided by the International Convention for the Conservation of Atlantic Tunas (ICCAT). One of the Recommendations of the Commission established by the Convention requires the parties to adopt the measures necessary "to prohibit landings from fishing vessels, placing in cages for farming and/or the transshipment within their jurisdiction of tunas or tuna-like species caught by IUU fishing activities." Once again, a potentially trade-restricting rule we once could only find in an environmental instrument can now also be found in a trade agreement. According to Article 24.21 of USMCA, for instance, "in support of international efforts to combat IUU fishing and to help deter trade in products from IUU fishing," each party shall adopt, maintain, review, or revise measures to "address the transshipment at sea of fish caught through IUU fishing or fish products derived from IUU fishing."[158]

---

155 PTPA Forest Annex, Art. 3.c.ii.

156 Ibid., Art. 3.f.

157 WT/CTE/M/57 (Sept. 30, 2014), para. 1.27.

158 ICCAT Recommendation to Adopt Additional Measures Against Illegal, Unreported and Unregulated Fishing (June 19, 2004). USMCA, Art. 24.21(2)(b)(ii).

3 The Power of Ideas

The examples provided in the previous paragraphs are evidence of the adoption of approaches previously held 'in contempt' by the trade community with regards to the environment. The introduction of environmental exemptions, for instance, stands in contrast with the idea that non-discrimination represents the rule and countries' freedom to protect the environment should be pigeonholed in narrow exceptions to avoid the risk that they might be used to introduce economic protection and lead to abuse. Even the decision of the Appellate Body to rely on external non-WTO sources to interpret GATT provisions represents an approach that would have been deemed unacceptable a few decades before, as panels were supposed to only rely on GATT law. The drafting of new rules prohibiting certain types of subsidies not only—and primarily—because trade-distorting but, most importantly, because environmentally harmful, marks a stark departure from the motives that had inspired the negotiations on subsidies during the first years of the GATT/WTO, where government subsidies were disciplined "as part of the broader quest for free trade."[159]

These new approaches, it is argued in this book, are the result of a gradual change in the perception of the trade/environment nexus, which largely originated in the environmental community and was facilitated by its increasing interactions with the trade community. The progress made since the 1970s, is considerable. For many years, the *trade policy elite,* "deploying traditional conceptual frameworks" had played "the role of gatekeeper of policy ideas, monopolizing not only the production but also the legitimation and authorization of acceptable policy proposals."[160] While members of the environmental community demanded incessantly to be heard, their protests stopped at the doors of the WTO, and the lack of support from developing countries, among other factors, contributed to maintaining the wall between the trade and environmental community.

159 Gary Clyde Hufbauer, 'Subsidies', in Jeffrey J. Schott (ed.), *Completing the Uruguay Round* (Institute for International Econimcs, 1990), p. 93. As aptly explained by Hufbauer, without such disciplines, "each nation will be reluctant to lower its own trade barriers. Indeed, it can be argued that the elimination of tariffs and quotas, without comparable discipline on subsidies and other behind-the-border barriers, will simply promote the growth of these opaquer forms of protection." Ibid.

160 Andrew Lang, 'The Role of the Human Rights Movement in Trade Policy-Making: Human Rights as a Trigger for Policy Learning' (2007) 5 *New Zealand Journal of Public International Law* 77, 90.

Although, during those first years, environmentalists were not successful in forming a united front and standing up to free-traders and ended up playing by free-trade rules, rather than creating their own,[161] they gradually began to question the underlying principles and norms of the trading system, and to frame them in a new light. Rather than focusing only on the impact of trade on growth and resource allocation, the environmental community has given voice to a different set of preoccupations and have provided impetus for an alternative discourse.[162] For instance, environmentalists have stimulated collective thinking and knowledge production about the impact of trade and trade instruments on the different components of the global environment, as well as on the potential use that can be made of trade instruments for environmental protection.[163] By starting these new kinds of discourses, the environmental community has planted the seeds of new ideas, acknowledging the instrumental role of trade liberalization and the positive relation with environmental protection. Once the *trade policy elite* ceased to be an impregnable fortress, these new ideas could begin to grow and further develop. This process, it is argued, has been facilitated by two series of factors: first, progress in the degree of interaction between the trade and environmental communities and, second, an increasing convergence of the environment and development agendas.

3.1 *From Weak to Strong Integration*

The creation of the CTE in 1994 marked the end of the clinical isolation in which the trade and environmental communities had coexisted for many years, at least at the international level. At first, however, the integration between the two communities within the CTE, and the WTO more broadly—i.e. in other committees where issues at the intersection between trade and environment were treated—was more nominal than real.[164] International relation scholars

---

161 See e.g. the approach adopted during the 1987 negotiations on the *Montreal Protocol for the Protection of the Ozone Layer*, or the fact that environmentalists have, for many years, framed the debate as 'trade and', just like the trade community has.

162 As explained by Finnemore and Sikkink, this act of calling attention to certain issues or even 'creating' issues through a process of reinterpretation or renaming is generally referred to by social movement theorists as 'framing'. See Martha Finnemore and Kathryn Sikkink, 'International Norm Dynamics and Political Change' (1998) 52(4) *International Organization* 887, 897. Andrew Lang describes in these terms the approach towards the trade/human rights nexus. Lang, 'The Role of the Human Rights Movement' (n 160).

163 See e.g. some of the opinions expressed at the GATT Symposium on Trade, Environment and Sustainable Development on July 28, 1994.

164 As an example, the CBD (observer at the CTE), has not been granted such status at the TRIPS Council, despite the continuous requests and despite dealing with overlapping issues, such as access to genetic resources and benefits sharing. In a March 2011 meeting,

refer to this type of integration as 'weak integration' or as 'low institutional capacity for reciprocal learning', which occurs when, among other things, communities' actors have unequal access to each other's discussions, linkages are based on informal arrangements, and relations are predominantly hierarchical.[165] In fact, during the first years of the CTE's existence, only a handful of environmental international organizations had been granted observer status,[166] the criteria for being granted such status were unclear, and their role within the Committee was mostly limited to an 'act of presence': as a representative described it, "you give them a flag. They come to the meetings and they sit there. That is it."[167]

As years went by, the number of 'environmental' observers grew, including most MEAs Secretariats, which had been initially excluded.[168] Moreover, their role slowly became substantially more active, first simply presenting on certain topics and later intervening in the debates, next to Member states representatives.[169] The interactions between the CTE and environmental organizations have become more formalized and frequent, the relationship between the two communities and the interests they represent less hierarchical, the two communities have gained a more equal access to each other's discussions,

the Members gathered in the TRIPS Council could not even agree on whether to invite the CBD Secretariat to give a briefing on the Nagoya Protocol right after it was adopted. See IP/C/M/65 (May 10, 2011).

165 Melissa Gabler, 'Norms, Institutions and Social Learning: An Explanation for Weak Policy Integration in the WTO's Committee on Trade and Environment' (2010) 10(2) *Global Environmental Politics* 80, 91.

166 The organizations having observer status since the beginning were: the UN, UNCTAD, the International Monetary Fund (IMF), UNEP, the United Nations Development Program (UNDP), the Commission on Sustainable Development (CSD), FAO, the International Trade Centre (ITC), the Organization for Economic Cooperation and Development (OECD), and EFTA. See WT/CTE/M/1 (Mar. 6, 1995).

167 Gabler, 'Norms, Institutions and Social Learning' (n 165) 107.

168 The first two MEAs Secretariats to be granted observer status at the CTE were CITES and the United Nations Framework Convention on Climate Change (UNFCCC) in 1997. As of today, the other MEAs Secretariats that have been granted such status are the CBD and ICCAT.

169 For the first 14 meetings of the CTE, observer environmental organizations did not have any active role. In 1997, for the first time, "in order to deepen the CTE's understanding of the linkages between the multilateral environment and trade agendas," the Secretariats of several MEAs were invited to make presentations and prepare background papers for the discussions. WT/CTE/M/14 (June 26, 1997) and WT/CTE/M/15 (Nov. 20, 1997). In 2000, the CTE began organizing 'MEAs Information Sessions', which have been planned several times after that and have been an important forum to discuss several issues at the intersection between trade and the environment. WT/CTE/M/24 (Sept. 19, 2000).

and they have become more open in their deliberations. In other words, the integration has become stronger and the institutional capacity for reciprocal learning higher.

The presence of the environmental community in discussions on issues at the intersection between trade and the environment—a presence that has become stronger, more formalized, and on an equal footing—has the power to influence policy outcomes and deliberations.[170] The discussions in the CTE, for instance, have been evolving, as environmental voices have become more frequent. A main concern that was constantly raised at nearly every single meeting over the first years of the Committee was that the WTO was not an environmental protection agency and the role of the CTE should be limited to trade-related issues and it should in no way engage "in adopting rules specifically aimed at protecting the environment."[171] As a result, discussions under *Item 1* of the Agenda dealt with the compatibility of trade measures in MEAS with the WTO, assuming the WTO legal framework adequately accommodated environmental concerns: as it appears from the record of a CTE meeting in 1995, "environmental measures with significant trade effects must be compatible with the open, equitable and non-discriminatory nature of the multilateral trading system, which meant that these measures must conform to its fundamental provisions"[172] and Article XX was sufficient to address any concern of the environmental community. In the early years, even when certain members began to argue that it was necessary to better "reconcile the need to accommodate the legitimate goal of environmental protection ... with the need to preserve the open, equitable and non-discriminatory character of the WTO,"[173] they would do that by proposing amendments to the existing exception clause, thus reflecting a clear hierarchy between trade and non-trade issues. And cross-community interactions tended to be similarly hierarchical, with the representatives from environmental organizations being very marginally involved in the discussion, compared to their involvement today.

As years went by, the presence and role of members of the environmental community became more significant and new issues came to be introduced in

170 The CTE is not here considered as a homogeneous block, but rather as a forum where representatives from Member states of the WTO meet to discuss matters at the intersection between the environment and trade. It is however argued that these representatives belong to the larger trade community and are seldom exposed to the discussions occurring in environmental fora, unless appropriate communication channels are established.

171 WT/CTE/M/21 (July 26, 1999), para. 39. See also WTO, *Trade and the Environment at the WTO* (2004).

172 WT/CTE/M/4 (Oct. 10. 1995), para. 8.

173 Ibid.

the discussions—such as logging, environmental labelling, fisheries subsidies, and environmental goods and services. Although some Members initially questioned the competence of the Committee or the WTO more broadly to address some of these issues,[174] they slowly gained ground and began featuring in all the more recent meetings. Two of these even began topics of negotiations.[175]

One should not forget that institutional integration occurred, first and foremost, at the domestic level, where it played a crucial role not only in the context of domestic and bilateral discussions but in influencing international politics as well. In regional and bilateral trade negotiations, the cooperation between representatives of the trade and environmental communities has become more formal and, in certain cases, mandatory. While during the final phases of the NAFTA negotiations, environmental experts were involved on an ad-hoc basis, in 1994 the Trade and Environment Policy Advisory Committee was created, and the 2002 revision of the US *Trade Act* required its involvement in the negotiations of trade agreements, making its report—as those of the other committees involved—a mandatory requirement before the country could enter into any trade negotiations. To the same effect, preventive environmental reviews have now become mandatory, after Clinton's Executive Order 13,141. As a result, those countries that have experienced a stronger integration of environmental and trade voices within their territory have been able to bring 'greener' proposals to the negotiating table. Moreover, their representatives have brought their heightened state of awareness to the CTE or other WTO bodies, influencing, brick by brick, multilateral discussions as well.

3.2 *Watching the Seeds Grow*

> For the longest time, many viewed the WTO architecture on subsidies as static, as not capable of change. But civil society soon came to knock on our doors, drawing our attention to the perilous state of much of the world's fish stock. Its message was clear, the WTO has

174 See e.g. WT/CTE/M/35 (Nov. 19, 2003), para. 16 [regarding illegal logging]; WT/CTE/M36 (May 19, 2004), para. 18 [regarding environmental labelling].

175 See supra Section 2.1 for an analysis of the current fisheries subsidies' negotiations. The other issue that has become object of negotiations is that of the liberalization of environmental goods and services (EGS). The discussions on this topic started to be conducted regularly within the CTE and its Special Sessions after Doha, which envisaged it as one of the Committee's task (Article 31(iii)). These discussions created a perfect breeding ground for the current plurilateral negotiations on an Environmental Goods Agreement. In 2014, 14 WTO Members, in the margins of the World Economic Forum in Davos, started negotiations on an Environmental Goods Initiative and were later joined by four more Members.

> a vital role to play in protecting the world's fish stock, in saving it from depletion.[176]
>
> PASCAL LAMY, WTO Public Forum 2007

The fisheries subsidies negotiations provide a great example of the way in which the interactions between the trade and environmental community have grown and become more open, dense, and formal over time. In this context, environmental organizations have played a crucial role in their contribution to advancing the discussions on this issue, in particular over the course of the first years, both within the CTE and later in the NGR. Several information sessions were held with UNEP and the CBD Secretariat, precisely to facilitate the CTE Members' understanding of the issues,[177] and work done on the topic by international organizations such as UNEP and FAO was reviewed carefully by the CTE Secretariat and used as a basis for discussions.[178] In 2007, UNEP and the World Wide Fund (WWF) prepared a document entitled *Sustainability Criteria for Fisheries Subsidies: Options for the WTO and Beyond*, which was supposed to provide technical input to the negotiations.[179] The two organizations emphasized the importance of setting certain minimum criteria—in the areas of fish stock, fishing capacity, and fisheries management—to eliminate the negative impacts of subsidies on fisheries conservation. In fact, the criteria set out in the UNEP/WWF document, which reflected the requirements under current international fisheries instruments for responsible fisheries,[180] were used by WTO negotiators when drafting the new regulations. In the study, for instance, overcapacity is recognized as a critical problem and as "the most important link between subsidies and overfishing,"[181] and capacity-enhancing subsidies to any fishery that is not substantially under-capacity are presented as inherently very risky.[182] As a result, most of the textual proposals submitted by WTO Members to the NGR have included capacity-enhancing subsidies among the

176 Pascal Lamy, Address at the 2007 WTO Public Forum: Civil Society is Influencing the WTO Agenda, Oct. 4, 2007.

177 WT/CTE/W/187 and WT/CTE/W/149.

178 WT/CTE/W/167 and WT/CTE/W/167/Add.1.

179 David K. Schorr and John F. Caddy, 'Sustainability Criteria for Fisheries Subsidies: Options for the WTO and Beyond' (2007) UNEP/WWF Working Paper. See WT/CTE/M/45, para. 17.

180 These international instruments include the United Nations Convention on the Law of the Sea (UNCLOS), the Code of Conduct for Responsible Fisheries, and the Fish Stocks Agreement.

181 Schorr and Caddy, 'Sustainability Criteria for Fisheries Subsidies' (n 179) 15.

182 Ibid.

list of *prohibited* subsidies, and so does the most recent text presented by the Chair.[183]

Outside of the specific case of fisheries subsidies negotiations, where the cooperation between environmental and trade officials has directly affected the outcome of the negotiations, representatives of the environmental community have stimulated collective thinking about the trade/environment nexus from an environmental standpoint, rather than merely a trade-centered one, as well as knowledge production about the potential use that can be made of trade instruments for environmental protection. In a 2011 meeting of the CTE, for instance, the Secretary-General of the 2012 United Nations Conference on Sustainable Development discussed the notion of 'green economy,'[184] and stated that he hoped the international community, including the CTE, "would consider how the international trading system could assist countries that choose to embark on a green economy path."[185] Only a few months later, the representative from UNEP briefed the Committee on the 'green-economy potential' of different economic sectors and emphasized the role of international trade in transitioning to a green economy.[186] Those were the very first times that the notion of 'green economy' was introduced in the Committee.[187] Until then, the concept was well known in environmental circles, but not necessarily among trade officials or among the national delegates sitting in the CTE: as rightly emphasized by Pauwelyn, "delegates representing a state in the WTO context are mostly not the same as those representing the same state in UNEP."[188]

Since then, the 'green economy', in all its different components, has become a permanent feature of nearly all subsequent CTE meetings. Representatives of several countries have been sharing their own experience with green economy initiatives and tracked their progress year after year, at times agreeing

183 See TN/RL/GEN/181/Rev.1 (EU), proposed Article 1.1(a); TN/RL/GEN/189/Rev.1 (Indonesia) proposed Article 2.1(a); TN/RL/GEN/192 (ACP Group) proposed Article 2.1(c); TN/RL/GEN/187/Rev.2 (Argentina, Colombia, Costa Rica, Panama, Peru, Uruguay) proposed Article 2.1.3(a); TN/RL/GEN/193 (LDC Group) proposed Article 2.1(d)-(e). The exceptions are the proposal from New Zealand, Iceland, Pakistan and the one from Norway. See also TN/RL/W/274/Rev. 6, Art.3.7.

184 WT/CTE/M/52 (Sept. 6, 2011), paras. 97–111.

185 Ibid., para. 106.

186 WT/CTE/M/53 (Jan. 27, 2012), para. 19. See also UNEP, *Towards a Green Economy* (n 38).

187 The first time was actually during the meeting which took place on November 9, 2010. WT/CTE/M/51 (May 31, 2011).

188 Joost Pauwelyn, *Conflict of Norms in Public International Law* (Cambridge University Press, 2003), p. 15.

to cooperate in the context of specific projects. During a 2013 meeting, for instance, Mr. Alberto Parenti, representing the European Union, presented on the *Single Market for Green Products* (SMGP) *initiative*, adopted as a Commission communication and recommendation on April 9, 2013, aimed at addressing the proliferation of green labels and methods to prove green credentials by levelling the playing field for green producers.[189] During the course of the very same meeting, the representative from Switzerland, to support the implementation of environmental schemes as a way to increase sustainable trade, expressed interest in participating in the pilot phase of the European SMGP initiative.[190] At the same time, he presented Switzerland's own project, the so-called *Green Economy Action Plan*, which spurred significant interest in a number of countries, in particular developing ones. In fact, not only developed but less-developed countries as well have been briefing the CTE on their own initiatives.[191]

In a handful of years, the notion of green economy had become something to be discussed by both the environmental and trade community, as well as something they could even discuss together. In the context of one of the most recent WTO Public Forums, for instance, the 'green economy' was at the center of most discussions, involving both trade and environment specialists. Significantly, during a meeting of the Committee in March 2019, the WTO Secretariat briefed the members on the outcome of the Forum explaining that:

> The discussions had emphasized the need for ever closer and positive links between open, rules-based and inclusive trade on the one hand, and a healthy environment on the other. The role that trade and the WTO could play in supporting the achievement of environmental goals was also considered. Trade could serve as a tool to disseminate and scale up environmentally sound technologies, and to accelerate the transition to a green economy. More green investment was needed in developing countries, not least to improve access to energy and sanitation.[192]

The increasing openness of the *trade elite* and the increasing interactions with the environmental community have allowed the spreading of environmental

189 Commission Communication on Building the Single Market for Green Products, Apr. 9, 2013, COM(2013)196 Final. WT/CTE/M/55 (Aug. 16, 2013), paras. 1.28–1.30.

190 Ibid., para. 1.58.

191 See e.g. Thailand's Product Carbon Footprint Program or Costa Rica's Carbon Neutrality Program (Ibid., paras. 1.56–57).

192 WT/CTE/M/66 (Mar. 22, 2019), para. 2.15.

concepts and notions: while there was a time when the two communities spoke different languages—when the word 'protection' warmed the heart of environmentalists and sent chills down the spine of free traders—now they have started to understand each other and the trade community has begun to use certain environmental terms and concepts on a daily basis. These interactions have facilitated the production of new knowledge regarding how certain aspects of the trading system operate.

Another instrument that has proven very useful in this regard is the carrying out of environmental impact assessments, which, it has been argued, can contribute to providing 'feedback loops', by monitoring the outcomes of policy choices, in this case, the impact of trade agreements on the environment.[193] According to organizational theorists, this feedback function can provide the impetus for policy-makers to learn—that is to rethink the "beliefs which these policy-makers hold concerning how the trading system operates, and what the outcomes of their interventions are likely to be."[194]

The idea that trade can be a powerful tool to promote sustainable development and environmental protection is now largely shared by the trade community and is not simply a possibility environmentalists discuss in their circles. And the negotiations on fisheries subsidies, the new environmental provisions in FTAs, and the European strategy towards a sustainable development future are all signals that the knowledge that has been produced thanks to these interactions can indeed impact the actions of policy-makers, helping them to reformulate their strategies and their policy preferences.

3.3 *The Development Factor*

Normative changes towards a system that envisions trade and trade norms as a powerful tool to promote sustainable development and environmental protection largely depend on the internal dynamics of each country, as well as on the relative power in the international arena of countries that are more or less supportive of 'green' agendas.

As the previous chapters have shown, at least two lessons can be learned from the unfolding of the trade/environment story. First, that it is not exclusively a 'trade and environment' story, but rather a story that, to capture the evolution of the relationship between the two regimes in its entirety, takes into account the development agenda as well, and the role it played in said

193 See e.g. Bo Hedberg, 'How Organizations Learn and Unlearn', in Paul C. Nystrom and William H. Starbuck (eds.), *Handbook of Organizational Design* (Oxford University Press, 1981).

194 Lang, 'The Role of the Human Rights Movement' (n 160) 97.

evolution. Second, that it is not just an 'international' story. How the environment is perceived within each country vis-à-vis its development and economic needs contributes greatly to the position each country adopts in both regional and international fora and, indirectly, to the concrete development of the nexus.

The latter has evolved towards what the author has defined *promotion-based* model at a greater speed in certain regional contexts than at the level of WTO rules and decisions. This discrepancy should not come as a surprise. It is precisely the need to constantly balance environmental and developmental considerations that can explain, at least in part, the difficulties encountered by the members of the environmental community in pushing their agenda through and in being able to spread new ideas and produce new knowledge within multilateral trade institutions.

With the development agenda gaining ground both in environmental and trade fora, the principle of sustainable development becoming the overarching principle guiding future negotiations, and the principle of common but differentiated responsibilities (CBDR) a fundamental component underlying them, addressing the role of trade as a meaningful means to achieve environmental goals in the context of multilateral negotiations became increasingly difficult.[195]

Previous chapters in this book have already provided several examples of these difficulties. In the context of the CTE, as the members of the Committee started preparing its first Report to be issued in 1996, representatives from developed countries were the ones who were proposing more integrated solutions, recognizing that existing WTO provisions did not have adequate scope to accommodate MEAs' trade related environmental measures (TREMS). The strongest positions suggested an *ex ante* MEA accommodation through a formal amendment or collective interpretation of Article XX.[196] On the other side

195 Many MEAs contain a caveat such as the one we can find in the chapeau of GATT Article XX. See e.g. United Nations Framework Convention on Climate Change, May 9, 1992, 1771 U.N.T.S. 107, 31 I.L.M. 849, Article 3.5. See Chapter 4, note 38.

196 See WTO, Committee on Trade and Environment (CTE), *Non-Paper by the European Communities on Item 1*, Feb. 19, 1996; CTE 1996 Report, para. 169. The EU and EFTA countries, had advanced this proposal years before within the EMIT Group. See GATT, *GATT Council Meeting, 6 February*, C/M/247; GATT, Standing Group on Environmental Measures and International Trade (EMIT Group), *The GATT and the Trade Provisions of MEAs*. Submission from the EC, TRE/W/5, 1992; *Report of the Meeting Held on 19 November 1992*. Note by the Secretariat, TRE/8, 1992; *Report of the Meeting Held on 4–5 February 1993*. Note by the Secretariat, TRE/9, 1993; *Report of the Meeting Held on 5–6 October 1993*. Note by the Secretariat, TRE/13, 1993. Other developed countries settled for proposals arguing for more moderate reforms. See CTE, *Non-Paper. Submission by Switzerland on Item 1*,

of the barricade, the vast majority of developing and least-developed countries (and only a handful of developed ones) strenuously opposed to all these suggestions, presenting counterproposals that were far more compatible with GATT philosophy and did not require elaborate changes to the existing trade legal framework.[197] Ultimately, this latter position had the best, with the Chair tabling a draft that fit well with the existing WTO frame.[198]

The position of developing countries vis-à-vis the introduction of trade/environment discussions within the WTO was made particularly clear at the dawn of the Doha Round. As well summarized by Steinberg, "developing countries wanted to exclude environment, labor, investment, and competition policy and include their issues."[199] Developing and least-developed countries' concerns are also partly to blame for the delay in concluding a WTO agreement on fisheries, especially given the issues raised by those countries "that have low income and poorly resourced fishers, achievement of these goals will depend in most part on the fisheries sector and with the removal of subsidies, the consequences can be catastrophic."[200]

As explained by Biermann, "concerns over green protectionism limit the willingness of many WTO members to integrate environmental considerations further into trade agreements."[201] For discussions to move forward, rules and

May 20, 1996; *The Relationship between the Provisions of the MTS and Trade Measures for Environmental Purposes, including those Pursuant to MEAs—Submission by New Zealand*, WT/CTE/W/20.

197 In particular, see EMIT Group, *Report of the Meeting Held on 5–7 July 1993*. Note by the Secretariat, TRE/12, 1993, and CTE. *Non-Paper Submission by India on Items 1 and 5* (July 23, 1996).

198 During the several discussions on this topic, several developed country representatives slightly modified their proposals to meet developing countries' concerns. See, for instance, the evolution of proposals submitted by the EU. See CTE, *Non-Paper by the European Communities on Item 1* (Feb. 19, 1996).

199 Richard H. Steinberg, 'In the Shadow of Law or Power? Consensus-Based Bargaining and Outcomes in the GATT/WTO' (2002) 56(2) *International Organization* 339, 353.

200 Radika Kumar et al, 'The Effectiveness of Fisheries Subsidies as a Trade Policy Tool to Achieving Sustainable Development Goals at the WTO' (2019) 100 *Marine Policy* 132.

201 Frank Biermann, 'The Rising Tide of Green Unilateralism in World Trade Law: Options for Reconciling the Emerging North-South Conflict' (2001) 35(3) *Journal of World Trade* 421, as quoted in Rachel McCormick, 'A Qualitative Analysis of the WTO's Role on Trade and Environment Issues' (2006) 6(1) *Global Environmental Politcs* 102, 108. As noted by McCormick, several barriers exist "to developing-country support for the resolution of trade and environment issues: inherent mistrust of developed-country use of trade-related environmental measures, lack of perceived benefits available to developing countries, overstatement of resultant limitations on market access to developing country products, and limited understanding of and capacity to negotiate on many trade and environment issues." 109.

institutions need to evolve in ways that are equally acceptable and beneficial to the environmental community and to developing countries.

3.4 *It's Not All about the Environment*

> So, let's redouble our efforts to continue this work. Let's build a more inclusive trading system, which supports the SDGs, keeps pace with the evolving nature of trade, and which paves the way for a better world.
>
> ROBERTO AZEVÊDO, WTO Public Forum, October 2, 2018

Development has indeed become an essential part of the equation and it is no longer all about the environment. If it is true that the principle of sustainable development, by replacing 'economic growth' pure and simple as the ultimate goal to be pursued with trade rules, procedures, and institutions, has brought significant changes to the international trade regime, a similar paradigm shift has affected the environmental regime. In fact, both elements—*development* and *sustainability*—have contributed to shifting the debate "from traditional environmentalism with its primary focus on environmental protection, to the notion of sustainability, which requires a much more complex process of trading off social, economic, and environmental priorities."[202]

As already discussed at length, while, during the 1972 Stockholm Conference, the environment was center stage in the international domain and Maurice Strong had to organize the famous Founex meeting to convince developing countries to take part in the Conference, as years went by, these countries found a stronger voice and by the time the *Brundtland Report* was being drafted, environment and development had become inseparably linked in the international agenda. In Rio, 20 years after Stockholm, instead of *The Human Environment*, the focus was on *Environment and Development*. The environment found itself forced to step aside and share the stage with development: they had become "co-stars in a new show—the international agenda for sustainable development."[203]

According to the *2030 Agenda,* the Sustainable Development Goals to be pursued by 2030 include:

---

202 Neil Carter, *The Politics of the Environment: Ideas, Activism, Policy* (Cambridge University Press, 2018), p. 215.

203 Ibid. See United Nations Conference on Environment and Development, Rio de Janeiro, Brazil, June 3–14, 1992, *Rio Declaration on Environment and Development*, U.N. Doc. A/CONF.151/26/Rev.1 (Vol. I), Annex I (Aug. 12, 1992) [hereinafter Rio Declaration], Principles 5, 6, and 7.

> to end poverty and hunger everywhere; to combat inequalities within and among countries; to build peaceful, just and inclusive societies; to protect human rights and promote gender equality and the empowerment of women and girls; and to ensure the lasting protection of the planet and its natural resources. We resolve also to create conditions for sustainable, inclusive and sustained economic growth, shared prosperity and decent work for all, taking into account different levels of national development and capacities.[204]

It follows that, while environmental protection is certainly an important component of sustainable development and is given an important place within the *2030 Agenda*, it also needs to be balanced and integrated with all the other components and goals. Over the years, a major challenge has in particular been posed by the need to balance and integrate environmental protection with development. The overarching goal of the *2030 Agenda* is to eradicate "poverty in all its forms and dimensions, including extreme poverty,"[205] and all the other goals are envisioned as stepping stones towards it. Underlying all these goals is the acknowledgment that developing and least-developed countries face particular difficulties in this process and the enunciation of the principle of common but differentiated responsibilities.[206]

As a consequence, the majority of targets related to the environmental goals of the *2030 Agenda* reflect the CBDR principle and integrate the need to take into account the conditions of less-developed countries and support them in the attempt to achieve these goals at their very core. Here are some relevant examples:

> 13.a Implement the commitment undertaken by developed-country parties to the United Nations Framework Convention on Climate Change to a goal of mobilizing jointly $100 billion annually by 2020 from all sources to address the needs of developing countries in the context of meaningful mitigation actions and transparency on implementation and fully

204 2030 Agenda, para. 3.

205 2030 Agenda, Preamble.

206 2030 Agenda, para. 12, which refers to Principle 7 of the Rio Declaration: "States shall co-operate in a spirit of global partnership to conserve, protect and restore the health and integrity of the Earth's ecosystem. In view of the different contributions to global environmental degradation, States have common but differentiated responsibilities. The developed countries acknowledge the responsibility that they bear in the international pursuit of sustainable development in view of the pressures their societies place on the global environment and of the technologies and financial resources they command."

> operationalize the Green Climate Fund through its capitalization as soon as possible.[207]
>
> 14.a Increase scientific knowledge, develop research capacity and transfer marine technology, taking into account the Intergovernmental Oceanographic Commission Criteria and Guidelines on the Transfer of Marine Technology, in order to improve ocean health and to enhance the contribution of marine biodiversity to the development of developing countries, in particular small island developing States and least developed countries.[208]
>
> 15.b Mobilize significant resources from all sources and at all levels to finance sustainable forest management and provide adequate incentives to developing countries to advance such management, including for conservation and reforestation.[209]

The need to take into account the interests and needs of less-developed countries should characterize all means to implement environmental goals, including trade. If, on the one hand, the *2030 Agenda* contains a specific mention of "unilateral economic, financial, or trade measures" countries might decide to pursue one or more of the 17 goals set out therein, on the other hand, it adds an important *caveat*:

> States are strongly urged to refrain from promulgating and applying any unilateral economic, financial or trade measures not in accordance with international law and the Charter of the United Nations that impede the full achievement of economic and social development, particularly in developing countries.[210]

As a result, trade can be framed as a means to pursue environmental protection goals only as long as the other components of sustainable development are not undermined.

---

207 2030 Agenda. Goal 13 refers to the need to "take urgent action to combat climate change and its impacts."

208 Ibid. Goal 14 refers to the conservation and sustainable use of "the oceans, seas and marine resources for sustainable development."

209 Ibid. Goal 15 refers to the need to "protect, restore and promote sustainable use of terrestrial ecosystems, sustainably manage forests, combat desertification, and halt and reverse land degradation and halt biodiversity loss."

210 Ibid., para. 30.

This *caveat* is significantly different from the one that was included in the Rio Declaration, which was first penned by the GATT drafters in the *chapeau* of Article XX, and which reflects the more traditional neoliberal narrative. Under this model, the limits within which countries were allowed to adopt trade-related measures to protect the environment were dictated by the trade community—as mentioned earlier, it was the trade community, relying on the prevailing neoliberal narrative, who determined what constituted the rule and what the exception, as well as the requirements of that exception.

Principle 12 of the Rio Declaration, after declaring that "States should co-operate to promote a supportive and open international economic system that would lead to economic growth and sustainable development in all countries, to better address the problems of environmental degradation," significantly added:

> Trade policy measures for environmental purposes should not constitute a means of arbitrary or unjustifiable discrimination or a disguised restriction on international trade ... Unilateral actions to deal with environmental challenges outside the jurisdiction of the importing country should be avoided.[211]

Principle 16 further clarified that "national authorities should endeavor to promote the internalization of environmental costs and the use of economic instruments ... without distorting international trade and investment."[212] The language used in these two Rio principles was clearly inspired by the *chapeau* of Article XX of the GATT—"subject to the requirement that such measures are not applied in a manner which would constitute a means of arbitrary or unjustifiable discrimination ... or a disguised restriction on international trade."[213] As explained in chapter 3, the *chapeau* had been added to the original formulation of Article XX to avoid the adoption of domestic measures that would constitute (unnecessary) barriers to trade and would (unduly) burden commerce.

The language used in the *2030 Agenda* is different from the one we find in Principles 12 and 16 of the Rio Declaration. In this new context, the only limit to the adoption of "unilateral economic, financial, or trade measures" to pursue any of the Goals enshrined in the *Agenda* is the respect of the development needs of less-developed countries.[214] No mention is made with regards

211 Rio Declaration, Principle 12.

212 Ibid., Principle 16.

213 GATT, Article XX, Chapeau.

214 To be precise, this limit was already envisioned in the Action Plan agreed on in Stockholm. In that context, however, reference was also made to the need for these measures not to

to the disturbance of trade flows and international commerce. This caveat, however, does pose certain limits to the use of trade instruments to protect the environment—or achieve any other sustainable development goals. As a matter of fact, the *Agenda* defines the Goals and Targets as "integrated and indivisible,"[215] meaning that each of them should be pursued without prejudice to the attainment of the others.

3.5 *Two Birds with One Stone*

The mainstreaming of the notion of green economy as a fundamental component of sustainable development has led to a gradual convergence of the environmental and development agendas. Going 'green' has accordingly become a necessary step to development, requalifying the whole idea of environmental protection in the eyes of the strenuous promoters of the development agenda. In other words, discussions have been moving forward when development was factored in the equation. The fisheries subsidies issue can once again be used as a helpful example. Since the very beginning, in the context of the debates on whether and how to modify trade rules to prohibit certain types of fisheries subsidies harmful for the environment, both within the trade and environmental communities, a lot of weight has been given to the special needs of less-developed countries and in particular of vulnerable coastal states. The importance of these special needs was already acknowledged in the 1999 Communication from Iceland to the General Council in preparation for the Seattle Ministerial Conference.[216] Since then, all proposals from developed countries have always emphasized the need to account for developing and least-developed countries concerns in any future draft of the agreement.[217]

Since the adoption of the Chair text in 2007, the negotiations have been characterized by an equal attention to the environmental benefits that can be obtained with a revised ASCM discipline and to the need to safeguard and protect the needs of less-developed members, providing an excellent example of

hamper trade. Recommendation 103 recommended that Governments would take the necessary steps to ensure, on the one hand, that "where environmental concerns lead to restrictions on trade, or to stricter environmental standards with negative effects on exports, particularly from developing countries, appropriate measures for compensation should be worked out," and on the other, that "all States participating in the Conference agree not to invoke environmental concerns as a pretext for discriminatory trade policies or for reduced access to markets." Stockholm Action Plan.

215 2030 Agenda, Preamble.

216 WT/GC/W/229.

217 See e.g., WT/CTE/W/105, paras. 32–9; WT/CTE/W/51, paras. 18(e) and 20; TN/RL/GEN/186 (proposed Article 1.4); and TN/RL/GEN/181/Rev.1 (proposed Article 4.1).

the 'integrated and indivisible' nature of the sustainable development goals and targets. And once the Chair text was concluded, both environmentalists and less-developed WTO members welcomed it with enthusiasm: WWF released a statement calling the draft "a serious and constructive text" and "a solid basis for negotiations to proceed," while the African, Caribbean, and Pacific Group of States (ACP), small and vulnerable economies, and Pacific Island members likewise echoed support for the Chair's treatment of S&D treatment.[218] As a matter of fact, developing and least-developed countries had been deeply involved in the discussions since the very beginning.[219]

Environmental organizations as well, working on the subject, have paid particular attention to this aspect. In July 2005, for instance, a representative from UNEP briefed the CTE on the result of a recent Roundtable on Promoting Development and Sustainability in Fisheries Subsidies Disciplines, which addressed different options to advance the sustainable development of artisanal fisheries while disciplining subsidies and investigating how special and differential treatment in the context of fisheries subsidies could link new trade rules to development, poverty reduction and environmental issues.[220] Ten years later, FAO, UNEP and UNCTAD submitted a joint statement on fisheries subsidies, aiming to move forward the trade-related targets under the SDGs and signing onto a roadmap to end harmful fisheries subsidies,[221] and 91 countries, four intergovernmental organizations, and 15 civil society groups signed on to this global roadmap to eliminate damaging subsidies by 2020.[222] In the statement, the three organizations have identified certain minimum outcomes that would contribute to the members' efforts to meet Target 14.6,

---

218 International Centre for Trade and Sustainable Development, 'Fisheries Subsidies Text Provides a Good Starting Point, Delegates Say', 7(22) *Bridges Trade BioRes* (Dec. 18, 2007). The S&D treatment foreseen in the more recent text of the proposed amendment to the ASCM include transition periods where certain provisions do not apply to LDCs and the complete exclusion of LDCs from the articles on prohibited subsidies, with the exception of the prohibition of subsidies to IUU fishing and in overfished conditions. TN/RL/W/274/REV.6, proposed Article 5.

219 See e.g., submissions from China (TN/RL/W/88), Brazil (TN/RL/W/176), and Antigua and Barbuda, Belize, Fuji Islands, Guyana, the Maldives, Papua New Guinea, Solomon Islands, St. Kitts and Nevis (TN/RL/W/136).

220 WT/CTE/M/40 (Sept. 2, 2005) and WT/CTE/GEN/20 (July 13, 2005). See UNEP, *Reflecting Sustainable Development and Special and Differential Treatment for Developing Countries in the Context of New WTO Fisheries Subsidies Rules* (2005).

221 UNCTAD-FAO-UNEP, Joint Statement: *Regulating Fisheries Subsidies Must Be an Integral Part of the Implementation of 2030 Sustainable Development Agenda* (2016) [hereinafter UNCTAD-FAO-UNEP Joint Statement].

222 WT/CTE/M/63, para. 1.63.

which include the "clear prohibition of subsidies that contribute to overfishing and overcapacity, including subsidies linked to IUU fishing, and those that undermine sustainable development," and special attention and treatment to be given to "developing countries, in particular, the least developed ones and Small Islands Developing States (SIDS), so that they can continue to use their marine resources sustainably."[223] And as a result, most SIDS signed on to the joint statement.[224]

In other words, as long as appropriate and effective special and differential treatment is an integral part of the negotiations, developing and least-developed countries have proven to be eager to participate in the discussions on reforming ASCM rules to prohibit those fisheries subsidies which might harm the sustainability of marine resources. It was precisely some of these countries—Indonesia, the least-developed countries (LDC) Group, and the ACP Group, to be specific—that proposed the exclusion from the overall discipline those fisheries subsidies that do produce a positive environmental impact. And those were the same countries that in 1972 had to be 'convinced' to send a representative to Stockholm.

The free trade agreements signed by the United States with Chile and Peru offer another example of the integration of development and environmental concerns within the same instrument. Since the adoption of the *Lacey Act*, which prohibits trade in wood products manufactured from illegally harvested and traded timber, the United States had tried to combat illegal logging and trade and promote trade in legal wood products, and recently the country has been pursuing this goals through free trade agreements.[225] In addition, these agreements offer an opportunity to, simultaneously, engage in capacity building.[226] In the Annex on Environmental Cooperation of the *US-Chile* FTA, for instance, the two countries committed to work together to build capacity to improve wildlife protection and management, among other things.[227] Because

223 UNCTAD-FAO-UNEP Joint Statement.

224 Antigua and Barbuda, Bahamas, Barbados, Cuba, Dominica, Dominican Republic, Fiji, Grenada, Guinea-Bissau, Guyana, Haiti, Jamaica, Kiribati, Marshall Islands, Mauritius, Micronesia, Nauru, Palau, Papua New Guinea, Samoa, Sao Tome and Principe, Seychelles, St. Kitts and Nevis, St. Lucia, St. Vincent and the Grenadines, Suriname, Timor-Leste, Trinidad and Tobago, Tong, Tuvalu, Vanuatu, all part of the ACP group.

225 Lacey Act, 16 U.S.C. §§ 3371–3378. WT/CTE/M/57, para. 1.27.

226 WT/CTE/M/57, para. 1.27.

227 US-Chile FTA, Annex 19.3, Art. 1(g). Other areas of cooperation include developing a pollutant release and transfer register in Chile, reducing mining pollution, improving environmental enforcement and compliance assurance, sharing private sector expertise, improving agricultural practices, reducing methyl bromide emissions, and increasing the use of cleaner fuels.

of the Annex, the parties even established a Joint Commission, which contributed greatly to strengthening and improving Chile's laws. And forests protection is just one of the many areas where this cooperation has benefitted Chile's environmental legal framework, others including energy efficiency and conservation and environmental law enforcement more broadly. As a result, many US Government agencies, such as the EPA, the National Science Foundation, and the National Park Service, are actively engaged in Chile, carrying out the objectives set out in the FTA Annex.

When the FTA was being negotiated, Chile—just like other countries the US signed similar agreements with—lacked the resources necessary to improve the environmental legal framework. These improvements might of course have occurred without the cooperation with the United States but "without the 'external' impulse given by the negotiation of this kind of provision, these changes may not have occurred, or would have occurred at a later stage."[228] For the very same reason, several initiatives have been established within the CTE to provide developing and least-developed countries with the assistance they need to be able to improve their environmental legal and institutional framework.[229] And even when discussing national initiatives, industrialized countries make sure to explain how these initiatives would impact less-developed country members and to what extent they foresee S&D treatment.[230]

A final example of a topic negotiated within the WTO—and already addressed in one FTA[231]—which is aimed at protecting the environment while advancing the development agenda is the Joint Statement on Fossil Fuel Subsidy Reform (FFSR), signed by 16 countries during the 11th WTO Ministerial Conference. In the statement, the signatories "confirmed their intention to seek the rationalization and phase out of inefficient fossil fuel subsidies that encouraged wasteful consumption, while recognizing that reform should take into account the specific needs and conditions of developing countries and

228 OECD, *Environment and Regional Trade Agreements* (2007), 48.

229 WT/CTE/M/43 (Feb. 12, 2007), Annex 1; WT/CTE/M/45 (Jan. 9, 2008), Annex 1; WT/CTE/M/46 (Jan. 12, 2009), Annex 1. WT/CTE/M/47 (Aug. 31, 2009), paras. 59–66; WT/CTE/M/48 (Jan. 12, 2010), Annex 1; WT/CTE/M/54 (Mar. 15, 2013), paras. 2.1–2.3.

230 In a 2013 meeting, for instance, the representative of Switzerland "explained that the needs of developing countries were being taken into account in the implementation of the Green Economy Action Plan through sector policies, as well as development and economic cooperation, bilateral experience exchanges and initiatives." WT/CTE/C/56 (Jan. 31, 2014), para. 1.42.

231 EU-Sing. FTA, Art. 13.11(3).

to minimize the possible adverse impacts on their development in a way that protected poor and affected communities."[232]

The negotiations on liberalizing environmental goods can, on the other hand, be used as a counterexample. Begun in 2014, and involving 18 WTO members, it has been argued that it was precisely the lack of support of developing countries that contributed to the stall of the negotiations.[233] Two of the lists of environmental goods used in the context of the negotiations—the Asia-Pacific Economic Cooperation (APEC) list and the WTO list—mostly contained industrial products, representative of the interests of developed countries, as opposed to the list comprising 108 so-called environmentally preferable products (EPP), which would have better reflected developing countries' interests.[234]

3.6 *Missed Opportunities*

Changes in ideas have led, as this book has argued, to an evolution in the rules and procedures of the international trade regime. This evolution has unveiled, removing one layer after another, the instrumental role of trade liberalization in protecting the environment and promoting sustainable development. As long as the trading system is anchored to traditional neoliberal ideas, however, it will remain impossible for the synergetic nature of the relationship between the trade and environmental regimes to fully come to life. As such, several areas are still 'lagging behind', the most emblematic probably being the determination of 'likeness' and the treatment of process and production methods (PPM s) under international trade law.[235]

The non-discrimination norm, which constitutes the cornerstone of the international trade regime, is translated into rules—most-favored nation and national treatment—which prohibit countries from discriminating between

---

232 WT/CTE/M66 (Mar. 22, 2019).

233 See Jaime de Melo and Jean-Marc Solleder, 'Barriers to Trade in Environmental Goods: How Important They are and What Should Developing Countries Expect from their Removal' (2018) FERDI Working Paper No. 235.

234 Ibid.

235 See generally on PPM s, Christiane R. Conrad, *Processes and Production Methods (PPMs) in WTO Law: Interfacing Trade and Social Goals* (Cambridge University Press, 2011). See also Steven Charnovitz, 'The Law of Environmental 'PPMs' in the WTO: Debunking the Myth of Illegality' (2002) 27 *Yale Journal of International Law* 59. Jason Potts, 'The Legality of PPMs Under the GATT' (2008) IISD 23; David Sifonios and Andreas Ziegler, '"*Tuna—Dolphin* Forever"? The Development of the PPM Debate Related to Trade and Environment in the WTO' (2020) 12 *Indian Journal of International Economic Law* 106.

and among 'like' products. According to the characterization of 'likeness' given by the Working Group on Border Tax Adjustment (BTA) in 1970[236] and further developed by the Appellate Body,[237] four elements should be taken into account to determine whether two products are 'like':

> (i) the physical properties of products; (ii) the extent to which the products are capable of serving the same or similar end-uses; (iii) the extent to which consumers perceive and treat the products as alternative means of performing particular functions in order to satisfy a particular want or demand; and (iv) the international classification of the products for tariff purposes.[238]

In *Japan—Alcoholic Beverages II*, the Appellate Body stated that the focus of the 'likeness' determination was on the BTA criteria, while no proof of trade effects was required.[239] As years went by, the determination of 'likeness' has gradually become, as explained by the Appellate Body in *EC—Asbestos*, "a determination about the nature and extent of a competitive relationship between and among products."[240] As argued by Trachtman, by focusing the 'likeness' determination solely on competitive relationship,

> the Appellate Body has diminished 'like products' from its ordinary meaning in an important way, because it has excluded national governmental

236 Report by the Working Group on Border Tax Adjustment, L/3464 (November 20, 1970).

237 Pierre M. Dupuy and Jorge E. Viñuales eds., *Harnessing Foreign Investment to Protect the Environment* (Cambridge University Press, 2013), p. 484.

238 Appellate Body Report, *European Communities—Measures Affecting Asbestos and Products Containing Asbestos*, WT/DS135/AB/R (Mar. 12, 2001) [hereinafter *EC—Asbestos*], para. 101. It was the Appellate Body in *Japan—Alcoholic Beverages II* that added the fourth criterion—international tariff classification—to the three already set by the Working Group on Border Tax Adjustment. See Appellate Body Report, *Japan—Taxes on Alcoholic Beverages*, WT/DS8/AB/R (Nov. 1, 1996) [hereinafter *Japan—Alcoholic Beverages II*], 21–2.

239 Appellate Body Report, *Japan—Alcoholic Beverages II*, at 16–23. With this pronouncement, the Appellate Body rejected the argument that judges consider 'aims and effects' in the context of discrimination cases. See Robert E. Hudec, 'GATT/WTO Constraints on National Regulation: Requiem for an "Aim and Effects" Test' (1998) 32 *International Law* 619, 620. See also Joel P. Trachtman, 'WTO Trade and Environment Jurisprudence: Avoiding Environmental Catastrophe' (2017) 58(2) *Harvard Journal of International Law* 273, 278.

240 Appellate Body Report, *EC—Asbestos*, para. 99. See Trachtman, 'WTO Trade and Environment Jurisprudence' (n 239) 277. After its decision in *Philippines—Distilled Spirits*, the Appellate Body has extended this determination of 'likeness' beyond para. 4 of Article III. See Appellate Body Report, *Philippines—Taxes on Distilled Spirits*, WT/DS403/AB/R (Dec. 21, 2011).

> determinations of regulatory categories from consideration in connection with the determination of likeness. The result is that when two products are sufficiently in competition, they are determined to be like products even if they differ in exactly the dimension that gives rise to the regulatory concern.[241]

This interpretation of 'likeness' has obvious consequences for the trade/environment nexus. Let us consider two scenarios, one where a government decides to adopt a domestic environmental regulation to address *consumption externalities* (i.e. based on how much a product pollutes), and a second one where the environmental regulation is aimed at addressing *production externalities* (i.e. based on the environmental impact of the process used to manufacture the product).

In the first scenario, according to the interpretation of 'likeness' outlined above, the products would most likely be found to be 'like', unless consumers are affected to the point that competition is altered. However, considering that consumers are generally victims of information asymmetries compared to producers and are by definition indifferent when it comes to externalities,[242] this outcome would appear to be extremely rare. In *EC—Asbestos,* after the panel found that chrysotile asbestos fibers and fibers that can be substituted for them were 'like' products under Article III:4 of the GATT, the Appellate Body reversed this finding arguing instead that the two products were not 'like' because the different composition of the two products had important health implications.[243] Notwithstanding its importance, this pronouncement is not particularly helpful from an environmental perspective for two reasons. First, the Appellate Body considered health risks in its 'likeness' determination insofar as they affected competitiveness.[244] Second, the health risks were considered as part of the existing criteria (physical properties)[245] and asbestos fibers do affect the physical properties of a product (product-related PPM), while from an environmental perspective, the way in which a product is produced, despite being an essential component of the product itself, often leaves no detectable traces in the final product (non-product-related PPM). It is

241 Trachtman, 'WTO Trade and Environment Jurisprudence' (n 239) 277–8.

242 Ibid., 278. Frieder Roessler, 'The Scope of Regulatory Autonomy of WTO Members under Article III:4 of the GATT: A Critical Analysis of the Jurisprudence of the WTO Appellate Body' (2015) Robert Schuman Center for Advanced Studies Policy Paper 3.

243 Appellate Body Report, *EC—Asbestos,* para. 113.

244 Ibid., para. 114.

245 Ibid., para. 113.

therefore likely that an environmental regulation that addresses *consumption externalities* would be found in violation of Article III:4. The only possibility for the Member adopting the regulation would be to try and justify it under GATT Article XX.

In the context of regulations that address *production externalities*, the outcome does not seem to be much different. In *Tuna/Dolphin*, the panel had argued that these kinds of regulations, because thy regulate processes rather than products, could not fall under Article III:4 of the GATT, but the strict scrutiny of Article XI would apply instead.[246] Although, after the establishment of the WTO, the Appellate Body did not have the opportunity to pronounce itself on the applicability of Article III:4 to regulations of processes, even if this provision applied, the determination of 'likeness' outlined above, as linked to the competitive relationship of the products, would make it very unlikely for two products with different non-product related PPMs to be found 'not like'.[247] In the recent *US—Tuna II (Mexico)* dispute, the Appellate Body did acknowledge that "it is permissible in theory under the national treatment obligation to differentiate among products on the basis of how they have been produced.[248] However, this pronouncement was made in reference to the TBT Agreement (and in particular Article 2.1), which includes certain PPMs explicitly under its scope,[249] and the possibility to extend this reasoning to the national treatment obligation under GATT is questionable. Once again, the one viable solution is to attempt a justification of the regulation via GATT Article XX.

What this analysis shows is that, in either scenario, the WTO does not prohibit countries from adopting environmental regulations to address either consumption or production externalities and to differentiate products based

246 Report of the GATT Panel, *United States—Restrictions on Imports of Tuna,* DS21/R-39S/155 (Sept. 3, 1991) (not adopted), 155.

247 This outcome would be possible once again in case consumers differentiated between the products to the point that competition could be considered altered. Trachtman, 'WTO Trade and Environment Jurisprudence' (n 239) 283.

248 Appellate Body Report, *United States—Measures Concerning the Importation, Marketing and Sale of Tuna and Tuna Products,* WT/DS381/ABR (May 16, 2012) [hereinafter *US—Tuna II (Mexico)*], para. 211. See also Trachtman, 'WTO Trade and Environment Jurisprudence' (n 239) 282.

249 The Appellate Body found that "Article 2.1 should not be read … to mean that any distinctions, in particular ones that are based exclusively on particular product characteristics or on particular processes and production methods, would per se constitute 'less favourable treatment' within the meaning of Article 2.1." Appellate Body Report, *US—Tuna II (Mexico)*, para. 211. See Trachtman, 'WTO Trade and Environment Jurisprudence' (n 239) 283.

on their process and production methods,[250] but their 'legality' is dependent on passing the 'Article XX-test'. In other words, the WTO does allow PPM-based measures, but only as long as they are eligible under an exception clause.[251] As explained by Charnovitz, "whenever it violates GATT Articles I, III, or XI, a PPM will be reviewed under GATT Article XX(b) or (g) and the chapeau to the Article."[252]

This approach, where trade liberalization remains the rule and environmental protection merely the exception, relies heavily on the neoliberal narrative, firm in depicting PPM s—and in particular those that are non-product related—as a slippery slope, as allowing Member states to discriminate products on these grounds would risk setting off a protectionist tide and disrupting international trade.[253] This approach shows a strong reluctance in introducing environmental differentiation in a WTO rule,[254] motivated by the fear that "if a nation is allowed to use the process characteristic as the basis for trade restrictive measures, then the result would be to open a Pandora's box of problems that could open large loopholes in the GATT."[255] However, excluding PPM s

250 See e.g. the pronouncement of the Appellate Body in *US—Shrimps*: "We have *not* decided that the protection and preservation of the environment is of no significance to the Members of the WTO. Clearly, it is. We have *not* decided that the sovereign nations that are Members of the WTO cannot adopt effective measures to protect endangered species, such as sea turtles. Clearly, they can and should. And we have *not* decided that sovereign states should not act together bilaterally, plurilaterally or multilaterally, either within the WTO or in other international fora, to protect endangered species or to otherwise protect the environment. Clearly, they should and do." Appellate Body Report, *US—Shrimps* WT/DS58/AB/R (Oct. 12, 1998), para. 185 (emphasis in original).

251 See Charnovitz, 'The Law of Environmental 'PPMs' in the WTO' (n 235) 59. Potts, 'The Legality of PPMs' (n 235) 23.

252 Charnovitz, 'The Law of Environmental 'PPMs' in the WTO' (n 235) 110.

253 Robert Housman, 'The North American Free Trade Agreement's Lessons for Reconciling Trade and the Environment' (1994) 30 *Stanford Journal of International Law* 379, 407; Jagdish Bhagwati, 'On Thinking Clearly About the Linkage Between Trade and the Environment' (2000) 5 *Environment & Development Economics* 483, 491, and 'Afterword: The Question of Linkage' (2002) 96(1) *American Journal of International Law* 126, 133.

254 The GATT's reluctance to take into account PPM s reflects one of the underlying differences between the trade and environmental communities: the former concerned only with products and the latter with processes. *But see* how environmental differentiation has been addressed in recent investment disputes. See *Parkerings v. Lithuania*, Award, para. 392.

255 John H. Jackson, 'World Trade Rules and Environmental Policies: Congruence or Conflict?' (1992) 49 *Washington & Lee Law Review* 1227, 1243. The same fear has been surrounding the possibility to rely on the exception provided in GATT Article XXI as well (national security). However, surprisingly to many, a WTO panel in the recent *Russia—Transit* case, has indeed opened the Pandora's box, by ruling that "WTO panels have jurisdiction to review aspects of a Member's invocation of Article XXI(b)(iii), that Russia had met the

from the 'likeness' analysis proves to be problematic in the context of environmental measures as, more often than not, their environmental footprint is not reflected in the composition of a product, just like a can of tuna does not tell us whether that tuna was caught with nets that injured dolphins, a bag of shrimps does not tell us whether they came from a country that requires turtle excluder devices, and electricity does not tell us whether it is sourced from renewables.

By describing the evolution undergone by the relationship between the international trade and environmental regimes, this book has emphasized the discrepancy between its true nature, evidenced by the recent developments described in this book, and the prevailing neoliberal narrative of the trading system, which fails to fully capture a system which is increasingly working for the protection of the environment and the promotion of sustainable development goals. However, the approach towards the determination of 'likeness' and the treatment of PPMs under WTO law, or even the discussions over the applicability of Article XX to the ASCM, can be read as a signal that, although rules and procedures have begun to change, the norms and principles of the trading system, and the underlying narrative, have not. In other words, the conditions that have made the evolution of the trade/environment nexus possible have run aground at the first, shallower level of learning: new provisions have been introduced, but the pillars on which the prevailing normative narrative rests are yet to be shaken.

This narrative, however—just like any narrative—is not eternal: "over time, other stories have been told about trade's purpose, producing different policies and encouraging different politics"[256] and the time may be ripe to tell a new story. It may be time to rethink the overarching purpose of the liberal trade project and of the trading system, precisely in light of the evolution described here.

---

requirements for invoking Article XXI(b)(iii) in relation to the measures at issue, and therefore, that the transit bans and restrictions were covered by Article XXI(b)(iii) of the GATT 1994." The panel continued stating that "*Unlike evaluations of whether measures are covered by the exceptions in Article XX,* an evaluation of measures under Article XXI(b)(iii) does not necessitate a prior determination that the measures would be WTO-inconsistent had they been taken in 'normal times' (para. 7.108). The Panel therefore considered that, "once it had found that the measures at issue were within its terms of reference and that Ukraine had established their existence, the 'most logical next step' was to determine whether the measures were covered by Article XXI(b)(iii)" (para. 7.109) (emphasis added). Panel Report, *Russia—Measures Concerning Traffic in Transit*, WT/DS512/R (Apr. 5, 2019).

256 Harlan Grant Cohen, 'What is International Trade Law For?' (2019) 113(2) *American Journal of International Law* 326, 327.

CHAPTER 6

Conclusions

The picture that emerges from these chapters is of two parallel normative 'forces' at work within the fields of international trade and environmental law. On the one hand, the prevailing neoliberal narrative, which emerged as a salient political force during the 1970s and, drawing from the tradition of neoclassical economics, emphasizes the superiority of free markets, deregulation, and anti-interventionism.[1] This is a vision that creates a clear-cut distinction between 'trade issues', which fall under the scope of trade law, and 'non-trade issues', which are excluded from it. And even if one were to add one or more 'non-trade issues' to the trade agenda, a clear hierarchy would automatically characterize the relationship between what is 'trade' and what is not. The environment, as any other non-trade issue, would be limited to exceptions, while non-discrimination and trade liberalization would always constitute the rules of the system. It is in fact the narrative itself which defines what constitutes the *rule* and the *exception*: even when environmental components are 'added' to the trade agenda, the space they are provided is always designed as exceptional.

On the other hand, the previous chapters have unveiled a trade regime that was never meant to be only for trade liberalization and also a relationship between trade liberalization and environmental protection—as well as between the international trade and environmental regimes—that was always characterized by a synergetic nature. This nature, however, has remained largely unnoticed under the prevailing narrative. The developments described in Chapter 5, in particular, are evidence of trade rules, procedures, and institutions that can positively contribute to the achievement of sustainable development goals, including environmental protection. A new generation of free trade agreements frames environmental protection as a *rule*,[2] rather than

1 Narratives provide principles that guide the interpretation of a regime's rules, "suggesting answers that better fit the goals or values that rules are meant to achieve." They "capture the basic, shared understanding of why a policy is worthwhile. In the case of trade, these narratives help explain why in a political-moral sense, trade liberalization is worth pursuing. They provide a political-moral story of what trade law and policy should look like and why." See Harlan Grant Cohen, 'What is International Trade Law For?' (2019) 113(2) *American Journal of International Law* 326, 329. See Andrew Lang, *World Trade Law After Neoliberalism. Re-Imagining the Global Economic Order* (Oxford University Press, 2013), pp. 1–3.

2 Supra Chapter 4, Section 3.

 | DOI:10.1163/9789004467569_007

merely as an exception, able to be enforced on the same basis as trade rules.[3] Environmental non-governmental organizations (NGOs) and the civil society at large are increasingly involved in the various procedures—from the negotiation of trade agreements to the submission of amicus curiae briefs in the context of trade/environment disputes.[4] And the World Trade Organization (WTO) itself is regarded, by both members of the trade and environmental community, as "the most promising" forum to deal with some of the thorniest issues at the intersection of trade and environmental law.[5]

The neoliberal ideas that have provided the shared normative narrative supporting the trading system since the 1970s have been the object of considerable criticisms over the past 20 years, when alternative narratives have been proposed as a result of the WTO's legitimacy crisis of the late 1990s.[6] Furthermore, in more recent years, the international trade regime has been struggling to cope with a whole new set of challenges, including the increasingly blurred boundaries between economic and national security, or between market and state. Many have shared their concerns about the inadequacy of the neoliberal vision to account for these new realities and about its tendency to prioritize the value of economic efficiency and the goal of economic growth to the detriment of other non-economic goals.[7]

3 Supra Chapter 5, Section 2.

4 Supra Chapter 4, Section 2 and Chapter 5, Section 2.

5 See e.g. Roberto Azevêdo, WTO Director-General, Address at the High-Level Panel on Making Trade Work for the Environment, Prosperity, and Resilience (Oct. 2, 2018); WT/CTE/M/45 (Jan. 9, 2008), para. 15.

6 The literature is extremely rich in this regard. See e.g., Jeffrey L. Dunoff, 'Rethinking International Trade' (1998) 19(2) *University of Pennsylvania Journal of International Economic Law* 347; 'Death of the Trade Regime' (1999) 10(4) *European Journal of International Law* 733; and 'The WTO in Transition: Of Constituents, Competence, and Coherence' (2001) 33 *George Washington International Law Review* 979. Andrew Lang, 'The Role of the Human Rights Movement in Trade Policy-Making: Human Rights as a Trigger for Policy Learning' (2007) 5 *New Zealand Journal of Public International Law* 77; 'Reflecting on "Linkage": Cognitive and Institutional Change in the International Trading System' (2007) 70(4) *Modern Law Review* 523; and *World Trade Law After Neoliberalism* (n 1). Ernst-Ulrich Petersmann, 'The WTO Constitution and Human Rights' (2001) 3 *Journal of International Economic Law* 19; and 'Time for a United Nations "Global Compact" for Integrating Human Rights into the Law of Worldwide Organizations: Lessons from European Integration' (2002) 13 *European Journal of International Law* 621. Susan A. Aaronson and Jamie M. Zimmerman, *Trade Imbalance: The Struggle to Weigh Human Rights Concerns in Trade Policymaking* (Cambridge University Press, 2008); Cohen, 'What is International Trade Law For?' (n 1). Gregory Shaffer, 'Retooling Trade Agreements for Social Inclusion' (2019) 1 *University of Illinois Law Review* 1.

7 See e.g. Sungjoon Cho, 'Linkage of Free Trade and Social Regulation: Moving Beyond the Entropic Dilemma' (2005) 5 *Chicago Journal of International Law* 626; Philip Nichols, 'Trade

This book intends to contribute to this debate, and the interest in performing this exercise has been triggered by the analysis of the evolution of the trade/environment nexus over the years and of the unique characteristics of the more recent developments described in Chapter 5. Such an evolution requires calling into question the prevailing narrative, which appears incapable of providing an accurate description of the nexus, and risks undermining its further development. Unlike other proposals, this book does not argue for a better balance of economic and non-economic values, for a further incorporation of non-trade issues within trade law, or for its democratization. It does not argue for a reinstatement of embedded liberalism, to better balance trade liberalization with domestic interventionism. The developments that have been observed present us with agreements and rules that do not simply *allow* domestic (environmental) policies but rather *facilitate* them. Trade liberalization and cooperation is not, in other words, simply *embedded* in domestic policy-making but rather *instrumental* to the achievement of certain legitimate policy goals.

In so doing, this book has attempted to reconceptualize the international trade regime by calling into question the prevailing 'thin' vision of the nature and purpose of trade law—largely limited to trade liberalization—which has attained something of a "natural and self-evident quality," as aptly described by Lang.[8] In this spirit, this final chapter intends to continue said reconceptualization by proposing a narrative where sustainable development and environmental protection are part of the nature and purpose of trade law, rather than simply 'added to' or 'accommodated within' it. And it intends to do so by slowly pulling the thread that has been underlying the book since its very first pages.

1 Ideational Change

The evolution of the trade/environment nexus can be ascribed, among other factors, to the development and spreading of new ideas regarding the intersection between trade and environmental law, and the purpose of the international trade regime at large.

In the 1930s, Cordell Hull was able to convincingly convey the message that "unhampered trade dovetailed with peace [while] high tariffs, trade barriers, and unfair economic conditions, with war,"[9] and his attachment to this idea

Without Values'(1996) 90 *Northwestern University Law Review* 658; Marco C. E. J. Bronckers, 'More Power to the WTO?' (2001) 4 *Journal of International Economic Law* 41.

8 Lang, *World Trade Law After Neoliberalism* (n 1) p. 348.

9 Cordell Hull, *The Memoirs of Cordell Hull* (Macmillan, 1948), p. 81.

was later followed by a change in collective ideas.[10] The Smoot-Hawley Tariff Act of 1930 was soon associated in the public eye with the Great Depression, while multilateral cooperation to reduce tariffs came to be identified with expanding trade and increasing peaceful relations among nations. Until then, tariffs had always been regarded as a domestic concern and international trade cooperation did not seem to be in the cards until the Senator from Tennessee stepped onto the scene. Yet, despite Hull's constant efforts and calls for an international conference to kick off the process of international trade cooperation, his voice remained for a long time an isolated one. It was only after years of disappointment and setbacks that his vision for a multilateral trading system found the necessary support to become a reality.

In a not too different way, the idea that trade can be used to protect the environment was first discussed only in environmental circles. From a very early stage, environmental treaties have introduced trade-related environmental measures as means to achieve the goals they were designed for, whether to artificially control the supply of a given product, provide incentives both to join the agreement and to comply with its obligations, or ensure the integrity of the regulatory framework created with the treaty itself. To the contrary, the trade community has been arguing, in line with traditional public policy theory, that trade measures do not represent the 'best' environmental policies,[11] regarding them with suspicion and framing them as 'barriers to trade'.[12] It was only after several decades, in March 2019, that the WTO Secretariat commented on "the role that trade and the WTO could play in supporting the achievement of environmental goals," declaring that "trade could serve as a tool to disseminate and scale up environmentally sound technologies, and to accelerate the transition to a green economy."[13]

---

10 Changes in collective ideas are thought to occur whenever a policy generates "consequences for societies that deviate from their collective expectations" and that are "starkly undesirable," and when a socially plausible alternative policy exists. Jeffrey W. Legro, 'The Transformation of Policy Ideas' (2000) 44 *American Journal of Political Science* 419, 420, 427.

11 See e.g. Kym Anderson and Richard Blackhurst, 'Trade, the Environment and Public Policy', in Kym Anderson and Richard Blackhurst (eds.), *The Greening of World Trade* (University of Michigan Press, 1992).

12 See John W. Evans, *The Kennedy Round in American Trade Policy: the Twilight of the GATT?* (Harvard University Press, 1971); Daniel K. Tarullo, 'Logic, Myth and the International Economic Order' (1985) 26 *Harvard International Law Journal* 553; Judith Goldstein, 'Ideas, Institutions and American Trade Policy' (1988) 42(1) *International Organization* 179; and Robert Howse, 'From Politics to Technocracy—And Back Again: The Fate of the Multilateral Trading Regime' (2002) 96 *American Journal of International Law* 94.

13 WT/CTE/M/66, para. 2.15.

This statement demonstrates that the idea that not only trade, but trade rules and institutions, can play a significant role to protect the environment, is no longer limited to environmental circles, but has gained ground among the trade community and has had a direct impact on trade law- and policy-making. It was this idea that allowed the launch of multilateral trade negotiations aimed at protecting fisheries, that explained the inclusion of environmental rules in the text of trade agreements, and that motivated the recent attitudes of many states towards the nexus. And the very same idea that underlay the launch in November 2020, within the WTO, of the *Structured Discussions on Trade and Environmental Sustainability*, conveying the message that the WTO could and should be the place to deliver progress on issues related to trade, the environment, and sustainability.[14]

This process, however, has been in no way automatic or easy, just like it had not been easy for Hull to impose his multilateral vision of trade cooperation and tariff reduction at a time when contrary views prevailed. In fact, the *trade policy elite*, in its confidence, has been advocating and prescribing free trade as a timeless truth, monopolizing the production and authorization of legitimate policy ideas. Cognitive frameworks tend to be deeply embedded in society, and the isolated and closed nature of the trade community has made its understanding of the purpose of the trading system even more resistant to change.

Even after the environmental movement was formed and the notion of sustainable development introduced—asking all nations of the world to pursue social, economic, and environmental goals in a mutually supportive manner—as long as the trade and environmental communities remained isolated, did not have access to each other's discussions, and framed their relationship on a hierarchical basis, trade rules kept being negotiated without any concern for the environment, as the trade community gave precedence to free trade principles and non-discrimination norms over environmental objectives.[15] Over the years, several changes have occurred in the relationship between the two communities: changes in the degree of openness of the trade community and in the degree to which the trade and environmental communities are interconnected through actual linkages; changes in the level of formality of such linkages, in the hierarchical relationship between them; and in the degree to which their institutional arrangements and venues are integrated.[16] All these factors have

14 Sofía Baliño, 'Trade and Environment Structured Discussions among WTO Member Group Get Underway', IISD Policy Brief (Mar. 10, 2021), available at http://sdg.iisd.org/commentary/policy-briefs/trade-and-environment-structured-discussions-among-wto-member-group-get-underway/ (last accessed Mar. 26, 2021).

15 See supra Chapter 3.

16 See supra Chapter 4, Section 2 and Chapter 5, Section 3.

contributed to the creation of an environment far more conducive to learning than it used to be during the years of the General Agreement on Tariffs and Trade (GATT) and the first years of the WTO. The two communities have started to have more regular access to each other's discussions and their ties have gradually become more frequent. They even started learning about each other's values and the utter incomprehension that had characterized the first decades of their coexistence began to fade. As a result, the environment started being taken in greater consideration in the context both of treaty drafting and dispute settlement. However, despite the indisputable positive steps, for a long time the integration between the two communities remained weak, with their relationship still framed in hierarchical terms. Moreover, the diverging views of developed and developing countries on nearly every trade/environment issue acted as an obstacle to substantial changes in the prevailing trade-centered stance. As a result, the trade-centered neoliberal ideas continued to prevail, leading to a regime that increasingly incorporated environmental values, but only peripherally and still relying on the traditional *rule-exception* scheme.

It is only more recently that more formalized and frequent interactions between the two communities, the gradual disappearance of a clear-cut hierarchy, and the convergence of environment and development interests on many fronts, have opened the door to more radical changes. The two agendas together—environment and development—have begun to allow the creation of trade instruments that act as means of implementation of sustainable development goals. Over time, the increasing engagement of environmental law voices and actors in trade debates has been providing an impetus for the evolution of ideas regarding rational and desirable trade policies. By addressing the trade/environment nexus from an environmental standpoint, the environmental community has prompted reflection on the broader goals and values that the trading system is designed to achieve, opening discussions on the very meaning of the ideas of 'free trade' and 'trade liberalization'.[17]

17 Lang, 'Reflecting on "Linkage"' (n 6), 525 and 539. For a long time, outsiders have also refrained from discussing the meaning of 'free trade', as pointed out by Driesen. See David M. Driesen, 'What is Free Trade? The Real Issue Lurking Behind the Trade and Environment Debate' (2001) 41 *Virginia Journal of International Law* 279, 281; Dunoff, 'Rethinking International Trade' (n 6); Steve Charnovitz, *The Path of World Trade Law in the 21st Century* (World Scientific, 2014).

2 Historical Contingency

> If men could learn from history, what lessons it might teach us!
>
> SAMUEL COLERIDGE, 1831

To describe the evolution of the trade/environment nexus, this book has been tracing, chapter after chapter, the historical unfolding of the trade and environmental regimes, thus forcing the reader to look at history. As beautifully put by Samuel Coleridge, looking at history has its own inherent importance in that it helps us develop historical awareness. This awareness does not seem to characterize the prevailing neoliberal narrative. The latter, as a matter of fact, relies on the assumption that the ideas of 'free trade' and 'trade liberalization' have fixed meanings, and the rationale of the international trade regime is timeless. The history of the international trade regime, however, shows that the meaning of both 'free trade' and 'trade liberalization' is far from fixed, and the reasons underlying the trade regime itself, are anything but timeless.[18] Just like the meaning of 'free trade', the underlying narratives—intended as the shared understanding of why trade liberalization is worth pursuing and of what trade law and policy should look like and why—are not eternal. Rather, over time, different stories have been told about the meaning and purpose of the trade regime. These different stories have each materialized in the concrete rules, procedures, and institutions associated with the trading system.[19]

2.1 *The GATT and Embedded Liberalism*

After World War II, the idea of 'free trade' was linked to the absence of discriminatory treatment as a reaction to protectionism. In 1947, when the GATT was drafted, a strong set of shared understandings existed as to what the purpose of the trade regime was supposed to be: to ensure international stability—in the specific sense of avoiding the horrors of the two world wars[20]—which was seen as a "necessary precondition of the flourishing of the social democratic welfare state."[21] The compromise between multilateralism and domestic

---

18 Lang, *World Trade Law After Neoliberalism* (n 1); Driesen, 'What is Free Trade?' (n 17).

19 Lang, 'Reflecting on "Linkage"' (n 6) 529.

20 See e.g. Douglas A. Irwin, 'The GATT in Historical Perspective' (1995) 85 *American Economic Review* 323, 326. Gerard Curzon and Victoria Curzon, 'The Management of Trade Relations in the GATT', in Andrew Shonfield (ed.), *International Economic Relations of the Western World, 1959–1971. Vol. 1. Politics and Trade* (Oxford University Press, 1976), pp. 143, 144; Robert E. Hudec, *The GATT Legal System and World Trade Diplomacy* (Butterworths, 1990), p. 5.

21 Lang, *World Trade Law After Neoliberalism* (n 1) 196–7.

interventionism has been explained through the theory of *embedded liberalism*, which explains the need "to devise a framework which would safeguard and even aid the quest for domestic stability without, at the same time, triggering the mutually destructive external consequences that had plagued the interwar period."[22] These shared ideas were translated into a set of legal structures and institutional forms which went on to characterize the trade regime for more than two decades. As aptly described by Ruggie in 1986, "the *principle* that liberalized trade is good for global welfare and international peace was readily translated by states into such *norms* as non-discrimination,"[23] the whole idea being that discrimination against trading partners was seen as being closely linked to the very idea of protectionism.[24] And the *rules* of the GATT (most-favored nation rule in Article I and National Treatment in Article III) reflected such principle and norms. At the same time, the importance to strike a balance between the needs of globalization and multilateralism on the one hand, and domestic interventionism on the other, was reflected in the introduction of safety valves in the text of the Agreement, in the form of exception clauses, which were originally intended to allow the Parties to pursue certain legitimate domestic policy goals.

2.2 *The WTO and the Resurgence of Neoliberalism*

Between the Tokyo Round in 1973 and the establishment of the WTO in 1995, the international trade regime underwent a profound transformation: dispute settlement became judicialized and compulsory,[25] the scope of application of the trade regime expanded and so too did its normative content.[26] This fundamental transformation has been described in this book as being ascribable to two sets of factors. On the one hand, to the increasing expansion and diversity of the GATT/WTO membership, the globalization of the economy, as well

22 John G. Ruggie, 'International Regimes, Transactions and Change: Embedded Liberalism in the Postwar Economic Order' (1982) 36 *International Organization* 379, 393.

23 John G. Ruggie and Friederich Kratochwil, 'International Organization: A State of the Art on an Art of the State' (1986) 40(4) *International Organization* 753, 769.

24 As aptly noted by Howse, GATT Articles I and III were seen as a "means of preventing member states from instituting discriminatory domestic and imported products, not a mechanism for liberalization per se." Robert Howse, 'The World Trade Organization 20 Years On: Global Governance by Judiciary' (2016) 27(1) *European Journal of International Law* 9, 14.

25 See e.g. Arie Reich, 'From Diplomacy to Law: The Juridicization of International Trade Relations' (1997) 17 *Northwestern Journal of International Law & Business* 775.

26 New rules were introduced, regulating areas that were not traditionally considered part of the 'liberal trade project'—such as technical regulations, standards, services, and intellectual property rights.

as governments' increasing recourse to new kinds of interventions and trade restrictions to address the rampant recession and stagflation.[27] On the other, to the development of the idea of 'free trade' as a synonym of freedom from burdens rather than simply freedom from discrimination, and the consequent convergence between the idea of trade barriers and that of trade distortions.[28] The underlying force was the resurgence of economic liberalism in both developed and developing countries and of neoliberal ideas as the shared normative narrative underlying this transformation as well as the trade regime itself for the years that would follow.

2.3 *The 2030 Agenda and the Instrumental Role of Trade*

Over the course of the last decade, the trading system has undergone yet again a number of significant changes. Today's political, socio-economic, and cultural environment is not the same as it was when the Second World War ended or when the Uruguay Round was being negotiated. Environmental degradation, lack of access to clean and affordable water, and spreading hunger and poverty have become today as pressing concerns as ensuring peaceful inter-state relations was when American and British officials began negotiating the GATT, or driving growth and modernization was when the WTO was established. The *2030 Agenda for Sustainable Development* is the result of the leaders of the world coming together to plan the best strategy to face the new challenges the world is confronted with. And in doing so, trade is depicted as an instrument, as a 'means of implementation' to address these challenges. And the developments described in the previous chapter present us with trade rules, procedures, and institutions that positively contribute to the achievement of sustainable development goals, including environmental protection. The prevailing narrative, however, does not seem able to adequately capture and explain these new developments. Thus, the final argument made in this book draws the reader's attention precisely to the need to suggest a new narrative, design a new theoretical model for the trade regime, in other words, write a 'new trade story'.[29]

---

27 The most notorious of these new types of measures were 'voluntary export restraints'—trade restrictions on the quantity of a good that a country is allowed to export to another country—which were often accompanied by safeguards, balance-of-payments restrictions and other arrangements of questionable legality under the GATT.

28 As a matter of fact, any form of governmental action has a possible impact on trade. Identifying certain action as 'barriers to trade' and not others, requires a certain shared understanding of what constitutes an acceptable form of government intervention and what does not.

29 See Dunoff, 'Rethinking International Trade' (n 6).

3 A New Trade Story

The developments presented in this book paint a picture where not only the values embodied in the trade and environmental regimes can peacefully coexist but where the interaction between the two regimes is potentially tremendously constructive: rather than focusing only on conflicts, which can and do present themselves, the focus is now on the *synergies* between the two fields. The prevailing narrative, however, does not seem capable to adequately capture and explain these new developments. The neoliberal narrative, in its determination of what constitutes the *rule* and the *exception*, tends to frame non-discrimination and trade liberalization as rules while the environment, as any other non-trade issue, is limited to exceptions. In fact, even when environmental components are 'added' to the trade agenda, the space they are provided is always designed as exceptional.

Many have shared their concerns about the tendency of the trade regime to prioritize the value of economic efficiency and the goal of economic growth to the detriment of other non-economic goals. In the context of these discussions, one proposal has been to 're-embed' liberalism: to reinstate, in other words, the model of embedded liberalism, where countries would retain considerable space to address social inclusion, and would be built precisely on "states' obligations to their people."[30] If, on the one hand, it is true that embedded liberalism is more capable of balancing trade liberalization with domestic interventionism, and therefore trade and environmental concerns, on the other, while it made sense in the aftermath of the Second World War, it would not completely capture the recent developments described in this book. As explained by Ruggie, the theory of embedded liberalism depicts the market as 'embedded' in a broader social fabric, and multilateralism as predicated upon domestic interventionism.[31] The result was the use of exception clauses so that countries could retain some space to pursue domestic social policies.

The examples provided here, on the other hand, present us with agreements and provisions that do not simply *allow* domestic (environmental) policies but rather *facilitate* them. If new trade instruments are conceived as instrumental and conducive to the achievement of environmental goals, the environment can no longer be forced into exception clauses. And in fact, these new provisions are not any longer simple safety valves, but actual *rules*.

30 Ibid., 336. See also Shaffer, 'Retooling Trade Agreements for Social Inclusion' (n 6), and Howse, 'From Politics to Technocracy' (n 12).

31 Ruggie, 'International Regimes' (n 22).

Both narratives (neoliberalism and embedded liberalism) can be subsumed under what this book has defined as an *exception-based* model: they both frame the environment as a 'non-trade' issue to be more or less incorporated within more or less generous exception clauses. However, the developments described in the previous chapters present trade liberalization and cooperation as neither *antithetical* nor simply *embedded* in domestic policy-making, but rather as *instrumental* to the achievement of certain legitimate policy goals. The question is no longer how these goals might be simply accommodated within the hard-driving logic of trade,[32] but rather how trade instruments can serve broader social and environmental goals. Trade liberalization and increasing countries' wealth would undoubtedly remain an important aim, but it may come second to achieving other legitimate policy goals.

This is an invitation to suspend the mainstream discourse on the relationship between trade and the environment in terms of conflicts and to put the notion of trade liberalization as the *raison d'être* of the trade regime into question. This means questioning trade liberalization as an undisputed assumption, showing that it is not self-evident and can be instead challenged.

3.1 *The Trade Regime: Can't Live without It*

There have been suggestions to increase the role of other organizations, or even to create an international environmental organization that could act as counterpart to the WTO.[33] Although these proposals raise several important points, it can be useful to look once again at the historical development of the two regimes to assess the feasibility and desirability of this approach. One of

---

32 See e.g. Henrik Horn and Petros C. Mavroidis, 'The Permissible Reach of National Environmental Policies' (2008) 42(6) *Journal of World Trade* 1107; Gary Clyde Hufbauer et al., *Global Warming and the World Trading System* (Peterson Institute for International Economics, 2009); Andrew D. Mitchell and Christopher Tran, 'The Consistency of the EU Renewable Energy Directive with the WTO Agreements' (2010) 1(1) *Renewable Energy Law & Policy Review* 33; Patrick Low et al., 'The Interface between the Trade and Climate Change Regimes: Scoping the Issues' (2012) 46(3) *Journal of World Trade* 485.

33 See e.g. Jeffrey L. Dunoff, 'Institutional Misfits: The GATT, the ICJ & Trade-Environment Disputes' (1993) 15 *Michigan Journal of International Law* 1043, 1046 [Arguing that "trade-environment conflicts should be heard before an institution that recognizes the interdependent nature of global economic and environmental issues and that has a mandate to advance *both* economic development and environmental protection. This body should have ready access to the scientific and technical expertise that would enable it to resolve trade environment disputes knowledgeably. It should possess tools encourage nations to comply with its decisions. Finally, the institution should be able to look beyond the interests of the parties to a particular dispute to protect broader interests in the international economy and the global ecosystem."].

the main issues addressed by Maurice Strong and his 'men' in Stockholm dealt precisely with the choice of the institutional framework to produce, interpret, and apply this new body of law. The suggestions to create an international environmental organization and court were swiftly dismissed for two main reasons: first, unlike most subjects dealt by international law, the environment was not just another separate sectoral issue, but rather a system of interacting relationships that extends through all sectors of activity. Even if such organization or court had been created, they could not have avoided encountering the GATT first and the WTO later.[34] Second, an institutional framework had already been created, both within and outside of the United Nations (UN), and the decision to privilege efficiency and avoid replication prevailed during the debates. Throughout the years, the trade regime had developed a strong institutional backbone, and a dispute settlement system that, despite current attacks, has been considered for decades 'the jewel in the crown' of the whole system.[35] On the other hand, the environmental regime has been characterized by a certain 'softness' of its law and 'weakness' of its dispute resolution and enforcement mechanisms vis-à-vis the trade regime.[36] And for all these reasons, the approach adopted in this book starts from the assumption that the trade regime can indeed provide an efficient and promising framework to achieve sustainable development goals, including their environmental component. Therefore, if the system is retooled to serve these broader goals, this is a process that can only begin by asking a different set of questions.

3.2 *Asking the Right Question*

The traditional and still prevailing approach to the trade/environment nexus has been to ask by what modalities can or should the environment—a 'non-trade' issue—be linked to the trade regime,[37] assuming it can and assuming

---

34 See Joel P. Trachtman, 'Institutional Linkage: Transcending "Trade and …" ' (2002) 96(1) *American Journal of International Law* 77, 88.

35 See e.g. Joost Pauwelyn, 'WTO Dispute Settlement Post 2019: What to Expect?' (2019) 22(3) *Journal of International Economic Law* 297.

36 See e.g. Daniel Bodansky, *The Art and Craft of International Environmental Law* (Harvard University Press, 2010).

37 The literature is extremely rich on this point, see, among many other examples, Larry A. DiMatteo et al., 'The Doha Declaration and Beyond: Giving Voice to Non-Trade Concerns Within the WTO Trade Regime' (2003) 36 *Vanderbilt Journal of Transnational Law* 95. See also Nichols, *Trade Without Values* (n 7); Steve Charnovitz, 'Linking Topics in Treaties' (1998) 19 *University of Pennsylvania Journal of International Economic Law* 329; Jeffery Atik, 'Introductory Essay: Uncorking International Trade, Filling the Cup of International Economic Law' (2000) 15 *American University International Law Review* 1231; Bronckers, 'More Power to the WTO?'; Jose E. Alvarez, 'The WTO as Linkage Machine'

it should.[38] This 'linkage' approach is based on the assumption that trade and the environment belong to two separate issue areas. And, as this book has described, whenever attempts are made to 'link' the environment—or any other 'non-trade' issue—to the trade regime, a hierarchy is almost instantaneously established between what is and what is not, technically, 'trade'.[39] However, the developments subsumed under the *promotion-based* model are characterized by the absence of such a hierarchy. In the free trade agreements (FTAs) signed by the United States (US), for instance, all environmental obligations are "enforced on the same basis as the commercial provisions of our agreements—same remedies, procedures, and sanctions."[40] And these are agreements, as clearly presented in Chapter 5, that are aimed at both expanding trade and securing markets for goods and services, and promoting sustainable development and protecting the environment, not merely because of the language of the preamble but because of the actual norms they contain and mechanisms they provide for. The use of environmental exemptions rather than exceptions represents another sign that such a hierarchy is disappearing. The US proposal to add the enactment and enforcement of environmental standards below a certain level of environmental protection to the list of 'actionable subsidies' under the WTO subsidies agreement can be read under the same light, and so do the current negotiations on fisheries.

As an alternative, we could start asking a different question: what does the 'trade' substantive issue area include? Descriptively, defining the scope of an issue area would require observing state practice and the actual content of trade agreements and rules. As summarized by David Leebron in the context of a Symposium organized by the American Journal of International Law precisely on the topic of 'linkage', "the issue area of trade, for example, has evolved from the comparatively narrow conception of trade in goods (primarily limited to

---

(2002) 96(1) *American Journal of International Law* 146; Robert Wai, 'Countering, Branding, Dealing: Using Economic and Social Rights in and Around the International Trade Regime' (2003) 14 *European Journal of International Law* 35; Frank J. Garcia, 'The Salmon Case: Evolution of Balancing Mechanisms for Non-Trade Values in WTO', in George A. Bermann and Petros Mavroidis (eds.), *Trade and Human Health and Safety* (Cambridge University Press, 2003), p. 133; Chantal Thomas, 'Should the World Trade Organization Incorporate Labor and Environmental Standards?' (2004) 61 *Washington & Lee Law Review* 347; Andrew T. Guzman, 'Global Governance and the WTO' (2004) 45 *Harvard International Law Journal*.

38 A number of scholars disagree with the idea of linkage. See e.g. Jagdish Bhagwati, 'On Thinking Clearly About the Linkage Between Trade and the Environment' (2000) 5 *Environment & Development Economics* 483.

39 See e.g. Dunoff, 'Rethinking International Trade' (n 6) 383.

40 Office of the US Trade Representative, Bipartisan Agreement on Trade Policy (May 2007).

the issues of border treatment and discrimination) to a much broader regime encompassing services, intellectual property, and many aspects of domestic regulation."[41] If we consider new free trade agreements, the scope seems to have expanded even more. A 'new generation' of FTAs feature environmental principles, environmental obligations, and, in certain cases, apply to them the same remedies, procedures, and sanctions, that traditionally applied solely to their commercial provisions.

In other words, an alternative approach could entail revisiting the existing 'narrower' vision of what the scope, nature, and purpose of the trade regime is, and reconceptualizing it by taking into account the instrumentality of trade (trade is a means to an end rather than an end in itself) and the "contemporary political priorities"[42] (environmental degradation, lack of access to clean and affordable water, spreading hunger and poverty), to ensure that a wider variety of legitimate values "are upheld in a coherent and synergetic ... fashion."[43] In doing so, this book aims to follow in the steps of other scholars and commentators who have emphasized the importance, even the necessity, to begin this conversation and ask this very same question.[44]

3.3 *An Organizing Principle for the Trade Regime*

The 'telos' of the trade regime[45] in 1947, when the GATT was drafted, was to achieve economic growth through the gradual elimination of trade barriers. And it did. Successfully. In 1995, the WTO was established, and its preamble was slightly, yet significantly, different: the emphasis shifted from 'economic growth' pure and simple to 'sustainable development.' As this book has explained, the notion of *development* refers to a process of transformation which is not limited to economic growth but rather combines it with broader social and cultural changes, while the dimension of *sustainability* brings the recognition that growth and development "must ... adhere to the physical constraints imposed

---

41 David W. Leebron, 'Linkages' (2002) 96(1) *American Journal of International Law* 5, 7.

42 Lang, 'Reflecting on "Linkage"' (n 6) 542.

43 Cho, 'Linkage of Free Trade and Social Regulation' (n 7) 646. See also Sungjoon Cho, 'The WTO's Gemeinschaft' (2004) 56 *Alabama Law Review* 483.

44 Andrew Lang suggested to "re-conceptualize" the WTO, claiming that "trade lawyers must join the search for a new theoretical model of the trade regime, a new 'trade story' defining a new problematic for the trade regime to address." Cho has similarly argued that there is a need for a "new telos" for the trade regime. Lang, Reflecting on 'Linkage' (n 6) 542; Cho, 'Linkage of Free Trade and Social Regulation' (n 7).

45 Cho, 'Linkage of Free Trade and Social Regulation' (n 7).

by ecosystems, so that environmental considerations have to be embedded in all sectors and policy areas."[46]

The developments subsumed under the *promotion-based* model seem to go precisely in the direction of a trade regime that "is true to the preamble of the WTO."[47] This is a regime where trade rules are determined so as to maximize development potential, as well as to lead to environmental protection and preservation. This is a regime that, rather than addressing the question of how to simply maximize trade and market access, is centered around the question of how to enable countries to protect the environment and achieve sustainable development goals.[48]

The principle of sustainable development, in its broader definition and as exemplified in all its diverse manifestations in the 17 goals contained in the *Agenda 2030*, could be used to summarize this universe of legitimate policy goals.[49] It could be used as the organizing principle of trade agreements: rather than focusing on economic growth, trade agreements should be assessed in terms of their implications in terms of *development* and *sustainability*.[50] Already in 2005, former WTO Director General Pascal Lamy stated that "sustainable development is itself the end-goal of this institution [the WTO],"[51] and the very same ideas have been reaffirmed by former Director General, Roberto Azêvedo in several recent speeches.[52] This 'organizing principle' could explain, for instance, the fisheries subsidies negotiations, where countries have agreed to prohibit certain types of subsidies because they harm the marine environment and, at the same time, distort trade, while providing less-developed

46 Neil Carter, *The Politics of the Environment: Ideas, Activism, Policy* (Cambridge University Press, 2018), p. 211.

47 Dani Rodrik, *The Global Governance of Trade as is Development Really Mattered,* Report submitted to the UNDP (2001).

48 Ibid. Rodrik made this point in 2002 with reference solely to the development component of sustainable development.

49 See e.g. Christina Voigt, *Sustainable Development as a Principle of International* Law (Martinus Nijhoff, 2009); Nico Schrijver, 'The Evolution of Sustainable Development in International Law' (2007) *Collected Courses of the Hague Academy of International Law* (The Hague Academy of International Law), pp. 217–412; Virginie Barral, 'Sustainable Development in International Law: Nature and Operation of an Evolutive Legal Norm' (2012) 23 *European Journal of International Law* 377.

50 Charnovitz argued that "the WTO can no longer be (if it ever was) merely a trade agency. The WTO also has to be an environment agency," and that "environment and sustainable development are part of the purpose of the WTO." Charnovitz, *The Path of World Trade Law* (n 17) 472.

51 Pascal Lamy, Address at the WTO symposium on Trade and sustainable Development within the framework of paragraph 51 of the Doha Ministerial Declaration, Oct. 10, 2005.

52 See e.g. Roberto Azevêdo, Address at the 2018 WTO Public Forum.

countries with guarantees. This would represent a win-win-win scenario, which would benefit trade liberalization, sustainability, and development at the same time.

It would no longer be a matter of defining how trade law can accommodate non-trade values, but it would require revisiting the notion of 'trade' itself, and what the trade regime is for. Some scholars have proposed the reliance on the principle of sustainable development as an organizing principle of the debate, but they have largely been arguing that this principle should guide panels and the Appellate Body in their interpretation of WTO norms and in the resolution of disputes,[53] as this approach would allow a fairer balance between trade and environmental concerns. In the approach suggested in this book, on the other hand, it would not merely serve as a guiding principle in the interpretation of trade rules and in the settlement of trade/environment disputes, but would replace economic growth as the ultimate goal of the system, thus permeating every aspect of the nexus and the regime, including norms, rules, and procedures. It would not just allow the reduction or prevention conflicts, but it would promote synergies between trade and environmental law.

Not only would this re-conceptualization more accurately explain and capture the developments this book has described with reference to the trade/environment nexus, but it would also facilitate future attempts to further develop the *promotion-based* model. Without re-thinking the purpose of the trade regime and reconceptualizing, in fact, all these efforts are unlikely to be successful, as they will keep clashing against an outdated but seemingly unwavering narrative.

Furthermore, although this work has been focusing on the trade/environment nexus, 'sustainable development' embraces other areas of regulation as well—such as labor standards or human rights—where similar developments can be seen.[54] At the same time, these developments do not characterize solely

53 This approach has for instance been taken by the Appellate Body in *US-Shrimps* and has been adopted by investment tribunals as well when addressing disputes raised by FTAs (see *Al Tamimi v. Oman*). See e.g. Francesco Sindico, 'Unravelling the Trade and Environment Debate Through Sustainable Development Law Principles' (2005) *European Society of International Law*; Miguel A. Elizalde Carranza, 'MEAs with Trade Measures and the WTO: Aiming Towards Sustainable Development' (2007) 15 *Buffalo Environmental Law Journal* 43. See also Laurence Boisson de Chazournes and Makane Moïse Mbengue, 'A "Footnote as a Principle." Mutual Supportiveness in an Era of Fragmentation', in Holger P. Hestermeyer et al. (eds.), *Coexistence, Cooperation and Solidarity—Liber Amicorum Rüdiger Wolfrum—Vol. II* (Martinus Nijoff Publishers, 2011).

54 See e.g. Daniela Sicurelli, 'The EU as a Promoter of Human Rights in Bilateral Trade Agreements: The Case of the Negotiations with Vietnam' (2015) 11(2) *Journal of Contemporary European Research* 230; Cedric Ryngaert, 'EU Trade Agreements and Human

international trade law but other areas of international economic regulations, such as international investment law. Investment tribunals have been increasingly integrating environmental considerations in their decisions, and recent international investment agreements have been introducing new and updated provisions that reflect similar developments to those outlined in this book.[55] It follows that the arguments developed in this contribution can be relevant beyond the confines of the trade and environment debate. Rather, they intend to provide an analytical framework that can help better integrate sustainable development in different fields of international economic law, contributing to shaping the future of international economic law governance at large.

Rights: From Extraterritorial to Territorial Obligations' (2018) 20(3–4) *International Community Law Review* 374; Giovanni Gruni, 'Towards a Sustainable World Trade Law? The Commercial Policy of the European Union after Opinion 2/15 CJEU' (2018) 13 *Global Trade & Customs Journal* 5.

55 See Wolfgang Alschner and Elisabeth Tuerk, 'The Role of International Investment Agreements in Fostering Sustainable Development', in Freya Baetens (ed.), *Investment Law within International Law* (Cambridge University Press, 2013), p. 217–31; Makane M. Mbengue and Stefanie Schacherer, 'The "Africanization" of International Investment Law: The Pan-African Investment Code and the Reform of the International Investment Regime' (2017) 18 *Journal of World Investment and Trade* 414; Stefanie Schacherer and Rhea T. Hoffmann, 'International Investment Law and Sustainable Development', in Markus Krajewski and Rhea T. Hoffmann (eds.), *Research Handbook on Foreign Direct Investment* (Edward Elgar, 2019), p. 564; Elena Cima, 'Retooling the Energy Charter Treaty for Climate Change Mitigation: Lessons from Investment Law and Arbitration' (2021) 14(2) *Journal of World Energy Law and Business* 75–87.

Bibliography

Books

Amery, Leo. 1988. *The Empire at Bay: The Leo Amery Diaries,* 1929–1945 (John Barnes and David Nicholson eds., Hutchinson).

Anderson, Kym and Richard Blackhurst (eds.). 1992. *The Greening of World Trade* (University of Michigan Press).

Barbier, Edward B. 2010. *A Global Green New Deal: Rethinking the Economic Recovery* (Cambridge University Press).

Bergsten, Fred. 1975. *Toward a New International Economic Order* (Lexington Books).

Bernstein, William J. 2008. *A Splendid Exchange. How Trade Shaped the World* (Atlantic Monthly Press).

Bhagwati, Jagdish. 1988. *Protectionism* (MIT Press).

Bidwell, Percy W. 1939. *The Invisible Tariff. A Study of the Control of Imports into the United States* (Council on Foreign Relations).

Blyth, Mark. 2002. *Great Transformations: Economic Ideas and Institutional Change in the Twentieth Century* (Cambridge University Press).

Bookchin, Murray. 1962. *Our Synthetic Environment* (Knopf).

Bronowski, Jacob and Bruce Mazlish. 1962. *The Western Intellectual Tradition* (Harper Collins).

Brown Weiss Edith, John H. Jackson and Nathalie Bernasconi-Osterwalder (eds.). 2008. *Reconciling Environment and Trade* (Brill).

Butler, Michael A. 1998. *Cautious Visionary: Cordell Hull and Trade Reform, 1933–1937* (Kent State University Press).

Cairncross, Alec and Nita G.M. Watts. 1989. *The Economic Section,* 1939–1961 (Routledge).

Cameron, James et al. (eds.). 1994. *Trade & the Environment: the Search for Balance* (WM Gaunt & Sons).

Cameron, Maxwell A. and Brian W. Tomlin 2002. *The Making of NAFTA: How the Deal Was Done* (Cornell University Press).

Campiglio, Luigi et al. (eds.). 1994. *The Environment After Rio: International Law and Economics* (Springer).

Carson, Rachel. 1962. *Silent Spring* (Houghton Mifflin).

Carter, Neil. 2018. *The Politics of the Environment: Ideas, Activism, Policy* (Cambridge University Press).

Chalmers, Damian et al. 2010. *European Union Law* (Cambridge University Press).

Charnovitz, Steve. 2014. *The Path of World Trade Law in the 21st Century* (World Scientific).

Chen, Chen-Ju. 2010. *Fisheries Subsidies under International Law* (Hamburg Studies on Maritime Affairs, Springer).

Churchill, Winston S. 1985. *The Grand Alliance* (Houghton Mifflin).

Cobden, Richard. 1903. *The Political Writings of Richard Cobden* (Fisher Unwin).

Condliffe, John B. 1940. *The Reconstruction of World Trade* (Norton).

Conrad, Christiane R. 2011. *Processes and Production Methods (PPMs) in WTO Law: Interfacing Trade and Social Goals* (Cambridge University Press).

Cottier, Thomas, Olga Nartova, and Sadeq Z. Bigdeli (eds.). 2009. *International Trade Regulation and the Mitigation of Climate Change: World Trade Forum* (Cambridge University Press).

Curzon, Gerard. 1965. *Multilateral Commercial Diplomacy: the General Agreement on Tariffs and Trade and its Impact on National Commercial Policies and Techniques* (Praeger).

d'Aspremont, Jean. 2019. *The Critical Attitude and the History of International Law* (Brill).

Dabell, Rodney and Michael Henfeld (eds.). 1993. *Beyond NAFTA, The Western Hemisphere* (Oolichan Books).

Deere, Carolyn L. and Daniel C. Esty (eds.). 2002. *Greening the Americas. NAFTA's Lessons for Hemispheric Trade* (MIT Press).

Dodds, Felix et al. 2012. *Only One Earth: The Long Road Via Rio to Sustainable Development* (Routledge).

Dupuy, Pierre M. and Jorge E Viñuales (eds.). 2013. *Harnessing Foreign Investment to Protect the Environment* (Cambridge University Press).

Dupuy, Pierre M. and Jorge E Viñuales 2015. *International Environmental Law* (Cambridge University Press).

Eckes, Alfred E. Jr. 2000. *Opening America's Market: U.S. Foreign Trade Policy Since 1776* (University of North Carolina Press).

Ehlrich, Paul. 1970. *The Population Bomb* (Ballantine Books).

Epps, Tracey and Andrew Green. 2010. *Reconciling Trade and Climate* (Edward Elgar).

Esty, Daniel C. 1994. *Greening the GATT. Trade, Environment, and the Future* (Institute for International Economics).

Evans, John W. 1971. *The Kennedy Round in American Trade Policy: The Twilight of the GATT?* (Harvard University Press).

FAO. 1993. *Marine Fisheries and the Law of the Sea: A Decade of Change* (FAO Fisheries Department).

Farvar, M. Taghi and John Milton (eds.). 1969. *The Unforeseen International Ecologic Boomerang* (American Museum of National History).

Flippen, Brooks. 1994. *The Nixon Administration, Politics and the Environment* (University of Maryland and College Park).

Flippen, Brooks. 2000. *Nixon and the Environment* (UNM Press).

Fossedal, Gregory A., *Our Finest Hour: Will Clayton, the Marshall Plan, and the Triumph of Democracy* (Hoover Institution Press, 1993).

Gardner, Richard. 1980. *Sterling-Dollar Diplomacy in Current Perspective: The Origins and the Prospects of Our International Economic Order* (Columbia University Press).

Gartlan, Jean. 2010. *Barbara Ward: Her Life and Letters* (A&C Black).

Geradin, Damien. 1997. *Trade and the Environment. A Comparative Study of EC and US Law* (Cambridge University Press).

Giddens, Anthony. 1981. *A Contemporary Critique of Historical Materialism* (University of California Press).

Goldstein, Judith. 1993. *Ideas, Interests, and American Trade Policy* (Cornell University Press).

Goldstein, Judith and Robert O. Keohane (eds.). 1993. *Ideas and Foreign Policy, Ideas, Institutions, and Political Change* (Cornell University Press).

Gottlieb, Robert. 2005. *Forcing the Spring: The Transformation of the American Environmental Movement* (Island Press).

Goyal, Anupam. 2006. *The WTO and International Environmental Law* (Oxford University Press).

Grando, Michelle T. 2009. *Evidence, Proof, and Fact-Finding in WTO Dispute Settlement* (Oxford University Press).

Harrod, R.F. 1951. *The Life of John Maynard Keynes* (Harcourt, Brace).

Hasenclever, Andreas Peter Mayer and Volker Rittberger. 1997. *Theories of International Regimes* (Cambridge University Press).

Hays, Samuel P. 1989. *Beauty, Health, and Performance. Environmental Politics in the United States, 1955–1985* (Cambridge University Press).

Hinton, Harold B. 1942. *Cordell Hull. A Biography* (Doubleday, Doran & Company Inc.).

Hirschman, Albert O., 1945. *National Power and the Structure of Foreign Trade* (University of California Press).

Hirschman, Albert O., 1977. *The Passions and Interests* (Princeton University Press).

Hoekman, Bernard et al. 2002. *Development, Trade and the WTO. A Handbook* (The World Bank).

Howson, Susan. 2011. *Lionel Robbins* (Cambridge University Press).

Howson, Susan. 2016. *Collected Papers James Meade V1* (1st ed., Routledge).

Hudec, Robert E. 1975. *The GATT Legal System and World Trade Diplomacy* (Praeger).

Hudec, Robert E. 1999. *Essays on the Nature of International Trade Law* (Cameron May).

Hufbauer, Gary Clyde et al. 2000. *NAFTA and the Environment: Seven Years Later* (Peterson Institute for International Economics).

Hufbauer, Gary Clyde et al. 2009 *Global Warming and the World Trading System* (Peterson Institute for International Economics).

Hull, Cordell. 1948. *The Memoirs of Cordell Hull* (Macmillan).

Irwin, Douglas A. 1996. *Against The Tide* (Princeton University Press).

Irwin, Douglas A. 2017. *Clashing Over Commerce* (The University of Chicago Press).

Irwin, Douglas A., Petros C. Mavroidis and Alan O. Sykes. 2008. *The Genesis of the GATT* (Cambridge University Press).

Jackson, John H. 1969. *World Trade and the Law of the GATT* (Bobbs-Merrill Company).

Jackson, John H. 1989. *The World Trading System: Law and Policy of International Economic Relations* (MIT Press).

Kazazi, Mojtaba. 1996. *Burden of Proof and Related Issues: A Study of Evidence Before International Tribunals* (Martinus Nijhoff Publishers).

Kelsen, Hans. 1991. *General Theory of Norms* (Clarendon Press).

Keohane, Robert O. 1984. *After Hegemony: Cooperation and Discord in the World Political Economy* (Princeton University Press).

Keohane, Robert O. 1989. *International Institutions and State Power: Essays in International Relations Theory* (Westview Press).

Krasner, Stephen ed. 1983. *International Regimes* (Cornell University Press).

Lang, Andrew. 2011. *World Trade Law After Neoliberalism. Re-Imagining the Global Economic Order* (Oxford University Press).

Langer, William L. and S. Everett Gleason. 1953. *The Undeclared War, 1940–1941* (Harper and Brothers Publishers).

Lazarus, Richard J. 2004. *The Making of Environmental Law* (Chicago University Press).

Lee, Maria. 2005. *EU Environmental Law: Challenges, Change and Decision-Making* (Hart).

LeQuesne, Christian. 1996. *Reforming World Trade: The Social and Environmental Priorities* (Oxfam Publishing).

Meade, James E., 1940. *The Economic Basis of a Durable Peace* (Allen & Unwin).

Meade, James E., 1943. *Proposal for a Commercial Union.*

Meade, James E., 1982. *Wage-Fixing: Stagflation, Vol. I* (Allen & Unwin).

Meadows, Donella H. 1972. *The Limits to Growth: A Report for the Club of Rome's Project on the Predicament of Mankind* (Penguin).

Mill, John S. 1909. *Principles of Political Economy* 582 (Longman Green).

Montesquieu. 1748 *De l'esprit de lois.*

Muskie, Edmund. 1972. *Journeys* (Doubleday).

Nader, Ralph et al eds. 1993. *The Case Against Free Trade* (North Atlantic Books).

Newell, Peter. 2013. *Globalization and the Environment* (John Wiley & Sons).

Notter, Harley A. 1949. *Postwar Foreign Policy Preparation, 1939–1945* (Greenwood Press).

OECD. 2000. *Assessing the Environmental Effects of Trade Liberalization Agreements: Methodologies* (OECD Publishing).

OECD. 2001. *Environmental Goods and Services: The Benefits of Further Global Trade Liberalization: The Benefits of Further Global Trade Liberalization* (OECD Publishing).

Orakhelashvili, Alexander. 2008. *The Interpretation of Acts and Rules in Public International Law* (Oxford University Press).

Osborn, Fairfield. 1948. *Our Plundered Planet* (Little Brown).
Patrick, Stewart. 2008. *The Best Laid Plans* (Rowman & Littlefield Publishers).
Pauwelyn, Joost. 2003. *Conflict of Norms in Public International Law* (Cambridge University Press).
Pearce, David et al. 1990. *Blueprint For A Green Economy* (Earthscan).
Penrose, Ernest F. 1953. *Economic Planning for the Peace* (Princeton University Press).
Petersmann, Ernst-Ulrich. 1995. *International and European Trade and Environmental Law After the Uruguay Round* (Martinus Nijhoff).
Polanyi, Karl. 1996. *The Great Transformation: The Political and Economic Origins of Our Time* (Amereon Limited).
Polkinghorne, Donald. 1988. *Narrative Knowing and the Human Sciences* (State University of New York Press).
Prost, Mario. 2012. *The Concept of Unity in Public International Law* (Hart Publishing).
Qureshi, Asif H. 2006. *Interpreting WTO Agreements. Problems and Perspectives* (Cambridge University Press).
Reisman, David A. 2018. *James Edward Meade, Great Thinkers in Economics* (Palgrave Macmillan).
Rhodes, Carolyn. 1993. *Reciprocity, U.S. Trade Policy, and the GATT Regime* (Cornell University Press).
Ricardo. David. 1817. *On the Principles of Political Economy and Taxation.*
Robbins, Lionel. 1971. *Autobiography of an Economist* (Macmillan).
Robbins, Lionel et al. 2014. *The Wartime Diaries of Lionel Robbins and James Meade, 1943–45* (Palgrave Macmillan Springer).
Rodrik, Dani. 2008. *One Economics, Many Recipes: Globalization, Institutions, and Economic Growth* (Princeton University Press).
Rodrik, Dani. 2011. *The Globalization Paradox* (Norton & Company Inc.).
Runciman, David. 2013. *The Confidence Trap. A History of Democracy in Crisis from World War I to the Present* (Princeton University Press).
Schermers, Henry G. and Niels M. Blokker. 2003. *International Institutional Law: Unity Within Diversity* (Martinus Nijhoff).
Schon, Donald A. and Martin Rein. 1994. *Frame Reflection: Toward the Resolution of Intractable Policy Controversies* (Basic Books).
Smith, Adam. 1776. *An Inquiry into the Nature and Causes of the Wealth of Nations.*
Stiglitz, Joseph E. and Andrew Charlton. 2005. *Fair Trade for All* (Oxford University Press).
Stein, Robert E. and Brian D. G. Johnson. 1979. *Banking on the Biosphere* (Aero Publishing Ltd).
Strong, Maurice F. 2010. *Where on Earth Are We Going?* (Knopf Canada).
Sullivan, Kathleen M. and Noah Feldman. 2013. *Constitutional Law* (18th ed., Foundation Press).

Tarbell, Ida. 1911. *The Tariff in Our Times* (MacMillan).

Terrill, Tom E. 1973. *The Tariff, Politics, and American Foreign Policy* (Greenwood Press).

Tussie, Diana (ed.). 2009. *The Politics of Trade: The Role of Research in Trade Policy and Negotiation* (Brill Academic Publishers).

Udall, Stewart P. 1964. *The Quiet Crisis* (Avon Books).

U.S. Congress, Office of Technology Assessment. 1992. *Trade and Environment: Conflicts and Opportunities* (U.S. Government Printing Office).

Viñuales, Jorge E. 2012. *Foreign Investment and the Environment in International Law* (Cambridge University Press).

Viñuales, Jorge E. (ed.). 2015. *The Rio Declaration on Environment and Development: A Commentary* (Oxford University Press).

Vogt, William. 1948. *The Road to Survival* (W. Sloane Associates).

Ward, Barbara. 1966. *Spaceship Earth* (Columbia University Press).

Ward, Barbara and René Dubos. 1972. *Only One Earth* (W.W. Norton & Company).

Watson, James K.R. 2013. *The WTO and the Environment* (Routledge).

Weinberg, Philip and Kevin A. Reilly. 2013. *Understanding Environmental Law* (Lexis Nexis).

Welles, Sumner. 1944. *The Time for Decision* (Harper & Brothers).

Welles, Sumner. 1946. *Where Are We Heading?* (Harper & Brothers).

Wendt, Alexander. 1999. *Social Theory of International Politics* (Cambridge University Press).

Wilcox, Clair. 1949. *A Charter for World Trade* (Macmillan).

Wilson, Woodrow and Arthur S. Link. 1966. *The Papers of Woodrow Wilson* (Princeton University Press).

Winham, Gilbert R. 1985. *International Trade and the Tokyo Round Negotiations* (Princeton University Press).

World Bank. 1992. *World Development Report* (Oxford University Press).

World Commission on Environment and Development. 1987. *Our Common Future* (Oxford University Press).

Zaelke, Durwood et al eds. 1993. *Trade and the Environment. Law, Economics, and Policy* (Island Press).

Articles and Chapters in Books

Abbott, Kenneth W. 1996. '"Economic" issues and Political Participation: The Evolving Boundaries of International Federalism' 18 *Cardozo Law Review* 971.

Adede, Andronico O. 1994. 'The Road to Rio: The Development of Negotiations', in Luigi Campiglio et al. (eds.). *The Environment After Rio: International Law and Economics* 3–13 (Springer).

Adler, Emanuel. 1991. 'Cognitive Evolution: A Dynamic Approach for the Study of International Relations and their Progress', in Emanuel Adler and Beverly Crawford (eds.), *Progress in Postwar International Relations* 43–88 (Columbia University Press).

Adler, Emanuel. 1992. 'The Emergence of Cooperation: National Epistemic Communities and the International Evolution of the Idea of Nuclear Arms Control' 46 *International Organization* 101.

Adler, Emanuel and Peter M. Haas. 1992. 'Conclusion: Epistemic Communities, World Order, and the Creation of a Reflective Research Program' 46 *International Organization* 367.

Aguayo Ayala, Francisco and Kevin P. Gallagher. 2005. 'Preserving Policy Space for Sustainable Development', *International Institute for Sustainable Development* (IISD).

Alam, Shawkat. 2005. 'Trade-Environment Nexus in GATT Jurisprudence: Pressing Issues for Developing Countries' 17(2) *Bond Law Review* 1.

Allen, William R. 1953. 'The International Trade Philosophy of Cordell Hull, *1907–1993*' 43 *American Economic Review* 101.

Alvarez, Jose E. 2002. 'The WTO as Linkage Machine' 96(1) *American Journal of International Law* 146.

Appleton, Arthur E. 2000. 'Amicus Curiae Submissions in the Carbon Steel Case: Another Rabbit from the Appellate Body's Hat?' 3(4) *Journal of International Economic Law* 691.

Arden-Clarke, Charles. 1993. 'An Action Agenda for Trade Policy Reform to Support Sustainable Development: A United Nations Conference on Environment and Development Follow-Up', in Durwood Zaelke et al. (eds.), *Trade and the Environment. Law, Economics, and Policy* 71–82 (Island Press).

Audley, John. 1993. 'Why Environmentalists Are Angry about the North American Free Trade Agreement', in Durwood Zaelke et al. (eds.), *Trade and the Environment. Law, Economics, and Policy* 191–202 (Island Press).

Bacchus, James. 2002. 'Table Talk: Around the Table of the Appellate Body of the World Trade Organization' 35(4) *Vanderbilt Journal of Transnational Law* 1021.

Bailey, James E. 1992. 'Free Trade and the Environment–Can NAFTA Reconcile the Irreconcilable' 8 *American University Journal of International Law and Policy* 839.

Baldwin, Robert E. 1978. 'The Economics of the GATT', in Peter Oppenheimer (ed.), *Issues in International Economics* 82–93 (Oriel Press).

Baucus, Senator Max. 1993. 'Environmental Policy and Trade Agreements: The New Nexus', in Durwood Zaelke et al. (eds.), *Trade and the Environment. Law, Economics, and Policy* 257–266 (Island Press).

Beckerman, Wilfred. 1970. 'Economic Development and the Environment: A False Dilemma' 39 *International Conciliation* 57.

Benedek, Wolfgang. 1998. 'Relations of the WTO with Other International Organizations and NGOs', in Friedl Weiss, Erik M. G. Denters, and Paul J. I. M. de Waart (eds.), *International Economic Law with a Human Face* 479–495 (Martinus Nijhoff Publishers).

Berk, Richard A. 1988. 'Causal Inference for Sociological Data', in Neil J. Smelser (ed.), *Handbook of Sociology* (Sage).

Bhagwati, Jagdish. 1993a. 'Trade and the Environment: The False Conflict?' in Durwood Zaelke et al. (eds.), *Trade and the Environment. Law, Economics, and Policy* 159–190 (Island Press).

Bhagwati, Jagdish. 1993b. 'The Case for Free Trade' *Scientific American*.

Bhagwati, Jagdish. 2000. 'On Thinking Clearly About the Linkage Between Trade and the Environment' 5 *Environment and Development Economics* 485.

Bhagwati, Jagdish. 2001. 'After Seattle: Free Trade and the WTO' 77 *International Affairs* 15.

Bhagwati, Jagdish. 2002. 'Afterword: The Question of Linkage' 96(1) *American Journal of International Law* 126.

Bidwell, Percy W. 1930. 'The New American Tariff: Europe's Answer' 9(1) *Foreign Affairs* 13–26.

Bidwell, Percy W. 1942/43. 'Controlling Trade after the War' 21(2) *Foreign Affairs* 297–311.

Biermann, Frank. 2001. 'The Rising Tide of Green Unilateralism in World Trade Law: Options for Reconciling the Emerging North-South Conflict' 35(3) *Journal of World Trade* 421.

Bigdeli, Sadeq Z. 2014. 'Clash of Rationalities: Revisiting the Trade and Environment Debate in Light of WTO Disputes over Green Industrial Policy' 6(1) *Trade Law and Development* 177.

Billings, Leon G. 2015. 'Edmund Muskie: A Man with a Vision' 67(2) *Maine Law Review* 234.

Blank, Daniel P. 1996. 'Target-Based Environmental Trade Measures: A Proposal for the New WTO Committee on Trade and Environment' 15 *Stanford Environmental Law Journal* 61.

Blomquist, Robert F. 1990. '"Clean New World": Toward an Intellectual History of American Environmental Law, 1961–1990' 25(1) *Valparaiso University Law Review* 1.

Blomquist, Robert F. 1997. '"To Stir Up Public Interest": Edmund S. Muskie and the U.S. Senate Special Subcommittee's Water Pollution, Investigations and Legislative Activities, 1963–66—A Case Study in Early Congressional Environmental Policy Development' 22(1) *Columbia Journal of Environmental Law* 1.

Blomquist, Robert F. 1999. 'What is Past is Prologue: Senator Edmund S. Muskie's Environmental Policymaking Roots as Governor of Maine, 1955–58' 51(1) *Maine Law Review* 88.

Blomquist, Robert F. 2002. 'Senator Edmund S. Muskie and the Dawn of Modern American Environmental Law: First Term, 1959–1964' 26 *William and Mary Environmental Law and Policy Review* 509.

Boisson de Chazournes, Laurence. 2000. 'Unilateralism and Environmental Protection: Issues of Perception and Reality of Issues' 11 *European Journal of International Environmental Law* 315.

Boisson de Chazournes, Laurence and Makane Moïse Mbengue. 2004. 'GMOs and Trade: Issues at Stake in the EC Biotech Dispute' *Review of European, Comparative & International Environmental Law* 289.

Boisson de Chazournes, Laurence and Makane Moïse Mbengue. 2011. 'A "Footnote as a Principle". Mutual Supportiveness in an Era of Fragmentation', in Holger P. Hestermeyer et al. (eds.), *Coexistence, Cooperation and Solidarity—Liber Amicorum Rüdiger Wolfrum—Vol. II* (Martinus Nijoff Publishers).

Booth, Alan. 1986. 'Economic Advice at the Centre of British Government, 1939–1941' 29 *History Journal* 655.

Borgen, Christopher. 2005. 'Resolving Treaty Conflicts' 37 *George Washington International Law Review* 573.

Boulding, Kenneth E. 1966. 'The Economics of the Coming Spaceship Earth', in Henry Jarrett (ed.), *Environmental Quality in a Growing Economy* 3–14 (John Hopkins University Press).

Brand, Ronald A. 1996. 'Sustaining the Development of International Trade and Environmental Law' 21 *Vermont Law Review* 823.

Brighton, Claire. 2017. 'Unlikely Bedfellows: The Evolution of the Relationship Between Environmental Protection and Development' 66 *International and Comparative Law Quarterly* 209.

Bronckers, Marco C. E. J. 2001.' More power to the WTO?' 4(1) *Journal of International Economic Law* 41.

Brown, Bartram. 1994. 'Developing Countries in the International Trade Order' 14 *Northern Illinois University Law Review* 347.

Brown, Winthrop G. 1948. 'United States Economic Foreign Policy', *U.S. Department of State, Department of Public Affairs*.

Brown Weiss, Edith. 1992. 'Environment and Trade as Partners in Sustainable Development: A Commentary' 86 *American Journal of International Law* 728.

Brown Weiss, Edith. 2011. 'The Evolution of International Environmental Law' 54 *Japanese Yearbook of International Law* 1.

Brulle, Roberts J. 1996. 'Environmental Discourse and Social Movement Organizations: A Historical and Rhetorical Perspective on the Development of U.S. Environmental Organizations' 66(1) *Sociological Inquiry* 58.

Brusasco-Mackenzie, Margaret. 1994. 'The Role of the European Communities', in Luigi Campiglio et al. (eds.), *The Environment After Rio: International Law and Economics* 23–32 (Springer).

Burhenne, Wolfgang E. and Thomas J. Shoenbaum. 1973. 'The European Community and Management of the Environment: A Dilemma' 13 *Natural Resources Journal* 494.

Caldwell, Lynton K. 1973. 'A World Policy for the Environment' *The Unesco Courier*.

Cameron, James and Jonathan Robinson. 1991. 'The Use of Trade Provisions in International Environmental Agreements and their Compatibility with the GATT' *Yearbook of International Environmental Law* 3.

Cameron, James and Halina Ward. 1994. 'The Multilateral Trade Organization: A Revised Perspective', in James Cameron et al. (eds.), *Trade and the Environment: the Search for Balance* 96–124 (Cameron May).

Cameron, James and Kevin R. Gray. 2001. 'Principles on International Law in the WTO Dispute Settlement Body' 50 *International and Comparative Law Quarterly* 248.

Carranza, Miguel A. Elizalde. 2007. 'MEAs with Trade Measures and the WTO: Aiming Towards Sustainable Development' (2007) 15 *Buffalo Environmental Law Journal* 43.

Chang, Howard F. 1995. 'An Economic Analysis of Trade Measures to Protect the Global Environment' 83 *Georgetown Law Journal* 2131.

Chang, Seung Wha. 2003. 'WTO Disciplines on Fisheries Subsidies: A Historic Step Towards Sustainability?' 6(4) *Journal of International Economic Law* 879.

Charnovitz, Steve. 1991. 'Exploring the Environmental Exceptions in GATT Article XX' 25(5) *Journal of World Trade* 37.

Charnovitz, Steve. 1992. 'GATT and the Environment. Examining the Issues' 4(3) *International Environmental Affairs* 203.

Charnovitz, Steve. 1993a. 'A Taxonomy of Environmental Trade Measures' 6(1) *Georgetown International Law Review* 1.

Charnovitz, Steve. 1993b. 'Environmental Harmonization and Trade Policy', in Durwood Zaelke et al. (eds.), *Trade and the Environment. Law, Economics, and Policy* 267–286 (Island Press).

Charnovitz, Steve. 1993c. 'NAFTA: An Analysis of Its Environmental Provisions' 23 *Environmental Law Reporter* 10067.

Charnovitz, Steve. 1994a. 'Environmental Trade Sanctions and the GATT: An Analysis of the Pelly Amendment on Foreign Environmental Practices' 9(3) *American University Journal of International Law e Policy* 751.

Charnovitz, Steve. 1994b. 'No Time for NEPA: Trade Agreements on a Fast Track' 3 *Minnesota Journal of Global Trade* 195.

Charnovitz, Steve. 1994c. 'NAFTA's Social Dimension: Lessons from the Past and Framework for the Future' VIII(1) *International Trade Journal* 39.

Charnovitz, Steve. 1994d. 'The NAFTA Environmental Side Agreement: Implications for Environmental Cooperation, Trade Policy, and American Treatymaking' 8 *Temple International and Comparative Law Journal* 257.

Charnovitz, Steve. 1996. 'Participation of Nongovernmental Organizations in the World Trade Organization' 17(1) *University of Pennsylvania Journal of International Economic Law* 331.

Charnovitz, Steve. 1997. 'A Critical Guide to the WTO's Report on Trade and Environment' 14(2) *Arizona Journal of International and Comparative Law* 341.

Charnovitz, Steve. 1998. 'Linking Topics in Treaties' 19 *University of Pennsylvania Journal of International Economic Law* 329.

Charnovitz, Steve. 2002a. 'A World Environmental Organization' 27 *Columbia Journal of Environmental Law* 323.

Charnovitz, Steve. 2002b. 'The Law of Environmental "PPMS" in the WTO: Debunking the Myth of Illegality' 27 *Yale Journal of International Law* 59.

Charnovitz, Steve. 2002c. 'Triangulating the World Trade Organization' 96(1) *American Journal of International Law* 28.

Charnovitz, Steve. 2007a. 'A New WTO Paradigm for Trade and the Environment' 11 *Singapore Yearbook of International Law* 15.

Charnovitz, Steve. 2007b. 'The WTO's Environmental Progress' 10(3) *Journal of International Economic Law* 685.

Charnovitz, Steve and Carolyn Fischer. 2015. 'Canada-Renewable Energy: Implications for WTO Law on Green and Not-So-Green Subsidies' 14(2) *World Trade Review* 177.

Charnovitz, Steve and John Wickham. 1995. 'Non-Governmental Organizations and the Original International Trade Regime' 29(5) *Journal of World Trade* 111.

Cho, Sungjoon. 2004. 'The WTO's Gemeinschaft' 56 *Alabama Law Review* 483.

Cho, Sungjoon. 2005. 'Linkage of Free Trade and Social Regulation: Moving Beyond the Entropic Dilemma' 5 *Chicago Journal of International Law* 626.

Cho, Sungjoon. 2007. 'The Bush Administration and Democrats Reach a Bipartisan Deal on Trade Policy' 11(15) *ASIL Insights* (May 31, 2007).

Clawson, Marion. 1971. 'Economic Development and Environmental Impact: International Aspects' 10(4) *Social Science Information* 23.

Clinton, Bill. 1993. 'Expanding Trade and Creating American Jobs' 23 *Environmental Law* 683.

Cima, Elena. 2017. 'Caught between Trade and Climate Change. The Economic Rationale of 'Green Subsidies', in Klaus Mathis and Bruce R. Huber (eds.), *Environmental Law And Economics* 379–404 (Springer, 2017).

Cima, Elena. 2018. 'Promoting Renewable Energy through FTAs? The Legal Implications of a New Generation of Trade Agreements' 52(4) *Journal of World Trade* 663.

Cima, Elena and Makane M. Mbengue. 2021. 'ESIL Reflection—"Kind of Green". The U.S. Proposal to Advance Sustainability through Trade Rules and the Future of the WTO' 10(1) *ESIL Reflections*.

Cohen, Harlan Grant. 2019. ' What is International Trade Law For?' 113(2) *American Journal of International Law* 326.

Condon, Bradly J. 1994. 'NAFTA and the Environment: A Trade-Friendly Approach' 14 *Northwestern Journal of International Law and Business* 528.

Correa, Carlos M. 2013. 'Innovation and Technology Transfer of Environmentally Sound Technologies: The Need to Engage in a Substantive Debate' 22(1) *Review of European, Comparative and International Environmental Law* 54.

Culbert, Jay. 1987. 'War-time Anglo-American Talks and the Making of the GATT' 10 *The World Economy* 381–399.

Cullet, Philippe. 2015. 'Principle 7: Common but Differentiated Responsibilities', in Jorge E. Viñuales (ed.), *The Rio Declaration on Environment and Development* (Oxford University Press).

Curzon, Gerard and Victoria Curzon. 1973. 'GATT: Traders' Club', in Robert W. Cox and Harold K. Jacobson (eds.), *The Anatomy of Influence: Decision Making in International Organizations* (Yale University Press).

Curzon, Victoria. 1976. 'The Management of Trade Relations in the GATT', in Andrew Shonfield (ed.), *International Economic Relations of the Western World 1959–1971, Vol. I* 143–283 (Oxford University Press).

Cushman, Robert E. 1919. 'National Police Power under the Commerce Clause of the Constitution' 3 *Minnesota Law Review* 289.

Dam, Kenneth W. 2005. 'Cordell Hull, the Reciprocal Trade Agreements Act, and the WTO: An Essay on the Concept of Rights in International Trade' 1 *New York University Journal of Law and Business* 709.

d'Arge, Ralph C. and Allen V. Kneese. 1972. 'Environmental Quality and International Trade' 26(2) *International Organization* 419.

d Vries, Gijs M. 1992. 'How to Banish Eco-Imperialism' *Journal of Commerce* (Apr. 30, 1992).

Davey, William J. 1987. 'Dispute Settlement in GATT' 11(1) *Fordham International Law Journal* 52.

Destler, I.M. and Marcus Noland. 2002. 'Constant Ends, Flexible Means: C. Fred Bergsten and the Quest for Open Trade', in Michael Mussa (ed.), *Fred Bergsten and the World Economy* 15 (Columbia University Press).

Dillon, Sara. 1996. 'Trade and the Environment: A Challenge to the GATT/WTO Principle of "Ever-Freer Trade"' 11(2) *Journal of Civil Rights and Economic Development* 351.

Dillon, Sara. 2002. 'A Farewell to "Linkage": International Trade Law and Global Sustainability Indicators' 55 *Rutgers Law Review* 87.

DiMatteo, Larry A. et al. 2003. 'The Doha Declaration and Beyond: Giving Voice to Non-Trade Concerns Within the WTO Trade Regime' 36 *Vanderbilt Journal of Transnational Law* 95.

Drake, William J. and Kalypso Nicolaïdis. 1992. 'Ideas, Interests, and Institutionalization: "Trade in Services" and the Uruguay Round' 46(1) *International Organization* 37.

Driesen, David M. 2001. 'What is Free Trade? The Real Issue Lurking Behind the Trade and Environment Debate' 41 *Virginia Journal of International Law* 279.

Dunoff, Jeffrey L. 1992. 'Reconciling International Trade with Preservation of the Global Commons: Can We Prosper and Protect' 49 *Washington and Lee Law Review* 1407.

Dunoff, Jeffrey L. 1993. 'Institutional Misfits: The GATT, the ICJ and Trade-Environment Disputes' 15 *Michigan Journal of International Law* 1043.

Dunoff, Jeffrey L. 1994. 'Resolving Trade-Environment Conflicts: The Case for Trading Institutions' 27 *Cornell International Law Journal* 607.

Dunoff, Jeffrey L. 1996. 'Trade and: Recent Developments in Trade Policy and Scholarship–And Their Surprising Political Implications' 17 *Northwestern Journal of International Law and Business* 759.

Dunoff, Jeffrey L. 1998. 'Rethinking International Trade' 19 *University of Pennsylvania Journal of International Economic Law* 347.

Dunoff, Jeffrey L. 1999. 'The Death of the Trade Regime' 10(4) *European Journal of International Law* 733.

Dunoff, Jeffrey L. 2001. 'The WTO in Transition: Of Constituents, Competence, and Coherence' 33 *George Washington International Law Review* 979.

Elliot, Donald et al. 1985. 'Toward a Theory of Statutory Evolution: The Federalization of Environmental Law' 1 *Journal of Law Economics and Organization* 313.

Engfeldt, Lars-Goran. 1973. 'The United Nations and the Human Environment—Some Experiences' 27(3) *International Organization.*

Espa, Ilaria. 2019. 'New Features of Green Industrial Policy and the Limits of WTO Rules: What Options for the Twenty-First Century?' 53(6) *Journal of World Trade* 979.

Espa, Ilaria. 2021. 'Dissecting the Green Component of 21st Century Industrial Policy in the Energy Sector: Implications for the WTO System' in Elena Cima and Makane M. Mbengue (eds.), *A Multifaceted Approach to Trade Liberalization and Investment Protection in the Energy Sector* (Brill).

Esty, Daniel C. 1993a. 'Beyond Rio: Trade and the Environment' 23(2) *Environmental Law* 387.

Esty, Daniel C. 1993b. 'Integrating Trade and Environment Policy Making: First Steps in the North American Free Trade Agreement', in Durwood Zaelke et al (eds.), *Trade and the Environment. Law, Economics, and Policy* 45–56 (Island Press).

Esty, Daniel C. 1994. 'The Case for a Global Environmental Organization', in Peter B. Kenen (ed.), *Managing the World Economy: Fifty Years after Bretton Woods* 287 (Institute for International Economics).

Esty, Daniel C. 1998a. 'Non-Governmental Organizations at the World Trade Organization: Cooperation, Competition, or Exclusion' 1(1) *Journal of International Economic Law* 123.

Esty, Daniel C. 1998b. 'Linkages and Governance: NGOs and the World Trade Organization' 19(3) *University of Pennsylvania Journal of International Economic Law* 709.

Esty, Daniel C. 1999. 'Economic Integration and the Environment', in Regina S. Axelrod and Stacy D. VanDeveer (eds.), *The Global Environment. Institutions, Law, and Policy* 190 (Sage).

Esty, Daniel C. 2000. 'An Environmental Perspective on Seattle', Faculty Scholarship Series, Paper 439.

Esty, Daniel C. 2001. 'Bridging the Trade-Environment Divide' 15(3) *Journal of Economic Perspectives* 113.

Farber, Daniel A. 1997. 'Environmental Federalism in a Global Economy' 83 *Virginia Law Review* 1283.

Floum, Joshua R. 1995. 'Exporting Environmentalism: Thoughts on the Use of Market Power to Improve the Environment in the Free Trade Era' 35 *Santa Clara Law Review* 1199.

Foster, Mark Edward. 1998. 'Trade and Environment: Making Room for Environmental Trade Measures within the GATT' 71 *Southern California Law Review* 393.

Frankel, Jeffrey A. 2001. 'Assessing the Efficiency Gains for Further Liberalization', in Roger B. Porter et al. (eds.), *Efficiency, Equity, and Legitimacy: The Multilateral Trading System at the Millennium* 334 (Brookings Institution Press).

Gabler, Melissa. 2010. 'Norms, Institutions and Social Learning: An Explanation for Weak Policy Integration in the WTO's Committee on Trade and Environment' 10(2) *Global Environmental Policy* 80.

Gaines, Sanford E. and Albert E. Utton. 1993. 'Environmental Laws and Regulations After NAFTA' 1 *U.S-Mexico Law Journal* 199.

Galizzi, Paolo. 2005. 'From Stockholm to New York, via Rio and Johannesburg: Has the Environment Lost its Way on the Global Agenda?' 29(5) *Fordham International Law Journal* 952.

Galizzi, Paolo and Alena Herklotz. 2011. 'Environment and Development: Friends or Foes in the 21st Century', in Malgosia Fitzmaurice et al. (eds.), *Research Handbook of International Environmental Law* 69 (Edward Elgar).

Garcia, Frank J. 2003. 'The Salmon Case: Evolution of Balancing Mechanisms for Non-Trade Values in WTO', in George A. Bermann and Petros Mavroidis (eds.), *Trade and Human Health and Safety* (Cambridge University Press).

Gardner, Richard N. 1972. 'The Role of the UN in Environmental Problems' 26(2) *International Organization* 237.

Gardner, Richard N. 1985. 'Sterling-Dollar Diplomacy in Current Perspective' 62 *International Affairs* 21–33.

Gathii, James T. 2001. 'Re-Characterizing the Social in the Constitutionalization of the WTO: A Preliminary Analysis' 7 *Widener Law Symposium Journal* 137.

Goldman, Patti. 1992. 'Resolving the Trade and Environment Debate: In Search of a Neutral Forum and Neutral Principles' 49 *Washington and Lee Law Review* 1279.

Goldstein, Joel K. 2015. 'Edmund S. Muskie: The Environmental Leader and Champion' 67(2) *Maine Law Review* 226.

Goldstein, Judith. 1988. 'Ideas, Institutions and American Trade Policy' 42(1) *International Organization* 179.

Gonzalez, Carmen G. 2001. 'Beyond Eco-Imperialism: An Environmental Justice Critique of Free Trade' 78(4) *Denver University Law Review* 981.

Gray, Kevin. 2000. 'International Environmental Impact Assessment' 11 *Colorado Journal of International Environmental Law & Policy* 83.

Green, Andrew. 2006. 'Trade Rules and Climate Change Subsidies' 5 *World Trade Review* 377.

Gruni, Giovanni, 2018. 'Towards a Sustainable World Trade Law? The Commercial Policy of the European Union after Opinion 2/15 CJEU' 13 *Global Trade and Customs Journal* 5.

Guzman, Andrew T. 2004. 'Global Governance and the WTO' 45 *Harvard International Law Journal* 303.

Haagsma, Auke. 1988. 'The European Community's Environmental Policy: A Case-Study in Federalism' 12(2) *Fordham International Law Journal* 312.

Haas, Peter M. 1992. 'Introduction: Epistemic Communities and International Policy Co-ordination' 46 *International Organization* 1.

Hajost, Scott A. 1994. 'The Role of the United States', in Luigi Campiglio et al. (eds.), *The Environment After Rio: International Law and Economics* 15–21 (Springer).

Hare, F. Kenneth. 1988. 'World Conference on the Changing Atmosphere: Implications for Security, held at the Toronto Convention Centre, Toronto, Ontario, Canada, during 27–30 June 1988' 15(3) *Environmental Conservation* 282.

Hedberg, Bo. 1981. 'How Organizations Learn and Unlearn', in Paul C. Nystrom and William H. Starbuck (eds.), *Handbook of Organizational Design* (Oxford University Press).

Hill, Hamner. 1987. 'A Functional Taxonomy of Normative Conflict' 6 *Law and Philosophy* 227.

Horn, Henrik and Petros C. Mavroidis. 2008. 'The Permissible Reach of National Environmental Policies' 42(6) *Journal of World Trade* 1107.

Housman, Robert. 1994. 'The North American Free Trade Agreement's Lessons for Reconciling Trade and the Environment' 30 *Stanford Journal of International Law* 379.

Housman, Robert and Paul M. Orbuch. 1993. 'Integrating Environmental and Labor Concerns in the North American Free Trade Agreement: A Look Back and a Look Ahead' 8(4) *American University International Law Review* 719.

Housman, Robert and Durwood Zaelke. 1992. 'Trade, Environment, and Sustainable Development: A Primer' 15 *Hastings International and Comparative Law Review* 53.

Howse, Robert L. 2002a. 'The Appellate Body Rulings in the Shrimp/Turtle Case: A new Legal Baseline for the Trade and Environment Debate' 27 *Columbia Journal of Environmental Law* 491.

Howse, Robert L. 2002b. 'From Politics to Technocracy—And Back Again: The Fate of the Multilateral Trading Regime' 96 *American Journal of International Law* 94.

Howse, Robert L. 2006. 'Montesquieu on Commerce, Conquest, War, and Peace' 31(3) *Brooklyn Journal of International Law* 1.

Howse, Robert L. 2009. 'Do the World Trade Organization Disciplines on Domestic Subsidies Make Sense? The Case for Legalizing Some Subsidies', in Kyle W. Bagwell et al. (eds.), *Law and Economics in Contingent Protection in International Trade* 85–102 (Cambridge University Press).

Howse, Robert L. 2016. 'The Word Trade Organization 20 Years On: Global Governance by Judiciary' 27(1) *European Journal of International Law* 9.

Howse, Robert L. and Henrik Horn. 2009. 'European Communities—Measures Affecting the Approval and Marketing of Biotech Products' 8(1) *World Trade Review* 49.

Hudec, Robert E. 1970. 'The GATT Legal System: A Diplomat's Jurisprudence' 4 *Journal of World Trade Law* 615.

Hudec, Robert E. 1996a. 'Differences in National Environmental Standards: The Level-Playing-Field Dimension' 50 *Minnesota Journal of Global Trade* 1.

Hudec, Robert E. 1996b. 'GATT Legal Restraints on the Use of Trade Measures Against Foreign Environmental Practices', in Jagdish N. Bhagwati and Robert E. Hudec (eds.), *Fair Trade and Harmonization: Prerequisites for Free Trade*? 95 (MIT Press).

Hudson, Stewart. 1992. 'Trade, Environment and the Pursuit of Sustainable Development in International Trade and the Environment', in Patrick Low (ed.), *World Bank Discussion Papers: International Trade and the Environment* 55 (World Bank).

Hufbauer, Gary Clyde. 1989. 'Beyond GATT' 77 *Foreign Policy* 64.

Hull, Cordell. 1934. 'International Trade and Domestic Prosperity', U.S. Dept. of State Commercial Policy Series No. 3 (Washington, D.C.).

Hurlock, Matthew H. 1992. 'Note. The GATT, U.S. Law and the Environment: A Proposal to Amend the GATT in Light of the Tuna/Dolphin Decision' 92 *Columbia Law Journal* 2098.

Ikenberry G. John. 1992. 'A World Economy Restored: Expert Consensus and the Anglo-American Postwar Settlement' 46 *International Organization* 289.

Irwin, Douglas A. 1995. 'The GATT in Historical Perspective' 85 *American Economic Review* 323.

Irwin, Douglas A. 1998. 'From Smoot-Hawley to Reciprocal Trade Agreements: Changing the Course of U.S. Trade Policy in the 1930s', in M.D. Bordo (ed.), *The Defining Moment: The Great Depression and the American Economy in the Twentieth Century* 325–350 (University of Chicago Press).

Irwin, Douglas A. 2008. 'Trade Liberalization: Cordell Hull and the Case for Optimism', Council on Foreign Relations.

Jackson, John H. 1979a. 'International Economic Problems and their Management in the 21st Century' 9 *Georgia Journal of International and Comparative Law* 497.

Jackson, John H. 1979b. 'Governmental Disputes in International Trade Relations: A Proposal in the Context of GATT' *Journal of World Trade Law* 1.

Jackson, John H. 1992a. 'Dolphins and Hormones: GATT and the Legal Environment for International Trade after the Uruguay Round' 14(3) *University of Arkansas at Little Rock Law Journal* 429.

Jackson, John H. 1992b. 'World Trade Rules and Environmental Policies: Congruence or Conflict?' 49 *Washington and Lee Law Review* 1227.

Jackson, John H. 1992c. 'GATT and the Future of International Trade Institutions' XVIII(1) *Brooklyn Journal of International Law* 11.

Jackson, John H. 1993. 'Changing GATT Rules', in *The Greening of World Trade* (U.S. Environmental Protection Agency).

Jackson, John H. 1994. 'Greening the GATT: Trade Rules and Environmental Policy', in James Cameron et al. (eds.), *Trade & the Environment: the Search for Balance* 39 (Cameron May).

Jackson, John H. 1995. 'International Economic Law: Reflections on the "Boilerroom" for International Relations' 10(2) *American University Journal of International Law and Policy* 595.

Jackson, John H. 1996a. 'Reflections on International Economic Law' 17(1) *University of Pennsylvania Journal of International Economic Law* 17.

Jackson, John H. 1996b. 'Reflections on Constitutional Changes to the Global Trading System' 72 *Chicago-Kent Law Review* 511.

Jackson, John H. 1998. 'Dispute Settlement and the WTO. Emerging Problems' 1(3) *Journal of International Economic Law* 329.

Jackson, John H. 2001. 'The WTO "Constitution" and Proposed Reforms: Seven "Mantras" Revisited' 4(1) *Journal of International Economic Law* 67.

Jackson, John H. 2005. 'Justice Feliciano and the WTO Environmental Cases: Laying the Foundations of a "Constitutional Jurisprudence" with Implications for Developing

Countries', in Steve Charnovitz et al (eds.), *Law in the Science of Human Dignity* 29 (Cambridge University Press).

Jadot, B. 1990. 'Observations—Mesures Nationales de Police de l'Environnement, Libre Circulation des Marchandises et Proportionnalité' *Cahiers de Droit Européen* 408.

Jenks, C. Wilfred. 1951. 'Co-Ordination in International Organization: An Introductory Survey' 28 *British Yearbook of International Law* 29.

Jenks, C. Wilfred. 1953. 'The Conflict of Law-Making Treaties' 30 *British Yearbook of International Law* 401.

Jerome, Robert. 1991. 'Traders and Environmentalists' *Journal of Commerce* (Dec. 27, 1991).

Kalen, Sam. 1993. 'Commerce to Conservation: The Call for a National Water Policy and the Evolution of Federal Jurisdiction Over Wetlands' 69 *North Dakota Law Review* 873.

Kennedy, David. 2006. The "Rule of Law," Political Choices, and Development Common Sense', in David M. Trubek and Alvaro Santos (eds.), *The New Law and Economic Development: A Critical Appraisal* (Cambridge University Press).

Keohane, Robert O. and Joseph S. Nye Jr. 2001. 'The Club Model of Multilateral Cooperation and Problems of Democratic Legitimacy', in Roger B. Porter et al. (eds.), *Efficiency, Equity, and Legitimacy: The Multilateral Trading System at the Millennium* 334 (Brookings Institution Press).

Kindall, M.P.A. 1993. 'Talking Past Each Other at The Summit' 4 *Colorado Journal of International Environmental Law and Policy* 69.

Kindleberger, Charles P. 1975. 'The Rise of Free Trade in Western Europe, 1820–1875' 35 *Journal of Economic History* 20.

Kindleberger, Charles P. 1981. 'Dominance and Leadership in the International Economy' 25(2) *International Studies Quarterly* 242.

Kindleberger, Charles P. 1989. 'Commercial Policy between the Wars', in Peter Mathias and Sidney Pollard (eds.), *The Cambridge Economic History of Europe VIII* (Cambridge University Press).

King, Alexander. 1971. 'New Ethic for Survival', in Clifton Fadiman and Jean White (eds.), *Ecocide—And Thoughts Toward Survival* (Center for Study of Democratic Institutions).

Kirgis, Frederic L. Jr. 1972. 'Effective Pollution Control in Industrialized Countries: International Economic Disincentives, Policy Responses, and the GATT' 70 *Michigan Law Review* 859.

Knox, John H. 2004. 'The Judicial Resolution of Conflicts Between Trade and the Environment' 28 *Harvard Environmental Law Review* 1.

Knox, John H. 2010. 'The Neglected Lessons of the NAFTA Environmental Regime' 45(2) *Wake Forest Law Review* 391.

Kovar, Jeffrey D. 1993. 'A Short Guide to the Rio Declaration' 4 *Colorado Journal of International Environmental Law and Policy* 119.

Kuijper, Pieter Jan. 1994. 'The Law of GATT as a Special Field of International Law' *Netherland Yearbook of International Law* 227.

Kumar, Radika et al. 2019. 'The effectiveness of Fisheries Subsidies as a Trade Policy Tool to Achieving Sustainable Development Goals at the WTO' 100 *Marine Policy* 132.

Lallas, Peter L., Daniel C. Esty and David J. van Hoogstraten. 1992. 'Environmental protection and International Trade: toward Mutually Supportive Rules and Policies' 16 *Harvard Environmental Law Review* 271.

Lamy, P. 2006. 'The Place of the WTO and Its Law in the International Legal Order' 17(5) *European Journal of International Law* 969.

Lang, Andrew. 2007a. 'The Role of the Human Rights Movement in Trade Policy-Making: Human Rights as a Trigger for Policy Learning' 5 *New Zealand Journal of Public International Law* 77.

Lang, Andrew. 2007b. 'Reflecting on "Linkage": Cognitive and Institutional Change in the International Trading System' 70(4) *Modern Law Review* 523.

Lang, Winfried. 1995. 'Is the Protection of the Environment a Challenge to the International Trading System?' 7 *Georgia International Environmental Law Review* 463.

Lash, William H. III. 1993. 'Green Gang's GATT Holdup' *Journal of Commerce* (Dec. 10, 1993).

Lazarus, Richard. 2015. 'Senator Edmund Muskie's Enduring Legacy in the Courts' 67(2) *Maine Law Review* 240.

Leal-Arcas, Rafael. 2013. 'Climate Change Mitigation from the Bottom Up: Preferential Trade Agreements to Promote Climate Change Mitigation' 7 *Carbon and Climate Law Review* 34.

Leebron, David W. 2002. 'Linkages' 96(1) *American Journal of International Law* 5.

Lefton, Ira Steven. 1977. 'Constitutional Law—Commerce Clause: Local Discrimination in Environmental Protection Regulation' 55(2) *North Carolina Law Review* 461.

Legro, Jeffrey W. 2000. 'The Transformation of Policy Ideas' 44 *American Journal of Political Science* 419.

Lerner, Stephen. 1993. 'The Maquiladoras and Hazardous Waste: The Effects under NAFTA' 6 *Transnational Law* 255.

Lomas, Owen, 'Environmental Protection, Economic Conflict and the European Community' 33 *McGill Law Journal* 506 (1988).

Long, Bill L. 1972. 'Identifying Environmental Options in Development' IX(1) *Development Digest*.

Low, Patrick et al. 2012. 'The Interface between the Trade and Climate Change Regimes: Scoping the Issues' 46(3) *Journal of World Trade* 485.

Magraw, Daniel. 1994. 'Environment and Trade: Talking Across Cultures' *Environment*.

Mann, Howard. 1992. 'The Rio Declaration' 86 *Proceedings of the American Society of International Law* 405.

Marceau, Gabrielle. 2001. 'Conflicts of Norms and Conflicts of Jurisdictions. The Relationship between the WTO Agreements and MEAs and Other Treaties' 35(6) *Journal of World Trade* 1081.

Marceau, Gabrielle. 2015. 'The Primacy of the WTO Dispute Settlement System' *Questions of International Law.*

Marceau, Gabrielle and Julian Wyatt. 2013. 'The WTO's Efforts to Balance Economic Development and Environmental Protection: A Short Review of Appellate Body Jurisprudence' 1(1) *Latin American Journal of International Trade Law.*

Martin, Gene S. and James W. Brennan. 1989. 'Enforcing the International Convention for the Regulation of Whaling: The Pelly and Packwood-Magnuson Amendments' 17 *Denver Journal of International Law & Policy* 293.

Mavroidis, Petros C. 2000. 'Trade and Environment after the Shrimps-Turtles Litigation' 34(1) *Journal of World Trade* 73.

McAlpine Jan C. and Pat LeDonne. 1993. 'The United States Government, Public Participation, and Trade and Environment', in Durwood Zaelke et al. (eds.), *Trade and the Environment. Law, Economics, and Policy* 203–218 (Island Press).

McCormick, Rachel. 2006. 'A Qualitative Analysis of the WTO's Role on Trade and Environment Issues' 6(1) *Global Environmental Politics* 102.

McDorman, Ted L. 1991. 'The GATT Consistency of U.S. Fish Import Embargoes to Stop Driftnet Fishing and Save Whales, Dolphins and Turtles' 24 *George Washington Journal of International Law and Economics* 477.

McDorman, Ted L. 1992. 'The 1991 U.S.—Mexico GATT Panel Report on Tuna and Dolphin: Implications for Trade and Environment Conflicts' 17 *North Carolina Journal of International Law and Commercial Regulation* 461.

McEvoy, James. 1972. 'The American Concern with the Environment', in William Burch et al. (eds.), *Social Behavior, Natural Resources and the Environment* (Harper & Row).

McGeorge, Robert L. 1994. 'The Pollution Haven Problem in International Law: Can the International Community Harmonize Liberal Trade, Environmental and Economic Development Policies?' 12(2) *Wisconsin International Law Journal* 277.

McHale, John. 1973. 'The Changing Pattern of Futures Research in the USA' 5(3) *Futures.*

Meltzer, Christina Ruth. 1990. 'The Environmental Policy of the European Economic Community to Control Transnational Pollution—Time to Make Critical Choices' 12 *Loyola of Los Angeles International and Comparative Law Review* 579.

Mensah, Chris K. 1994. 'The Role of Developing Countries', in Campiglio et al. (eds.), *The Environment After Rio: International Law and Economics* 33–52 (Springer).

Milewicz, Karolina et al. 2016. 'Beyond Trade: The Expanding Scope of the Nontrade Agenda in Trade Agreements' 62(4) *Journal of Conflict Resolution* 743.

Mitchell, Andrew D. and Christopher Tran. 2010. 'The Consistency of the EU Renewable Energy Directive with the WTO Agreements' 1(1) *Renewable Energy Law and Policy Review* 33.

Morgera, Elisa. 2012. 'European Environmental Law', in Shawkat Alam et al. (eds.), *Routledge Handbook of International Environmental Law* (Routledge).

Morin, Jean-Frédéric, Andreas Dür and Lisa Lechner. 2018. 'Mapping the Trade and Environment Nexus: Insights from a New Data Set' 18(1) *Global Environmental Politcs* 122.

Moss, Ambler H. Jr. 1993. 'Free Trade and Environmental Enhancement: Are They Compatible in the Americas?' in Durwood Zaelke et al. (eds.), *Trade and the Environment. Law, Economics, and Policy* 109–120 (Island Press).

Muskie, Edmund S. 1968. 'Role of the Federal Government in Air Pollution Control' 10 *Arizona Law Review* 17.

Nader, Ralph and Lori Wallach. 1996. 'GATT, NAFTA, and the Subversion of the Democratic Process', in Jerry Mander and Edward Goldsmith (eds.), *The Case Against the Global Economy: and for a Turn Toward the Local* 92–107 (Sierra Club Books).

Nanda, Ved P. 2005. 'Sustainable Development, International Trade and the Doha Agenda for Development' 8 *Chapman Law Review* 53.

Nichols, Philip. 1996. 'Trade Without Values' 90 *Northwestern University Law Review* 658.

Nolde, Boris. 1924. 'Droit et technique des traités de commerce (Volume 003)', in *Collected Courses of the Hague Academy of International Law* (The Hague Academy of International Law).

O'Brien, Denis. 1976. 'Customs Unions: Trade Creation and Trade Diversion in Historical Perspective' 8(4) *History of Political Economy* 540.

OECD. 1972. 'Guiding Principles Concerning International Economic Aspects of Environmental Policies'.

Ogle, Flint B. 1993. 'The Ongoing Struggle Between Private Property Rights and Wetlands Regulation: Recent Developments and Proposed Solutions' 64 *University of Colorado Law Review* 573.

Ostry, Sylvia. 2016. 'Energy Security and Sustainable Development: The WTO and the Energy Charter Treaty', in Marina Larionova (ed.), *Making Global Economic Governance Effective: Hard and Soft Law Institutions in a Crowded World* (Routledge).

Ozorio de Almeida, Miguel A. 1970. 'The Confrontation Between Problems of Development and Environment' 39 *International Conciliation* 37.

Patterson, Eliza. 1991. 'International Trade and the Environment: Institutional Solutions' 21(10) *Environmental Law Reporter.*

Patterson, Eliza. 1992. 'GATT and the Environment—Rule Changes to Minimize Adverse Trade and Environmental Effects' 26(3) *Journal of World Trade* 99.

Pauwelyn, Joost. 1998. 'Evidence, proof and Persuasion in WTO Dispute Settlement. Who Bears the Burden?' 1 *Journal of International Economic Law* 227.

Pauwelyn, Joost. 2001. 'The Role of Public International Law in the WTO: How Far Can We Go?' 95(3) *American Journal of International Law* 535.

Pauwelyn, Joost. 2002. 'The Use of Experts in WTO Dispute Settlement' 51(2) *International and Comparative Law Quarterly* 325.

Pauwelyn, Joost. 2004. 'Recent Books on Trade and Environment: GATT Phantoms Still Haunt the WTO' 15 *European Journal of International Law* 575.

Pauwelyn, Joost. 2012. 'Carbon Leakage Measures and Border Tax Adjustments under WTO Law,' in Denise Prevost and Geert Van Calster (eds.), *Research Handbook on Environment, Health and the WTO* (Edward Elgar).

Pauwelyn, Joost. 2015. 'The Rule of Law Without the Rule of Lawyers? Why Investment Arbitrators Are from Mars, Trade Adjudicators from Venus' 109 *American Journal of International Law* 761.

Pauwelyn, Joost. 2016. 'The WTO 20 Years On: 'Global Governance by Judiciary' or, Rather, Member-Driven Settlement of (Some) Trade Disputes between (Some) WTO Members?' 27(4) *European Journal of International Law* 1119.

Pauwelyn, Joost. 2020. 'Defenses and the Burden of Proof in International Law', in Lorand Bartels and Federica Paddeu (eds.), *Exceptions and Defences in International Law* (Oxford University Press).

Pearson, Charles S. 1993. 'The Trade and Environment Nexus: What is New Since '72?' in Durwood Zaelke et al. (eds.), *Trade and the Environment. Law, Economics, and Policy* 23–32 (Island Press).

Peel, Jacqueline. 2001. 'Giving the Public a Voice in the Protection of the Global Environment: Avenues for Participation by NGOs in Dispute Resolution at the European Court of Justice and the World Trade Organization' *Colorado Journal of International Environmental Law and Policy* 47.

Petersmann, Ernst-Ulrich. 1993. 'International Trade Law and International Environmental Law. Prevention and Settlement of International Environmental Disputes in GATT' *Journal of World Trade* 43.

Petersmann, Ernst-Ulrich. 2000. 'From "Negative" to "Positive" Integration in the WTO: Time for "Mainstreaming Human Rights" Into WTO Law?' 37 *Common Market Law Review* 1363.

Phillips, David. 1993. 'Dolphins and GATT', in Ralph Nader et al. (eds.), *The Case Against Free Trade* 133–138 (North Atlantic Books).

Pilon, Roger. 1982. 'Property Rights, Takings, and a Free Society' 6 *Harvard Journal of Law and Public Policy* 165.

Pires de Carvalho, Nuno. 2000. 'Requiring Disclosure of the Origin of Genetic Resources and Prior Informed Consent in Patent Applications Without Infringing the TRIPS

Agreement: The Problem and the Solution' 2 *Washington University Journal of Law and Policy* 371.

Porras, Ileana M. 1995. 'The Puzzling Relationship Between Trade and the Environment: NAFTA, Competitiveness and the Pursuit of Environmental Welfare Objectives' 3 *Indiana Journal of Global Legal Studies* 65.

Prévost, Denise. 2000. 'WTO Subsidies Agreement and Privatised Companies. Appellate Body Amicus Curiae Briefs' 27 *Legal Issues of Economic Integration* 279.

Qureshi, Asif H. 1999. 'Extraterritorial Shrimps, NGOs and the WTO Appellate Body' 48 *International and Comparative Law Quarterly* 199.

Redish, Martin H. and Shane Nugent. 1987. 'The Dormant Commerce Clause and the Constitutional Balance of Federalism' *Duke Law Journal* 569.

Rodgers, William H. Jr. 2000. 'The Most Creative Moments in the History of Environmental Law: "The Whats"' *University of Illinois Law Review* 1.

Rodrik, Dani. 2001. 'The Global Governance of Trade as is Development Really Mattered, Report submitted to the UNDP'.

Röpke, Wilhelm. 1954. 'Economic Order and International Law', in *Collected Courses of the Hague Academy of International Law* (The Hague Academy of International Law).

Rubini, Luca. 2012. 'Ain't Wastin' Time No More: Subsidies for Renewable Energy, the SCM Agreement, Policy Space and Law Reform' 15 *Journal of International Economic Law* 525.

Ruggie, John G. 1982. 'International Regimes, Transactions and Change: Embedded Liberalism in the Postwar Economic Order' 36 *International Organization* 379.

Ruggie, John G. 1998a. 'Epistemology, Ontology, and the Study of International Regimes', in John G. Ruggie (ed.), *Constructing the World Polity: Essays on International Institutionalization* 85 (Routledge).

Ruggie, John G. 1998b. 'The New Institutionalism in International Relations', in John G. Ruggie (ed.), *Constructing the World Polity: Essays on International Institutionalization* (Routledge).

Ruggie, John G. and Friederich Kratochwil. 1986. 'International Organization: A State of the Art on an Art of the State' 40(4) *International Organization* 753.

Ruggiero, Roberto. 2000. 'Reflections After Seattle' 24(9) *Fordham International Law Journal* 9.

Runciman, Leslie. 1927. 'Note and Memoranda. The World Economic Conference at Geneva' *Economic Journal* 465.

Russell, Clifford S. and Hans H. Landsberg. 1971. 'International Environmental Problems: A Taxonomy' 172(3990) *Science* 1307.

Salzman, James. 2001. 'Seattle's Legal Legacy and Environmental Review of Trade Agreements' 31(3) *Environmental Law* 501.

Sanchez, Roberto A. 1990. 'Health and Environmental Risks of the Maquiladora in Mexicali' 30(1) *Natural Resources Journal* 163.

Sands, Philippe. 1991. 'European Community Environmental Law' 100 *Yale Law Journal* 2511.

Sands, Philippe. 1992. 'Danish Bottles and Mexican Tuna' 1(1) *Review of European, Comparative & International Environmental Law* 28.

Saunders, J. Owen. 1992. 'Trade and Environment: The Fine Line Between Environmental Protection and Environmental Protectionism,' 47(4) *International Journal* 723.

Schechter, Cheryl and David Frill Jr. 1992. 'Maquiladoras: Will the Program Continue' 23 *St. Mary's Law Journal* 697.

Schloemann, Hannes L. and Stefan Ohlhoff. 1999. '"Constitutionalization" and Dispute Settlement in the WTO: National Security as an Issue of Competence' 93 *American Journal of International Law* 424.

Schultz, Jennifer. 1995. 'The GATT/WTO Committee on Trade and the Environment—Toward Environmental Reform' 89 *American Journal of International L.aw* 423.

Sexton, Toni R.F. 1991. 'Enacting National Environmental Laws More Stringent than Other States' Laws in the European Community: *Re Disposable Beer Cans: Commission v. Denmark*' 24(3) *Cornell International Law Journal* 563.

Shaffer, Gregory C. 2001. 'The World Trade Organization under Challenge: Democracy and the Law and Politics of the WTO's Treatment of Trade and Environment Matters' 25 *Harvard Environmental Law Review* 1.

Shaffer, Gregory C. 2002. 'The Nexus of Law and Politics: The WTO's Committee on Trade and Environment', in Richard Steinberg (ed.), *The Greening of Trade Law* 81 (Rowman & Littlefield Publishers).

Shaffer, Gregory C. 2019. 'Retooling Trade Agreements for Social Inclusion' 2019(1) *University of Illinois Law Review* 1.

Shoenbaum, Thomas J. 1992. 'Free International Trade and Protection of the Environment: Irreconcilable Conflict?' 86 *American Journal of International Law* 700.

Shoenbaum, Thomas J. 1997. 'International Trade and Protection of the Environment: The Continuing Search for Reconciliation' 91 *American Journal of International Law* 268.

Shoenborn, Brian. 1995. 'Public Participation in Trade Negotiations: Open Agreements, Openly Arrived At?' 4 *Minnesota Journal of Global Trade* 103.

Shrybman, Steven. 1990. 'International Trade and the Environment: An Environmental Assessment of the General Agreement on Tariffs and Tradeo' 20(1) *The Ecologist* 30.

Shrybman, Steven. 1991/92. 'Trading Away the Environment' 9(1) *World Policy Journal* 93–110.

Sikkink, Kathryn. 2002. 'Transnational Advocacy Networks and the Social Construction of Legal Rules', in Yves Dezalay and Bryant G. Garth (eds.), *Global Prescriptions: The Production, Exportation, and Importation of a New Legal Orthodoxy* (Ann Arbor).

Simma, Bruno. 1985. 'Self-Contained Regimes' *Netherlands Yearbook of International Law* 111.

Simma, Bruno. 2006. 'Of Planets and the Universe: Self-Contained Regimes in International Law' 17(3) *European Journal of International Law* 483.

Sindico, Francesco. 2005. 'Unravelling the Trade and Environment Debate Through Sustainable Development Law Principles' *European Society of International Law.*

Sinha, Manisha. 2013. 'An Evaluation of the WTO Committee on Trade and Environment' 47(6) *Journal of World Trade* 1285.

Skilton, Thomas E. 1993. 'GATT and the Environment in Conflict: The Tuna-Dolphin Dispute and the Quest for an International Conservation Strategy' 26 *Cornell International Law Journal* 455.

Sorsa, Piritta. 1992a. 'GATT and the Environment: Basic Issues and Some Developing Country Concerns,' in Patrick Low (ed.), *World Bank Discussion Papers: International Trade And The Environment* 325.

Sorsa, Piritta. 1992b. 'Trade and Environment' 15(1) *World Economy* 115.

Srinivasan, T.N. 2005. 'Nondiscrimination in GATT/WTO: Was there Anything to Begin with and is there Anything Left?' 4 *World Trade Review* 69.

Stairs, Kevin and Peter Taylor. 1992. 'Non-Governmental Organizations and the Legal Protection of the Oceans: A Case Study,' in Andrew Hurrell and Benedict Kingsbury (eds.), *The International Politics of the Environment* 110 (Clarendon Press).

Stein, Arthur A. 1984. 'The Hegemon's Dilemma: Great Britain, the United States, and the International Economic Order' 38 *International Organization* 355.

Steinberg, Richard H. 1997. 'Trade-Environment Negotiations in the EU. NAFTA, and WTO: Regional Trajectories of Rule Development' 91 *American Journal of International Law.*

Steinberg, Richard H. 2002. 'In the Shadow of Law or Power? Consensus-Based Bargaining and Outcomes in the GATT/WTO' 56(2) *International Organization* 339.

Stewart, Richard B. 1992. 'Environmental Law in the United States and the European Community: Spillovers, Cooperation, Rivalry, Institutions' 1 *University of Chicago Legal Forum* 41.

Strauss, Andrew L. 1998. 'From GATTzilla to the Green Giant: Winning the Environmental Battle for the Soul of the World Trade Organization' 19(3) *University of Pennsylvania Journal of International Economic Law* 769.

Strong, Maurice. 1991. 'ECO'92: Critical Challenges and Global Solutions' 44 *Journal of International Affairs* 287.

Strong, Maurice. 1993. 'Beyond Rio: Prospects and Portents' 4 *Colorado Journal of International Environmental Law and Policy* 21.

Subramanian, Arvind. 1992. 'Trade Measures for Environment: A Nearly Empty Box?' 15(1) *The World Economy* 135.

Tarasofsky, Richard G. 1996. 'Ensuring Compatibility between Multilateral Environmental Agreements and GATT/WTO' 7(1) *Yearbook of International Environmental Law* 52.

Tarasofsky, Richard G. 1999. 'The WTO Committee on Trade and Environment: Is It Making a Difference?' 3 *Max Planck Yearbook of United Nations Law* 471.

Tarullo, Daniel K. 1985. 'Logic, Myth and the International Economic Order' 26 *Harvard International Law Journal* 553.

Tarullo, Daniel K. 1987. 'Beyond Normalcy in the Regulation of International Trade' 100 *Harvard Law Review* 546.

Tester, Frank . 1988. 'Free-Trading the Environment', in Duncan Cameron (ed.), *The Free Trade Deal* (Lorimer and Company).

Thomas, Chantal. 2004. 'Should the World Trade Organization Incorporate Labor and Environmental Standards?' 61 *Washington and Lee Law Review* 347.

Tobey, James A. 1990. 'The Effects of Domestic Environmental Policies on Patterns of World Trade: An Empirical Test' 43(2) *Kyklos* 191.

Tobey, James A. 1993. 'The Impact of Domestic Environmental Policies on International Trade', in Herbert Giersch (ed.), *Economic Progress and Environmental Concerns* 181–200 (Springer).

Trachtman, Joel P. 1998. 'Trade and ... Problems, Cost-Benefit Analysis and Subsidiarity' 9 *European Journal of International Law* 32.

Trachtman, Joel P. 2002. 'Institutional Linkage: Transcending "Trade and ..."' 96(1) *American Journal of International Law* 77.

Trachtman, Joel P. 2017. 'WTO Trade and Environment Jurisprudence: Avoiding Environmental Catastrophe' 58(2) *Harvard Journal of International Law* 273.

Trentmann, Frank. 1998. 'Political Culture and Political Economy: Interest, Ideology, and Free Trade' 5 *Review of International Political Economy* 217.

Usher, Peter. 1989. 'World Conference on the Changing Atmosphere: Implications for Global Security, Environment, Science and Policy for Sustainable Development'.

Van Calster, Geert. 1996. 'The World Trade Organisation Committee on Trade and Environment: Exploring the Challenges of the Greening of Free Trade' *European Environmental Law Review* 44.

Vandermeersch, Dirk. 2003. 'The Single European Act and the Environmental Policy of the European Economic Community', in Ludwig Kramer (ed.), *European Environmental Law: A Comparative Perspective* (Routledge).

Vaughan, Scott. 1994. 'Trade and Environment: Some North-South Considerations' 27 *Cornell International Law Journal* 591.

Verhoosel, Gaetan. 1998. 'Beyond the Unsustainable Rhetoric of Sustainable Development: Transferring Environmentally Sound Technologies' 11 *Georgetown International Environmental Law Review* 49.

Viner, Jacob. 1947. 'Conflicts of Principle in Drafting a Trade Charter' 25 *Foreign Affairs* 612.

Viñuales, Jorge E. 2019. 'Foreign Investment and the Environment in International Law: The Current State of Play', in Kate Miles (ed.), *Research Handbook on Environment and Investment Law* (Edward Elgar).

Viñuales, Jorge E. 2020.' Seven Ways of Escaping a Rule: Of Exceptions and Their Avatars in International Law', in Lorand Bartels and Federica Paddeu (eds.), *Exceptions and Defences in International Law* (Oxford University Press).

Von Moltke, Konrad. 1993. 'A European Perspective on Trade and the Environment', in Durwood Zaelke et al. (eds.), *Trade and the Environment. Law, Economics, and Policy* 93–108 (Island Press).

Vranes, Erich. 2006. 'The Definition of "Norm Conflict" in International Law and Legal Theory' 17 *European Journal of International Law* 395.

Wallach, Lori. 1993. 'Hidden Dangers of GATT and NAFTA', in Ralph Nader et al. (eds.), *The Case Against Free Trade* 23–64 (North Atlantic Books).

Walter, Ingo. 1972. 'Environmental Control and Patterns of International Trade and Investment: An Emerging Policy Issue' *Banca Nazionale del Lavoro Review* 82.

Walter, Ingo. 1974. 'Pollution and Protection: U.S. Environmental Controls as Competitive Distortive' 110 *Weltwirtschaftliches Archiv* 104.

Weiler, Joseph. 2001. 'The Rule of Lawyers and the Ethos of Diplomats: Reflections on the Internal and External Legitimacy of Dispute Settlement', in Roger B. Porter et al. (eds.), *Efficiency, Equity, and Legitimacy: The Multilateral Trading System at the Millennium* 334 (Brookings Institution Press).

Weiler, Joseph and Andreas L. Paulus. 1997. 'The Structure of Change in International Law or Is There a Hierarchy of Norms in International Law?' 8 *European Journal of International Law* 545.

Williams, Mark. 1993. 'International Trade and the Environment: Issues, Perspectives and Challenges' 2(4) *Environmental Politics* 80.

Willoughby, Woodbury. 1948. 'American Trade Policy', U.S. Dept. of State Publication 3091, *Commercial Policy Series* 110.

Wirth, David A. 1993. 'The International Trade Regime and the Municipal Law of Federal States: How Close a Fit?' in Durwood Zaelke et al. (eds.,) *Trade and the Environment. Law, Economics, and Policy* 33–44 (Island Press).

Wirth, David A. 1994. 'Reexamining Decision-Making Processes in International Environmental Law' 79 *Iowa Law Review* 769.

Wirth, David A. 1995. 'The Rio Declaration on Environment and Development: Two Steps Forward and One Back, or Vice Versa?' 29 *Georgia Law Review* 599.

Wofford, C. 2000. 'A Greener Future at the WTO: The Refinement of WTO Jurisprudence on Environmental Exceptions to GATT' 24 *Harvard Environmental Law Review* 563.

Woody, Kristin, 1996. 'The World Trade Organization's Committee on Trade and Environment' 8 *Georgetown International Environmental Law Review* 459.

Wu, Mark and James Salzman. 2014. 'The Next Generation of Trade and Environment Conflicts: The Rise of Green Industrial Policy' 108(2) *Northwestern University Law Review* 401.

Yandle, Bruce. 1992. 'Escaping Environmental Feudalism' 15 *Harvard Journal of Law and Public Policy* 517.

Zaelke, Durwood et al. 1993. 'Frictions between International Trade Agreements and Environmental Protection', in *The Greening of World Trade. A Report to epa from the Trade and Environment Committee of the National Advisory Council for Environmental Policy and Technology* 44–77 (U.S. Environmental Protection Agency).

Reports, Working Papers, and Other Nonperiodic Materials

Bagwell, Kyle and Robert W. Staiger. 2000. 'GATT-Think, Working Paper 8005', NBER Working Paper Series (Nov. 2000).

Bartels, Lorand and Tibisay Morgandi. 2017. 'Options for the Legal Form of a WTO Agreement on Fisheries Subsidies', International Centre for Trade and Sustainable Development.

Bhagwati, Jagdish. 1999. 'Third World Intellectuals and NGOs Statement Against Linkage' (TWINS-SAL).

Bhagwati, Jagdish and T.N. Srinivasan, 1995. 'Trade and the Environment: Does Environmental Diversity Detract from the Case for Free Trade?' Discussion paper Series No. 718 (January 1995).

Bidwell, Percy W. 1933. 'Tariff Reform: The Case for Bargaining', The American Economic Review, 23, 1, Supplement, Papers and Proceedings of the Forty-fifth Annual Meeting of the American Economic Association, 137–146.

Bidwell, Percy W. 1944. 'A Postwar Commercial Policy for the United States', The American Economic Review, 34, 1, Part 2, Papers and Proceedings of the Fifty-sixth Annual Meeting of the American Economic Association, 340–353.

Cosbey, Aaron. 2002. 'Taking the Doha Language Seriously: the WTO as if Sustainable Development Really Mattered', Paper presented at the Conference on Sustainable Development in the New Trade Round: Trade, Investment, and Environment after Doha, Royal Institute of Affairs (May 2002).

de Melo, Jaime and Jean-Marc Solleder. 2018. 'Barriers to Trade in Environmental Goods: How Important They are and What Should Developing Countries Expect from their Removal', FERDI Working Paper No. 235.

Elliot, Geoffrey. 1994. 'Internalization of Environmental Costs and Implications for the Trading System', Papers presented at the GATT Symposium on Trade, Environment and Sustainable Development, July 28, 1994, 38–48.

FAO. 2001.' International Plan of Action to Prevent, Deter, and Eliminate Illegal, Unreported and Unregulated Fishing'.

'Feedback and Way Forward on Improving the Implementation and Enforcement of Trade and Sustainable Development Chapters in EU Free Trade Agreements', Non-paper of the Commission services (Feb. 26, 2018).

Ferretti, Janine. 1994. 'The Internalization of Environmental Costs and the Implications for the Trading System', Papers presented at the GATT Symposium on Trade, Environment and Sustainable Development, July 28, 1994, 33–37.

Gehring et al. 2013. 'Climate Change and Sustainable Energy Measures in Regional Trade Agreements (RTAs). An Overview', ICTSD Issue Paper No. 3, Aug. 2013.

Grossman Gene M. and Alan B. Krueger. 1994. 'Economic Growth and the Environment', NBER Working Paper Series, Working Paper No. 4634.

Horlick, Gary and Peggy Clarke. 2016. 'Rethinking Subsidy Disciplines for the Future', E15 Task Force on Rethinking International Disciplines—Policy Options Paper, ICTSD (January 2016).

Horn, Henrik and Petros C. Mavroidis. 2009. 'Burden of Proof in Environmental Disputes in the WTO: Legal Aspects' (Research Institute for Industrial Economics, IFN Working Paper No. 793).

Howse, Robert. 2010. 'Climate Mitigation Subsidies and the WTO Legal Framework', IISD.

Howse, Robert and Makau Mutua. 2002. 'Protecting Human Rights in a Global Economy: Challenges for the World Trade Organization', International Center for Human Rights and Democratic Development, Policy Paper.

IISD. 2011. 'International Investment Law and Sustainable Development: Key Cases from 2000–2010'.

IISD. 2018. 'International Investment Law and Sustainable Development: Key Cases from the 2010s'.

IUCN, UNEP, WWF, FAO, UNESCO. 1980. 'World Conservation Strategy: Living Resource Conservation for Sustainable Development'.

Letter from Michael B.G. Froman, US Trade Rep., to Magali Silva Velarde-Alvarez, Minister of Trade and Tourism, Republic of Peru (Feb. 26, 2016).

Mavroidis, Petros C. and Aaron Cosbey. 2014. 'A Turquoise Mess: Green Subsidies, Blue Industrial Policy and Renewable Energy: The Case for Redrafting the Subsidies Agreement of the WTO', EUI Working Paper RSCAS 2014/17.

McNeely, Jeffrey A. 1994. 'Trade and Biological Diversity: The Internalization of Environmental Costs', Papers presented at the GATT Symposium on Trade, Environment and Sustainable Development, July 28, 1994.

OECD. 2000. 'International Environmental Issues and the OECD 1950–2000. An Historical Perspective', by Bill L. Long (OECD Publishing).

OECD. 2007. 'Environment and Regional Trade Agreements'.

Papers Presented at the GATT Symposium on Trade, Environment and Sustainable Development (July 28, 1994).

Porter, Gareth. 2001. 'Fisheries Subsidies and Overfishing', UNEP—Economics and Trade Unit (Feb. 12, 2001).

Potts, Jason, 2008. 'The Legality of PPMs Under the GATT', IISD.

Press Release, Office of the US Trade Rep., 'USTR Announces Unprecedented Action to Block Illegal Timber Imports from Peru' (Oct. 19, 2017).

Prudencio, Rodrigo J. and Stewart J. Hudson. 1994a 'The Road to Marrakech: An Interim Report on Environmental Reform of the GATT and the International Trade System', National Wildlife Foundation.

Prudencio, Rodrigo J. and Stewart J. Hudson. 1994b. 'Suggestions on an Environmental Reform Agenda at the World Trade Organization', Papers presented at the GATT Symposium on Trade, Environment and Sustainable Development, July 28, 1994, 9–14.

Ruggiero, Renato. 1997. 'A Shared Responsibility: Global Policy Coherence for our Global Age', Address to the Conference on Globalization as a Challenge for German Business: Export Opportunities for Small and Medium-sized Companies in the Environmental Field (Dec. 9, 1997).

Runnalls, David. 1994. 'Trade Liberalization and Sustainable Development', Papers presented at the GATT Symposium on Trade, Environment and Sustainable Development, July 28, 1994, 19–22.

Runnalls, David and Aaron Cosbey. 1992. Trade and Sustainable Development. A Survey of the Issues and A New Research Agenda, IISD Report.

Sands, philippe. 1994. 'GATT 1994 and Sustainable Development: Lessons from the International Legal Order', Papers presented at the GATT Symposium on Trade, Environment and Sustainable Development, July 28, 1994, 27–30.

Satterthwaite, David. 2006. 'Barbara Ward and the Origins of Sustainable Development' (International Institute for Environment and Development).

Schorr, David K. and John F. Caddy. 2007. 'Sustainability Criteria for Fisheries Subsidies: Options for the WTO and Beyond,' UNEP/WWF Working Paper.

Sharma, Ravi. 1994. 'Ownership and Governance: Keys to Ensure Sustainable Development with Trade Liberalization', Papers presented at the GATT Symposium on Trade, Environment and Sustainable Development, July 28, 1994, 15–18.

Sykes, Alan. 2003. 'The Economics of WTO Rules on Subsidies and Countervailing Measures', University of Chicago Law & Economics, Olin Working Paper No. 186.

The Federalist No. 10 (James Madison).

The Federalist No. 22 (Alexander Hamilton).

Thomson, Peter. 2019. '2019: The Year to End Harmful Fisheries Subsidies', IISD SDG Knowledge Hub (Jan. 8, 2019).

UNCTAD. 1992. 'A New Partnership for Development: The Cartagena Commitment'.

UNCTAD. 2015a. 'Investment Policy Framework for Sustainable Investment'.

UNCTAD. 2015b. 'Trade and Climate Change Policy Beyond 2015', Policy Brief No. 36 (Sept. 2015).

UNCTAD-FAO-UNEP. 2016. 'Joint Statement: Regulating Fisheries Subsidies Must Be an Integral Part of the Implementation of 2030 Sustainable Development Agenda'.

UNEP. 2001. 'UNEP Fisheries Subsidies Workshop Geneva'. Chairman's Summary (Feb. 12, 2001).

UNEP. 2004. 'Incorporating Resource Impact into Fisheries Subsidies Disciplines: Issues and Options, a Discussion Paper'.

UNEP. 2005. 'Reflecting Sustainable Development and Special and Differential Treatment for Developing Countries in the Context of New WTO Fisheries Subsidies Rules'.

UNEP. 2009. 'Global Green New Deal', Policy Brief.

UNEP. 2011. 'Towards a Green Economy: Pathways to Sustainable Development and Poverty Eradication'.

UN Environment/IISD. 'A Sustainability Toolkit for Trade Negotiators: Trade and Investment as Vehicles for Achieving the 2030 Sustainable Development Agenda'.

US Interagency Committee on Trade in Timber Products from Peru, Statement Regarding Implementation of the PTPA Forest Annex and Peru's July 2018 Verification Report (Sep. 17, 2018).

US-Chile Joint Commission for Environmental Cooperation. 2012. 2012–2014 Work Program.

US/Mexico Hazardous Waste Work Group, 'Hazardous Waste Management and Maquiladora Industry Manual'.

USTR. 2018. '2018 Trade Policy Agenda and 2017 Annual Report of the President of the United States on the Trade Agreements Program' (Mar. 2018).

WTO/UNEP. 2009. 'Trade and Climate Change'.

WTO/UN Environment. 2018. 'Making Trade Work for the Environment, Prosperity, and Resilience'.

Papers of Maurice Strong Collection

'Canadian Praised as Ecologists Meet', *The Gazette*, Montreal, June 5, 1972.

Committee for International Environmental Programs National Academy of Sciences (Washington D.C.). 1971. United Nations Conference on the Human Environment,

Panel of Experts on Development and Environment, Background Paper No. 2 (June 4, 1971).

'Development and Environment': Report and Working Papers of a Panel of Experts Convened by The Secretary-General of The United Nations Conference on The Human Environment (Mouton Publishing 1971).

'Environmental Costs and Priorities. A Study at Different Locations and Stages of Development', United Nations Conference on the Human Environment, Panel of Experts on Development and Environment, Working Paper No. 4 (June 4, 1971).

FAO. 1971. 'The Environment and Agricultural Development', United Nations Conference on the Human Environment, Panel of Experts on Development and Environment, Background Paper (June 4, 1971).

Hess, John. 1972. 'What We Hope to Accomplish at Stockholm', *International Wildlife*, 20 (Mar.-Apr. 1972).

Iglesias, Enrique. 1971. 'Development and the Human Environment', United Nations Conference on the Human Environment, Panel of Experts on Development and Environment, Working Paper No. 1 (June 4, 1971).

Institute on Man and Science, 'International Organization and the Human Environment: Proceedings of an International Conference', Rensselaerville, N.Y., May 1971.

Jessup, Phillip C., 'Do New Problems Need New Courts?' (unpublished paper).

Kapp, K. William. 1971. 'Implementation of Environmental Policies', United Nations Conference on the Human Environment, Panel of Experts on Development and Environment, Working Paper No. 8 (June 4, 1971).

Lee, J. 1971. 'Environmental Considerations in Project Appraisal', United Nations Conference on the Human Environment, Panel of Experts on Development and Environment, Working Paper No. 7 (June 4, 1971).

Muskie, Edmund. 1971. 'Address at the Conference on International Organization and the Human Environment,' New York: An Alliance for Survival.

Pant, P. 1971. 'Environmental Problems and Economic Development', United Nations Conference on the Human Environment, Panel of Experts on Development and Environment, Working Paper No. 5 (June 4, 1971).

Populi, 'The Environment: A Global Issue'. Maurice Strong Interviewed by Kurt R. Swinton, Interview for Populi (1972–75).

Populi, 'Maurice Strong: Can Savages Learn Self-Reliance?' Interview for Populi (1972–75).

Press Release, Statement by the Secretary General of the Conference on the Human Environment at the 2nd Session of the Preparatory Committee for the Conference, Geneva, 8 February 1971, HE/2 (Feb. 9, 1971).

Sachs, Ignacy (on behalf of UNESCO Secretariat). 1971. 'Environmental Quality Management and Development Planning: Some Suggestions for Action', United

Nations Conference on the Human Environment, Panel of Experts on Development and Environment, Working Paper No. 2 (June 4, 1971).

Strong, Maurice F. 1970a. Opening Remarks at Informal Meeting of Preparatory Committee for the Conference (Nov. 9, 1970).

Strong, Maurice F. 1970b. Lecture delivered at Carlton University, Ottawa: Development, Environment and the New Global Imperative—The New Technological Order (1970–1).

Strong, Maurice F. 1971a. Statement to the Economic Commission for Latin America in Santiago, Chile (May 3, 1971).

Strong, Maurice F. 1971b.Address at the Man and Science Institute, Rensselaerville (May 23, 1971).

Strong, Maurice F. 1971c. Address at the University of Toronto Study Conference on The Crisis of the Human Environment and International Action (May 27, 1971).

Strong, Maurice F. 1971d. Address at the International Youth Conference on the Human Environment, McMaster University (Aug. 27, 1971).

Strong, Maurice F. 1971e. Address at the National Foreign Trade Convention, The Waldorf Astoria NY: The Crisis of Our Environment and the Quality of Life (Nov. 17, 1971).

Strong, Maurice F. 1972a. 'The Institutional Aspects of the Environment' (unpublished outline) (May 20, 1972).

Strong, Maurice F. 1972b. Address before the 24th Session of the International Geological Congress: Science and Society in the Environment Age (Aug. 21, 1972).

Strong, Maurice F. 1973a. Montague Burton Lecture: The United Nations Conference on the Human Environment at Stockholm (Jan. 19, 1973).

Strong, Maurice F. 1973b. Address as the Southwestern Economic Association Meetings, Dallas: Economic Development and International Response to Environmental Decay (Mar. 23, 1973).

Strong, Maurice F. 1975. interview for the Canadian Broadcasting Corporation on 'Limits to Growth' (Mar. 1975).

'The Implication of Environment Measures for International Trade and Development', Background Paper prepared by the UNCTAD Secretariat (June 3, 1971).

UNCTAD. 1971. 'The Implications of Environment Measures for International Trade and Development', United Nations Conference on the Human Environment, Panel of Experts on Development and Environment, Background Paper, Preliminary Version (June 3, 1971).

Periodic Materials

Cairncross, Alec, 'Economic Forces in a Social Context: James Meade: Obituary', *Guardian,* Dec. 28, 1995.

Caldwell, Lynton K., 'A World Policy for the Environment', *The Unesco Courier,* Jan. 1973.

Carson, Rachel, 'Silent Spring—I', *New Yorker,* June 16, 1962.

Dodwell, Patricia, 'Trade Row Looms over U.S.'s Dolphin-Friendly Tuna Policy', *Financial Times,* Jan. 30, 1992.

Drozdiak, William., 'Poor Nations Resist Tougher Trade Rules', *The Washington Post,* Apr. 14, 1994.

Eckholm, Erik P. 'Cheaper Than Oil but More Scarce', *The Washington Post,* July 27, 1975.

Eckholm, Erik P. 'The Deterioration of Mountain Environments', 189 *Science* 764 (1975).

'Environment. The Downing of Earth Day', *Time,* Apr. 27, 1970.

Gardner, Richard N., 'Global Pollution III: U.N. as Policeman, in Environment and the Quality of Life', 54 *Saturday Review,* Aug. 7, 1971.

Hill, Gladwin, 'Environment May Eclipse Vietnam as College Issue', *New York Times,* Nov. 29, 1970.

Hills, Carla A., 'The Trade Pact is Our Best Deal', *New York Times,* Aug. 17, 1993.

International Centre for Trade and Sustainable Development, 'Fisheries Subsidies Text Provides a Good Starting Point, Delegates Say', 7(22) *Bridges Trade BioRes* (Dec. 18, 2007).

Kennan, George F., 'To Prevent a World Wasteland: A Proposal', 48(3) *Foreign Affairs,* April 1970.

Kohr, Martin, 'The GATT and Environmental Protection', *Greenpeace* (1990).

Lash, William H. III, 'Green Gang's GATT Holdup', *Journal of Commerce,* Dec. 10, 1993.

Lear, John, 'Global Pollution I: The Chinese Influence, in Environment and the Quality of Life', 54 *Saturday Review,* Aug. 7, 1971.

Mathews, Jessica. 'Dolphins, Tuna and Free Trade', *The Washington Post,* Oct. 18, 1991.

Mathews, Jessica. 'The Great Greenless GATT', *The Washington Post,* Apr. 11, 1994.

Nader, Ralph. 'The Corrosive Effects of NAFTA', *The Washington Post,* Nov. 15, 1993.

New York Times, Apr. 30, 1933.

New York Times, Oct. 31, 1947.

'Oil Exploration, Environment, Immigration Should Not Be in FTA, Mexican Official Says', *International Trade Reporter,* Oct. 31, 1990.

Pelham Burn, Henry, 'Packaging Paradise', 60 *Sierra Club Bulletin* 25 (1975).

Postrel, Virginia I., 'The Big Green Trade-Killing Machine', *The Wall Street Journal,* Sept. 21, 1990.

'Strong Confident Environment Talks Will Be a Success', *The Intelligencer,* June 12, 1972.

Todaro, Lenora, 'Attack of the Killer Kapitalists', *The Village Voice,* Nov. 30, 1999.

'Toronto Climate Conference Calls for Sharp Cuts in Carbon Dioxide Emissions', *Climate Alert* 1(3) (Fall 1988).

Udall, Stewart P., 'We Must Save the Beauty of Our Land', *The Carpenter,* Apr. 1964.

'USTR Reluctance to Debate Social Aspects of Mexico Pact Worries FTA Backers', *Inside U.S. Trade,* Jan. 4, 1991.

Vogel, David, 'A Big Agenda', *Wilson Quarterly* (1987).

Weisman, Steven R., 'Bush and Democrats in Accord on Trade Deals', *New York Times,* May 11, 2007.

Wilford, John Noble, 'Crew of Crippled Apollo 13 Starts Back After Rounding Moon and Firing Rocket; Men Appear Calm Despite Low Reserves', *New York Times,* Apr. 15, 1970.

Zoellick, Robert B. 'Clinton's Seattle Straddle', *The Washington Post,* Dec. 14, 1999.

Index

Actionable subsidies 233, 290
Agenda 21 92, 232
Agreement on Anti-dumping (ADA) 188
Agreement on Sanitary and Phytosanitary Measures (SPS) 196, 199, 203
Agreement on Subsidies and Countervailing Measures (ASCM) 4, 188–190, 229–233, 269–270, 277
Agreement on Technical Barriers to Trade (TBT) 196, 203, 275
Agreement on Trade-related Aspects of Intellectual Property Rights (TRIPS)
Amicus curiae 27, 184, 279
Anti-dumping duties 234
Appellate Body (AB) 253
  case history 149, 176–185, 199–202, 273–277
  composition 26, 177, 179–180
  impact 26, 104, 175, 179, 274
  See also Tribunals
Argentina 1
Asia-Pacific Economic Cooperation (APEC) 171, 272
Association of Southeast Asian Nations (ASEAN) 118
Atlantic Conference 46–48
Atlantic Charter 47–48, 57, 63, 223
Australia 82, 103, 202
Austria 118, 125, 251

Balance of payments 82
Baldwin, Robert 15
Bergsten, Fred 13
Bhagwati, Jagdish 120, 127, 158
Boulding, Kenneth 60
Brazil 82
Bretton Woods system 20
Brown-Weiss, Edith 88
Brundtland
  Commission 148, 153
  Gro Harlem 116, 153
  Report 148, 151, 153, 166, 183, 194, 264
Burden of proof 141–143, 182, 198

Canada 63–64, 95–96, 115–116, 162, 195, 202, 235, 244–245
Carson, Rachel 58
Carve-outs 195–201, 231, 233, 238–239, 253, 291
Chile 82, 245–247, 270–271
China 82, 155
Churchill, Winston 46–48, 63
Clean Water Act 74, 77
Climate change 115–116, 182, 215, 224, 247
Clinton, Bill 125, 150, 159, 161, 257
Club model of cooperation 25, 115, 171, 245
Club of Rome 61
Cobden, Richard 41
Commerce Clause 70, 77–79, 133
Commission on Sustainable Development (CSD) 161
Committee on Trade and Environment (CTE) 162, 165, 167, 172–176, 185, 192–193, 212, 215, 228–229, 231, 252, 254–262, 269, 271
Common But Differentiated Responsibilities (CBDR) 205, 262, 265
Conflict
  arguments/theories 6
  of goals 87–88, 251
  of norms 149
Conservation 57, 59, 153, 271
Constructivism 25, 111, 245
Convention on International Trade in Endangered Species of Wild Fauna and Flora (CITES) 125, 183, 242, 244, 246, 250–252
Countermeasures 125
Countervailing duties 234
Cultures, clash of 112–115, 148

DDT 58
Decolonization 121
Denmark 124
Developing countries 220
  assistance 28, 219, 226, 231, 265–266

in the GATT/WTO 119–120, 149, 171–172, 185, 192, 260
role in environmental negotiations 67–68, 111, 121–123, 154–155
role in trade negotiations 119, 167, 171, 228, 232, 269
support for trade regime status quo 110, 118–120, 253, 263
Development 68, 122
Agenda 28, 121, 157, 261–262, 268, 283
movement 121
Dispute settlement
participation 114, 146
procedures 135, 144–145
Dispute Settlement Understanding (DSU) 184, 202
Doha Round 119, 191, 217, 228–229, 263
Dormant Commerce Clause 133
Dubos, René 60, 152
Dumping 112, 126

Earth Summit. *See* Rio Conference on Environment and Development
Eco-imperialism 109, 126
Eco-labelling 125, 237, 251, 257, 260
Economic Section, War Cabinet Secretariat (UK) 45, 48–50
Embedded liberalism 19, 87, 105–106, 285
Environment
as an international issue 56, 62–63, 70–71
domestic dimension 56, 59, 223
interest 58–59, 71–72
Environmental agreements. *See* Multilateral environmental agreements
Environmental differentiation 99, 275–276
Environmental goods 171, 214, 218, 257, 272
Environmental impact assessment (EIA) 159–162, 167, 205, 207, 261
Environmental imperialism. *See* eco-imperialism
Environmentalists
challenge to free trade 109
defensive agenda 159
fragmentation 92, 111, 254
offensive agenda 129, 142
trade perspective 91, 129
trade propositions 168
Environmental Kuznets Curve (EKC) 158
Environmental Measures in International Trade GATT (EMIT) Group 91, 119, 150, 171–173
Environmental movement 58–60, 70, 169
Environmental organizations 26–27, 113, 117, 256, 258, 269, 283
Environmental protection
aim of 8
trade liberalization linkage 7–9, 89, 93
Environmental Protection Agency (EPA) 169, 245, 271
Environmental standards
competitiveness factor 126, 234
convergence or harmonization 96–98, 203, 247
diversity of 96–97, 112, 235, 245
enforcement of 233–235
high 112, 147, 235
international 203
low 96, 98, 113, 126, 147, 164, 234–235, 245, 247
process, product, 234
trade attacks on 96–97
trade disputes over 126, 202–203
Environmental trade measures. *See* Trade-Related Environmental Measures
Epistemic communities 25, 111
Esty, Daniel 112, 204, 221
European Commission 103, 148, 225, 247
European Community (EC). *See also* European Union
environmental policy 70, 80–81
case history 95
common market 96–98
goals 80
European Court of Justice (ECJ) 102, 136, 138, 249
European Economic Community (EEC) Treaty 98
Article 2 80–81, 96
Article 30 103
Article 36 100, 102, 104, 137–138
Article 100 80–81, 97
Article 235 80, 97
European Free Trade Area (EFTA) 118, 171, 236
European Parliament 2, 247

European Union (EU) 118, 236
  environmental policy 161–162, 167, 239, 261
  official GATT/WTO statements 168, 186
  trade policy 118, 149, 195, 249
Exception clauses. *See also* GATT, Article XX 195–201, 278
  aim 81–83, 99–100, 104, 285
  drafting 81–83, 100, 130–132, 186–190, 233
  interpretation 135–141, 180–185, 199–202
  origin 81–83, 100–104, 285
Exemptions. *See* carve-outs
Exhaustible natural resources 100, 183–184
Experts
  environmental 170, 225–226, 257
  in trade disputes 135
  trade 24, 92, 111, 135, 185, 225–226
Exploitation of natural resources 56
Extraterritoriality 139, 267

Fisheries
  Negotiations 2, 228–232, 259, 261, 291, 292
  sector 124, 214, 226–232, 252
  subsidies 214–215, 218–210, 220, 226–232, 235, 238, 257, 259, 268–270
Food and Agricultural Organization (FAO) 84, 227, 258, 269
Fossil fuels
  subsidies 214, 219
  subsidies reform 220, 223, 238, 271–271
Founex meeting 68, 110, 122–123, 154–155, 224, 264
France 201–202
Free trade 90
  agenda 121
  environmentalist challenge to 159
  history of 16–19, 22, 50–52
  meaning 16–19, 23, 94, 283–285, 287
Free traders 114, 120, 127, 158–159, 254
Free trade agreements (FTAs)
  dispute settlement 95, 142, 207–210, 240–244, 252
  environmental provisions 149, 187–190, 197, 203–207, 209, 234–244, 246–247, 249, 252, 261, 278
  investment chapter 196, 208–209
  negotiation 159, 188, 196, 257, 279
Friends of the Earth 160
Future generations 152, 206

General Agreement on Tariffs and Trade (GATT)
  Article I 199, 276, 285
  Article III 95, 99, 104–105, 107, 130, 199, 273–276, 285
  Article XI 104, 106, 199, 275–276
  Article XX 82–83, 99–100, 103–104, 130–132, 137–141, 157, 168, 175–177, 180–191, 196, 251, 256, 262, 275–277
  Article XXIII 143
  environmental criticism 108, 129
  evolution of 23, 218
  negotiation of 53–55, 81–83, 93, 101–104, 117–118, 130–132, 136, 284
  objective 90, 106, 127, 129, 135, 153–154
  preamble 13, 127, 153, 218
  Secretariat 24, 87, 89–90, 92, 97, 111, 171, 224–225
General Agreement on Trade in Services (GATS) 188
General exceptions. *See* Exceptions; GATT, Article XX
General principles of international law 145
Germany 98
Global Environmental Organization (GEO) 204, 288–289
Global warming. *See* Climate change
Government procurement 195, 201, 239–240
Government Procurement Agreement 195–196
Great Depression 17, 35, 49, 106, 281
Green economy 27, 220, 222–223, 259–260, 268
Group of 77 119

Harmonized system 170
Havana Charter 54–55, 82–83, 146, 211
Hull, Cordell 23, 35–45, 48, 76, 217, 280–282

Iceland 228, 268
Ideas 10–11, 21, 23, 37, 107, 253–254, 262, 272, 280–284
Illegal unreported and unregulated (IUU) fishing 219–220, 226, 231, 238, 252, 270
Imperial preferences 48

Import bans 202
Import restrictions 244
India 82, 167
Institutional cooperation 27, 171, 174, 192, 215
Institutional integration 254–261, 282–283
International Convention for the Protection of Birds 57
International Court of Justice (ICJ) 136
International environmental agreements. *See* Multilateral environmental agreements
International environmental law, history of 64–70
International Institute for Sustainable Development (IISD) 225
International investment law 294
International standards. *See* Environmental standards
International Trade Organization (ITO) 20, 54, 146
Italy 82, 101

Jackson, John 137, 175
Japan 131, 162, 236
Jurisdiction 139, 209, 267

Kennedy Round 93

Labelling. *See* Eco-labelling
Laissez-faire 20
Lang, Andrew 15
League of Nations 36, 42–43
Learning 10–12, 21, 23
Least-Developed Countries (LDCs) 28, 167, 219–220, 226, 231, 263, 265, 269–271
Less favourable treatment 104
Likeness 99, 104, 107, 272–277

Marine Mammal Protection Act 128
Meade, James 23, 45, 48–54
Mercantilism 16, 22, 52
Mexico 131, 156, 163–164, 235
Mill, John Stuart 40–41
Millennium Development Goals (MDGs) 152
Montesquieu, Charles-Louis de Secondat 40
Montreal Protocol on Substances that Deplete the Ozone Layer 92, 225
Most-favoured nation (MFN) 51, 273, 285
  See also GATT, Article I
Multilateral Environmental Agreements (MEAs) 243
  GATT/WTO compatibility 192, 225–226, 251, 256
  negotiation 92, 113
  secretariats 174, 228, 255, 258
  with trade provisions 109, 186, 193–194, 212–213, 225
Multilateralism 17, 50, 52–54, 281
Mutual supportiveness 148, 210, 282
Muskie, Edmund 73–75

National Environmental Policy Act (NEPA) 72–73, 160
National sovereignty. *See* Sovereignty
National treatment 51, 104, 134, 273, 275, 285
  See also GATT, Article III
Natural resources 56, 104, 128–129
Natural Resources Defence Council (NRDC) 169
Necessity test 137, 180–183, 187, 202
Neoliberalism 13, 89–90, 92, 94, 105–107, 110, 127, 129, 140, 223–224, 278–279, 283–284
Nixon, Richard 72–73
Non-actionable subsidies 190
Non-discrimination 105, 107, 134, 204, 253, 273, 278, 285
  See also Most-favoured nation; National treatment
Non-governmental organizations (NGOs) 27, 114, 117, 120, 146, 170–171, 184, 214, 216, 279
Non-tariff barriers (NTBs) 89, 93–94, 104, 134, 239
North American Agreement on Environmental Cooperation (NAAEC) 118, 161–162, 164
North American Free Trade Agreement (NAFTA) 150, 201, 215
  environmental provisions 163–164, 166, 190, 193, 203, 234–235, 251
  environmental review 161, 163
  negotiations 113–114, 117, 160, 167, 169–170, 249–250
Norway 124

Organization for Economic Cooperation and Development (OECD) 134, 161, 170

Panels
  composition 135, 144
  GATT 103, 108–109, 129, 134–136, 140–141, 157, 177–178, 183, 253, 275
  WTO 175, 177–178, 202, 274
Paris Agreement 2, 247
Peace 40–42, 50, 106, 217–218, 285
Peace-making value of trade 40–42, 50, 217, 280–281
Pelly Amendment 124–125, 251
Peru 1, 241–244, 252, 270
Pesticides 58, 96, 244
Polluter pays principle 205
Pollution 56, 74, 127
Pollution haven 164
Pollution-haven package 164–165, 206, 234
Population growth 61–62
Prevention principle 205
Process and production methods (PPMs) 99, 115, 147, 272–277
Prohibited subsidies 259
Protectionism 17, 35, 87, 94, 110, 120, 126–127, 129, 132, 156, 204, 263
Public health 82, 100, 102–103, 201–202, 274
Public participation
  in environmental decision-making 113, 206
  in environmental negotiations 113
  in trade negotiations 113–114, 161
  in the WTO 161, 174
Public procurement. *See* Government procurement

Quantitative restrictions 51, 104
  See also GATT, Article XI

Race to the bottom 109, 126, 161, 164
Reciprocal Trade Agreements Act (RTAA) 44–45, 76
Regimes
  conflict 6, 8, 148
  integration 272, 278, 293
Renewable energy 189, 214, 220, 237
Ricardo, David 16
Right to development 122, 155–156
Right to regulate 127, 201–202, 238, 240
Rio Conference on Environment and Development 153–155, 171–172, 194, 216, 264
Rio Declaration on Environment and Development 154, 156–157, 267
Robbins, Lionel 45, 49–50, 53
Roosevelt, Franklin Delano 46–48, 63, 221
Roosevelt, Theodore 57, 223
Ruggie, John Gerard 19, 285

Safeguards 234
Schuman, Robert 79
Scientific community 65–66
Seattle Ministerial of the World Trade Organization 159, 215, 268
Sierra Club 160, 169
Single European Act (SEA) 81
Smith, Adam 16, 22
Smoot-Hawley Tariff 17, 35, 281
South Africa 130
Sovereignty 127, 185, 202
Spaceship Earth 55, 60–62, 151, 153
Special and differential treatment 226, 231, 269–272
Standards. *See* Environmental standards
Stockholm Conference on the Human Environment 63, 65–70, 84, 89, 91, 110, 121–122, 134, 151–155, 264, 270
Stockholm Declaration on the Human Environment 69, 204, 206
Strong, Maurice 63–71, 89, 121, 123, 152, 264, 290
Subsidies 126, 218
  definition of 231
  discipline reform 217, 229, 231
  environmental 197, 231, 238
Sustainable development 14, 148–149, 151, 159, 166, 176, 178, 217–220, 223–226, 228, 237, 246, 248–249, 261–262, 264–269, 282, 291–293
Sustainable development goals (SDGs) 2–3, 28, 148, 152–154, 157, 216, 218–220, 225–226, 230, 265–266, 268–269, 278, 292
Sweden 64–65, 118
Switzerland 82, 101, 118, 236

Taiwan 125, 251
Tariffs
  domestic dimension 37–39, 281
  international dimension 39–40, 51
  regulation 37, 51
Technical barriers to trade 97
Technology, environmentally friendly 214, 237
Tokyo Round 23, 93, 106–107, 144, 285
Trade community 89, 129, 214
Trade liberalization 251, 278
  aim 8, 13, 283–284
  benefits 50, 94
  environmental perspectives on 159
  relationship with environmental protection 6, 120, 127, 194, 224, 235, 254, 278
Trade measures
  sanctions 124–125, 157, 240–244, 251–252
  unilateral 124–126, 157, 175, 234
Trade negotiations 113–114, 159, 167, 215
Trade policy, convergence with environmental policy 118, 223
Trade policy *élite* 24–26, 87, 110, 117, 135, 175, 177–179, 215, 253–254, 260, 282
Trade regime
  aim 13–15, 87, 90, 105, 107, 120, 127, 153–154, 176, 213, 218, 261, 264, 279, 280, 283, 286–291
  history of 51–55, 105, 218, 284–286, 291
  theories 13, 107, 128
Trade-Related Environmental Measures (TREMS) 192, 212, 238, 262, 267, 281
Trade restrictions. *See* Trade measures
Trade sanctions. *See* Trade measures
Trade remedies 233–234
Transboundary harm 56, 77
Transparency 113–114, 161
Treaty on the European Union (TEU) 249
Treaty on the Functioning of the European Union (TFEU) 249
Tribunals
  failure to consider environmental issues 144–145, 175, 253, 276
  introduction of environmental considerations 176–179, 183–185, 209, 283
  jurisdiction 209
  problems with scientific evidence 144–145
  use of external sources 144–145, 176–179, 183, 253

Udall, Stewart 71
UNCED. *See* Rio Conference on Environment and Development
Unilateralism 17, 124–126, 139, 157, 175, 234, 266–266
United Kingdom (UK) 17, 45–54, 131–132, 225
United Nations (UN) 54, 58, 64, 68, 84–85
United Nations Conference on Trade and Development (UNCTAD) 121, 162, 224, 269
United Nations Convention on the Law of the Sea (UNCLOS) 145, 183
United Nations Development Programme (UNDP) 121
United Nations Environment Programme (UNEP) 70, 83–86, 115, 162, 215, 221, 225, 228, 258–259, 269
United Nations 2030 Agenda for Sustainable Development 2–3, 28, 213, 216, 219, 226, 230, 265–268, 286, 292
United States (US) 3–4, 95, 227, 232–235, 240–247, 270–271
  Constitution 70, 75–79, 133
  environmental impact assessment procedures 159, 246, 257
  environmental legislation 72, 74–75
  environmental policy 57, 72, 118, 128, 162
  federalism 70, 75–77, 133
  role in post-war economic reconstruction 17, 41, 45–48, 53–55
  tariff policy 37–39
  trade policy 17–18, 118, 124–125, 128, 149, 162, 195, 243
  unilateralism 124
United States-Canada Free Trade Agreement (USCFTA) 95–96, 116
United States-Mexico-Canada (USMCA) 235, 238–239, 252
United States Supreme Court
  case history 77–78, 133–134, 180
  composition 180

United States Trade Representative (USTR) 1, 108, 160, 163, 169–171, 243–246
Uruguay Round 20, 117–120, 128, 161, 167, 171–172, 176, 196, 234
Utilitarism 56–58

Vienna Convention on the Law of Treaties (VCLT) 178–179

Ward, Barbara 61, 151
Water
  management 77–78
  pollution 74
Wetlands 77–78
Wilcox, Clair 45, 54, 83
Wildlife, protection of 241–244, 246, 250
Wilson, Woodrow 41–42
World Bank 158
World Commission on Environment and Development. *See* Brundtland, Commission
World Health Organization (WHO) 84–85
World Meteorological Organization (WMO) 84
World Trade Organization (WTO)
  history of 19, 218
  membership 20, 23, 149, 171, 285
World Trade Organization Agreement, preamble 14, 176, 183, 210, 291
World War I 39–42
World War II 17, 44–45, 121, 284
World Wild Fund (WWF) 169, 258

www.ingramcontent.com/pod-product-compliance
Lightning Source LLC
LaVergne TN
LVHW021725021026
849161LV00004BA/680
* 9 7 8 9 0 0 4 4 6 7 5 5 2 *